SELLING SEX

Sexuality Studies Series

This series focuses on original, provocative, scholarly research examining from a range of perspectives the complexity of human sexual practice, identity, community, and desire. Books in the series explore how sexuality interacts with other aspects of society, such as law, education, feminism, racial diversity, the family, policing, sport, government, religion, mass media, medicine, and employment. The series provides a broad public venue for nurturing debate, cultivating talent, and expanding knowledge of human sexual expression, past and present.

Other volumes in the series are:

Masculinities without Men? Female Masculinity in Twentieth-Century Fictions, by Jean Bobby Noble

Every Inch a Woman: Phallic Possession, Femininity, and the Text, by Carellin Brooks

Queer Youth in the Province of the "Severely Normal," by Gloria Filax

The Manly Modern: Masculinity in Postwar Canada, by Christopher Dummitt

Sexing the Teacher: School Sex Scandals and Queer Pedagogies, by Sheila L. Cavanagh

Undercurrents: Queer Culture and Postcolonial Hong Kong, by Helen Hok-Sze Leung

Sapphistries: A Global History of Love between Women, by Leila J. Rupp

The Canadian War on Queers: National Security as Sexual Regulation, by Gary Kinsman and Patrizia Gentile

Awfully Devoted Women: Lesbian Lives in Canada, 1900-65, by Cameron Duder

Edited by Emily van der Meulen,
Elya M. Durisin, and Victoria Love

SELLING SEX

Experience, Advocacy, and Research
on Sex Work in Canada

UBCPress · Vancouver · Toronto

© UBC Press 2013

21 20 19 18 17 16 15 14   5 4

Printed in Canada on FSC-certified ancient-forest-free paper
(100% post-consumer recycled) that is processed chlorine- and acid-free.

Library and Archives Canada Cataloguing in Publication

Selling sex : experience, advocacy, and research on sex work in Canada / Emily van der Meulen, Elya M. Durisin, and Victoria Love, eds.

Includes bibliographical references and index.
Also issued in electronic format.
ISBN 978-0-7748-2448-4 (bound); ISBN 978-0-7748-2449-1 (pbk.)

1. Prostitution – Canada. 2. Sex-oriented businesses – Canada. 3. Prostitutes – Labor unions – Organizing – Canada. 4. Prostitution – Government policy – Canada. 5. Sex-oriented businesses – Law and legislation – Canada. I. Van der Meulen, Emily, 1977- II. Durisin, Elya M., 1979- III. Love, Victoria, 1969-

HQ148.S44 2013   306.740971   C2012-906702-4

Canadä

UBC Press gratefully acknowledges the financial support for our publishing program of the Government of Canada (through the Canada Book Fund), the Canada Council for the Arts, and the British Columbia Arts Council.

This book has been published with the help of a grant from the Canadian Federation for the Humanities and Social Sciences, through the Awards to Scholarly Publications Program, using funds provided by the Social Sciences and Humanities Research Council of Canada.

The preparation of the index was supported with a grant provided by the office of the Dean of Arts, Ryerson University.

Printed and bound in Canada by Friesens
Set in Kozuka Gothic and Minion by Artegraphica Design Co. Ltd.
Copy editor: Deborah Kerr
Proofreader: Lana Okerlund
Indexer: Christine Jacobs

UBC Press
The University of British Columbia
2029 West Mall
Vancouver, BC V6T 1Z2
www.ubcpress.ca

This book is dedicated
to the sex workers' rights movement.

In solidarity, we have included the red umbrella,
an important symbol of the movement,
on the book's cover.

Contents

Acknowledgments

This collection would not have been possible without the courage, perseverance, and vivacity of the sex workers' rights movement. We are most grateful to Maggie's: Toronto Sex Workers Action Project and other sex workers' rights organizations for the inspiration for this book. Emily and Elya first met at Maggie's, where we were both on the board of directors. From there we met Victoria and other sex worker activists and researchers from across the country, many of whom are featured in this collection. We are proud to consider ourselves members of this broad community of sex workers, advocates, and academics dedicated to the fight for social legitimacy, labour protections, and legislative change.

We would also like to thank the staff at UBC Press for their assistance, encouragement, and thoughtful commentary throughout the process, as well as the Social Sciences and Humanities Research Council of Canada for providing publication support and doctoral scholarships for both Emily and Elya. Emily would also like to acknowledge and thank Rob Heynen for his enduring patience, thoughtful insight, and endless compassion.

Finally, we have been fortunate to work with a dynamic group of contributors who so generously shared their wisdom and experiences with us. We are indebted to each of you.

SELLING SEX

Introduction

EMILY VAN DER MEULEN, ELYA M. DURISIN, AND VICTORIA LOVE

There are few subjects that garner more interest and intrigue than prostitution and other forms of sex work. This interest, however, often takes the form of sensationalist or inflammatory reaction to concerns – real or imagined – about who is participating, where it is happening, and the particular form it takes. Nuanced understandings of sex work coming from sex workers, advocates, and researchers in Canada are too often neglected in favour of polemics that are not grounded in the lived experiences of people in the industry. This collection is, in part, our collaborative intervention into dominant discourse. Key to the methodological approach adopted in this text is the location of sex workers as legitimate sources of knowledge about their work, which does not necessarily mean unanimity and agreement on all aspects of it. As the chapters in this collection attest, there are many differing positions, opinions, and perspectives. By presenting the diverse voices of a range of contributors, we aim to advance sex work theorizations, research praxis, and political organizing in support of sex workers' rights.

This collection represents a unique dialogue between and among academics, sex workers, and advocates, emphasizing the importance of personal perspectives and experiences as the basis for new and more nuanced conceptualizations of sex work. Our three-member editorial team exemplifies this dialogue since we ourselves occupy these three categories. From our different vantage points we are able to draw on our respective experiences researching, advocating, and/or working within the sex industry to ground our analyses in sex workers' lived realities. Thus, we alternate between using the first person (our, we) and the third person (their, them) when we talk about sex work; this is to allow each editor to locate herself.

We begin this introduction with a note on language and a discussion of the central themes, concepts, and structure of *Selling Sex*. From there we move to a brief overview of the history of prostitution policy and politics in Canada from 1860 to the present. Since a major priority of this collection is to provide an in-depth analysis of the contemporary politics of criminalization in Canada and sex workers' resilience and resistance to it, it is important to contextualize the present in its historical context. We then turn our attention to the controversial and politically charged topic of conceptualizations of sex work. Our aims are to briefly recount the feminist and legislative debates, and to advance the sexual labour or 'sex-work-is-work' paradigm drawn on throughout this book.

"Sex Work" and "Prostitution"

Within the sex workers' rights movement, the language used to talk about prostitution and sex work constitutes a critical framework through which sex workers articulate their realities. As Kempadoo (1998, 3) explains, "The idea of the sex worker is inextricably related to struggles for the recognition of women's work, for basic human rights and for decent working conditions." We choose to use "sex work" and "sex workers" because this language is used by our sex-working friends and colleagues, and also by the Canadian and international sex workers' rights movements. We understand sex work as both a type of labour and an income-generating activity (Kempadoo and Doezema 1998). It is also a useful term because of its flexibility in describing activities related to the exchange of sexual services for remuneration. This can include, but is not limited to, escorting, street-based sex work, massage, prostitution, dance, pornography acting/performing, professional domination and submission, fetish, and phone sex work. We recognize, however, that this term also has its limitations. Since sex work is a highly stigmatized and criminalized activity, many do not identify themselves as sex workers or even as people who are employed in the industry. This is a challenge for a political movement focused on the identity "sex worker." We highlight this as an issue for sex work activism, one that will continue to shape the focus and goals of the movement.

Some of our academic and sex-working colleagues use the words "prostitution" or "prostitute" to describe their own sex industry activities or when a differentiation of labour arrangements is relevant for the context of the situation. "Prostitution" is also used in this collection when certain policies, such as specific sections of the Canadian Criminal Code, are being analyzed, or when it's historically relevant to the ways in which sex workers are identified. Thus, our use of "prostitute" and "prostitution" does not necessarily reflect how individual sex workers engage with this language, but signals the relevance of these terms for legal and policy matters.

Themes, Concepts, and Structure of the Collection

A number of overarching themes and concepts have been interwoven throughout the chapters that make up this book. Perhaps the most significant of these include sex-work-related stigma, sex workers as knowledge producers, and sex workers' perseverance and resilience. Stigma in particular is raised as an issue by a number of the contributors. Sex workers report being routinely confronted with multiple forms of stigma, ranging from the institutional stigma experienced in our relationships with the police to that faced in our personal lives, as workers, friends, and activists. Although we work in the sex industry, we simultaneously live our lives as daughters, sons, sisters, brothers, mothers, fathers, students, friends, lovers, and numerous other identities. Because of sex-work-related stigma and its relationship to criminalization, however, many of us must live our lives with some degree of secrecy and fear of exposure. The salience of stigma throughout this collection speaks to a particular dimension of sex workers' lived realities.

Our struggle to be understood as knowledge producers, not simply as objects of research or study, is another theme that unites the chapters. Central to our knowledge production as members of the sex workers' rights movement is the social legitimacy of our labour. Although each of us has developed different knowledge based on our unique experiences, and though we do not all share the same opinions or have the same concerns, we are nevertheless in near unanimity about our understanding of sex work as a form of labour. Despite stigma and resistance to locating our knowledge as legitimate knowledge, sex workers have shown tremendous perseverance and resilience. Thus, this text is also unified by our endurance and strength as we continue to live and work in the face of harmful legal regimes and social prejudice. This collection is a testament to our agency and ability to take action, whether as workers trying to get by day-to-day or as activists trying to change the legal system. Regardless of where in the industry we are located or the understanding we have of our work, we are wilful actors; to say we are anything less simply doesn't reflect our experiences.

In order to unpack these themes and concepts, we have divided the book into three parts, each of which includes writing by sex workers, advocates, and researchers. Part 1 focuses on sex workers' diverse realities, experiences, and perspectives to add nuance and complexity to conceptualizations of sex work. The contributors in Part 1 come from a variety of social locations, and they challenge many of the existing theories of prostitution both by illuminating the remarkable diversity of the industry and by illustrating how interlocking systems of oppression (including racism, classism, sexism, colonialism, homophobia, and transphobia) shape one's experiences of and feelings about sex work. The chapters make visible the complex experiences that are often rendered invisible in both academic and mainstream discourse – namely, those of Aboriginal, youth, male, and trans sex workers. Part 1 also highlights the changing organization of labour within exotic dance, as well as sex workers' challenges with transitioning from sex work to mainstream jobs. Through their analyses, contributors are steadfast that sex work is a socially valuable form of labour and that despite the challenges many face, it can be fulfilling and can offer numerous benefits.

Building on the complexity and diversity of experience presented in Part 1, Part 2 is an exploration and analysis of sex workers' social movements and organizing for social change. Contributors highlight the historical unfolding of the contemporary sex workers' rights movement in Canada and sex workers' attempts to organize against not only poor working conditions in the industry, but also against misperceptions about the work itself. Chapters focus on sex workers' labour organizing with mainstream unions, as well as organizing and struggles for sex workers' rights in various cities, such as Vancouver, Montreal, and Halifax. This part also explores some of the challenges and barriers to the advancement of a sex workers' rights agenda, in particular anti-prostitution feminism and the persistence of stigma and discrimination. Despite the challenges, sex workers across the country, and across the world, continue to organize for improved rights and protections.

Part 3 concludes the book with an analysis of the politics of regulation in Canada. Its chapters are unified through their analyses of the contradictions of Canada's prostitution laws and the significance of the ways in which sex workers have been and continue to be produced as subjects in political discourse. By looking at a recent federal review of prostitution policy and the Ontario constitutional challenge of aspects of the Criminal Code, Part 3 opens with an examination of the impact of differing discourses on policy processes. It also examines anti-trafficking initiatives, procuring laws, and youth prostitution policy to consider the ways in which laws and policies that purport to protect sex workers may instead produce the conditions for harm. Part 3 concludes with a consideration of the politics of regulation in municipal jurisdictions,

Emily van der Meulen, Elya M. Durisin, and Victoria Love

looking at police abuse of power in Ottawa as well as various complex and often contradictory municipal bylaw systems across the country. The afterword closes the text with a call for legal changes that will allow sex workers to work in safe and secure conditions.

Selling Sex covers an expansive range of topics, which reflects and encourages a broader shift in research and writing toward increasingly complex understandings of sex work in Canada. Inevitably, though, some important areas of research are not included here. Perhaps the most significant in this respect is the body of work by francophone authors (see Thiboutot 1994; Nadeau 2003; Parent et al. 2010; Mensah, Thiboutot, and Toupin 2011). Important work has also been done in other areas that are considered, but not fully explored, in this book; these include clients and John Schools (see Lowman and Atchison 2006; Atchison 2010; Khan 2011), bondage, domination, and sadomasochism (see Young 2003; Khan 2009), HIV/AIDS and other sexually transmitted infections (see Maticka-Tyndale et al. 1999; Betteridge 2005), and street-based sex work (see Allinott et al. 2004).

Canadian Sex Work Policy and Politics

Prostitution Policy Development in Canada (1860-1915)

Contemporary configurations of sex work and sex work policy in Canada have emerged out of a complex and contested history. Before criminal law became the jurisdiction of the federal government in 1867, the criminalization of prostitution-related activities in Canada was primarily focused in two areas: provisions were aimed at reducing residential brothels, street prostitution, and vagrancy, and at protecting girls and women under twenty-one years of age from defilement by "false pretenses" (McLaren 1986). The laws were, in part, based on a social understanding of the monetary and proprietary value of women in relation to a male counterpart, their husband, brother, or father. Some cities and communities tolerated a certain level of prostitution in recognition "of the need to service the large surplus male population" (ibid., 127). Other cities, however, saw prostitution as a nuisance, and police focused on reducing the trade. Prostitution was classified as a status offence, which meant that women were subject to vagrancy charges and detention merely for *being* prostitutes.

Canadian criminal laws and social values at the time were greatly influenced by the moral and social purity movements in Britain, including those surrounding the Contagious Diseases Acts (CDA) (Walkowitz 1982; Phoenix 1999) and white slavery panics in the United States (Rosen 1982). Canada implemented its own Contagious Diseases Act from 1865 to 1870, which meant that women could be detained on the suspicion of having a venereal disease, as it was called at the time, and forcibly confined in a certified "lock hospital" for up to three months (McLaren 1986). Because no such hospitals were certified during this time, the Canadian CDA was never really enacted, and it expired with very little impact in 1870.

In 1869, the year before the Canadian CDA was to end, Canadian politicians passed a law intended to prevent occurrences of prostitution. Titled An Act Respecting Vagrants, the Vagrancy Act maintained the existing status offence for prostitution and added new provisions that criminalized men who were found to be "living on the avails."[1] On paper, the Vagrancy Act was relatively more equitable as it equally targeted and criminalized the procurers, prostitutes, and managers/owners of bawdy-houses. In practice, however, women were disproportionately charged (C. Backhouse 1991). Major social and political changes occurred at the federal level between the 1869 Vagrancy Act and the 1892 ratification of Canada's first Criminal Code. Legal historian Backhouse (ibid., 255) has argued that these changes were a "response to a growing outcry from middle-class social reformers against the sexual exploitation of women." The campaign for social and moral reform, she continues, was really an attempt to eradicate sexual double standards and to encourage the same (female) standard of chastity and purity for both genders. Moral reformers saw the strengthening of family values as a way to save society from moral decay, and since women were viewed as the guardians of the family's welfare, they in particular needed to be shielded from male licentiousness; eradicating prostitution was seen as a good place to start. In response, Canadian laws pertaining to prostitution were developed into a highly complex series of provisions that sought to protect women from the wiles of the procurer, pimp, and brothel keeper, and also included increased penalties for convictions (McLaren 1986).

Codified in 1892, Canada's first federal Criminal Code contained an inclusive and wide-ranging series of provisions against prostitution and other "offences against morality," including: the seduction of "previously chaste girls" of fourteen to sixteen years of age as well as women under twenty-one "with promise of marriage"; the protection from procuring for women who were under twenty-one and were not prostitutes or "of known immoral character"; the provision that no woman or girl could be enticed into a "house of ill-fame" for the purposes of prostitution; and the protection from procurement by their parent or guardian to have "carnal connection" with a man (*Criminal Code, 1892,* ss. 181-82, 185(a), 185(b), 186). Bawdy-house offences, previously dealt with under the Vagrancy Act, were also made stricter and subsumed into the Criminal Code.

Emily van der Meulen, Elya M. Durisin, and Victoria Love

Despite the rhetoric of saving innocent girls and women from the evils of carnal knowledge and those who would force it upon them, the first Criminal Code did not contain legislation directed at prostitutes' customers. It is here that the unique, and somewhat contradictory, social positioning of prostitution is most apparent. On the one hand, it was argued that prostitutes were victims in need of legal protection. On the other hand, it was thought that prostitution provided a necessary and inevitable outlet for male sexual needs, which should not be criminalized; thus, prostitution was both a necessary evil and a social ill. As the moral reform movement grew and gained mainstream popularity across North America during the early twentieth century, the social positioning of prostitution as a necessary evil that could be regulated began to erode, and it was increasingly characterized as a social ill that needed to be prohibited (Rosen 1982). This ideological and legislative shift also corresponded to the early-twentieth-century white slavery panic (Ringdal 2004), whereby Canadian and international policies were created to prohibit occurrences of white girls and women being lured into prostitution (Donovan 2006).[2] In 1913, the Canadian Criminal Code was accordingly adapted to include additional punishments for offenders, both in number and severity.

In the subsequent decades, the federal government did little to modify the Criminal Code in relation to prostitution. In effect, during the fifty-five years surrounding the enactment of the first Criminal Code, from 1860 to 1915, Canada's laws on prostitution developed from a set of segmented offences directed at protecting young women and girls and reducing street nuisances to complicated and far-reaching measures applied to a series of unlawful activities with stricter penalties for all in violation (F.M. Shaver 1996). For the next fifty-five years, from 1915 to 1970, the Criminal Code remained almost entirely unchanged in its criminalization of prostitution-related activities.

Recent Changes to Prostitution Legislation (1970-2000)

Since it had remained almost entirely unmodified since 1892, the vagrancy section of the Criminal Code relating to sex work continued to read that a woman, if found walking alone at night, needed to "give a satisfactory account of herself" or risk arrest (Robertson 2003; see also *Criminal Code, 1892*, s. 207(i)). Thus, women could be charged for what they were presumed to be, not for what they actually did. Police officers subjected women to overnight detentions and mandatory medical exams, all of which were legitimate according to the vagrancy laws (Brock 1998). It wasn't until 1972, when it was argued that the status offence of vagrancy was in violation of the 1960 Bill of Rights, that the whole of the vagrancy legislation was revoked and replaced by laws that prohibited soliciting. Since the original bawdy-house and procuring sections of the Criminal Code were separate from the vagrancy sections, they remained in effect along with the new soliciting offence. Thus, *being* a prostitute was no longer illegal; instead, the law criminalized the activities that surrounded it.

In the years directly following the ratification of the solicitation law, both the police and the courts were confused and unsure as to how to interpret the legislation. Further, despite the gender neutrality in the wording of the law, the police were still predominantly arresting and charging women. After six years of confusion and conflicting court rulings, in 1978, the Supreme Court ruled in *Hutt v. R.* that if a prostitute were to be criminally charged, solicitation must be "pressing or persistent," which reduced police powers of arrest (Sturdy 1997; Boritch 2005; Jeffrey 2004; see also *Hutt v. R.* 1978). Residents' groups, politicians, and the police publicly critiqued the now almost unenforceable law: residents' groups charged that street prostitution was increasing; municipalities attempted to control the trade through city bylaws (which were later deemed *ultra vires,* or invalid); and the police complained that they were left with little power to lay charges (Brock 1998).

It was around the same time that sex workers themselves were beginning to form organizations across North America, partially in response to increased public focus on their work. In 1977, Canada saw its first sex work organization, BEAVER (Better End All Vicious Erotic Repression), which soon changed its name to CASH (Committee against Street Harassment). Not long after, in 1982, sex workers and allies in Vancouver created the Alliance for the Safety of Prostitutes (ASP), and in 1983, the Canadian Organization for the Rights of Prostitutes (CORP) was formed in Toronto. Also, at the same time, urban spaces were gentrifying as middle-class residents were increasingly moving from suburban areas into what were then becoming more desirable downtown locations. Inner-city geographies, which had been home to sex workers and the urban poor, were becoming contested spaces. Further, the second wave of the women's movement was engaged in heated arguments around issues of gender and sexuality. These extra- and intra-movement debates, commonly called the sex wars, would see conceptualizations of prostitution and pornography as disputed terrain (Vance 1984; Duggan and Hunter 1995).

With mounting pressure from the courts, police associations, residents' groups, and mayors of the country's largest cities, the federal minister of justice, appointed by the ruling Liberal Party, decreed that the national "problems" of prostitution and pornography needed a national solution. In June of 1983, the Special Committee on Pornography and Prostitution was created. Commonly called the Fraser Committee after its chairperson, Paul Fraser, it was to research, through a socio-legal frame, pornography and prostitution in Canada (Special Committee on Pornography and Prostitution 1985). During its nearly three years of public consultation and research, the committee heard from only a small number of sex workers.

Public reaction to the release of the committee's final report varied considerably, with the media focusing on one of the most controversial of its 105 recommendations – the loosening of brothel, pimping, and licensing laws. The Fraser Committee argued that it should be allowable for "small numbers of prostitutes to organize their activities out of a place of residence" and that the Criminal Code should not prevent the "provinces from permitting and regulating small-scale, non-residential commercial prostitution establishments employing adult prostitutes" (ibid., 684). Although some women's organizations and civil liberties associations as well as individual social workers and sex workers were in support of the findings, criticisms came from many radical feminists, municipal politicians, and representatives of religious groups. Less than a week after its release, the newly appointed Progressive Conservative minister of justice introduced Bill C-49, which would come to have devastating effects on sex workers in Canada.

The main crux of Bill C-49 was its proposal to make "communication" for the purpose of engaging in prostitution a Criminal Code offence for both sex workers and clients, and to eradicate the earlier ruling that solicitation had to be pressing or persistent, which would make sex workers liable for arrest at the mere suggestion of sex. Additionally, Bill C-49 proposed to turn parked cars into public places, making it illegal to engage in commercial sex in one's own vehicle. Within six months, and in direct contravention of the Fraser Committee recommendations, Bill C-49 was passed by Parliament with a wide majority vote.[3] Shortly afterward, it became section 195.1 of the Criminal Code (now section 213). Three years later, the mandatory review of the communication law concluded there was a drastic inequity in enforcing prostitution laws and that many sex workers "simply have longer criminal records" (DoJ-C 1989, 118). It also stated that the criminalization of communication had not succeeded in curbing prostitution, as originally intended, claiming "the main effect was to move street prostitutes from one downtown area to another, thereby displacing the problem" (ibid., 119). In addition to being disproportionately charged and displaced under the new legislation, sex workers, many of whom began working after the 1978 "pressing or persistent" ruling, were also reporting an increase of violence on the streets and more punitive policing measures including detentions, curfews, and strict bail conditions (Brock 1998).

In the late 1980s, the constitutionality of the communication and bawdy-house laws was put to the test and challenged on the basis that they violate the Charter of Rights and Freedoms, particularly the freedom of expression and freedom of association. In 1990, the Supreme Court upheld the constitutionality of both laws, concluding that the prohibition against keeping a common bawdy-house does not violate one's Charter rights, and that although the communication section might indeed be an infringement, this infringement was within reasonable limits (*Reference re ss. 193 and 195.1(1)(c)* 1990).[4]

Another review of Canada's prostitution policy was initiated in 1992. Called the Federal-Provincial-Territorial Working Group on Prostitution, it focused primarily on youth sex workers and street-based sex work (Working Group 1998). Among its recommendations, the Working Group suggested that youth prostitution laws be made easier to enforce and that sentences for procurers and customers should be increased and/or made mandatory.

After the constitutional challenge of the communication and bawdy-house laws in the late 1980s, the early 1990s saw three other cases brought before the Supreme Court on the basis that the prostitution-related sections of the Criminal Code were in violation of the Charter.[5] In each instance, the Supreme Court ruled against the challenges and concluded that when and if the prostitution laws have infringed one's rights, this infringement was again a justifiable reasonable limit.

Between 1991 and 1995, sixty-three known prostitutes, sixty of whom were women, were murdered in Canada. It was thought that most were killed by men posing as clients (Lowman 1998). In a study of violence toward sex workers in British Columbia before and after the communicating law, Lowman and Fraser (1996) found that twelve sex workers were murdered in the six years preceding the legislative change (an average of two per year) compared to the four murders in 1985, the year the new law was enacted, and an average of five murders per year from 1986 through to 1995. From 1996 to 2006, an average of seven sex workers were murdered per year (*Bedford v. Canada* 2010, 296). Lowman and Fraser argue that the communicating law created a symbolic marginalization of sex workers that contributed to their displacement and made them easier targets of violence.

Current Policy Status (2000-Present)

The most recent federal review of Canada's prostitution laws was initiated in response to the continued violence against sex workers, in particular those who worked in Vancouver's Downtown Eastside and went missing or were murdered. Called the Subcommittee on Solicitation Laws Review (SSLR), it included

Emily van der Meulen, Elya M. Durisin, and Victoria Love

representatives from all the major political parties, and its mandate was to review Canada's prostitution policies in order to make recommendations to reduce exploitation and violence (Davies 2003). Over the course of 2005, the SSLR held consultations, both closed session and public, with nearly three hundred witnesses representing police services, community and residents' associations, women's groups, advocacy and rehabilitation organizations, researchers, and sex workers themselves. Unlike the previous Fraser Committee, which saw only a limited number of sex workers, the SSLR heard, either directly or indirectly, from well over a hundred (Allinott et al. 2004; Clamen 2005a, 2005b). Sex workers' and researchers' near unanimous support for decriminalization did influence the subcommittee, with all but one member endorsing at least partial decriminalization, saying "sexual activities between consenting adults that do not harm others, whether or not payment is involved, should not be prohibited by the state" (SSLR 2006, 90). Despite this, in their final report, SSLR members agreed on just six recommendations, including increased resources to combat youth sex work and trafficking, increased education to prevent people from entering sex work, and better exit strategies for those who want to leave. The Conservative Party's framing of sex work as exploitation and (most) sex workers as powerless to protect themselves may be one reason why the SSLR failed in its mandate to improve safety and reduce exploitation; instead, the status quo for sex workers has continued to exist over the past decade.

As it currently stands, prostitution and the sale of sexual services are not illegal in Canada, yet the laws that surround prostitution-related activities make it extremely difficult to work without breaking the law. Indeed, sex workers are forced to choose between working safely or risking arrest. Four areas of federal law continue to regulate how, where, and between whom transactions can take place, and each produces its own set of problems and dangers for workers. The first area of law criminalizes keeping, being an inmate of, or being found in a common bawdy-house (*Criminal Code, 1985*, s. 210). Since section 197.1 of the Criminal Code defines a common bawdy-house as any location that is "kept or occupied, or resorted to by one or more persons, for the purpose of prostitution or the practice of acts of indecency," it is unlawful for sex workers to work in any fixed location by themselves or with others. In 2010, keeping a bawdy house was further defined as a "serious offence" for the purposes of the organized crime provisions of the *Criminal Code,* which could impact sex workers who work together in a fixed location. As well, Canadian case law dictates that neither sexual intercourse nor full nudity have to take place for the act to be considered prostitution; "the definition of prostitution merely requires proof that the woman offered her body for lewdness or for the purposes of the commission of an unlawful act in return for payment" (Bruckert, Parent, and Robitaille 2003, 13). Therefore, the broad bawdy-house section of the Criminal Code can encompass many more workplaces than simply brothels; strip clubs, massage parlours, dungeons, and other locations can also be criminalized.

The second area of legislation adds to the criminalization of a sex worker's common work activities through the prohibition of directing or transporting, or offering to direct or transport, someone to a bawdy-house (*Criminal Code, 1985,* s. 211). While rarely used, this law applies to an individual who drives another to work as well as, conceivably, to referrals among and between clients, sex workers, hotel concierges, taxi drivers, and the like who provide "directions" to a bawdy-house (these types of referrals are also criminalized under the procuring provisions). Thus, section 211 can both detract from sex workers' business by prohibiting word-of-mouth recommendations and add to their vulnerability by criminalizing drivers, who are often the first people to be contacted by workers in instances of an undesirable or difficult client, and who are also responsible for safely transporting workers to various locations.

The third major area of law that prohibits prostitution activities is related to procuring offences, including living on the avails of a sex worker's earnings and owning or operating an establishment where sexual services are provided for a fee (ibid., s. 212). It further deems guilty any individual who is "habitually in the company of a prostitute ... in the absence of evidence to the contrary." Canadian case law has determined that the "habitually in the company of" relationship needs to be "parasitic" (*R. v. Grilo* 1991; *R. v. Bramwell* 1993; *R. v. Celebrity Enterprises* 1998), yet the definition of parasitic remains vague (Barnett 2008; van der Meulen 2010). In effect, this section potentially exposes sex workers' partners and friends to charges of pimping, even if coercion cannot be proven. It further disallows employer-employee relationships and prevents sex workers from being able to organize unions to protect their labour rights. Section 212 additionally includes specific provisions, with increased penalties, for paying for the sexual services of youth.

The final area of federal law – used in over 90 percent of prostitution-related charges – criminalizes public communication for the purposes of engaging in prostitution (*Criminal Code, 1985,* s. 213). Communication is prohibited in any public place, or place open to public view, including the inside of a car, hotel lobbies, restaurants, and bars. Because of this section, sex workers are often forced to go with clients to private and potentially dangerous locations before the negotiation of sexual services can take place. This law disproportionately affects sex workers in outdoor and public locations, yet Canadian research has

Emily van der Meulen, Elya M. Durisin, and Victoria Love

indicated that outdoor sex work accounts for less than 20 percent of the overall sex trade (F. Shaver 1993; Lowman 2005; Childs et al. 2006).

Despite the sanctions outlined in sections 210-13 of the Criminal Code, there are ways in which sex workers are able to provide their services without putting themselves in legal jeopardy; for example, they may work independently, see clients in a different location each time, communicate only in private areas, and remain isolated from co-workers, family, and friends. Needless to say, though such measures might prevent criminal charges, they can dramatically decrease both safety and quality of life (Allinott et al. 2004; Betteridge 2005). Thus, sex workers and allies have been steadfast in their endorsement of decriminalization and have engaged in social and legal efforts to remove these sections from the Criminal Code.

In 2007, one current and two former sex workers in Ontario and a registered non-profit society run by and for current and former sex workers from Vancouver's Downtown Eastside, with an individual former sex worker, filed constitutional challenges in their respective provinces against the prostitution-related sections of the Criminal Code. The BC challenge was initially dismissed in 2008 for lack of standing, on the grounds that a group could not be considered at risk of the laws in question and the individual plaintiff was a former sex worker to whom the laws no longer applied. In the fall of 2012, the Supreme Court of Canada ruled that the BC constitutional challenge could indeed proceed and that the group could be granted public interest standing. This was a significant decision in Canadian constitutional law as it opened the door for additional Charter challenges to be brought forward by groups and organizations, not solely by individuals.

Two years preceding the Supreme Court decision in BC, history was made in Ontario when Madam Justice Himel of the Ontario Superior Court of Justice released her momentous decision in the Ontario Charter challenge *Bedford v. Canada*. She concurred with the three applicants that laws preventing keeping a common bawdy-house, living on the avails of prostitution, and communicating for the purpose of prostitution violate Charter rights to freedom of expression and security of the person, and cannot be saved by the reasonable limits clause. Basing her argument on the evidence before her, Himel stated that the Criminal Code provisions endangered the lives of sex workers: "These laws, individually and together, force prostitutes to choose between their liberty interest and their right to security of the person" (*Bedford v. Canada* 2010, 3). The decision was stayed until the appeal was heard in June 2011.

Nearly a year later, in March 2012, the Ontario Court of Appeal (OCA) released its decision, which upheld the law against communicating, modified the law against living on the avails, and struck down the law against operating a common bawdy-house in Ontario (*Canada (Attorney General) v. Bedford* 2012). The appeal judges concluded that the communication provision does not violate the principles of fundamental justice and is reasonable given the negative effects of prostitution on neighbourhoods. Although this was the majority opinion, two judges out of five issued a strong dissenting opinion and concluded that the communicating provision was indeed unconstitutional. Changes to the bawdy-house law have been stayed, giving the government time to draft new legislation that is compliant with the Charter. The modification to the living on the avails provision should mean that living on the avails will be considered illegal only if it is "exploitative," although it's uncertain how future courts will define exploitation. This decision, though significant, is only a partial success for sex workers. Indoor workers in Ontario could benefit from the legal changes, but street-based workers, who experience higher rates of violence, as well as more arrests and contact with law enforcement, are left unprotected.

The OCA decision was appealed by the Crown, and cross-appealed by the complainants. In October 2012 the Supreme Court of Canada granted leave to hear the case in June 2013.

Conceptualizations of Sex Work

Feminist Positions and Legislative Frameworks
Feminists have been extremely vocal in debates on sex work, with differing positions espoused. Feminists and women's movements have also worked to affect prostitution policy and legislation, to varying degrees of success (Outshoorn 2004). Despite the diversity of politics, however, most conceptualizations tend to conform to one of three positions: sex work as sexual slavery, as a necessary evil, or as labour. In turn, each conceptualization is linked to a particular legislative framework, namely prohibitionism, legalization, or decriminalization.

In an effort to protect prostitutes from perceived harms, the first position – often called prohibitionism, abolitionism, or radical feminism – criminalizes only those actions of individuals who are seen to be controlling or coercing sex workers (Scibelli 1987; Ekberg 2004). In this collection, we have chosen to call this grouping "prohibitionists," as the term "abolitionist" often has a positive association with the movement to end slavery. Although many anti-prostitution radical feminists call themselves abolitionists, in part because they liken sex work to sexual slavery, we feel that the term "prohibitionist" is more appropriate for this book. Prohibitionist and anti-prostitution feminists, who are highly politically organized and often aligned with conservative religious, government, and policing interests, support the view that the sex industry can be abolished by punishing those who support it and helping those who are exploited within it. Therefore, "johns," "pimps," and "traffickers" are charged and penalized, but sex workers are not. Female sex workers are understood to be the victims of male sexual violence and in need of rescue.

In their arguments in support of criminalizing the "demand-side" of prostitution, prohibitionist feminists have tended to neglect nuanced analyses and to disregard discussions of sex worker agency and self-determination (see Barry 1979, 1995; Farley 1998, 2004; Dworkin 2004). Instead, they conceptualize sex work as a form of gendered exploitation and slavery. Their use of highly emotive and controversial language to describe the commercial sex industry and the people who work in it (as, for example, prostituted women who are bought and sold as sexual slaves, and who suffer from post-traumatic stress disorder) is indicative of their passionate zeal for the topic. Intended to evoke sympathy for victims of abuse and to prompt anger toward male perpetrators of violence, the terminology not only is misleading, but often makes "sweeping claims ... not supported by empirical studies" (Weitzer 2005b, 212) and "is designed for maximum shock value" (Weitzer 2005a, 935). Nevertheless, radical and prohibitionist feminists have been successful in influencing prostitution policy both in Canada and internationally. Indeed, some countries have incorporated the prohibitionist perspective into their legal systems, including Finland, Iceland, Norway, and Sweden. Thus, this policy framework has been dubbed the Swedish Model or the Nordic Model. In practice, however, a number of countries that have taken this approach have continued to criminalize sex workers themselves (NSWP 2011, 3).

The second major framework involves the regulation or legalization of sex work by the state in an effort to control and manage the negative implications of the industry. In this context, sex work is simultaneously understood to be a necessary service and a public nuisance. Unlike prohibitionism, where sex work is seen as a social evil that needs to be eradicated (by punishing the perpetrators and those in demand of sexual services), the legalization stance perceives sex work as a necessary evil that requires strict rules to keep it under control (F. Shaver 1985; Wijers 2004). In this way, sex work is conceptualized as a social problem that will never go away and should therefore be regulated to reduce the most undesirable effects. The three best-known examples of regulation include Nevada in the USA, the Netherlands, and Germany.

Legalized systems also differ from prohibitionist frameworks in that sex workers are recognized as having self-determination and as voluntarily entering the industry. Consequently, discussions of prostitution are often underscored by a distinction between forced and voluntary sex work. This distinction refers to how one enters the trade: forced workers are generally understood to be victims of trafficking or of unscrupulous third parties, whereas voluntary workers are those who willingly chose the trade. Some researchers have argued that this characterization is imbued with gendered and racialized assumptions of guilt and innocence (Doezema 1998; Ditmore 2005). Others have critiqued regulated contexts for the overly onerous and strict penalties that are applied to those who violate various laws and bylaws (Scibelli 1987; Wijers 2004). Due to the restrictions associated with legalization, it is not uncommon for sex workers to opt to work illegally in underground areas out of state view (Chapkis 1997).

The third framework – often referred to as decriminalization – is supported by feminists and others who define sex work as a form of labour and who support efforts to establish rights and protections for sex industry workers. Unlike legalization, where criminal justice policies are most often used in an attempt to manage and control the industry, decriminalized contexts remove oppressive criminal regulations targeting sex work, such as the prostitution-related offences in the Criminal Code. Instead, labour and other policies are relied on to regulate sex workers' activities, thus recognizing the importance of workplace rights and responsibilities. While sex workers are still protected by and subject to the Criminal Code in all work-related, private, and public activities, under decriminalization, sex workers should enjoy improved workplace standards and benefits as defined by labour law (Bindman 1998).

Those who argue against decriminalization, for example prohibitionists, often claim that without the Criminal Code sex workers would be left unprotected from violence. However, with decriminalization, workplace harms and grievances can be judged under more appropriate federal, provincial, or municipal policies. For example, there are existing federal provisions that protect against extortion, sexual assault, forcible confinement, and threat with a weapon – crimes that prohibitionists claim are inherent to sex work. Additionally, businesses causing public disturbances (brothels, for instance) or engaging in illegal activities can face fines and closure. Indeed, in a decriminalized system, bawdy-houses and other commercial sex establishments would be subject to rules, regulations, and standards similar to other businesses. Street solicitation, like other public activities, would be subject to nuisance, loitering, littering, and trespassing laws where appropriate. Further, sex workers could be eligible for worker's compensation, health and disability insurance, and statutory holidays under provincial employment standards and occupational health and safety acts. They could also organize into unions, guilds, and associations to protect their labour rights with greater ease. Since decriminalizing its sex industry in 2003, New Zealand has seen an improvement in sex work rights and protections (Abel et al. 2010).

Sex-Work-Is-Work Paradigm

The recognition of sex work as a category of labour denotes an important ideological and political shift away from prohibitionist and radical feminist understandings of sex work as sexual slavery, misogyny, or sexual assault (see Barry 1979; Dworkin 1981; Rich 1983; Farley 2007). It is also a shift away from regulationist conceptualizations of sex work as a necessary evil (C. Backhouse 1991; Wijers 2004) or in relation to the forced/voluntary dichotomy (van Doorninck 2002; Gregory 2005).

Conceptualizations of sex work as a form of labour, as existing within a sex-work-is-work paradigm, have been developed in Canada and internationally by sex workers, often through labour and harm reduction advocacy. According to sex worker activist Carol Leigh (2004), also known as Scarlot Harlot, she coined the term "sex work" at the 1978 Women Against Violence in Pornography conference to better describe the diversity of labour performed within the industry. A significant feature of this paradigm is that it permits a shift from conceptualizing sex work exclusively in terms of a gender perspective (prostitution as a metaphor for women's experiences under patriarchy) to an understanding of how sexual labour is organized within the broader capitalist context, including its class and racial dimensions. Marx (1959, v) who is often credited as the first to analogize prostitution as work, wrote that "prostitution is only a *specific* expression of the *general* prostitution of the *labourer*" (emphasis in original). Whereas some feminist researchers have interpreted this analogy to mean that the prostitute and the labourer are alike in that both sell their bodies (see van der Veen 2001), others have expanded upon Marx's thinking to explain that because sexual and reproductive labour produces life, satisfies human needs, and reproduces the labouring population, it is a form of productive labour (Truong 1990; Agathangelou 2004).

The sex-work-is-work paradigm also creates space for discussing the complex and varied experiences of people in the industry. In recent decades, a broad range of experiences have been documented within the growing body of writing by sex workers (Bell 1987; Delacoste and Alexander 1998; Leigh 2004; Milne 2005; Sterry and Martin 2009), which highlights not only sex workers' differing experiences and meanings they attach to their work, but also the operation of racism, classism, and citizenship within the specific hierarchies of a highly complex global industry. These labour-based discourses support the argument that violence and other forms of criminal exploitation are *not* inherent features of sex work. Instead, they are produced by structural factors, including legal regimes that criminalize prostitution and illegalize migrants, the capitalist organization of the labour process, and gendered and racialized devaluations of work. Given this, calls for the decriminalization of prostitution are among the first demands of the sex workers' rights movement globally.

Looking more closely at the wide variety of sex workers' experiences undermines the assumption that there is a stable and universal object of inquiry (Agustin 2007). Sex workers are differently positioned within the multifaceted sex industry based on our intersecting social locations, which in turn can affect our labour-related experiences. These diverse realities further complicate the notion that sex work is only about sex, or the physical mechanics of two bodies coming together in a specific way, for money (ibid.). Instead, complex emotional and intimate relations can develop and be satisfied. Sex work researchers have built upon Hochschild's (1983) concept of emotional labour, first developed in relation to the labour activities of flight attendants, explicating that sex work is indeed a form of sexual and emotional work (Chapkis 1997; Sanders 2005; van der Meulen 2012). Agustin (2007, 65) suggests that the production of feelings of intimacy is a common feature of work in service occupations and explains that "it is *only* possible to isolate sexual services from other services if sexual communication and touching are accepted as utterly different from all other contact" (emphasis in original). In a similar vein, Bernstein (2007, 6) explains that the consumer marketplace has become intertwined with private-sphere emotional needs in commercial sexual exchanges and coins the term "bounded authenticity" to describe a "recreational sexual ethic [that] derives its primary meaning from the depth of physical sensation and from emotionally bounded erotic exchange." Understanding sex work as a form of labour enables connections to be drawn between it and other forms of emotional, caring, and/or service work, and also – importantly – between the working conditions and experiences of those employed in these respective industries.

Transnational, anti-racist, and Indigenous feminists have drawn attention to the centrality of race in the organization, and stratification, of labour in the sex industry as well as to the manifestation of racism in both the sex workers' rights movement and academic writing on the topic. Histories of colonialism and racism have resulted in the exoticization of women who are considered to be different from the dominant group because of their ethnic, racial, and/or cultural backgrounds. Kempadoo (1998), for example, explains that this exoticization, in addition to economic factors, is particularly important in positioning groups of women, specifically women of colour, in sex work.[6] Not unlike other

Emily van der Meulen, Elya M. Durisin, and Victoria Love

industries, the sex industry is stratified, with white workers (i.e., those defined by others as white or those who can enact whiteness) often occupying the better paying jobs in safer working conditions, and with racialized and Indigenous workers overrepresented as the targets of state, police, neighbourhood, and male violence.

Despite their decades of resisting these conceptualizations and realities, some Western academic feminists have tended to portray racialized women/ sex workers from the global South as homogeneous, ignorant, and easily duped (Mohanty 1991), a construct that lines up easily with contemporary discourses and impulses to 'save' the victims of sex slavery and trafficking.[7] Relatedly, there has been a tendency within North American sex workers' rights movements, like other social movements, to decentre the lived experiences and concerns of Indigenous and racialized sex workers as well as their presence in organizing and resistance efforts (see Kempadoo 1998; $pread Magazine 2011).

Sex workers have been organizing in international contexts for longer than in North America and Western Europe (see Kempadoo and Doezema 1998; Jeffrey 2002). Many of the sex worker groups in the South are highly organized and similarly articulate their demands through a language of "rights" and "labour." However, their struggles reflect the local circumstances of the workers and are not exported versions of North American or Western European discourses (Kempadoo 1998). Even so, there are a number of similarities in the demands expressed across international contexts, such as those for sexual autonomy and self-determination, access to health information, broader social understandings of prostitution as work, and the eradication of police and other violence against sex workers.[8] Comparable demands are also being made by organizations advocating for and with sex workers in a number of Eastern European states, such as the Czech Republic and Hungary, among others.[9]

Sex worker organizing in international contexts has also sought to redefine discourses of migration and human trafficking, and to position migrant sex workers as definitive sources of expertise on issues of forced and coerced labour in the global industry. As international attention to prostitution, migration for sex work, and sex tourism continues to increase, so too does sex worker organizing against feminist prohibitionist and anti-prostitution campaigns that largely define sex workers as victims (Pattanaik 2002). Writers such as Agustin (2007), Andrijasevic (2010), and Zheng (2010) capture the complexity of the situation of migrant workers in the sex industry, showing how workers' own experiences of labour and migration undermine dominant narratives of trafficking. These authors illustrate how women's migration projects are complex, develop from a variety of motivations and circumstances, and involve varying degrees of agency and coercion. Careful attention to the experiences of sex workers globally is imperative given the trend toward the criminalization of prostitution and reduction of legal avenues for women's migration in the name of anti-trafficking efforts and initiatives. Defining sex workers as victims or as necessary but undesirable makes it possible to dismiss their experiential knowledge. The labour-based positioning of sex work as work and the advocacy of decriminalization locate sex workers as actors and agents deserving of full labour rights both on and off the job; the chapters in this collection are a testament to precisely this understanding.

An appreciation of the Canadian context in relation to its global counterpart is increasingly significant for understanding the complexity of sex work experiences but also for the formation of policy. The Canadian state's conceptualization of and approach to prostitution are evidenced not only within its criminal law, but also in development initiatives, projects designed to combat international organized crime, and changes in domestic criminal laws and immigration policies in light of concerns about human trafficking. Its actions affect the experiences of people working in both the domestic and the global sex industry, though in the latter, in ways that are only beginning to be perceptible.

The chapters in this book, then, take up the challenges and possibilities faced by sex workers, advocates, and researchers in the current Canadian legal and policy context. Court decisions striking down key provisions in the criminalization of sex work have left the field in flux, providing the opportunity for new ways of conceptualizing sex work as work but also potentially opening the door to renewed forms of criminalization, regulation, or prohibition. The contributors to this volume, who come from differing positions within and in relation to the sex industry, as well as from various geographic locations across Canada, offer powerful accounts that can help us navigate these changing contexts.

Notes

1 The Vagrancy Act criminalized "1) all common prostitutes, or nightwalkers wandering in the fields, public streets or highways, lanes or places of public meeting or gathering of people, not giving a satisfactory account of themselves; 2) all keepers of bawdy houses and houses of ill-fame, or houses for the resort of prostitutes, and persons in the habit of frequenting such houses, not giving a satisfactory account of themselves; and 3) all persons who have no peaceable profession or calling to maintain themselves by, but who do for the most part support themselves by the avails of prostitution" (quoted in C. Backhouse 1985, 394-95).

2 Moral and social reformers in Europe and North America coined the term "white slavery" to describe the moral panic of white girls and women being lured into prostitution. There are conflicting reports as to the extent of white slavery and whether it accurately described women's entry into prostitution (C. Backhouse 1985; McLaren 1986).

3 The vote was 111 for to 35 against.

4 Over the ten-year period following the enactment of the communication law, from 1986 to 1995, between six and ten thousand prostitution-related charges were generally laid per year (Duchesne 1997). Although the communication section of the Criminal Code was deemed a reasonable infringement of freedom of expression and freedom of speech, 92 percent of the 7,165 charges laid in 1995 alone came under that section (ibid.).
5 *R. v. Stagnitta* [1990]; *R. v. Skinner* [1990]; *R. v. Downey* [1992].
6 In certain geographic locations, Eastern European women are similarly exoticized in relation to Western European women (Stenvoll 2002; Marttila 2008).
7 The "global North and South" refers to a political and socio-economic divide between wealthier countries, generally located in Western Europe and North America (the North), and poorer nations, often called "developing countries," such as those in Africa and Asia (the South).
8 For relevant organizations, see South Africa's SWEAT, http://www.sweat.org.za; India's Durbar Mahila Samanwaya Committee, http://www.durbar.org/; Thailand's Empower Foundation, http://www.empowerfoundation.org/; the Global Network of Sex Work Projects, http://www.nswp.org/; and the Asia Pacific Network of Sex Workers, http://apnsw.wordpress.com/.
9 For relevant organizations, see the Sex Worker's Rights Advocacy Network, http://swannet.org/.

References

Abel, G., L. Fitzgerald, C. Healy, and A. Taylor. 2010. *Taking the crime out of sex work: New Zealand sex workers' fight for decriminalization.* Bristol: Policy Press.

Agathangelou, A.M. 2004. *The global political economy of sex: Desire, violence, and insecurity in Mediterranean nation states.* 1st ed. New York: Palgrave Macmillan.

Agustin, L.M. 2007. *Sex at the margins: Migration, labour markets and the rescue industry.* New York: Zed Books.

Allinott, S., et al. 2004. *Voices for dignity: A call to end the harms caused by Canada's sex trade laws.* Vancouver: Pivot Legal Society.

Andrijasevic, R. 2010. Deported: The right to asylum at EU's external border of Italy and Libya. *International Migration* 48, 1 (February): 148-74.

Atchison, C. 2010. *Report of the preliminary findings of Johns' Voice: A study of adult Canadian sex buyers.* http://www.johnsvoice.ca.

Backhouse, C. 1985. Nineteenth-century Canadian prostitution law: Reflection of a discriminatory society. *Histoire sociale/Social History* 18, 36: 387-423.

–. 1991. Prostitution. In *Petticoats and prejudice: Women and law in nineteenth-century Canada,* ed. C. Backhouse, 228-59. Toronto: Osgoode Society.

Barnett, L. 2008. *Prostitution in Canada: International obligations, federal law, and provincial and municipal jurisdiction.* http://www.parl.gc.ca/.

Barry, K. 1979. *Female sexual slavery.* Englewood Cliffs: Prentice-Hall.

–. 1995. *The prostitution of sexuality: The global exploitation of sexuality.* New York: New York University Press.

Bell, L., ed. 1987. *Good girls/bad girls: Feminists and sex trade workers face to face.* Toronto: Seal Press.

Bernstein, E. 2007. *Temporarily yours: Intimacy, authenticity, and the commerce of sex.* Chicago: University of Chicago Press.

Betteridge, G. 2005. *Sex, work, rights: Reforming Canadian criminal laws on prostitution.* Toronto: HIV/AIDS Legal Network.

Bindman, J. 1998. An international perspective on slavery in the sex industry. In *Global sex workers: Rights, resistance, and redefinition,* ed. K. Kempadoo and J. Doezema, 65-68. New York: Routledge.

Boritch, H. 2005. The criminal class revisited: Recidivism and punishment in Ontario, 1871-1920. *Social Science History* 29, 1: 137-70.

Brock, D. 1998. *Making work, making trouble: Prostitution as a social problem.* Toronto: University of Toronto Press.

Bruckert, C., C. Parent, and P. Robitaille. 2003. *Erotic service/erotic dance establishments: Two types of marginalized labour.* Ottawa: Law Commission of Canada.

Chapkis, W. 1997. *Live sex acts: Women performing erotic labor.* New York: Routledge.

Childs, M., et al. 2006. *Beyond decriminalization: Sex work, human rights and a new framework for law reform.* Vancouver: Pivot Legal Society.

Clamen, J. 2005a. Submission to the Subcommittee on Solicitation Laws of the Standing Committee on Justice, Human Rights, Public Safety and Emergency Preparedness. 16 March. Unpublished manuscript.

–. 2005b. Recommendations for law reform: A sex worker rights perspective. Submission to the Subcommittee on Solicitation Laws of the Standing Committee on Justice, Human Rights, Public Safety and Emergency Preparedness. 30 May. Unpublished manuscript.

Criminal Code, 1892, 55-56 Vict., c. 29.

Criminal Code (R.S.C., 1985, c. C-46).

Davies, L. 2003. Libby succeeds: Parliamentary committee to review sex trade laws. News release. 9 February. http://www.libbydavies.ca/.

Delacoste, F., and P. Alexander, eds. 1998. *Sex work: Writings by women in the sex industry.* 2nd ed. San Francisco: Cleis Press.

Ditmore, M. 2005. Trafficking in lives: How ideology shapes policy. In *Trafficking and prostitution reconsidered: New perspectives on migration, sex work and human rights,* ed. K. Kempadoo, J. Sanghera, and B. Pattanaik, 107-26. London: Paradigm.

Doezema, J. 1998. Forced to choose: Beyond the voluntary v. forced prostitution dichotomy. In *Global sex workers: Rights, resistance, and redefinition,* ed. K. Kempadoo and J. Doezema, 34-50. New York: Routledge.

DoJ-C (Department of Justice – Canada). 1989. *Street prostitution: Assessing the impact of the law.* Ottawa: Communications and Public Affairs.

Donovan, B. 2006. *White slave crusades: Race, gender, and anti-vice activism, 1887-1917.* Chicago: University of Illinois Press.

Duchesne, D. 1997. *Street prostitution in Canada.* Ottawa: Canadian Center of Justice Statistics.

Duggan, L., and N.D. Hunter. 1995. *Sex wars: Sexual dissent and political culture.* New York: Routledge.

Dworkin, A. 1981. *Pornography: Men possessing women.* London: Women's Press.

–. 2004. Pornography, prostitution, and a beautiful and tragic recent history. In *Not for sale: Feminists resisting prostitution and pornography,* ed. C. Stark and R. Whisnant, 137-48. North Melbourne: Spinifex Press.

Ekberg, G. 2004. The Swedish law that prohibits the purchase of sexual services: Best practices for prevention of prostitution and trafficking in human beings. *Violence against Women* 10, 10: 1187-1218.

Farley, M. 1998. Prostitution, violence, and posttraumatic stress disorder. *Women and Health* 27, 3: 37-49.

–. 2004. "Bad for the body, bad for the heart": Prostitution harms women even if legalized or decriminalized. *Violence against Women* 10, 10: 1087-1125.

–. 2007. Prostitution research and education website. http://www.ProstitutionResearch.com.

Gregory, K. 2005. *The everyday lives of sex workers in the Netherlands.* New York: Routledge.

Hochschild, A.R. 1983. *The managed heart: Commercialization of human feeling.* Berkeley: University of California Press.

Jeffrey, L.A. 2002. *Sex and borders: Gender, national identity and prostitution policy in Thailand.* Vancouver: UBC Press.

–. 2004. Prostitution as public nuisance: Prostitution policy in Canada. In *The politics of prostitution: Women's movements, democratic states and the globalization of sex commerce,* ed. J. Outshoorn, 83-102. London: Cambridge University Press.

Kempadoo, K. 1998. Introduction: Globalizing sex workers' rights. In *Global sex workers: Rights, resistance, and redefinition,* ed. K. Kempadoo and J. Doezema, 1-28. New York: Routledge.

Kempadoo, K., and J. Doezema, eds. 1998. *Global sex workers: Rights, resistance, and redefinition.* New York: Routledge.

Khan, U. 2009. Putting a dominatrix in her place. *Canadian Journal of Women and the Law* 21, 1: 143-76.

–. 2011. Running in(to) the family: 8 short stories about sex workers, clients, husbands, and wives. *American University Journal of Gender, Social Policy and the Law* 19, 2: 495-528.

Leigh, C. 2004. *Unrepentant whore: Collected works of Scarlot Harlot.* San Francisco: Last Gasp.

Lowman, J. 1998. Prostitution law reform in Canada. In *Toward comparative law in the 21st century,* ed. The Institute of Comparative Law in Japan, 919-46. Tokyo: Chuo University Press.

–. 2005. Submission to The Subcommittee on Solicitation Laws of the Standing Committee on Justice, Human Rights, Public Safety and Emergency Preparedness. Unpublished manuscript.

Lowman, J., and C. Atchison. 2006. Men who buy sex: A survey in the Greater Vancouver Regional District. *Canadian Review of Sociology/Revue canadienne de sociologie* 43, 3: 281-96.

Lowman, J., and L. Fraser. 1996. *Violence against persons who prostitute: The experience in British Columbia.* Technical Report No. TR1996-14e. Ottawa: Department of Justice Canada.

Marttila, A.M. 2008. Desiring the 'other': Prostitution clients on a transnational red-light district in the border area of Finland, Estonia and Russia. *Gender, Technology and Development* 12, 1 (January-April): 31-51.

Marx, K. 1959. *Economic and philosophic manuscripts of 1844.* Translated by M. Mulligan. Moscow: Progress. (Orig. pub. 1844.)

Maticka-Tyndale, E., J. Lewis, J. Clark, J. Zubick, and S. Young. 1999. Social and cultural vulnerability to sexually-transmitted infection: The work of exotic dancers. *Canadian Journal of Public Health* 90, 1: 19-22.

McLaren, J.S. 1986. Chasing the social evil: Moral fervour and the evolution of Canada's prostitution laws, 1867-1917. *Canadian Journal of Law and Society* 1: 125-65.

Mensah, M.N., C. Thiboutot, and L. Toupin. 2011. *Luttes XXX: Inspirations du mouvement des travailleuses du sexe.* Montreal: Les Éditions du remue-ménage.

Milne, C., ed. 2005. *Naked ambition: Women who are changing pornography.* New York: Carroll and Graf.

Mohanty, C.T. 1991. Under Western eyes: Feminist scholarship and colonial discourses. In *Third World women and the politics of feminism,* ed. C.T. Mohanty, Chandra Talpade, Ann Russo, and Lourdes Torres, 51-80. Indianapolis: Indiana University Press.

Nadeau, R. 2003. *Pute de Rue.* Montreal: Les Intouchables.

NSWP. 2011. *Briefing paper #02: The criminalization of clients.* Global Network of Sex Work Projects. http://www.nswp.org.

Outshoorn, J. 2004. *The Politics of Prostitution: Women's Movements, Democratic States and the Globalization of Sex Commerce.* New York: Cambridge University Press.

Parent, C., C. Bruckert, P. Corriveau, M.N. Mensah, and L. Toupin, eds. 2010. *Mais oui c'est un travail! Penser le travail du sexe au-delà de la victimisation.* Montreal: Presses de l'Université du Québec.

Pattanaik, B. 2002. Conclusion: Where do we go from here? In *Transnational prostitution: Changing global patterns,* ed. S. Thorbek and B. Pattanai, 217-30. New York: Zed Books.

Phoenix, J. 1999. *Making sense of prostitution.* New York: Palgrave.

Rich, A. 1983. Compulsory heterosexuality and lesbian existence. In *Powers of desire: The politics of sexuality,* ed. A. Snitow and C. Stansell, 177-205. New York: Monthly Review Press.

Ringdal, N.J. 2004. *Love for sale: A world history of prostitution.* Translated by Richard Daly. New York: Grove Press.

Robertson, J.R. 2003. *Prostitution.* Ottawa: Library of Parliament.

Rosen, R. 1982. *The lost sisterhood: Prostitution in America, 1900-18.* London: Johns Hopkins University Press.

Ross, B.L. 2009. *Burlesque west: Showgirls, sex, and sin in postwar Vancouver.* Toronto: University of Toronto Press.

Sanders, T. 2005. 'It's just acting': Sex workers' strategies for capitalizing on sexuality. *Gender, Work and Organization* 12, 4: 319-42.

Scibelli, P. 1987. Empowering prostitution: A proposal for international legal reform. *Harvard Women's Law Journal* 10: 117-57.

Shaver, F. 1985. Feminist defense of the decriminalization of prostitution. *Resources for Feminist Research* 14, 4: 38-39.

–. 1993. Prostitution: A female crime? In *In conflict with the law: Women and the Canadian criminal justice system,* ed. E. Adelberg and C. Currie, 153-73. Vancouver: Press Gang.

Shaver, F.M. 1996. The regulation of prostitution: Setting the morality trap. In *Social control in Canada,* ed. B. Schissel and L. Mahood, 204-26. London: Oxford University Press.

Special Committee on Pornography and Prostitution. 1985. *Pornography and prostitution in Canada: Report of the Special Committee on Pornography and Prostitution.* Vol. 1. Ottawa: Canadian Government Publishing Center.

$pread Magazine. 2011. Race and the sex industry. *$pread Magazine* 5, 4 (Summer).

SSLR (Subcommittee on Solicitation Laws of the Standing Committee on Justice and Human Rights). 2006. The challenge of change: A study of Canada's criminal prostitution laws. Ottawa: House of Commons. http://www2.parl.gc.ca.

Stenvoll, D. 2002. From Russia with love? Newspaper coverage of cross-border prostitution in northern Norway, 1990-2001. *European Journal of Women's Studies* 9, 2 (May): 143-62.

Sterry, D.H., and R. Martin. 2009. *Hos, hookers, call girls, and rent boys: Professionals writing on life, love, money, and sex.* Berkeley: Soft Skull Press.

Sturdy, S. 1997. *Prostitution in Canada: Crim 101.* http://records.viu.ca/www/crimweb/Student/Sturdy.htm.

Thiboutot, C. 1994. Le mouvement des prostitueés: bientôt vingt ans. *Perspectives* 7, 1: 14-16.

Truong, T.D. 1990. *Sex, money, and morality: The political economy of prostitution and tourism in South East Asia.* London: Zed Books.

van der Meulen, E. 2010. Illegal lives, loves, and work: How the criminalization of procuring affects sex workers in Canada. *Wagadu: A Journal of Transnational Women's and Gender Studies* 8: 217-40.

–. 2012. When sex is work: Organizing for labour rights and protections. *Labour/Le Travail* 69: 147–69.

van der Veen, M. 2001. Rethinking commodification and prostitution: An effort at peacemaking in the battles over prostitution. *Rethinking Marxism* 13, 2: 30-51.

van Doorninck, M. 2002. A business like any other? Managing the sex industry in the Netherlands. In *Transnational prostitution: Changing global patterns,* ed. S. Thorbek and B. Pattanai, 193-200. New York: Zed Books.

Vance, C., ed. 1984. *Pleasure and danger: Exploring female sexuality.* Boston: Routledge.

Walkowitz, J.R. 1982. *Prostitution and Victorian society: Women, class, and the state.* New York: Cambridge University Press.

Weitzer, R., ed. 2005a. Flawed theory and method in studies of prostitution. *Violence against Women* 11, 7: 934-49.

–. 2005b. New directions in research on prostitution. *Crime, Law and Social Change* 43: 211-35.

Wijers, M. 2004. Criminal, victim, social evil or working girl: Legal approaches to prostitution and their impact on sex workers. *Trabajador@s del sexo: derechos, migraciones y tráfico en el siglo XXI.* Madrid, Spain. http://www.nswp.org/.

Working Group (Federal-Provincial-Territorial Working Group on Prostitution). 1998. *Report and recommendations in respect of legislation, policy and practices concerning prostitution-related activities.* Ottawa: Department of Justice.

Young, A.N. 2003. *Justice defiled: Perverts, potheads, serial killers and lawyers.* Toronto: Key Porter.

Zheng, T., ed. 2010. *Sex trafficking, human rights and social justice.* New York: Routledge.

Cases Cited

Bedford v. Canada, 2010 ONSC 4264.

Canada (Attorney General) v. Bedford, 2012 ONCA 186.

Hutt v. R. (1978), 82 D.L.R. (3d) 95.

R. v. Bramwell (1993), 86 C.C.C. (3d) 418 (BC CA).

R. v. Celebrity Enterprises (1998), 41 C.C.C. (2d) 540 (BC CA).

R. v. Downey, [1992] 2 S.C.R. 10.

R. v. Grilo (1991), 64 C.C.C. (3d) 53 (Ont. CA).

R. v. Skinner, [1990] 1 S.C.R. 1235.

R. v. Stagnitta, [1990] 1 S.C.R. 1226.

Reference re ss. 193 and 195.1(1)(c) of the Criminal Code (Man.), [1990] 1 S.C.R. 1123.

Realities, Experiences, and Perspectives

PART 1 OF THIS COLLECTION highlights the diversity of work in Canada's sex industry through the contributions of sex workers and advocates from a variety of social locations. Each chapter presents a differing perspective or experience of sex work; together, they challenge many existing theories and conceptualizations by illuminating various realities and by illustrating how interlocking systems of oppression shape one's experiences of and feelings about sex work.

In her exploration of the history of exotic dancing in Toronto, and her analysis of dancers' identity formation and material experience, Deborah Clipperton (Chapter 1) opens this part of the book by addressing the complex question of whether stripping is a performance or part of the sex industry. The following chapters present personal narratives focusing on experiences and perspectives on sex work often rendered invisible in both academic and mainstream discourse. River Redwood (Chapter 2) looks at the intersection of class and masculinity, and draws on his extensive experiences in the sex industry to dispel myths and explore the realities of male sex work. Victoria Love (Chapter 3) reflects on shifts in her subjectivity and class positioning during her sex work career, discussing the emotional impact of anti-prostitution feminist theorizing and the complexity of worker-client relationships. Drawing on conversations with trans sex workers, Tor Fletcher (Chapter 4) considers sexual and gender identity to highlight the experiences, benefits, and challenges of being a transsexual/transgender person in the sex industry.

The next two chapters explore the experiences and perspectives of youth and Aboriginal sex workers, who are often spoken for. Through a conversational-narrative style, JJ (Chapter 5) interviews Ivo about state oppression and youth prostitution policies, topics that are further developed later in the collection. As young people with experience in sex work, JJ and Ivo explore how colonialism, prostitution laws, and age-related sex laws create intersecting oppressions for youth in the sex trade, particularly for Indigenous youth. Sarah Hunt (Chapter 6) continues this discussion of Aboriginal people involved in sex work, advancing a decolonizing approach that is grounded in Indigenous and women's rights frameworks. Tuulia Law (Chapter 7) concludes this part of the book with her chapter on sex workers' experiences in transitioning out of the industry and into mainstream work. Her primary research challenges conventional understandings of exiting by examining sex workers' complex reasons for leaving the industry and by arguing that transitioning needs to be understood as part of the trajectory of one's working life.

1

Work, Sex, or Theatre?
A Brief History of Toronto Strippers and Sex Work Identity

DEBORAH CLIPPERTON

For strippers, feminists, and academics alike, the question of whether stripping is a performance or part of the sex trade is complex, unresolved, and further complicated by certain changes that have occurred within the industry during the past fifty years. In order to comprehend the complexities of stripper identity, it is important to situate its development historically. Drawing on my fifteen years of experience as a Toronto-area stripper and the numerous interviews and archival materials I have collected since, this chapter argues that stripping is more properly aligned with theatrical performance than with sex work and that, though it may be a sex *act*, it is not an act of sex. For stripping, the shift away from its origins in the theatre and closer to activities associated with sex work has had profound consequences for women in the trade in terms of identity formation as well as material experience. Where originary theatre affiliations put performance at the core of stripper identity, more recent sex work affiliations have produced conflicts and divisions within the stripper community about whether strippers should consider themselves performers or sex workers. Although strippers have benefited in some ways from taking on a sex worker identity, many struggle to distinguish stripper from sex worker identity by retaining and developing the performance aspects of their work, even though the context of the theatre has been largely lost. In the past fifteen years, the appearance of the new burlesque in Toronto and across the globe may indicate a return to theatrical conceptualizations.

The Early Years of Burlesque: 1875-1964

From its earliest forms in vaudeville and burlesque at the turn of the twentieth century until the early 1960s, stripping took place in music halls, travelling shows, and theatres. Unlike prostitution, which was understood as the occasion of direct personal sin, early burlesque seems to have been a threat only insofar as its ideas were counter to prevailing norms. Burlesque featured comic bawdy sketches that satirized social standards, particularly those associated with the upper classes. From about 1850 through to the 1960s, challenging tradition often involved scantily clad women engaged onstage in witty, sexually suggestive dialogue. As early as 1912, the Toronto Vigilance Association on behalf of one Sam Scribner, accompanied by the Children's Aid Society and other organizations from the city, launched an effort to "safeguard the morals of our young" from the "salacious quality of the shows that are put on in the local houses of burlesque" (*The World* 1912, n.p.). It pressured Toronto City Council to pass a bylaw prohibiting any minor under the age of twenty-one from entering a burlesque house.

It is difficult to pinpoint the exact moment when burlesque dancers began to remove their clothes, the extent of which depended on the town and the audience. A series of individual acts combined to create a momentum of revelation that emerged as a new genre called striptease. Strippers took advantage of the moment and, competing with each other and with the new talkies, became more and more daring.[1] In 1923, a veteran entertainer named Carrie Finnell booked a three-week engagement at a Cleveland theatre (Liepe-Levinson 2002; Shteir 2004). Fifty-six years later, the *Toronto Globe and Mail Weekend Magazine* described this momentous and groundbreaking occasion: "Knowing that a girl's ability to fill the house was her most treasured asset, Carrie promised her audience the removal of one more article of clothing each week. It was an offer they couldn't refuse. Carrie lasted a year, in the course of which, many claim, she invented striptease" (Fifty Years of Striptease 1979, n.p.).

From the beginning of the Depression through to the late 1940s, what Shteir (2004, 4) calls the era of the "Literary Striptease" flourished. Shows became increasingly theatrical, lavish, and sexy, and strippers such as Gypsy Rose Lee and Ann Corio were household names. In Toronto, the burlesque tradition was carried on at the Star and the Gaiety Theatres. After the Second World War, as Rodger (1998, 10) tells us, Toronto's Casino, Lux, and Victory Burlesque became "many a young man's destination for fun on a Friday night. Although the live entertainment onstage would be considered tame by today's standards, it was pretty risqué stuff for Toronto The Good. It was hard work and long hours for

Deborah Clipperton

relatively low wages but according to some of the men who worked in these houses, there were some memorable, if not repeatable, moments."

In most burlesque theatres across the country, one or two to five or six strippers a day would perform shows. Often they worked very long hours, doing three to five shows per day, each show lasting thirty to forty minutes. The performances were, to varying degrees, carefully choreographed and rehearsed, with elaborate costuming that was often designed and made by the women themselves. Other women (often retired strippers) created costumes for girls who were still on the stage. Until the late 1960s, music was usually provided by a small band including drums, keyboard, guitar, sometimes a saxophone. Often a master of ceremonies cracked a few jokes and introduced the girls. After 1962, the invention of cassette tapes made it possible for strippers to choose their own music, which would be played over a speaker system by the sound man, who would also perform introductions: "Here she is, folks, the girl who put the shim in shimmy and the rock in rock 'n' roll! Put your hands together for – big, bold, and beautiful – Bridget!"[2]

Topless Dancing: 1965-70

As the second wave of the women's movement began and the sexual revolution was born, stripping moved out of burlesque theatres and into the bars and taverns of North America. Just as many women began to reclaim their right to an active sexuality and to reject the constraints of monogamy, so too did stripping start to open up, beginning with the advent of the go-go dancer. In the early 1960s, clubs in Paris, New York, and San Francisco were crowded with dancers wearing short boots called go-go boots. "Twist to the go-go rhythm!" ran an Eaton's department store ad for women's clothes (*Toronto Globe and Mail* 1963, 50). Go-go dancing as a form of entertainment originated when women at the Peppermint Lounge in New York City got up on the tables to dance the twist. Soon nightclub owners were hiring them as entertainers, and in 1965, when the Whiskey-a-go-go opened on the Sunset Strip in Los Angeles, they danced in cages suspended from the ceiling (Mann 1992). On 19 June 1964, Carol Ann Doda was working at the Condor Club in San Francisco. The breast-baring monokini had just been designed, and she was given one by the club's publicist.[3] She wore it that night and has since been credited as the city's, and perhaps North America's, first topless dancer. She was an instant hit, performing twelve shows a night to the music of a rock and roll band; within two months almost all the go-go girls in San Francisco were topless. Five years later, in 1969, the still-dancing Doda removed her bottom and thus became the first go-go dancer to perform completely nude. Both events are commemorated in a plaque at the site of the original Condor Club.

In Toronto, topless and bottomless dancing took a little longer to develop. Weeks after Carol Ann Doda shocked the USA, model Carol Craig was reported to have worn a topless bathing suit "patterned on the proposed new flag" with a "couple of extra maple leaves for the faint of heart" (Hanlon 1964, 9). Although the monokini and the bare-breasted evening gown were scintillating news items across North America, in Toronto, female nudity stayed in the burlesque theatres until 1965, when musician Rompin' Ronnie Hawkins started hiring go-go dancers as a feature of his rock 'n' roll act at Le Coq d'Or (Swan 1996).[4] Before long, these women, too, were topless, and thus the antecedents of table dancing came into being.

In topless dancing, there was no narrative, no tease or drama of the gradual revelation of the female body; the allure lay in the dancer's untouchability. Hanging in a cage like a bird, on a tiny pedestal, or even swinging on a giant swing above the audience, the topless dancer's tease was all about forbidden fruits: "You can look, but you can't touch." Enticing and unreachable, she was protected more by distance than by the conventions of the stage (though the stage was only two-foot square at the most) or the laws of the land.

Stripping Moves into the Bars: 1971-80

In 1973, Ontario amended its Liquor Control Act to expand the definition of "theatre," and suddenly nudity became legal in establishments where alcohol was served (Cooke 1987; *Act to Amend the Liquor Licence Act* 1973). Strippers were hired to perform in Toronto bars and taverns, but municipal laws required them to cover their genitalia with a G-string. Establishments in and around Toronto began to hire strippers according to their entertainment needs. Taverns that engaged a band at night, for example, might hire two or three girls to draw a crowd in the afternoon. Some taverns found it more cost-effective to dispense with bands altogether and become full-fledged "strip joints," with strippers performing all day and all night.

The organization and practice of stripping differed between smaller establishments and larger clubs. A small restaurant with an alcohol licence in a mall on the outskirts of Toronto, for example, might hire one dancer for the afternoon shift: she would do four to five twenty-minute shows per shift, five to six days a week. Sometimes another girl or perhaps a band would take over for the evening shift. In larger clubs, however, the format followed that of the burlesque theatre tradition: three to five girls would work approximately a seven-hour

Deborah Clipperton

shift, providing continuous entertainment from noon to one in the morning when the club closed. Strippers typically did four or five shows per shift and were paid twelve to twenty dollars per show, in cash, at the end of the week. They also relied on tips received from customers onstage to augment their incomes.

As with burlesque theatre, strippers considered themselves to be in "show business" (Cooke 1987, 94). They were still required to invest in costumes, music, and often photographs, sometimes work with agents, and follow a standard performance protocol. Generally, the show was at least four or five songs long, lasting fifteen to twenty minutes. Usually during the first song, the stripper focused on her dance performance and established her relationship with the audience. During the second and third songs, costumes were gradually removed in the order of dress or top, skirt, bra, and T-bar or underwear.[5] Depending on the establishment and the prevailing legal situation, the final song would be performed as a "floor show." In this, the stripper would spread a mat or rug on the floor of the stage and finish her act by executing moves while prone or in various positions on her hands and knees. If the G-string were removed, a negligee would be put on so she would not be totally nude. Strippers often took pride in their costumes, music, and the excellence of their shows, and in those years, the uniqueness and quality of the individual performances were reflected in how much money strippers had stuffed in their garters or stockings as they came offstage.

Both a stripper's ability to connect with her audience and the quality of her performance differed greatly according to individual skill, but there was also considerable variance according to venue. Girls had favourite places to work; good performers who were reliable and attractive, and who had a following of regular customers, could bring in and hold a crowd, so it was in the best interests of the club to create working conditions that would draw and keep quality dancers. It was also in the dancers' best interests to produce performances that would retain their position in the club and keep their customers coming back for more.

Although the quality of the work experience and the tips were strong incentives for a stripper to develop a good show, love of the work was also present, and many girls used the accepting atmosphere of clubs in the seventies to create something special. I recall Nurse Annie, for example, who danced exclusively to the music of her boyfriend, Mendelson Joe, coming onstage in full construction worker gear, juxtaposing nudity and the tease with the vigorous hammering of invisible nails perilously close to audience members' toes as she enthusiastically disrobed. She, of course, also dressed as a nurse, doing naughty things while she took customers' pulses. Another dancer, Gwendolyn, used the stage as an opportunity to develop her stand-up comedy skills at the same time as she delivered a pro-sex-worker feminist message; Ross (2009, xiii) reports sitting "in awe" of this performance. Maxine developed a shtick where her genitalia had a personality and voice of their own. Pussy Rabbit, or P Rab, or PR, as she was affectionately known in the dressing room, frequently delivered speeches on the importance of what she called genitalia freedom and complained that she was not given the respect she deserved.[6] Notorious Nadine and others developed wonderful dance routines, recorded in Kay Armatage's (1980) award-winning documentary *Striptease*. Many girls took pride in their shows, some as dancers and performance artists, others as strippers in what Gwendolyn referred to as the "neo-classical" style, by which she meant a carefully crafted seductive choreography combined with a frank celebration of female nakedness.

Strippers enjoyed other advantages as well. They were free to socialize with each other between shows, and with only five girls working a shift, they could spend time in the dressing room, where they developed friendships and support networks. These friendship networks created and maintained an environment in which they could continue performing what they called "proper" shows in the burlesque tradition, though labour conditions were not always optimal. Even when the club was small, or out of town, or dancers didn't know anyone, they could usually trust each other with their costumes, makeup, and money, which meant they could use their expensive costumes and music without fear of having them stolen and were able to continue the theatrical tradition of striptease.

Licensing, Table Dancing, and the Shift to the Sex Trade: 1981-94

In Toronto, this relatively self-regulated period of stripping came to an abrupt end in late July 1977 with the heinous sex murder of Emmanuel Jacques. At the time, Yonge Street had many strip clubs, body rub parlours, adult stores (for pornography), and head shops (Brock 1998). Emmanuel was a thirteen-year-old Portuguese shoeshine boy who worked there and who was part of the vibrant – or "seedy" – street culture of the day. He was lured upstairs above a body rub parlour called Charlie's Angels, where he was raped and murdered by three men. A fourth man was later acquitted. When Emmanuel's body was found, a media-generated moral panic ensued, mandating a vigorous "cleanup" of Yonge Street (ibid.). Because he had been killed by men, hostility focused on the gay

Deborah Clipperton

community, and an anti-gay backlash was only narrowly averted. Still, in the public eye, all the workers and members of the street culture of Yonge Street, gays, strippers, body rubbers, and street prostitutes alike, occupied sexualized, illicit, and threatening identities. In an effort to take control of a potentially explosive situation and to prevent the exploitation of under-age girls and boys, prostitutes were arrested, body rub parlours were closed down, bathhouses were raided, and strippers experienced increased surveillance and harassment by the Morality Squad of the Toronto police.

In 1981, in the wake of the moral outcry, the City of Toronto decided to license body rub parlours and workers, as well as both dancers and the taverns that wanted to hire them. For many strippers, sex trade workers, feminists, and gay activists, the murder of Emmanuel Jacques and the new move to licensing were linked and interpreted as evidence of a repressive and hostile government that saw the sex trade and gay life as equally transgressive, dangerous, and in need of regulation (Cooke 1987; Gulliver 2006). The licensing process was deeply resented by many strippers as it was time consuming and costly, and they saw no positive results from it (see also Chapter 20 in this volume). A stripper had to present herself at the licensing bureau, fill out a form requiring that she disclose both her address and her social insurance number, and obtain photo ID with her real name, which she was obliged to carry with her at all times. Further, she could not have a criminal record.

For a group of women who preferred to be anonymous and off the grid, who were sometimes underage or who *had* criminal records, who had no faith in bureaucratic authority structures, and who might not pay taxes, the idea of an official record that made them visible and traceable was not welcome. On top of that, the first licence issued was for an adult parlour attendant, grouping strippers with body rub parlour workers and suggesting that city hall understood stripping as part of the sex trade rather than theatrical performance, which was troubling to some strippers. They were particularly offended by a clause requiring that they be tested and cleared for venereal disease (Cooke 1987). The licence name was eventually changed to burlesque entertainer, but many strippers, who thought they should not be licensed at all, chose that moment to leave the business.

Also in the early eighties, table dancing was brought in from Montreal. During the late 1970s, Montreal owners and dancers had realized that customers would pay to have a girl dance exclusively for them. Owners provided small tables, which were made of wood, cube-shaped, about two-feet square, and perhaps a foot high. They were built to bear the weight of a dancer and were quite heavy to carry around. After completing her stage show, a girl would wander through the audience, carrying her table and soliciting a dance, which lasted for the duration of one song and cost five dollars. At the customer's request, she would place the table in front of him and dance for him personally (Arpin 1983). Although 363 Toronto-area clubs were engaging dancers in 1980, only sixty-three licences were granted in 1981, drastically reducing the number of clubs that were legally able to hire dancers. But twenty to thirty table dancers could work in a club where only five strippers had worked before, so even though they had to buy a licence, lots of table-dancing jobs were available in most of those few clubs. Since only a few small clubs still hired strippers, necessity ruled and though many girls were unwilling, most made the transition from stage show to table dancing.

The shift to table dancing entailed a change in skill set. No longer was it necessary to hold and manage the attention of a large audience in a theatrical venue. This opened the door for hundreds of young dancers who did not have, and did not need, stagecraft skills but could rely on personal charm and good looks to manage individual customers one-on-one. Certain big clubs in Brampton, Mississauga, and Scarborough brought in busloads of "French girls," table dancers from Montreal and Quebec City whose perceived exoticism and years of experience table dancing in the nude set a new standard of interpersonal interaction with the audience. In 1983, the *Montreal Gazette* ran a lengthy article characterizing the situation between Ontario and Quebec girls as the "battle of the strippers" (ibid.). Upward of two hundred Quebec strippers were being hired weekly by fourteen strip bars in the prosperous industrial belt around metropolitan Toronto, upsetting both the Canadian Association of Burlesque Entertainers (CABE) and the Brampton chapter of a citizens' group called Canadians for Decency.[7] They were both particularly incensed because Brampton did not have a municipal G-string law, and strippers were allowed to dance completely nude:

> Aside from cavorting around in the nude on stage, the Quebec entertainers outstrip their Ontario counterparts by doing it at patrons' tables, an innovation the more modest Ontario girls are reluctant to copy. Leaping up on tiny portable stages they lug around with them, the Quebec strippers thrust their *derrieres* to within inches of a customer's face and suggestively bend forward to touch their toes. At $5 a 'dance,' Ontario beer hall regulars are finding this form of 'adult entertainment' an incredible bargain. And the Quebec dancers who pocket the $5, plus tips, are cleaning up financially. (ibid., A1, emphasis in original).

Deborah Clipperton

As with licensing, the introduction of nude table dancing created another significant shift for strippers in Ontario; they were faced with the choice of changing their performance styles, going out of town, or leaving the business entirely.[8] Already upset with licensing and the loss of the stage show, and very uncomfortable with the physical intimacy of the table dance, many chose to leave.

Toronto girls who stayed watched and learned new techniques for making money, aware that a profound structural change had taken place in their work, one that required new skills and innovations. From being a performer paid for her shows, a stripper now had to hustle individual customers, and from an average $360 per week (not including tips), her weekly pay was slashed to $200 on the assumption that she would make up the difference in table dances. By the mid-1980s, clubs no longer paid dancers a salary, and in fact, girls were required to pay the club a fee for dancing, usually forty dollars per night, often in addition to paying the deejay as well. The girls became dependent on individual customers for their money, and much like street-based sex workers, they had to develop complex techniques for hustling dances in order to make their money. Instead of being remunerated for doing shows as a performer, the stripper now paid the club for the opportunity to dance for individual customers and was required to give the owner a percentage of her take, just as girls working in a brothel or escort service would pay the madam. Due to these developments, the working conditions in the industry shifted from those of the theatre, becoming much more congruent with other sectors of the sex trade.

The emphasis on table dancing also changed the nature and meaning of the stage show, where the purpose was not only to entertain the audience but to put performers on display. As in a brothel, customers could view their options and choose which woman they would later ask for a table dance. Girls did not dance so much as strut, like models on a runway; the emphasis shifted from theatricality to physical beauty. The understanding of the tease also moved from the gradual revelation of the nude woman beneath her layers of costume, sometimes associated with a narrative, to a sexual erotics onstage, mimicking seductive poses in pornographic films and magazines. Some dancers continued to exert themselves on stage, developing a unique style and care for the quality of their work, but they were constrained by the shortness of their time onstage and their limited costumes.

Managers wanted the girls to be on the floor, where they could individually entertain customers. To discourage them from staying in the dressing room together, change rooms were kept small and utilitarian, with hooks for street clothes, a table, makeup mirror, and nearby bathroom, but no space for sitting and talking away from the crowd. With so many girls working at one time, managers were not able to provide enough locker space to accommodate storage of a variety of elaborate costumes, so the strippers worked with one small outfit for the shift.

The invention of the pole in the early nineties added a new challenge to the stage show but still primarily in finding new angles of visual consumption. However, the high level of skill and stamina involved in using the pole did increase the respect given strippers who took advantage of it in a performance. "Pole-dancer" became a tag for strippers who put emphasis on their stage show, approaching it with enthusiasm and working hard to improve their performance skills.

Lap Dancing and the Champagne or VIP Lounge: 1994-Present

In the early 1990s, lap dancing made its appearance; audiences became customers and touching became part of the job expectation in some clubs. Initially, lap dancing was table dancing pushed to the limit, where the dancer, still working on the box, moved closer and closer to the customer and engaged in intimate touching behaviours designed to keep him aroused and buying more and more dances (Lewis 2000). Competition between the strippers on the floor for customers was increasingly intense, and as some girls were willing to allow physical contact, the others had to follow suit if they were to keep up. Dancers could see what each girl was doing, which involved sitting on or lying across a customer's lap, sometimes allowing him to touch her body.

There was a great deal of conflict among and between strippers and club owners regarding this activity. For some, lap dancing was an acceptable practice and a matter of personal choice; for others, it was clearly beyond the pale and even against the law. Some who opposed it thought that owners were forcing them to work as sex trade workers, not as performers. Those who accepted it felt that any attempt to legislate against lap dancing was an insult to a stripper's ability to handle herself and amounted to problematic protective legislation. The uncertainty was echoed in the shifting cost of a table dance, which was no longer fixed at five dollars, but could be ten or even twenty dollars. This state of affairs continued for some years, reflecting a series of overturned decisions as the issue of lap dancing and physical contact between dancers and customers made its way through to the Supreme Court of Canada.

In the clubs, however, it continued to be a matter of negotiation between stripper and customer, depending on who was watching and how much the

Deborah Clipperton

owner, manager, or bouncer was willing to regulate activities on the floor. A stripper negotiated with a customer before the table dance, either talking him into the more expensive lap dance or clarifying how much she would be paid so she would know how close to get to him. During an interview with me, Sugar, who danced for twelve years in Toronto, explained the process:

> I remember, see I had been dancing for a while at this point, and I heard girls start talking about twenty-dollar songs and I'm like, twenty dollars? How are you getting twenty bucks and I'm still doing ten bucks? Well, what's the difference? Well, they said, well then, you have to make it, ... This is what you got to do ... and this is what you got to say. So, for the ten dollars you'd make it a little further away. For twenty dollars you get a little closer. And they'd tell you little moves to make and little things to say. You might just want to brush the side of his head and, you know?

> Deborah: *So how would you negotiate this twenty dollars? Would you do it up front?*

> Sugar: *Yeah, well that's what I'd say ... Would you like to do a ten or a twenty? And they'd go, well what's the difference? And I would have to say, well twenty's a little bit closer. You have to be careful because you don't want to get busted you know, because it was only supposed to be ten dollars, you can get in trouble, you can get charged apparently if you did a twenty-dollar song.*

This negotiation is more complicated than it sounds, as the stripper must keep the customer in enough of a state of arousal to maintain his interest while they are discussing the fees for her dance.

Late in 1999, the Supreme Court of Canada ruled that lap dancing, including sexual touching, did not constitute prostitution and did not offend community standards as long as it took place in private or semi-private conditions, as in, for example, a private booth (*R. v. Pelletier* 1999).[9] This decision had the effect of institutionalizing the fourth of four types of performances that are featured in strip clubs today: the stage performance, table dancing, lap dancing, and dances in a private booth – sometimes called the Champagne Room or VIP Lounge. The use of the private booth made stripping so unarguably similar to work in a brothel that many strippers themselves began to identify as sex trade workers.

During the first few years, lap dancing was very popular and money was easy to come by. A 2008 *Toronto Star* article reports, "When Jane began working in strip clubs four years ago [2004], she earned between $600 and $1,000 a night.

'I used to just walk through the bar and men would come to me and ask for a dance. It was easy,' says the 23-year-old" (Popplewell 2008). However, by 2008, according to Jane, things had changed, and making money was much more difficult. Kitti, another Toronto-area dancer, described in an interview with me how it became harder for a stripper to find customers: *"Now, oh my God, I sit with them for fifteen minutes or more ... Before it was so easy to get them to go for a dance. It's either yes or no. Now you gotta spend half an hour with this guy or ten minutes talking to this knucklehead or fifteen minutes for that old fart ... They wanna talk to you. They wanna like, see what you're doing ... The worst is when you go up to them [and they say], 'I don't want a dance right now.'"*

The psychological pressure of asking customer after customer if he would like a dance, and being rejected time and time again, can be very difficult to manage. As Jane explained in the *Toronto Star* article, "I did really well for the first few years but then it got harder to get guys to buy a dance. It burns you out after a while. I would just go in for an hour or two and then leave" (Popplewell 2008). Similarly, Kitti was having such a hard time that she took a break from the Toronto scene and went to Kitchener to dance at a "no contact club," where the dancers would still provide lap dances, but the customers were not allowed to touch them: *"I enjoyed it [in Kitchener]. When I was working down here [in Toronto] ... it started eating at me a lot. And I started hating what I do. I didn't enjoy it any more ... When I was [in Kitchener], I took pride in, I was happy. I felt like I was a performer ... And when we did give a lap dance there was no contact, like they couldn't touch us, which was great. You still made twenty dollars in the horseshoe and outside of it."*

Difficulty managing the pressure to conform to the parameters of the sex trade meant that many strippers left the business and that their ranks were not replenished by new girls. During the ten years between 1998 and 2007, the number of strippers in Toronto decreased from 2,834 to 1,254 (Popplewell 2008). Kitti explained this by describing her own experience in one Toronto club: *"A lot of girls are leaving that club. No one wants to be there 'cause if I'm going up with some guy and he only gets a twenty-dollar dance from me, and I feel like shit that he just drooled over me and still I'm giving the club ten bucks every time I go, that means I only got ten bucks from the lap dance ... They make you feel like shit and they just get one song from you and if you don't let them touch you where they wanna touch you it's just one song."*

Although some Toronto strip clubs allow contact between dancers and customers, others are more highly regulated by owners, management, and bouncers, and the boundary between stripper and customer is strictly monitored. Even in these no contact clubs, some strippers have mixed feelings. With

Deborah Clipperton

strict management and controls over customers and strippers, most of these clubs do not charge dancers the ten-dollar fee for a visit to the VIP Lounge. On the other hand, there are explicit, and often strict, standards of behaviour: no touching, look busy on the floor, do not get drunk at work, absolutely no drugs, and, as Kitti comments, if a customer offers a drink, *"Do not say no, get a juice."* Strippers, who tend to be caught between wanting to be protected and wanting to be free to regulate themselves, sometimes find the rules and regulations patronizing and controlling.

On the whole, lap dancing seems to be the final frontier between striptease as a theatrical performance and striptease as sex work, and it marks a shift to a differing skill set for strippers. The audience member is now a customer, and the lap dancer is more occupied with negotiating levels of physical intimacy than she is with theatricality. She is no longer paid by salary, or even by the show, but rather she pays the club for the opportunity to work and often pays it a percentage of her take. Though many lap dancers have worked hard to develop their individual style, and retain a theatrical element in the execution of their work, lap dancing has merged with the realm of sex work.

Despite the shift in conditions for strippers over the past fifty years and the move from burlesque halls to commercial strip clubs, many strippers continue to find their work financially rewarding and take pride in aspects of it, even though the opportunities for creative expression have changed considerably. Many strippers are highly talented pole-dancers, demonstrating a remarkable level of physical strength and skill. They are often able to build and maintain friendships and supportive networks with other dancers, even given fierce competition, and to work in an environment that is more flexible and higher paying than many others.

The New Burlesque

In the 1990s, what is often referred to as the new burlesque emerged out of a culture of nostalgia that looked to ways of performing that recovered fantasy, style, costume, narrative, and the tease, elements many burlesque performers felt were lost to stripping when it entered the world of the sex trade. In the past ten years, the new burlesque has offered aficionados an alternative way of performing that gave men and women "in love with that combination of fun, glamour, and simple storytelling something to latch on to, to be inspired by – a place to start creating an act" (Baldwin 2004, 23). In a postmodern approach that collapses time and juxtaposes seemingly unrelated cultural elements to create something new, these performers draw on ideas of striptease in its theatrical form and use it as a venue for glamour, pleasure, comedy, satire, and political comment.

Many practitioners of the new burlesque in Toronto identify as strippers, although in practice, the focus of a burlesque show is as much on narrative, style, and fun as it is on sexuality. Sometimes burlesque performers are or have been professional bar strippers, table dancers, or lap dancers; more often they have chosen to perform striptease in neo-burlesque because it contains the narrative or fantasy elements now rare in Toronto strip clubs. Sauci Callahora, for example, explains that she prefers burlesque because, for her, contemporary stripping, including lap dancing, is *"arousing at a body level,"* but it *"doesn't really engage my brain."* She feels that it is important to arouse the imagination as well as the body:

> *In modern-day stripping, I mean, the main point of it is basically … to arouse people, like their bodies, right? And whether or not it engages their imagination doesn't really, at this point in time, unfortunately, doesn't really matter. That's not really the point of it. In the past I think that used to be part of it. And now, I guess it's just kind of veered away from that direction for whatever reason. I know there are some performers out there who obviously have like, really imaginative, great acts, but it's not a prerequisite, I guess, is what I'm trying to say.*

Some strippers who also work in burlesque are trying to reintroduce that imaginative component into the strip clubs, bringing professional stripping full circle back to its theatrical roots. During a press conference at the 2010 Toronto Burlesque Festival, Roxi Dlite, who started as a bar stripper and was crowned Miss Exotic World in 2010, rather astonished her audience by stating that she would like to bring burlesque back to the strip clubs.

Conclusion

Stripping has gone through profound structural changes in the past century, and changing working conditions in strip clubs complicate the relationship between strippers and a sex trade identity. The structures of stripping in Toronto rest on historical developments in the form, changing from the grand theatrical venues of vaudeville and burlesque to topless dancing, bar stripping, table dancing, and finally lap dancing. Each development moved stripping farther away from its theatrical elements, to clear membership in the sex trade.

Throughout this process, strippers both embraced and resisted the changes that took place within their industry: some responded by leaving the business;

Deborah Clipperton

others accepted them; and still others exploited the new forms to develop their performances, using smaller work spaces, new moves, and the close relation to the audience. As stripping finally sedimented into sex trade signification, some dancers decided not to participate in that environment, choosing instead to reconstitute striptease *outside* paid labour. In the late 1990s, the structure of erotic dance split into two distinct activities that each identify as stripping. On the one hand, professional stripping, associated with adult entertainment in bars and taverns, is licensed by the city and constituted as part of the sex industry. On the other, the new burlesque hearkens back to earlier theatrical performances and takes place outside those establishments regulated specifically for stripping. Strippers in the new burlesque tradition actively reassert the performative aspects of stripping and have more ties to performance art than contemporary sex work. With the new burlesque, stripping may have recovered its theatrical roots.

Notes

1 In 1927, Warner Brothers released *The Jazz Singer,* starring Al Jolson, the first feature-length film to have dialogue on its soundtrack, and thus began the decline of the silent film and the rise of talkies.

2 This position also drew its legacy from burlesque theatres, where the job often entailed technical responsibilities. It later developed into what we now call the deejay.

3 Rudolph Gernreich designed this one-piece bathing suit that left the breasts uncovered.

4 At this time, total nudity was not permitted. Dancers wore a G-string, and before removing it, they were required by law to put on a negligee or other garment so that they would not be totally nude. Many dancers disregarded this stipulation.

5 Slightly larger than a G-string, a T-bar is designed with fasteners that ensure easy and quick removal.

6 I saved a few of my phone messages from P Rab because they were so inspirational. One from some time in 2005 ran as follows (my stage name was Morgana Revere): *"Hi Schmorgana, it's PR. I know I've been forgotten and no one really asks about me any more, but I wanted to let you know I'm still alive and suffering under Pontius Pilate, and trying to work the magic for genitalia freedom, but frankly it's pretty rough ... Love you, bye!"*

7 From 1979 to 1982, CABE was the first strippers' union in Toronto, organized to improve working conditions (Cockerline, Gwendolyn, and Sorfleet 1993). It was displeased that Quebec girls were taking Toronto jobs.

8 Although table dancing quickly became de rigueur in the big suburban Toronto clubs, as well as in certain Ontario cities (London, Hamilton, Windsor), many small taverns outside the urban centres continued to hire one or two strippers to provide entertainment in the afternoons and early evenings before the musicians took the stage. Many older girls took to the road to keep stripping without having to table dance, leaving the new genre to the new girls.

9 In her oral judgment, Judge Louise Arbour said that the court was reinstating an earlier Quebec Superior Court decision that stated, "The court is of the opinion that the sole fact of touching does not constitute an act of prostitution ... The touching has to constitute a sexual exchange like masturbation, fellatio, penetration or sodomy" (Tibbetts, Reevely, and King 1999).

References

Act to Amend the Liquor Licence Act, R.S.O. 1973, c. 68, 69.

Armatage, K., dir. 1980. *Striptease.* Toronto: Lauron Productions.

Arpin, C. 1983. Quebec girls winning Ontario's 'battle of strippers.' *Montreal Gazette,* 5 December, A1, A2. http://news.google.com/.

Baldwin, M. 2004. *Burlesque and the new bump-n-grind.* Golden, CO: Speck Press.

Brock, D.R. 1998. *Making work, making trouble: Prostitution as a social problem.* Toronto: University of Toronto Press.

Cockerline, D., Gwendolyn, and A. Sorfleet. 1993. A brief history of sex worker activism in Toronto. Sex Workers Alliance of Toronto. http://www.walnet.org/.

Cooke, A. 1987. Stripping: Who calls the tune. In *Good girls, bad girls: Sex trade workers and feminists face to face,* ed. L. Bell, 92-99. Toronto: Women's Press.

Fifty years of striptease. 1979. *Toronto Globe and Mail Weekend Magazine,* 3 February, n.p.

Gulliver, T. 2006. Harnessed anger: Living history/the sound of smashing bathhouse doors in 1981 is still with us. *Xtra!* 2 February. http://www.xtra.ca/.

Hanlon, M. 1964. Commercials crash telephone weather. *Toronto Globe and Mail,* 29 July, 9.

Lewis, J. 2000. Controlling lap dancing: Law, morality, and sex work. In *Sex for sale: Prostitution, pornography, and the sex industry,* ed. R. Weitzer, 203-96. New York: Routledge.

Liepe-Levinson, K. 2002. *Strip show: Performances of gender and desire.* London: Routledge.

Mann, R., dir. 1992. *Twist.* Toronto: Sphinx Productions.

Popplewell, B. 2008. Bye lap dance, hello laptop. *Toronto Star,* 28 April. http://www.thestar.com/.

Rodger, D. 1998. A Reflection on the glorious history of: Local 58, I.A.T.S.E. Toronto, IATSE. http://www.iatse58.org/downloads/Local58History.pdf.

Ross, B.L. 2009. *Burlesque west: Showgirls, sex, and sin in postwar Vancouver.* Toronto: University of Toronto Press.

Shteir, R. 2004. *Striptease: The untold story of the girlie show.* New York: Oxford University Press.

Swan, S. 1996. Only a go-go girl in love. *Toronto Life,* November, n.p.

The World. 1912. Save morals of young from salacious burlesque. (As we were). 21 May, n.p.

Tibbetts, J., D. Reevely, and M. King. 1999. Top court swings toward lap dance. *Montreal Gazette,* 14 December, A1.

Toronto Globe and Mail. 1963. Eaton's: Another great fashion exclusive. 13 September, 50.

Case Cited

R. v. Pelletier, [1999] 3 S.C.R. 863.

2

Myths and Realities of Male Sex Work: A Personal Perspective

RIVER REDWOOD

My life as a sex worker started one night when my high school boyfriend and I were riding the streetcar home from a concert. We were both sixteen years old. An older guy sat down behind us, told us it was his birthday, and offered us money if we'd get off the streetcar and beat his ass with his belt. For every lash we gave him, we got two dollars. I'd charge much more by today's standards, but we were curious boys, and it was hard to say no. The guy ended up having a great birthday, it was fun for us both, and we got a good workout beating his butt bright red. My friend and I still joke about it today – and both of us continue to do sex work: a hardcore leather master top, he is also a graduate of the London School of Economics, and he holds a senior position in government; I'm a forty-one-year-old gay male porn performer, producer, and director. I'm also a male escort and have turned tricks in alleyways, stairwells, parks, and cars, and I've operated out of apartments, condos, dungeons, and hotels. I've had a long list of sugar daddies and can't even begin to tell you how many men I've slept with; it's definitely well into the several thousands. My life might seem really different or outrageous compared to most, but in reality I'm just a normal guy. Over my working years I've found that my biggest challenges have come not from sex work but from people's misperceptions, stereotypes, and prejudices. This chapter will attempt to bust some myths and present some realities about sex work and sex workers by drawing on my personal experiences in the industry.

Sex Workers Are Regular People

My partner and I have been together for fourteen years, I pay a mortgage and bills, and I've held down several regular good-paying "straight" jobs. I don't currently have a problem with substance use and never have. I'm attractive and work out regularly, but I'm not a bodybuilder or a supermodel. I eat and sleep like everyone else. In other words, I'm not only a male sex worker with a lengthy history in the industry, but at the end of the day, I'm a lot like everybody else.

Male sex workers are all over the place. All you have to do is Google the term "gay porn" to see them instantly pop up on your computer screen. There really is no shortage of guys out there having sex for money, yet in discussions of sex work, male workers and their experiences are often ignored. It's rare that male sex workers get to speak for ourselves in our own words. Few people seem to want to talk publicly about the nitty-gritty of hooking up and having gay sex, let alone spend time thinking about the realities of men paying other guys to have sex. Yet it's the daily reality for myself and an entire world of people I know and love dearly.

There are many reasons why men start doing sex work; people enter it at different points in their lives, for different motivations, and in many different ways. Some men choose sex work because they enjoy both it and the lifestyle that goes with it. Others do it for a short time as an experiment or fantasy or simply to see what it's like. Some do it part-time on the side for fun and to make extra money. And others do it because they simply have no other options. Like all occupations, it's best when you are in control of what you are doing and have choices about it. I have done sex work out of necessity and to meet my basic survival needs, but I'm much happier if I'm doing it when I have options. I've also worked in some totally terrible straight jobs because I've simply had to do them. Lots of people are stuck in jobs they don't like, but sometimes a job is the only means to an end.

I can't imagine how different and limited my world would have been had I not had the opportunity to engage in sex work. It's allowed me to make good money, to meet people, to travel, and to develop insights and experiences about society and myself. Most importantly, it has helped me to grow into a much fuller, better, and more rounded human being.

Sex Work Can Be a Good Job

I left what could only be described as an extremely dysfunctional home at age seventeen. I quickly realized that I had limited options and found the idea of spending the rest of my life in a minimum-wage job totally unappealing. At the time, I was working in a shoe store for $6.25 an hour; I also had a sugar daddy with a luxury condo. One perfect summer day, I was dreading having to leave his place to go in for another long shift of boring drudgery for little pay. My trick wasn't happy to see me go either. He asked me how much I would make at the shoe store that day; sad to say, it was about fifty bucks. He offered me three hundred dollars to call in sick and spend the day with him, hanging out and drinking by the pool. It doesn't take a rocket scientist to figure out which was the better choice.

The crucial components of male sex work, like many other types of work, include listening to the client, communication, and acting out a role (Sanders 2005). The mechanics don't have to be that difficult, but they do involve a distinct set of skills. Indeed, sex work takes skill and ability, like anything else in life, and at the end of the day, it is a job like any other. It's not uncommon to hear that the majority of people hate what they do for a living. I'm happy to say I'm not part of that percentage. I get to set my own hours and pick where, when, how, and with whom I work. I'm my own boss and often get to sleep in late during the week. I may not have a pension plan or health benefits, but realistically, when you look at the facts, male sex work really isn't very different from any other kind of freelance job.

However, because of the stigma and stereotypes about my work, it can be very difficult for me to get a non-sex-industry job (see Chapter 7 in this volume). Although I have a range of skills and experiences, I'm often forced to drop things off my resumé or just plain lie in job interviews. For example, I can edit and direct commercial movies – I've produced a number of films that are sold in stores across the country, some of which have been nominated for international awards. I've spent a good chunk of my time learning and working with video equipment and editing software. I've also designed many print advertisements and box-covers that have appeared in magazines. My interpersonal skills are the best in town. Sounds like the perfect dude to hire for your next commercial project, right? The problem is that my work experience has been sex-related. If I apply for work at a straight company that produces non-porn films or deals with non-sex-related material, this is a major issue. I can't be honest about my professional history or the projects I've worked on. I have a few pieces of work that are passable for a mainstream audience (for example, the thirty-second commercial I did for men's jockstraps), but my best work is my porn films.

When a mainstream employer wants to see my portfolio, I can't just walk into an interview, pull out my best collection of porn pieces, and say, "Look at the special effects in this tape," or "Don't you just love the angle of the camera for the cum-shot?" or "Doesn't the lighting design create the perfect environment for the anal sex dungeon scene?" Many sex workers have great professional skills, but they can't put them on their resumé for fear of stigma or the simple fact that their work isn't recognized as legitimate. If they worked in a strip club, escort agency, bathhouse, or massage parlour, they are forced to come up with a different name or alternative for how they've been employed. In other words, they are made to lie.

I once met with an employment counsellor to create a resumé. I put down all my straight jobs, educational information, and the usual junk you'd put in. However, I also included my full videography, porn, sex work, gay activist work, awards, and community group involvement. It filled five pages. But once we cut out everything that was gay- or sex-related, we ended up with a skimpy page and a half. It was hardly a true description of my abilities, and if I were competing for a job with my mainstream contemporaries, I'd barely be qualified to work in even a so-called low-skill job. I'm skilled enough to work for the CBC, but it's not likely I'll ever be given the chance. Thankfully, I'm happy where I am, doing the work I do, but if I weren't, it would be a difficult path to a different career.

Stigma, Stereotypes, and Homophobia Are Harmful

In my experience, I've become acutely aware of the striking similarities between issues related to male and female sex work. I've found that the stereotypes surrounding female sex workers can also be applied to men in the industry. For example, by mainstream societal standards, sex workers are often portrayed as worthless or disposable bodies who are doing a horrific job against their will (Hoigard and Finstad 1992; Jeffreys 2004; MacKinnon 2005). They are also commonly positioned as victims of abuse who are exploited by some older, nasty male figure (Barry 1979; Dworkin 1981). We are viewed as unethical, diseased, and suffering from post-traumatic stress disorder (Farley 1998). The list of myths goes on and on, with few people stopping to challenge them.

Male sex workers, especially those of us who are gay, face the same stigma and discrimination as women but have the additional burden of dealing with even greater invisibility and increased marginalization. Services and social supports are lacking for us, and we face the pressures of masculine stereotypes and intense homophobia from both straight people and within the gay community itself.

Many professionals have to endure stereotypes; for example, computer technicians are often seen as geeks, and bankers are perceived as conservative and uptight. However, none of these stereotypes can be equated to the harshness and discrimination that comes with being labelled a sex worker. It seems that no matter what people do for a living, even if their job has a bunch of negative outcomes for humanity or the environment, they still get more respect than someone who turns tricks on a street corner; most people aren't branded as sick or diseased for doing their job.

Sex-negative and homophobic attitudes can do extreme damage to our health and well-being. Too often I've seen male sex workers who have internalized negative homophobic beliefs engage in self-destructive behaviour. These men are often ashamed of the work they do and are sometimes even ashamed of their clients. Condemned to silence, we live in a world that is full of repressive systems and institutions, be they religious, legal, cultural, social, governmental, or medical. In these circumstances, is it any wonder that some people might find sex work unappealing?

I've found the best way to deal with these pressures is to surround myself with people whose belief systems are compatible with my own; for example, this would include a community of gay and straight sex workers from a variety of genders who are sex-positive with non-judgmental attitudes. I often find myself gravitating toward these people so that I can be open about what I do and who I am. I am much more closeted in mainstream environments, and it takes time before I'll fully disclose my past to someone. After a period of testing the waters and building trust, I'll disclose my work but otherwise I find it's often just not worth the effort.

Sex work stigma and homophobia are particularly evident in the context of health care. For example, when I disclose to a doctor that I'm a gay man or a sex worker, I'm often met with a host of questions, usually not at all related to the reason why I'm there. Suddenly my queerness and my work become the sole focus of who I am as a patient. Doctors want to do a battery of STI (sexually transmitted infections) and HIV tests regardless of how clear I make it that I practise safe sex and already get tested regularly. It's as though everything I say needs to be second-guessed, and I can't be trusted. I often find myself forced into the role of sex educator when I really just want to be treated for an in-grown toenail!

Sex Work and Pornography Are Not Always Exploitative

Everyone I know, including my seventy-year-old mother, has at some point viewed a piece of pornography. The majority of adults seem to enjoy it on some level; after all, it brings in more money every year than the entire Hollywood film industry. Yet few people attempt to understand or comprehend what's involved in the making of pornography. It's much easier to label certain things as bad, to go along with stereotypes, and to ignore the reality that there are many shades of grey in experiences of making porn. We shouldn't be so quick to say that the porn industry is bad just because people are getting paid to perform sex. Pornography is hardly the only industry we should be focusing on when we talk about labour abuses and unfair work practices; as has been widely documented, harm and exploitation are abundant in non-sex-industry workplaces (Vosko 2006; WAC 2007). In our capitalist economy, we are all subjected to and culprits of exploitation of one kind or another.

One time I was working on an amateur porn film with a group of guys; the film involved shooting an orgy scene. One of the guys had never done anything like this before and was extremely nervous about what was going to happen. We talked about it for a long time, and he was given many choices and chances not to do things. Needless to say, after the day was done and he'd had sex with his fill of multiple beautiful men, he couldn't stop talking about how great the shoot was. In fact, for months afterward, he was begging to be put into another movie.

Since working in gay and straight porn, I have found stories like this to be extremely common. Most people on the set, both in front of the camera and behind it, are glad to be there, and work tends to be fun and respectful. I have never seen anyone forced to do something he or she didn't want to do; if I did, I'd be headed straight out the door. Unless you're pumping someone full of Viagra, it's difficult for a man to perform in porn if he doesn't want to be doing it. Further, pornography is a highly controlled and regulated industry; there are a ton of rules and regulations that govern what we can and can't do on- and off-screen. Why don't stories like this get told more often? Why do we focus on the negative stories and stereotypes in porn?

Due to the stigma surrounding pornography, many sex workers feel that they cannot be open with family, friends, and service providers about their line of work. Can you imagine Hollywood actors not being allowed to talk about their acting or the movies they're making? This double standard simply allows for the further exploitation of sex workers; it doesn't help provide them with the ability to access services, such as employment standards and worker's compensation, that normally protect people in other industries. No one is ever going to stop pornography or prostitution from taking place; nor should it be attempted. They will always be around, and the sooner society embraces this, the better things will be for everyone. In my view, people working in the sex industry need to be empowered to have control over their bodies and workspaces, and to have the freedom to celebrate what they do.

Pornography Is about Acting and Performing

For nearly every porn film I have been involved with, the end result doesn't look anything like the actual process of making the film. A shoot of a single scene can take many hours to set up and perform, involving many different angles, stops, and starts. All of the materials from the day of the shoot are then chopped down and compressed into a few minutes. This means that all the humour or joking on set is cut out, and the viewer never sees the lights or other crew in the room. Even the personality of the performers gets dropped onto the cutting room floor. The final product is a reflection of what the producers and director think the consumer wants to buy. The names, situations, and narratives in porn are usually, if not always, fake.

To my mind, porn is best described as idealized sexual fiction. It's not the best place for people to learn about sexual communication in the real world; it is merely there to be enjoyed for what it is. When you see Superman jumping out a window in a movie, you wouldn't try to emulate it in reality, because you know it's fake and you'd probably end up hurting yourself if you tried. It's the same with porn. Yet so many people fall into the trap of believing that porn sex is real sex, which can cause no end of problems for them in reality. My job as a sex worker often involves reproducing fantasies for other people. This can be a lot of fun to do, and I definitely take pride in this and enjoy doing it. However, it's critically important for people to understand that what they are seeing in front of a camera is a performance; it's actors who are acting out a prescribed role that often does not reflect who they are or what they do in real life. If people want to believe that what they are viewing is real, they are setting themselves up for a big disappointment.

Clients Can Be Nice, Sweet, and Normal Guys

My ideal client is someone who is clean, treats himself and me with respect, understands the rules I set, doesn't pressure me to change things, and agrees to pay me for what I'm worth. The vast majority of my clients fall into this category. A lot of the guys I meet are nervous, shy, or just looking to have some NSA (no strings attached) fun. Quite often they have fantasies they want to try or experience and needs that they want to fulfill.

In contrast, for some of my more long-term sugar daddies, client relationships are often about projecting secret fantasies onto me. Some like to take the role of a mentor or enjoy having me there for companionship. They can fall in love with the person they think I am or even the real me should I decide to share that part of myself with them. I can't lie and say that every trick I've turned has been great or that I've never had a bad experience, but can anyone say this about every job he or she has worked in? I've definitely had my share of both crappy and fun stories! For me, doing sex work is 99 percent good and 1 percent not so cool. I think these are really good odds and probably way better than for other people, such as, for example, firemen, industrial tradespersons, construction workers, retail employees, or health care workers.

When I do have a bad client, it's usually someone who is really messed up by societal factors, his family life, or his own prejudices or stereotypes. He's not some happy-go-lucky guy looking for some dick to suck on, but someone who's deeply hurt and struggling with his own core issues; he needs help more than anything else. If sex education were better, it would go a long way to improving the lives of these clients and their families. Ultimately, we're all suffering in the current system of silence and sexual ignorance. There are usually telltale signs of a bad client, and I have no problem leaving, stopping something midway, or kicking somebody out. What's sad is that, under the current legal system, we sex workers can't even organize ourselves and teach each other techniques or run workshops about how to screen clients. Nor can we form unions and demand basic labour rights and protections (see Chapter 8 in this volume). This is frustrating to me and shows the disregard for sex workers' realities and our safety. Those of us with first-hand experience could and should be allowed to share our knowledge with other people who work in the profession.

Men Can Be Victims of Sexual Assault

Due to issues of masculinity, a man who has been sexually assaulted is rarely seen as a victim. It is more often the case that he will believe, or will be made to feel, that the assault was his own fault because he wasn't masculine enough. This situation can be doubly compounded if you're a male sex worker and are assaulted by another man. To this day, I would never call the police to help me in connection with a work-related issue. I shudder at the thought of how they would react and deal with the situation. If anything, I view the police as being more dangerous than the most horrendous trick. For similar reasons, I would never choose to engage with the legal system. My hesitation to involve myself with the law is not unique – it is a common feeling among many male sex workers, and it leaves us extremely vulnerable and unprotected against violence and assault.

If a male sex worker is assaulted, there are very few services and supports he can access. Rape crisis and sexual assault centres aren't places that my male sex worker friends, or even my female sex worker friends, would consider calling in an emergency. The sad reality is that it's often better to deal with the situation on your own or with close friends than to risk the ignorance and abuse of a professional. A clear message is being sent that my life experiences, safety, and needs are unimportant. Fortunately, I do have a group of people in my life that I can count on for support, and through hard work I have been able to find doctors and other professionals who treat me with respect and for whom my sex work is not an issue. Unfortunately, not everyone has access to these supports, a grim reality for many sex workers who are sexually assaulted.

Sex Workers Are Stigmatized as Drug Users with STIs

Too often, sex work and drugs are automatically linked in people's minds. If I say that I'm a sex worker, people often draw the conclusion that I'm also a drug user. Some sex workers do use drugs, just like some accountants and lawyers, but not all of us do. And for those of us who do, it's not necessarily a problem in our work or personal lives.

I used to have a client who was a doctor. I saw him over several months and he strangely started to deteriorate after a while; he was a nice guy but looked like he hadn't been sleeping. After he stopped showing up for our appointments, I went to his office one day, only to find that it was closed. Eventually I learned that he had lost his medical licence because of a crystal meth addiction. I saw him homeless and on the street a year later. A lot of people can become addicted to substances for a lot of different reasons, but nobody would ever say he started using crystal meth because he was a doctor.

I don't think sex work has to be about drugs. Lots of people in a range of different fields do drugs. Rich people are simply better able to hide their addiction problems than those with less money. People will do what is required to get what they need; some may end up stealing or doing sex work to pay for substances. Penalizing, blaming, and judging people for their addictions will not help them. I personally have never used chemical drugs and have no desire to start. I occasionally use marijuana, but drugs aren't a part of my life. I can't say the same for a lot of the lawyers I know! There are definitely sex workers who party when they are working, but there are lots out there who don't.

As with drugs, people love to assume that because I have sex for work, I must be walking around with a ton of sexually transmitted infections. This too is an unfair assumption that reflects the extent to which sex workers are stigmatized. We never think that because a hairstylist touches hair all day, she must have ringworm and lice. How about nurses and doctors, who are surrounded by sick people and who touch their bodies all day? It's assumed that because they are professionals, they care about protecting themselves, but for sex workers, well, that's a different story.

I personally don't know anyone who purposely goes out and wants to get sick or to contract an infection. Sex workers are no different in this regard. We are not out looking to give people HIV and certainly aren't in a hurry to get it. The majority of sex workers I know are super comfortable with condoms and know how to use them properly. Safer sex supplies are an integral part of our work because we use them regularly, yet it's often assumed that we don't know what we are doing. Could you imagine a construction worker not knowing how to wear a hardhat or safety boots? In my experience, sex workers communicate about sex and sexual health directly with their clients, and just like the construction worker, they know the tools of their trade.

Not All Male Sex Workers Are Gay and Have Male Clients

Although the majority of a male sex worker's clients are men, this doesn't mean that women never hire us; they definitely do and can sometimes be quite aggressive about it. I had a friend who worked as a stripper for women in Montreal. Often he was paid to go into the back area to do private lap dances, where some of the women would open their shirts and ask him to ejaculate on their breasts. For some men this would be a dream job! My friend, however, would never do it because of the potential implications. He was concerned that the women might return to the bar with his cum on their breasts and threaten to charge him with assault. It wasn't worth the risk, no matter how much money he was offered.

Many people believe that if you are a male sex worker, you must be gay. I know a lot of straight-identified male sex workers who will sleep with men for a variety of reasons (this is often called being gay for pay). Some do it to satisfy basic survival needs, others to get money for drugs, and others just to pay the rent. Some simply do it because it pays more than their mainstream jobs ever could. I know lots of straight men who prefer to spend their days working out at the gym; sex work gives them the time, money, and freedom to do this.

Some of my straight male friends who like to drink sometimes find themselves short on cash at the end of the month. Because they can't afford to buy drinks on their own, they'll come with me to the gay bar to flirt and tease the gay men there. Often, the gay guys are quite eager and happy to buy them drinks, and the situation works out well for everyone: the gay guy gets to hang out with a super-hot straight boy for the night, and the straight boy gets all the drinks he needs to keep him happy. Some male sex workers will similarly barter in this way; trading companionship for a necessity or a desired item is often an easy exchange. Sex doesn't have to be part of the equation.

For many straight-identified male sex workers, the threat of being found out by their peers or of being labelled bisexual or gay is often too big a risk. It pains me to think of all the men who work under these homophobic pressures and the difficulty it causes them. Ultimately, I think people should be able to label themselves as they wish without fear of reprisal. Yet so many people find this difficult to do and believe. When I was working in porn, I found that a lot of gay guys would make disparaging comments about the performers who engaged in gay sex for the camera but who insisted on being called straight afterward. A lot of these performers were happily married with wives and/or girlfriends and had families. Sex work was work for them, and they were acting in porn for the cash, pure and simple. If you choose to believe their performance is real, it just means they are good at their job. If you like what they do on the set, who cares how they identify afterward?

I have been hired by and have had sex with several women in my life, yet most people who meet me would never label me as straight. Usually, once they start talking to me, they figure out that I'm gay. I am not hyper-effeminate or anything, but I cannot pass for straight; nor do I desire to be straight or to pretend to be a heterosexual male. This can affect the type of clients I attract and the way I interact with them. Most of the time, it's a non-issue as I'm cute and good at what I do. However, it can cause difficulties for some clients who have internalized homophobia and masculine gender issues, even though I tend to be a top in the bedroom. Often these clients are uncomfortable having gay sex to begin with and can find that sex with a gay man triggers their issues and fears. This doesn't make for a good fit for either of us, and I'm happy there are other guys out there with whom they can pair up.

Sex Workers Are No More Susceptible to Body Issues than Anyone Else

I work out at the gym three to four times a week and follow a rigid diet plan. I have been doing this for years to ensure that my body is the best it can be; I'm very happy with how I look. I'm often told that I'm the most beautiful boy alive, and I get constant praise for my body from my clients. I personally think I'm a regular joe, but I'll gladly accept the flattery and the money that comes with it. That said, I was in a bathhouse once and a guy touched my stomach and said I was very beautiful except I could do with "eating a few less" hamburgers. The very next week I was in the same place, absolutely nothing had changed with my weight, and someone different said I needed to "eat a few more" hamburgers. Was I too big or was I too skinny? Should I even care what either person thought? For me, the key to sex work is having good self-esteem, being comfortable with the body you've got, and knowing you'll never be able to please everyone.

Like clients of a female sex worker who want her to have large breasts, clients of male sex workers often focus on dick size. Some men like muscle guys and some men like skinny boys. There is room for a great deal of diversity in the sex industry, and no one can ever be everyone's type. That's not to say that stereotypes don't exist or that we are not pressured to be fit or to look a particular way. We are all subject to the beauty myth (Wolf 1991) regardless of where we work or what gender we are. This might be more obvious for women, but men must also increasingly fit into idealized images of beauty. Not surprisingly, this can affect male sex workers directly in the work that they do. Despite what society leads us to believe, most men deal with intense body issues; and for those of us in the sex industry, they can be even more of a concern.

Like many people whose work directly involves the body, such as dancers, models, or actors, male sex workers can experience a lot of pressure to have a certain type of physique. They also encounter intense racism, classism, ageism, and almost any other "ism" you can think of. Interestingly, however, things often play out differently in the bedroom. For example, there is an assumption that big guys or bodybuilders are supposed to be a top. Yet more often than not, I find the bigger guys are eager to be on the bottom and can't wait to try taking it in the ass if given the chance. My feelings are that these "isms" and biases apparent in male sex work reflect the power dynamics that exist in larger society. I know from experience that you can never judge a book by its cover and that beauty comes in many different forms.

Conclusion

Despite all the myths and misconceptions, the reality is that sex work has been a great choice for me, and I will defend it passionately. That said, male sex work is not the job of choice for everyone. It has its share of pressures and issues like any other occupation. However, it has been a great experience for me, and my life has been deeply enriched by it. At the end of the day, it's my body, my life (which I enjoy very much), and my choice to do what I do. I hope that, one day, society will learn to accept the realities of sex work and see it for what it is – a lot more complex and diverse than most people think. This occupation is all about knowing and believing in who you are and being able to set strong boundaries. What makes the job difficult is not the work itself but the crap that society throws toward people who engage in it. Sucking cock for cash is easy; it's the moralistic judgments for doing so that create bigger problems and can be harmful for sex workers. Personally I've never understood why sex work is such a big deal, but clearly my life adventures make other people uncomfortable. If people would challenge their stereotypes and drop their stigmas, phobias, judgments, and biases, this would create more space for male sex workers to exist with respect. Ultimately, I think we'd all be a lot freer, healthier, and happier with ourselves, and would generally be on our way to having much more fun and better sex!

References

Barry, K. 1979. *Female sexual slavery.* Englewood Cliffs: Prentice-Hall.

Dworkin, A. 1981. *Pornography: Men possessing women.* London: Women's Press.

Farley, M. 1998. Prostitution, violence, and posttraumatic stress disorder. *Women and Health* 27, 3: 37-49.

Hoigard, C., and L. Finstad. 1992. *Backstreets: Prostitution, money, and love.* University Park: Pennsylvania State University Press.

Jeffreys, S. 2004. Prostitution as harmful cultural practice. In *Not for sale: Feminists resisting prostitution and pornography,* ed. C. Stark and R. Whisnant, 386-99. North Melbourne: Spinifex Press.

MacKinnon, C. 2005. Pornography as trafficking. *Michigan Journal of International Law* 26, 4: 993-1012.

Sanders, T. 2005. 'It's just acting': Sex workers' strategies for capitalizing on sexuality. *Gender, Work and Organization* 12, 4: 319-42.

Vosko, L.F., ed. 2006. *Precarious employment: Understanding labour market insecurity in Canada.* Montreal and Kingston: McGill-Queen's University Press.

WAC (Worker's Action Center). 2007. *Working on the edge.* Toronto: Worker's Action Center.

Wolf, N. 1991. *The beauty myth: How images of beauty are used against women.* New York: Anchor Books.

3

Champagne, Strawberries, and Truck-Stop Motels: On Subjectivity and Sex Work

VICTORIA LOVE

I grew up in a small farming community in rural Ontario, and not unlike many teenagers in rural communities, I remember feeling trapped by my life in the country and also by the difficulties of living with a severely alcoholic father. I was a very artistic teenager; I took ballet, jazz, and piano lessons for years, and though I was very shy, I loved to perform. I watched the movie *Fame* obsessively, found inspiration in the glossy pages of dance and fashion magazines, and dreamed of a much more interesting and exciting life far away from the one I found myself in.

I was about fourteen years old when Madam Alex, the infamous Los Angeles madam, was in the news. I came across a magazine article profiling her and some of her "call girls." I was immediately intrigued. I studied the article closely, paying attention to any information about how the women dressed, what lingerie they wore, and how they did their makeup. To me, the women in the photos espoused a beauty and glamour that I could only dream of. I didn't completely understand what it meant to be a call girl; I knew it involved sex, but that was about it. What I did know was that the women were beautiful and that I wanted to be like them.

Even when I consider the ups, downs, and sometimes difficult times working in the sex industry, this glamour does indeed exist for me, and it's part of what brings me back to the strip club, the parlour, or the agency time and time again. That moment when, as a young woman, I discovered the cultural mystique of the call girl, marked a point of departure as I journeyed through the rest of my life. In the following, I will discuss some of my experiences over my ten-year career in the sex industry, during which I have shifted from a working-class to middle-class subjectivity. I will also describe my experience of how feminist theories that conceptualize sex work as exploitation and violence have had a harmful impact on my understanding of both my work and myself.

Beginnings: Working Sex as a Young Woman

My family situation became increasingly difficult for me to deal with, and I left home when I was just fifteen. People who hear my story often want to impose narratives about familial abuse that caused me to enter prostitution, but that's not how I understand my situation. Growing up in a patriarchal nuclear family, where, because of his economic and gender privilege, my father was not held accountable for his actions, taught me about power. For me, starting to do sex work, in addition to satisfying a critical need for money, was an empowering way of saying "fuck you" to the family structure that had hurt me. It was also a way of gaining independence and avoiding the situation I saw my mom endure for so many years.

By the time I was seventeen, a friend and I were living in an apartment in a working-class city in southern Ontario. Although I had always excelled in academics, I had lost interest in high school and didn't return after the eleventh grade. Instead, I started working at a coffee shop down the street from my apartment. My roommate was trying to finish high school and was on welfare; together we dreamed about being fashion designers, and we plastered our apartment with images from *Vogue* magazine. We smoked pot, did drugs, and listened to techno music. My life was enjoyable in that it was carefree, but it was also tumultuous and difficult, especially financially.

Still holding on to that image of the call girls from years earlier, I picked up the local newspaper and phoned an advertisement for an escort agency. My first client was an older man; I wasn't really sure what to do, and I gave the guy a blow job. When it was over, I remember feeling that it wasn't as difficult as I'd expected, and I was happy to have some money in my hand. In one hour, I made as much money as I would have in two days of pouring coffee and having customers get angry at me if I got their order wrong. What I didn't like, though, was the agency owner; after a while he started to act as if I owed him something, expecting to have sex with me for free and pressuring me to work all the time.

I eventually left the agency for another one that turned out to be much better for me. I was still seventeen, and the new agency wanted to see my identification; I gave them my friend's driver's licence and pretended that I was twenty-two years old. I'd never had access to so much money – all of a sudden, I was able to pay my bills, buy food for myself and my roommate, and afford the clothing and perfume that made me feel beautiful. All of this made me feel quite powerful in the context of my life; for the first time, I felt that I was somebody and my self-confidence started to grow.

Although I held on to the image of the intriguing and glamorous call girl, my early years in the business were mostly not like this. I had a lot of fun times, but many moments were decidedly not glamorous. I'm sure I've spent more time in budget hotels and truck-stop motels than any of Madam Alex's girls ever did! I don't remember much about the clients, but the majority of calls were without any problems. Sometimes I'd work in the rich neighbourhood just outside the city I lived in, and I saw homes and met people who were unlike any I'd ever seen in my whole life. This gave me a host of new things to dream about. After seeing the good life of some of my clients, I set my sights on going to university.

Shifting Identity: Middle-Class Subjectivity and Anti-Sex-Work Sentiment

Eventually I saved my money, got breast implants, and started to work as an exotic dancer. I became involved with my first boyfriend, a man I met as a client, who was the first person I ever really loved. He bought a condo and I lived in it as I finished high school while dancing. Also around this time, negative values surrounding sex work started to affect my thoughts and feelings about my occupation. My feminist consciousness was beginning to develop, and as I searched the shelves of my local public library for information about prostitution (I was not familiar with the term "sex work" at the time), the books gave me the distinct feeling that what I was doing was very wrong. I started to wonder if I was being exploited, if I was doing something bad for women; I began to experience deep and crushing shame, and convinced myself that I was going to die of AIDS. To cope with the shame and judgment, I started to adopt a negative perspective on the sex industry and my place within it. I broke up with my boyfriend, applied for welfare, moved in with my mother, and passed on the judgment I felt to other women I knew in industry, wondering why they couldn't get their lives together like I had. I finally started university, intent on helping all the women who just weren't as lucky as I thought I was.

My change of perspectives about sex work was an attempt to cope with a new and profound shame and also marked the start of my transition into a bourgeois feminine subject position that seeks to save Others and to be understood as an ethical subject (see Heron 2007). In retrospect, I understand that this shift was about my own identity as a white working-class woman moving into a middle-class subjectivity and not about some realization of the "truth" about sex work. At the time, however, I felt that I had to prove to myself and others that I was something more than just a prostitute, even if that meant reinterpreting my history in ways that didn't reflect my lived experience. For years, I wished, more than anything in the world, that I could cut out or somehow amputate my sex-working past. I imagined scalpels, knives, and tools that draw blood and injure.

Although I was affected by the general stigma that society places upon all sex workers, my initial foray into feminist theorizing on prostitution caused me to loathe parts of my own history and experience, wresting from me a belief in my resilience and the pride I felt about being able to take care of myself as a youth in difficult circumstances. My encounter with anti-prostitution feminism while I was finishing high school and starting university produced a painful and significant rupture in my self-concept, reifying a division between a prostitute self and a straight self. The realization of how bad it was to be a prostitute made me feel disgusted; I was so ashamed that when I looked in the mirror, I almost couldn't bear the sight of myself. The only way I was able to speak of my involvement in sex work – if I ever did – was as a "reformed" prostitute. But when I stumbled upon other ways of understanding prostitution – initially through a history of sex work written by a sex worker (Roberts 1992) – I began to change the way I thought about myself.

Take 2: My Return to the Sex Industry

Whereas my initial involvement in sex work occurred when I was a youth with limited options for supporting myself financially, my return to it was marked by race and class privilege. While I was finishing my undergraduate degree, I was exposed to sex-radical theory (Rubin 1984), sex-positive feminism (Chapkis 1997), and the third wave of the women's movement (Baumgardner and Richards 2000), which changed almost everything I thought I knew about the sex industry. Maybe feminists who claimed that prostitution was exploitation had it wrong? Maybe the clients weren't misogynists? Maybe I wasn't such a fuck-up after all? I began to rethink my own history and started to feel the first stirrings of pride in my experiences rather than shame and disgust. Despite my burgeoning middle-class subjectivity and my new educational capital, I was still working-class economically, so my shift in thinking also reflected my material circumstances and the fact that I had few options to pay for the graduate education that I intended to pursue in Toronto.

When I was in my final undergraduate year, I started to work at a Toronto escort agency on the weekends. Just as I had nearly ten years before, I initially felt excited and empowered by the work, only this time I was embracing the side of myself that I had tried to obliterate through radical and anti-sex-work feminist ideas. In a number of ways this was a very affirming experience; it was again like giving a big "fuck you," but this time to the feminists and others who had caused me to feel such incapacitating shame that sometimes I wanted to die.

I worked at the agency for a number of years before moving to a massage parlour and then transitioning into independent escort work. For me, independent escort work was a wholly different experience from working at an agency. When I worked at agencies, I saw regulars with whom I had ongoing relationships, but I never established the sort of emotionally intimate and enduring connections that I've developed with my clients as an independent. I have clients whom I've been seeing for years, and others I expect to see for perhaps the rest of their lives. Some of my clients are part of my social life, some bring me gifts on my birthday, and in one case, we even celebrate the date of our first appointment as our anniversary.

My clients provide me with access to experiences that I could not afford on my own, such as using a car service or going out to expensive restaurants. On rare occasions, someone I meet as a client enters fully into my personal life, becoming a friend or lover. Sometimes my relationships with clients are neither fully personal nor fully commercial, existing in a space we don't have the language to describe. Likewise, my own feelings about clients exist somewhere between personal and commercial. Although the exchange for sexual services mostly takes a monetary form, there is also an exchange that exceeds the purely financial to encompass dinners, gifts, and opportunities for travel.

The Girlfriend Experience: Emotional Labour and Intimacy in Sex Work

Like many workers in many labour sectors, I don't have a firm boundary between my work life and my personal life, and my interactions with clients are simultaneously genuine and performative (see Sanders 2005). If some of my clients were to become ill or go into hospital, I know I would become a support person for them. Although I bring what I understand as my authentic self to interactions with clients (Bernstein 2007), what they often see are aspects of my personality that are strategically woven together to produce a particular effect or the persona that I seek to create. In other words, as much as I present authentic variations of who I am, the pieces are purposefully stitched together to present a confident,

Victoria Love

intelligent, and entertaining companion, one who can charge rates at the high end of the sex industry.

At some moments, my emotionally intensive relationships with clients are positive and affirming; at other times, the labour involved is draining. Many of my clients relate to me as a girlfriend, largely because there are few other frameworks or ways to understand our relationship. As a result, I am constantly trying to manage boundaries and maintain balance when my clients – perhaps unwittingly – attempt to take too much of my time and energy. Sometimes the things that I see as providing good service, such as allowing the appointment to go over time, talking to them on the telephone, and sending text messages, are interpreted as acts of intimacy and affection, further confusing the already complex relationship. It's not uncommon for clients to develop deep feelings for me, and though I care for them, I typically do not feel this level of emotional connection. It's also not uncommon for my clients to want to know what I enjoy sexually, how I feel about them, and if I'm just with them for the money. The management of clients' feelings and desire for access to my personal life is the part of the job I find most difficult.

When I reflect on my experiences, I see that I have very successfully used my time in the sex industry to achieve a level of material comfort and financial stability that I would not otherwise have attained. Indeed, were it not for my work in the industry, it's unlikely that I could have pursued post-graduate education, bought a home, or had access to a middle-class lifestyle and all the perks that go with it. Perhaps the irony of my situation is that the education I pursued in the expectation that it would lead to a job outside the sex industry is partly what has permitted me such success within it (see Bernstein 2007).

How my sexual labour is used in the industry is very much related to how I am positioned as a white, bourgeois, feminine subject; my rural working-class background, my family's immigrant status, and the marginalization I experienced as a youth have become hidden from view. At a young age, I identified with the subject position of the call girl, of which Madam Alex's girls are but one example, and in a sense, this created my persona as an "upscale escort." This image and the ideas associated with it are a component of what I sell to clients, rather than my self or body per se; the meanings associated with the call girl produce the experiences for which my clientele are willing to pay significant amounts of money.

Sometimes my clients tell me that they've chosen me in preference to other escorts because I'm "educated" or because they want to see someone whom they think is sophisticated (I include information about my educational background on my business website). For me, what this translates to is an observation on how bodies are located in the hierarchy of the sex industry. Because of my race and class positioning, I create a situation for clients to experience themselves as bourgeois subjects. I use my gendered labour to produce my clients' subjectivity – the meanings and feelings they have about themselves as middle-class men. This process is not unique to the sex industry; the production of identity through consumption is a feature of capitalist society (Langman 2003).

Conclusion

Reflecting on my thoughts and experiences over the fifteen years since I started to work in the sex industry, I have come to understand that feminism has conceptualized sex work in far too limiting a manner. Sex work is about emotionally complex relationships that involve genuine feelings of intimacy; it's about relationships of power; it's about the complex layers of meaning we attach to our lives and activities; and it's about having a job and making a living. As I write this, I'm happier in sex work than I was in any of the straight jobs that I've had, and I'm not planning to exit any time soon. I'd never be where I am today without the sex industry. I've made important differences in the lives of a number of people, more so than in many of my other jobs. Although the work can be hard, and occasionally shitty things do happen, I get a lot from it too. I get satisfaction from sharing myself with others, I love to feel beautiful and to be appreciated, and I love to perform. The sex industry has been a good fit for me, and I'm grateful to have a job that allows me to be independent and to enjoy my life.

References
Baumgardner, J., and A. Richards. 2000. *Manifesta: Young women, feminism, and the future.* New York: Farrar, Straus and Giroux.
Bernstein, E. 2007. *Temporarily yours: Intimacy, authenticity, and the commerce of sex.* Chicago: University of Chicago Press.
Chapkis, W. 1997. *Live sex acts: Women performing erotic labor.* New York: Routledge.
Heron, B. 2007. *Desire for development: Whiteness, gender, and the helping imperative.* Waterloo: Wilfrid Laurier University Press.
Langman, L. 2003. Culture, identity and hegemony: The body in a global age. *Current Sociology* 51, 3-4: 223-47.
Roberts, N. 1992. *Whores in history: Prostitution in Western history.* London: Harper Collins.
Rubin, G. 1984. Thinking sex: Notes for a radical theory of the politics of sexuality. In *Pleasure and danger: Exploring female sexuality*, ed. C. Vance, 267-319. Boston: Routledge and Kegan Paul.
Sanders, T. 2005. 'It's just acting': Sex workers' strategies for capitalizing on sexuality. *Gender, Work and Organization* 12, 4: 319-42.

4

Trans Sex Workers: Negotiating Sex, Gender, and Non-Normative Desire

TOR FLETCHER

Questions of decriminalization and human rights protections for sex workers are particularly salient for trans sex workers, who must contend with multiple layers of stigma, legal ambiguity, transphobia, and very often, classism, racism, and homophobia.[1] However, trans sex workers also hold some measure of power in hierarchical terms vis-à-vis non-trans sex workers. For example, their relatively small numbers ensure their exclusive access to clients who are interested in having sex with a trans person. These issues will be unpacked in this chapter after a brief introduction to trans concepts, followed by an examination of the interlocking issues that arise when a transgender body takes up space in both the sex industry and mainstream society.

I spoke with two transgender sex workers – Farah and Monica – who have been working in a large Ontario municipality for between five and twenty-two years. Both women are racialized; Monica describes herself as a trans woman and Farah identifies as a woman most of the time. My own background is also relevant here. I am a racialized trans man and queer/feminist activist living in Ontario. I volunteer on the board of a sex worker advocacy group and have engaged in sex work at various times in the past decade. I align myself with those living on the margins, and I have noticed that whereas the voices of sex workers are rarely heard or taken seriously, those of trans sex workers are almost completely silenced. This chapter, then, aims to provide a forum for the marginalized voices of trans sex workers to contribute to the discussion about sex work and sex workers' rights.

Gender and Sexual Diversity

In recent years, transsexuality has asserted itself as a challenge to accepted notions that gender is static, fixed, natural, and unchanging across a lifetime. The Canadian census (Statistics Canada 2006, 2011) has expanded its definition of "family" to include queer relationships and families; however, when it comes to the question of gender, there are only two options: male or female. Indeed, one of the first questions asked of new parents is "Is it a boy or a girl?" Gender expressions outside of these two categories are considered aberrant and Other. The erasure of trans bodies in official statistics not only means that they are ignored but more importantly, that trans people are unlikely to be considered in policy decisions. As a result, stigmatization and discrimination in employment, housing, social services, health care, and the justice system are not adequately addressed.

The existence of transgender people causes cognitive dissonance in a society that is built around the deeply held assumption that there are only two genders. Even within trans communities, there can be pressure to conform to one gender or another through sex reassignment, dress, and acceptance of concepts of passing.[2] Postmodern ideas about identity have provided new ways of thinking about gender (see Butler 1990; Bornstein 1994; Califia 2003; Serano 2007), which have allowed some trans people to maintain a trans identity, resisting identification on one side of the gender binary or the other as either woman or man. Apart from the high cost of surgery and hormones, which can severely limit a trans person's quest to traverse the gender binary and live fully in the chosen gender, the burgeoning genderqueer movement within queer and trans communities instead disrupts the binary (see Herdt 1993; Bornstein 1994; Halberstam 1994). A genderqueer person queers gender by refusing to conform to one or other of the categories "man" or "woman," instead locating somewhere in the middle or on the periphery, thereby declaring the existence of more than two genders.[3] Genderqueer individuals, either by personal or political choice, or through economic necessity, occupy a unique space, challenging society to reassess its insistence that only two gender categories, man and woman, exist.

The high cost of sex reassignment surgery and hormones can be prohibitive for people whose lives are deeply affected by anti-trans stigma, resulting in high levels of un- and under-employment (Bauer et al. 2011). For many trans people, workplace discrimination and an absence of anti-discrimination laws and policies addressing gender identity result in precarious employment and lack of job security. The impact of neoliberal economic policies that result in part-time and contract employment, no job security, and employment with no benefits or union representation compounds the barriers for trans workers.

The sex industry, itself set up on the margins, provides many trans people, primarily trans women, a platform from which to make a living as well as a place to find community among others who live outside of society's mainstream. However, sex work in Canada is currently in a state of legal ambiguity. In September 2010, Ontario's Superior Court of Justice ruled that existing laws that prohibit communication for sexual purposes, operating a common bawdy-house, and living on the avails of prostitution were unconstitutional (see Chapter 15 in this volume). More recently, in March 2012, the Ontario Court of Appeal partially agreed with the lower court's decision and again ruled that certain prostitution-related sections of the Criminal Code are unconstitutional. Currently, the case is making its way to the Supreme Court, which will have the final decision on Canadian prostitution laws. For sex workers, the decriminalization of prostitution would provide safer working conditions, allowing them to conduct business indoors and enabling street-based workers, for whom the potential for violence is significantly greater (Lowman 2000), to screen clients. Further, they will be able to report violent clients to police without the fear of being prosecuted themselves and can organize around both working conditions and health and safety standards (CBC News 2010). However, the potential triumph of decriminalization is bittersweet for trans sex workers. In June 2012, fifty years after the creation of Ontario's Human Rights Code, Toby's Act was enacted, making Ontario the first major North American jurisdiction to pass a law protecting trans people from discrimination based on gender identity and gender expression (CUPE 2012). The reach and power of this law are still to be determined. Heretofore lack of legal protection from transphobic violence and the continued prevalence of stigma and social exclusion have meant that trans sex workers are still at risk not only in their work, but also in society at large. Laws do not change attitudes and cannot legislate against stigma, exclusion, and transphobia.

Navigating Intersections of Oppression: Transphobia, Racism, and Sexism

Transphobia, homophobia, and racism play a large part in the experiences of trans sex workers and their clients. The majority of men who engage the services of trans sex workers identify as straight. Farah explains that most of the men who hire her do so precisely because she is trans. They are curious about sex with men and about what it would be like to be with a woman who has a penis, but they are not interested in men's bodies and would not identify as gay. Having sex with a trans woman is safer in terms of the client's identity because his heterosexuality is not questioned by society and the economic basis of the interaction ensures that any opinion held by the sex worker about the client's sexuality is not shared or even relevant. In my own experience, I was once hired by a man who was interested in playing with his sexual orientation. He enjoyed the external perception of gay masculinity – I wore a suit and tie to the appointment – while knowing that under my clothes, I had a woman's body. He was turned on by the fantasy of gay sex but at that time did not actually want to have sex with a male body.

Clients' desire to be with a trans body can also lead to expressions of transphobia. Farah expresses concern about her own safety and has at times experienced rejection because of her trans body. Sometimes clients have been surprised to discover she has male biology, causing them self-loathing and anxiety about their sexual orientation, which can lead to rejection and increases the possibility of violence. She understands that people prefer certain body types, but her experience of rejection is tinged with something else, specifically transphobia: *"You have a bit of an edge or whatever, but on the flip side you have a lot of rejection too, right? Like disclosure and all that stuff and questions, and, you know, about your body ... I assume they don't ask ciswomen all these questions about their bodies, right?"*[4]

Many trans people experience this sense of being exposed, as cisgender people ask very intrusive questions about genitalia, which would never be tolerated by a non-trans person. Non-trans people have a certain sense of entitlement about trans bodies, as if trans subjects are medical anomalies that warrant examination and study by even the most casual of researchers. This entitlement is magnified when the trans body belongs to a sex worker. Clients have a right to be specific about their desires, but the commercial nature of the relationship between client and worker can give the client perceived permission to act as if he owns this body for the duration of the appointment. Having to endure intrusive questions about one's genitals and sexual urges, mixed with the fear of rejection precisely because of being trans, is a daily occurrence for many trans sex workers. Of course, as Halberstam (1994, 212) states, "desire has a terrifying precision" and rejection is always a possibility in negotiating its parameters. However, the rejection of a trans body is edged with cultural messages about beauty, acceptable sexuality, and what constitutes a legitimate body.

Trans women's experiences reflect the deeply rooted ambivalence our culture has created regarding notions of masculinity and femininity. The presence of trans women in the sex industry complicates the gender binary, as well as the performance of masculinity and femininity. It also complicates sexuality and biology insofar as monogamous, loving, heterosexual relationships between cissexual women and men are privileged above other kinds of relationships, the legalization of gay marriage in a heterosexist paradigm notwithstanding.[5] The clients who engage trans sex workers experience a world where gender and sexuality are fluid categories that resist essentialism, but transphobia and cis-sexism, coupled with the stigma and current criminalization of prostitution activities, mean that these sexual and gender adventurers must constantly remain vigilant against discovery. Although discovery of having engaged the services of a cisgender sex worker may very well lead to prosecution and public shaming, at least the heterosexuality of the client is reinforced; his masculinity is not questioned.[6] Being outed as a man who seeks sex with a transsexual is very different in a society that largely insists on compulsory heterosexuality and requires adherence to rigid gender categories.

However, for the trans sex worker, the stakes are, in many ways, higher than for the male client. She is a potential target for the anger and self-loathing of the closeted client; only recently and only in Ontario have her human rights been recognized, but as has already been discussed, this legislative change has yet to be tested. Elsewhere in Canada, she has little to no recourse in law because not only does she face prosecution and societal judgment for prostitution, but she is also trans, which means that she is not protected from transphobic violence, harassment, and discrimination.

Being racialized adds yet another layer of oppression to the trans sex worker's identity. Monica describes feeling that, because she is a person of colour, society already sees her as not good enough. She said that the police have regularly targeted her for being brown and that some clients have been aggressive or tried to dominate her because she is a racialized trans sex worker:

> Being racialized ... has kept me silent to the systemic abuse I've experienced due to not being validated as a person. It has allowed me to be silent to the physical and sexual abuse I've experienced by clients, society, lovers due to not being believed or [with the belief that] I perpetrated it. The experience has led me to speak out ... about the injustices women of colour, immigrant, and migrant sex workers experience through police brutality. It has also pushed me as an advocate to make sex work and trans a platform to bring awareness, inclusion, and accessibility to many communities and community services.

These realities form an important part of the working conditions that trans sex workers must navigate. For example, Monica spoke about systemic violence as a result of being trans and racialized, and Farah has been in situations where she has felt unsafe. The potential for violence creates the context for their decisions. Both Monica and Farah do mostly indoor work now, although both go to the corner to visit their friends who work outdoors. This connection to their community is a way of standing in solidarity with other workers. The women operate with safety uppermost in their minds, developing strategies such as having a personal driver, working indoors, and doing in-calls only. Perhaps this is why, relying on sophisticated, shared, and thus far successful standards, these women have experienced relatively little violence.

The Benevolent Edge: Benefits of Being a Trans Sex Worker

Despite transphobia and racism, Monica and Farah were quick to point out that there are simultaneously many benefits to being a trans sex worker. When thinking about the ratio of trans sex workers to clients, and to cissexual women, one can quickly discern a trans woman's competitive edge in the market. There are far fewer trans sex workers advertising their services than ciswomen, making the ratio of trans sex workers to clients much larger and hence creating a niche for trans women. The trans body is taboo and exotic, forbidden and dangerous, and therefore highly sought after. Monica discussed this sense of advantage when she spoke of the benefits of being a trans sex worker: *"I think me being trans and [a] sex worker has its benefits because we are looked at as special women with a little extra."* She adds, *"Also, trans is a taboo erotic form, which the opposite sex find intriguing ... Trans women will always be sexualized in society, which can be a good thing or a bad thing depending on the individual."* Monica became a sex worker over twenty years ago for many reasons and continues it today because of the benefits it has afforded her:

> I became a sex worker in 1990 because the only community that existed for trans women was the sex-working community and at that time it was a way of survival and ... the scene was very vibrant with clubbing, dancing, and partying. Sex work also allowed me to live a life that was comfortable, such as a beautiful home, status, and allowed me to transition and have surgeries to make me more feminine ... Also, due to the social attitudes towards transgender people, it was an outlet to meet people that were attracted to trans women and also validate that my body is admired by many people.

She also spoke about the complex interplay of standpoints (Smith 1987) that trans women often adopt, depending on the situation: *"To me I guess it has its negatives and positives. In the sex-working community I have what the clients want. In society I feel sometimes I'm not taken serious because of being [a] trans woman and sex worker, and for some reason people think we have no other skills besides being sex workers and that allows society to oppress us."* Thus, standpoint plays an important role in the way that trans sex workers navigate society's structures. In choosing sex work, either by preference or economic necessity, they have discovered a niche at the margins of society, among other sex workers, and among other trans women who are not employed in the industry. Within the industry, trans women experience certain advantages over ciswomen, whereas in larger society the double stigma of being trans and a sex worker is marginalizing. The ways that trans sex workers negotiate their space in society are very much self-generated as these women are social actors in their own lives. They experience different outcomes depending on whom they are interacting with and whether or not they are working. By reading from and interpreting the standpoints of subjects, we can gain insight into life at the margins and learn about the multiple contingencies, contradictions, and negotiations that trans sex workers must navigate to survive and thrive in a transphobic anti-sex culture such as ours (Gately 2010).

Farah's standpoint when she is working is as a racialized trans sex worker. She spoke of the unique position of trans women as sex workers and added another layer to the conversation by commenting on ciswomen in the industry: *"Well, first off, they think that we're not women ... There's a disassociation and an exclusion, and the ciswomen feel intimidated by the trans women, because of the fact that there's not many, and you know, there's such a demand for [trans workers], and there's ... I won't say hatred, but there's some jealousy."* This statement reveals that there are advantages to being trans in the sex industry, but that those advantages can provoke jealousy and envy from non-trans sex workers. So, though having an edge in terms of the sexual desire of clients and the relative rarity of trans sex workers is beneficial on the level of economics and self-esteem, it can also result in negative treatment from co-workers, who may see trans sex workers as stealing clients away from "legitimate" women.

The trans sex workers with whom I talked were unequivocal that they very much enjoyed their time in the industry. These women, who come from various ethnic and educational backgrounds, challenge the ideological belief that sex work is practised solely as a last resort to survive or to pay for substance use. They told me that they have supportive families and large networks of friends who identify as both trans and non-trans, sex workers and not. Both are involved in their communities, striving to bring about change and transform attitudes about trans people and sex workers. Neither of them expressed self-loathing;

nor do they see themselves as victims despite having experienced stigma and systemic discrimination for aspects of their identities. Both women are professional, resilient, political, and passionate about their work and their identities. They make no apologies for who they are or what they do. They take pride in making pleasure their business.

Conclusion

We are witnessing a sea change in Canada: trans people are standing up and fighting back, and queer communities are re-examining their own assumptions about sexual orientation and gender. The existence of transgender and transsexual individuals, whose sex, gender, and sexuality exist on a continuum, and who are being forced to address the historical erasure of their embodied experiences as legitimate, presents society with opportunities to expand its understanding of the complexities of sex and gender. At the same time, the legal framework of sex work is undergoing serious reconsideration in the Ontario courts. People are suffering because of archaic and repressive government policies, not because there is anything inherently unhealthy about being trans or doing sex work. Sex workers and trans people, uniting in solidarity to demand law reform, are providing the numbers needed to build on the momentum for change. Collaboration and solidarity among groups with a common cause will bring about lasting change more effectively than working separately. Change is inevitable; it's simply a question of when.

Notes
1 In this essay, I will use the terms "trans," "transgender," "genderqueer," and occasionally "transsexual" interchangeably in an effort to acknowledge the dynamic and contested meanings attached to the trans lexicon.
2 Sex reassignment refers to the act of changing one's biological sex to align with one's gender, typically by the use of hormones and/or surgery.
3 "Genderqueer" can be used interchangeably with "genderfuck," "liminal" (meaning betwixt and between), "T-girl," and, less commonly, "T-boy" to signify those who do not conform to society's rules about gender.
4 A ciswoman is a non-trans woman, or a woman whose gender expression conforms to the sex she was assigned at birth. Other terms include "cisman," "cissexual," and "cisgender."
5 See Serano's (2007) *Whipping Girl*, 11-20 for a compelling rationale for using the term "cissexual" instead of "cisgender." Many queers believe that legalized gay marriage will never shake its roots as a sexist institution. They suggest that activists are better off advocating for a re-examination of the fundamental assumptions that underlie heterosexual marriage and creating different forms of relationships that more accurately reflect the myriad ways we love one another.

6　Many men who identify as heterosexual engage the services of male sex workers, but trans men are poorly represented in the industry. For information about trans men in the industry, see the work of Buck Angel, an FTM (female-to-male) porn actor.

References

Bauer, G., N. Nussbaum, R. Travers, L. Munro, J. Pyne, and N. Redman. 2011. We've got work to do: Workplace discrimination and employment challenges for trans people in Ontario. *Trans PULSE e-Bulletin* 2, 1 (30 May). http://transpulseproject.ca/documents/E3English. pdf.

Bornstein, K. 1994. *Gender outlaw: On men, women and the rest of us.* New York: Routledge.

Butler, J. 1990. *Gender trouble.* New York: Routledge.

Califia, P. 2003. *Sex changes: Transgender politics.* San Francisco: Cleis Press.

CBC News. 2010. Prostitution laws struck down by Ont. court. 28 September. http://www. cbc.ca/.

CUPE. 2012. Passage of Toby's Law a historic victory for transgender rights. 18 June.

Gately, C. 2010. Solidarity in the borderlands of gender, race, class and sexuality: Racialized transgender men. Master's thesis, Ontario Institute for Studies in Education, University of Toronto.

Halberstam, J. 1994. F2M: The making of female masculinity. In *The lesbian postmodern,* ed. L. Doan, 210-28. New York: Columbia University Press.

Herdt, G., ed. 1993. *Third sex, third gender: Beyond sexual dimorphism in culture and history.* New York: Zone Books.

Lowman, J. 2000. Violence and the outlaw status of (street) prostitution in Canada. *Violence against Women* 6, 9: 987-1011.

Serano, J. 2007. *Whipping girl: A transsexual woman on sexism and the scapegoating of femininity.* Berkeley: Seal Press.

Smith, D.E. 1987. *The everyday world as problematic: A feminist sociology.* Boston: Northeastern University Press.

Statistics Canada. 2006. *2006 Census.* Ottawa: Government of Canada. http://www12.statcan. gc.ca/.

–. 2011. *2011 Census.* Ottawa: Government of Canada. http://www12.statcan.gc.ca/.

5

We Speak for Ourselves: Anti-Colonial and Self-Determined Responses to Young People Involved in the Sex Trade

JJ

In discussion and debate over the sex trade and sex industries, the voices of young people are seldom heard. Young people involved in the sex trade, whether other options have run out or were not accessible in the first place, are rarely seen as possessing any form of agency and are often excluded from a rights-based approach that meets them where they are at. Further, the interconnections between the legacy of colonialism and approaches that try to "rescue" or "save" Indigenous youth involved in the sex trade, often through punitive measures of criminalization and detainment, aren't even discussed. Instead, it is common for policy makers, service providers, and others to speak on our behalf, as though they have the best knowledge of our experiences and our needs.

Below, I speak with a dear friend, colleague, and community member, Ivo, about our experiences working in, and working with, youth who are involved in the sex trade. And here we are speaking for ourselves.

An Interview with Ivo

Youth in the Sex Trade: Shame, Stigma, and Self-Determination

JJ: Can you tell me about your experiences working with young people who have been involved in the sex trade? Also, what has been your experience when other people bring up this issue of young people who are in the sex trade, particularly when other opportunities to get by may not be an option in their lives?

Ivo: To be honest, it's not something that we as young people disclose about ourselves or identify as – we don't always see ourselves as "sex workers." Even the phrase itself – "sex work" – is rarely talked about, but when people do bring up youth involved in the sex trade, it comes from the point of view that "we need to save these young people because they don't know what's good for them." The consensus that we as youth have the ability to make our own decisions, even if options are limited, is not there, and often our decisions are either not listened to, or they are second-guessed. In our society we are rarely consulted, when in fact we are the people most impacted by any decision really, and this goes for service providers as well. The interactions I've had with other youth in the sex trade is that on some level we're ashamed of what we've had to do and that on some level we feel fucked over. The sex industry is rarely talked about, even less so when we talk about the trade in North America or with youth. People often think that sex work is a "profession of desperation," and although I think that's sometimes true, a lot of people get jobs out of desperation. Whether it's working at McDonald's or whether it's working at some corporation, everyone needs a job to survive in this society – and so, any job could be considered a profession of desperation.

Add to that stigma, which prevents us from accessing so many things, and being younger, maybe we're not even eighteen yet, and you get a social context that isn't working. Younger people need jobs, but a lot of people don't hire younger folks, which means we need to find jobs under the table. I'm really fortunate that I've just turned eighteen and have a stable job at a health organization, but that doesn't happen for a lot of us. When we might be in bad situations and we need money to survive, the sex trade becomes one of the few options available to us.

JJ: When you are young, say, sixteen, seventeen, eighteen, for example, and living on your own, you need to make more than minimum wage to survive. Given all those things you describe – living in a capitalist society, lack of employment opportunities, stigma and discrimination against both youth and people in the sex industry – what do you think are the important things that people need to know about young people who may be trading sex to get by and live, for money, shelter, or basic needs?

Ivo: I want people to know that like any job, we need support; we need some form of security. There are so many organizations that want to save us, and many of them rely on traumatizing stories of youth exploitation to get funding.

However, they don't employ people who have real lived experiences to guide the work, and they don't talk to us to see what we actually need. When it comes down to it, if you don't have the lived experience or personal knowledge, how can you really understand something? How can you truly advocate for it? I want to be talked to by a peer, or someone who is Indigenous, or someone with life experience in the sex trade. I want to see more of those people talking to me! And talking about the trade in a way where the only option is *not* just about being a victim.

JJ: Why do you think people feel so uncomfortable talking about the reality of youth sex trade work?

Ivo: In our society, young people are viewed as sacred. And we are. We represent so many things, like light, hope, love. When we look at the sex industry, a lot of people think, "That could be my daughter." So it's this conflicting feeling where as a society we want to protect the younger generation, but at the same time we're constantly shaming them and telling them what they can and can't do; we're not providing ways for them to support themselves. I'm tired of being a young person and always having someone telling me what to do. As someone with life experience in the sex trade, I have the ability to identify when my body is able to accept someone else. I should have sovereignty over my own body.

JJ: Why is it important to recognize youth self-determination in relation to the sex trade? Or to put it differently, what do you think self-determination for young people looks like? Like you said, there's a lot of speaking for, or speaking on behalf of, youth, particularly youth in the sex trade. For example, I hear older folks say things like "I'm doing this for the next generation," which is great, but I wonder why aren't we as young people speaking on behalf of ourselves? Why aren't we taking up that space? So, what does self-determination mean to you?

Ivo: It means having a voice in decision-making processes – whether that be in our personal lives, in employment, in society, or in government. In terms of what self-determination means for youth in the sex trade, it's about having safe spaces for us to disclose what we're doing without fear of prosecution, or fear of being "saved." It's about healthy dialogues that are productive and supportive. We need spaces to talk honestly about the sex trade and what that means for people under eighteen, for example, without the fear of having someone call the cops, or family services, or priests, or whatever. For us as Indigenous peoples, we've faced those people before through the process of colonization, and we don't want to deal with them again.

Anti-Colonial Critiques of "Youth Exploitation"

JJ: What you are offering is what I would call an anti-colonial critique or perspective on both the sex trade and the so-called saving people approach. People don't look at this approach as colonizing, and really, "colonization" doesn't need to be this big fancy academic word. They conveniently forget that one of the initial purposes of colonization of cultures, of communities, and of lands was to save. Ulterior motives in the saving approach included genocide and trying to wipe Indigenous peoples and anyone who didn't conform off the map to make it easier for the Europeans and settlers to take over. Do you agree that these similar approaches that aim to save youth are working to further colonize us?

Ivo: Yes. It's about imposing one's ideals and lifestyle on others. People who do work from the saviour mode are perpetuating a form of colonization. Society has given us few other options, but it's also important to recognize that some people might be ok with where they are at and there may be some of us who don't want to change. We should be respected for our decisions and supported for where we are at.

JJ: So really what this comes down to is many of the organizations and agencies that use selected narratives about youth involved in the sex trade, use them to advance their own ideological agendas of making themselves feel better for "helping the less fortunate" or wanting to work with so-called marginalized communities. That is, in the name of ending youth exploitation, for instance, they themselves are appropriating the experiences of youth. However, they don't recognize that these very efforts are so oppressive.

Ivo: I have an image in my head of a fence, with a community on both sides. Someone from one side decides that they want someone from the other, so they hop the fence to get them. They convince the other person that the way their community lives is wrong. I feel like that's what a lot of these saving organizations are trying to do. They are trying to convince one community that they are better than the other; it's a slow, hostile takeover. This is an image that we as Indigenous people have seen many times before: the preachers or missionaries who haven't lived on our side of the fence are trying to tell us that how we are living is wrong and that there's a better way.

In relation to the sex trade, it reminds me of my previous work with a local anti-violence group. The group helped me recognize the interconnectedness of discrimination; I came to the realization that so many things are violent. Through the act of trying to save youth, organizations are not only exploiting the experiences of youth, they are harming us. We are harmed because they say our experiences are invalid when we don't agree with what they're saying, and our struggles are not important; this is a kind of violence.

JJ: They only want to hear our negative experiences. It's as though only the negative parts of our lives are relevant. It's almost as if consciously or subconsciously they only want to see you as someone needing to be saved. And if you don't fit this picture, they will manipulate your understanding of your lived experiences to the point where they can impose on you their efforts to "help."

Ivo: Or manipulate you to the point that you are vulnerable, and that vulnerability makes you agree to being converted or saved.

Youth Sexuality, Sex Education, and Social Services
JJ: In my work I find the saving perspective everywhere – not just in agencies or organizations, but in the way that a lot of people view youth sexuality in general. Do you think that it has a negative impact on health outcomes for youth? If that's the so-called dominant discourse or the way that people approach youth sexuality, what kind of effect does this have on young people?

Ivo: A lot of youth sexual education information is hella oppressive and hella violent. Our society robs young people of the knowledge of how to be safe. We have all these images projected at us saying "Be sexy, be sexy, be sexy – but don't actually have sex." Even among our peers we aren't really supposed to talk about sexuality; you are supposed to fit this mould, and if you break it, there are severe social punishments. The only time we can talk openly about sex is when we are bragging or joking about it. Social expectations and sexual standards are loaded on us like cinder blocks, and we have to carry them wherever we go. Added to that is the barrier of not having access to good sex-positive sexual health education, and we are left very vulnerable. For example, when I was in the sex trade, no one told me that I should use a condom, and I didn't even know about things like HIV. I thought it was something in Africa; no one told me it was in Canada too. I knew that in a situation with two men there wasn't a chance of pregnancy, but I didn't know there were other reasons to use a condom. I feel like society robbed me of so much knowledge that I could have used to keep myself safe in the sex trade. I never understood why men would pay me more not to use a condom! Even now in the work that I do, we hear from many youth that condoms are boring and gross. Just touching or seeing one can make people uncomfortable!

Then there's the lack of education – and I'm talking about real education, not about a nurse coming in Grade 7 and saying, "This is a condom, having babies is bad." True education is more than an hour-long workshop; it's more than one conversation, and as a young person I feel robbed. Who was it that robbed me of this knowledge? It was the legacy of the church and the morals it imposes on its devotees and followers. Those morals have had a huge effect on our society to the point where we as young Indigenous peoples have limited ways to identify ourselves in terms of both sexuality and gender. In my home territory of Cowessess First Nation, we had over 120 different words for sexuality and over 40 for gender alone; we viewed sex very differently. Instead of getting married, we had our life partners and carried many different roles. I come from a family of medicine men and women who held very sacred roles in our community. We had our teachings taken away in the name of the church and colonization, and we now have to deal with a stigmatization of sex and sexuality that wasn't there before. Through this, our bodies are policed.

JJ: With you all the way, brother! Keep speaking the truth! I also think it's important for people to know that we're not saying that youth exploitation doesn't exist, and we're not saying that age isn't a major factor in the oppression experienced in young people's lives. We are *all* against violence and abuse. However, so many age-related regulations exist that exacerbate the already limited options available to youth, and these regulations can often result in increased violence when young people are turned away from, for example, harm reduction or housing services. Of course, another major problem with these regulations is that they haven't included youth voices in their creation, and they don't or won't take into consideration youth having agency and autonomy.

Another pressing issue on the topic of youth exploitation is that some mainstream sex work and social service organizations are really uncomfortable even discussing how to take a supportive stance that meets young sex trade workers where they are at. When the stigma of the sex industry and discrimination are compounded with the "save the youth" perspective, a lot of sex work organizations feel the need to distance themselves from the topic of youth; they need to announce "We're consenting adults, and our work is legitimate." Some organizations have policies or funding agreement stipulations that say they can only offer support services to people who are eighteen and older. Needless to say, even if they want to provide services to youth, they might not be able to. What kind of effect do you think this has on addressing the reality of young people who are in the sex trade? Do you think organizations can offer services like harm reduction from a supportive place that affords the right to youth self-determination?

Ivo: I myself was never able to go to a sex work or social service organization, because I was only fifteen and then sixteen. I never had the opportunity to discuss what I wanted from an organization like that. My only option was to stay where I was because that was the safest. There should be some kind of exception that allows youth to access services and to make our own fucking decisions.

We have specific needs and realities that should be supported. There are fundamental reasons why we do what we need to do to get by – for money, housing, food – but we have other needs as well, like security, safety, support, and autonomy. We survive on our own because we know that we might be in jeopardy if we access a social service outreach program; we might be shamed, stigmatized, or even prosecuted by being put into custody.

I do feel for organizations that have funding considerations that prevent them from working with youth, and I'm sure there are good employees who are supportive of youth rights. However, I've heard people say things like, "You are just a kid – you shouldn't be living this life." This kind of sentiment doesn't actually help me; in fact, it tokenizes my knowledge and disregards my experiences. Youth should have an inherent right to freedom of choice and freedom to survive in the best way we can.

JJ: And really, young people are getting turned away at a time in their lives when they may need support the most. What kind of organizational, social, or community change do you think needs to happen?

Ivo: I don't want to make the generalization that all sex work or social service agencies disregard youth voices – certainly many do not. Similarly, I don't want to make the generalization that all people in the sex trade even need access to support services! But I do know that when I've needed support as an Indigenous youth in the sex trade, it was rarely available. And when it was available, it wasn't the right kind of support; instead, it put me in further danger of criminalization.

I would like to see organizations stop turning people away because of their age and stop telling us what we can and can't do with our bodies. I'd also like to see people's views change about youth in the sex trade in general – we're not doing this because we are bored; we're doing it because we need to support ourselves, just like everyone else. And like anything else, we should have access to support services that actually support us without compromise. Meaning we should not be asked to compromise our trade or the protection we receive from law enforcement in order to do what we have to do. Yes, sex work needs to be decriminalized so we stop getting arrested and have more violence come from the police themselves, but we also need a lot more than that. People need to recognize that their way is not the only way; youth voices need to be listened to so people can understand that there are many ways that people survive – don't stigmatize us for what we do. Instead, support us unconditionally. Youth with lived experience in the sex trade have valuable, legitimate, and expert knowledge – we deserve rights and we deserve to be recognized.

Conclusion

Ivo and JJ: There's so much stigma for younger folks involved in the sex trade. There's also a lot of shame and discomfort around youth sexuality in general, whether it's who we have sex with or why, as well as not wanting to discuss the root issues of young people not having options to begin with or that increased punishment and detainment may actually result in more violence in someone's life, not less. Some deem us invalid or irrelevant because of our experiences, and others can't or won't provide services to help us because of our age, unless – again – it's about rescuing us or forcing us to comply with a system where all we can be is a victim. Yet stigma and shame don't help anyone, and youth are being further oppressed because of it!

There's so much more to say on the topic of youth involved in the sex trade – and this chapter isn't ever going to be done. It's a work in progress that is coming from our hands, which in turn is coming from the hands of those before us and our peers, and now we're passing this on to you. As a closing remark, we'd like to say – no actually, the people who are reading this *are* the closing remark! There is so much potential for where you can take this information and the new perspectives you can have. You decide.

6

Decolonizing Sex Work: Developing an Intersectional Indigenous Approach

SARAH HUNT

In the early 1990s, I attended my first Valentine's Day Memorial March for women who had gone missing from, or been murdered in, Vancouver's Downtown Eastside. There, violence had come to be expected, and police were slow to respond to the deaths and disappearances of female residents (Cameron 2010). The community's proud history as the home of vibrant immigrant populations and the site of diverse social justice and arts movements is often overshadowed by its current concentration of visible street-level drug use, poverty, and sex work. As a young mixed-blood Kwakwaka'wakw woman, I was familiar with the struggle to get attention from police and the media about the violence in our communities. This was not unique to the Downtown Eastside but was prevalent in rural and urban on-reserve and off-reserve First Nations communities. In my late teens, my passion for breaking the silence about intergenerational violence and abuse was fuelled by the writing of Indigenous women that I had been introduced to in university women's studies classes (Campbell 1973; Chrystos 1988, 1995; Allen 1992; Brant 1994; Acoose 1995; Dumont 1996; Maracle 1996).[1] But that Memorial March made the silences even clearer for me.

Before the march began, as I listened to elders and families speak about their lost loved ones, I scanned the lists of names that lined the painted banners. I stopped when I read the name Sheila Hunt. Until then, the missing women had been members of a broader community, both Indigenous and non-Indigenous – women who were marked as "outsider" by a society that shuns sex workers, substance users, the poor, and the homeless, among many others. But this stopped my heart. It suddenly occurred to me that if I were related to this woman, or any of the other missing women, I might never hear about her life because of the shame and silence in our communities. Women and girls who leave smaller communities to go to the city and end up on the streets of the Downtown Eastside are often not talked about. They, like those of us who break the silence about abuse or who dare to leave a violent relationship, are often pushed away rather than being supported. At times, it feels that the shame has deeper roots than the love. From that day on, this added layer of silence informed my work and became the measuring stick for my ethics and accountability.

Soon after the march that year, I began looking for research on the overrepresentation of Indigenous women in the sex trade. Surprisingly, I found that very little work had been done in Canada, at least the sort of work that made it into written form, such as research, scholarly writing, or community publications. Due to this lack of research and publication, I became inspired to write my honours thesis about the colonial stereotypes of Indigenous women that were integral to the colonial project. The same stereotypes that were used to justify keeping us confined to reserves, that barred us from cities, prohibited our spiritual practices, and took away our children, were alive and well in this ongoing invisibility in the Downtown Eastside. Since that time, I have been involved in community-based research, program development, and education on violence, sexual exploitation, and a range of other issues in Indigenous communities across British Columbia. And, since then, both nothing and everything have changed.

In recent years, increasing recognition has been given to the reality that large numbers of Indigenous women have gone missing from, or been found murdered in, communities across Canada. A national study reported that over five hundred Indigenous women have been identified as missing or murdered, their cases largely remaining unsolved (NWAC 2010). Awareness about the national scale of this issue emerged only after the police identified a serial killer in Vancouver's Downtown Eastside and pressed charges for the deaths of twenty-six of the sixty-seven women officially identified as missing from that community. The first trial focused on six of the cases, and the offender was convicted of second-degree murder. Today, many Canadians are aware of the missing women from Vancouver and the horrors some of them experienced at the hands of a serial killer. Although we know that not all were Indigenous, thirty-nine of the sixty-seven were (Pratt 2005). It has become commonplace for the image of the missing women to be invoked whenever violence against Indigenous women is mentioned, thus muddling the complexity of their lives. After years of community advocacy, the police have finally been forced to sit up and pay attention as the world looks on. But that's usually where the story ends: the missing women. What about the women who are still working in the sex trade today, right now, in cities and towns, on highways and street corners, in communities across Canada? And what is the relationship between violence targeted at sex workers in the Downtown Eastside and the broader racialized violence experienced by Indigenous women at a national level?

In order to have a view to the present and the future, as well as of the injustices of the past, this chapter argues for a shift in the way that sex work is talked about in Indigenous communities. It is based on the available literature and the insights I've gained from my work in this area, and it recommends a series of approaches that I believe provide a strong foundation for decolonizing our views about sex work; these include centring the voices, agency, freedom, and mobility of Indigenous sex workers.

Colonialism in Canada: Situating Sex Work in Relation to Colonial Violence

Diverse and distinct Indigenous groups have lived in what is now called North America since time immemorial. The cultural and political practices of Indigenous peoples prior to contact with Europeans, and their experiences since colonialism began, vary widely. Thus, there is no single history of colonialism in Canada – each Indigenous nation has its own cultural identity and set of practices, and its own engagement with the Canadian and provincial governments. However, some common colonial ideologies and practices have been imposed on Indigenous peoples through the formation of the Canadian state and its continued relationship with them.

The country of Canada officially formed in 1867, formalizing the claims that European settlers had been slowly making over the vast territories of Canada since first arriving in the fifteenth century. Confederation signalled the formal dismissal of Indigenous sovereignty and governance, which pre-dated contact with Europeans and continue to be practised in diverse ways to this day. In 1876, the federal government instituted the Indian Act, which established Canada as the paternal figure to Indigenous people, with the power to decide how the lives of "Indians" were to be lived (RCAP 1996). All aspects of their lives were covered in this act, including governance of Indian reserves and details of daily life in these communities, which were to be mediated by agents of the federal Department of Indian Affairs (Moss and Gardner-O'Toole 1991).

Although the Indian Act has been changed many times since then, it remains in effect today, shaping Indian bands, Indian status, and reserves. Other

Sarah Hunt

significant legal documents work in complex relationship with the Indian Act, including section 35(1) of the 1982 Constitution Act, which recognizes and affirms the rights of Indigenous peoples as pre-existing the formation of Canada (see Borrows 2010). Indigenous people continue to navigate the relationship between Canadian and Indigenous law in broader efforts toward sovereignty and self-determination. However, as Coulthard (2007) has argued, Indigenous struggles to gain recognition and justice under Canadian law serve to reinforce the power of the colonial state, as the terms of recognition are always set by the state rather than within the terms of Indigenous nations. Thus, given that Canadian law provides the primary avenue for seeking justice for Indigenous people, some argue that this approach will always have limitations because of the colonial relationship between the state and Indigenous peoples. Although the Assembly of First Nations and some individual Indigenous leaders continue to work closely with the Canadian government, many Indigenous people are looking to self-affirmation, assertions of Indigenous sovereignty, and the resurgence of Indigenous legal and cultural traditions alongside (or instead of) greater recognition in Canadian law (Alfred 2005; Coulthard 2007; Corntassel 2008) under models of legal pluralism (Borrows 2010).

The Indian Act comprises colonial ideas about Indians, including racist and sexist stereotypes and ideologies, beginning with the beliefs that Indigenous people are inferior to Europeans and that women are inferior to men. For example, it legislated that only male band members could vote or hold office in band governance, which limited women's power in band politics until revisions were made to the act in 1951 (Peters 1998). Further, until 1985, when the act was again modified, Indian women lost their status if they married non-status men, whereas non-Indian women gained Indian status by marrying status men (*Indian Act,* ss. 20, 109-13). The repercussions are still felt today as many women and their children continue to be denied status due to administrative and legislative issues.

Ideas about Indigenous people, including Indigenous women's sexuality, existed in the colonial imagination prior to contact between Europeans and Indigenous people in Canada. Colonial agents in Europe imagined a world available for seizure, settlement, and development, envisioning Indigenous people as savages who were in need of being saved from their heathen ways, either by force or surrender (Williams 1990). As Said (1978) has shown in his analysis of Orientalism, the European or dominant identity has been fabricated in relation to representations of racialized Others in order to construct essentialized difference between dominant and marginalized groups.[2] In the colonial imagination, Indigenous women were portrayed as sexually licentious savages or beasts of burden and were conflated with an imagined colonial landscape, which signified that it was open for settlement (Acoose 1995). Imagining Indigenous people as savage rendered them less than human, allowing settlers and colonizers to deny them rights and their humanity. Though colonial strategies changed over time and space, Indigenous people were often portrayed as inferior Others in need of being saved for their own good (Francis 1992).

At a material level, colonial ideologies in Canada came to be rendered real through law, violent acts of dispossession, and grounded and embodied colonialism. The Indian Act is one way that colonial ideologies became, quite literally, the law of the land. Colonial measures were justified partially through depicting Indigenous women as lewd and licentious, as colonial agents worked to legitimize the constraints placed on their activities and movements (Carter 1993). In some areas, this included a pass system in which Indigenous women must obtain permission from Indian Agents (federal employees) to leave their reserves (RCAP 1996). This 1885 measure, which kept Indigenous women away from cities, was justified by fears of white settlers and government agents that they would bring their supposed immorality to virtuous white women or end up working as prostitutes. The confinement of First Nations on Canadian reserves remained until about the 1950s, when Indigenous people began moving to urban areas in efforts to access resources and opportunities. The connection between First Nations people and reserves is determined by the Indian Act, which funnels resources and rights through bands and their reserve lands.

Violence and sex were also intertwined through colonialism and the Indian Act, as is evident in the widespread sexual and physical abuse in church-run residential schools.[3] Indeed, as Smith (2005, 12) writes, "The extent to which Native peoples are not seen as 'real' people in the larger colonial discourse indicates the success of sexual violence, among other racist and colonialist forces, in destroying the perceived humanity of Native peoples." In the early days of Canadian colonialism and settlement, Indigenous women were partners of white men, fulfilling a reproductive and familial role until the arrival of European women. However, the sexual availability of Indigenous women became seen as a threat when greater numbers of European women immigrated to Canada, and in 1921, the House of Commons considered a Criminal Code amendment that would make it an offence for any white man to have "illicit connection" with an Indigenous woman (Carter 1993). Thus, ideas about Indigenous women were linked to the powerful technologies of the law, as "officials propagated an image of Aboriginal women as dissolute, as the bearers of sinister influences, to deflect criticism from government agents and policies" (ibid., 150).

Sarah Hunt

The legacy of colonialism lives on, as poverty and unsettled land claims shape the lives of Indigenous people to this day, with First Nations band governance defined and overseen by Ottawa. Interpersonal violence is just one of the ongoing manifestations of Canada's colonial relationship with Indigenous people. Although they cannot replace experiential knowledge, statistics do shed light on these violent realities. In the 2004 General Social Survey on Victimization, 4 in 10 self-identified Aboriginal people aged fifteen and over reported that they were victimized at least once in the past year (Brzozowski, Taylor-Butts, and Johnson 2006).[4] This proportion was well above the level of 2.8 out of 10 for non-Indigenous Canadians. In the same study, Aboriginal people were three times more likely than other Canadians to be victims of violent crime, specifically sexual assault, robbery, and physical assault; this trend was highest among people aged fifteen to thirty-four, which was 2.5 times higher than for other age groups. The 2009 General Social Survey found that Aboriginal women were three times more likely to be victims of violence than non-Indigenous women (Brennan 2011), with 13 percent of Indigenous women reporting violence in the previous year. The mortality rate due to violence is three times higher for Indigenous women than for non-Indigenous women, a rate that rises to five times higher for the twenty-five- to forty-four-year-old age group (Health Canada 2000).

Indigenous people have responded to the racist and sexist stereotypes and the realities of violence in our communities through writing, art, advocacy, and other acts of resistance. A number of Indigenous women writers have spoken back to the stereotypes of squaw, Indian princess, and sexually available brown woman, as well as the violence justified by these images of us (see Acoose 1995; Dumont 1996; Maracle 1996).

But has Indigenous women's refusal of these sexual stereotypes resulted in simultaneously distancing ourselves from women who are working in the sex trade? We need to examine the moralistic stance against sex work, and the conflation of sex work with exploitation, to see how we have internalized both this stereotype and its opposite. Although resistance to degrading and dehumanizing stereotypes of Indigenous people is important, it is simultaneously essential to look at how our responses affect – or fail to affect – the material reality of violence. In discussions about colonial violence, Indigenous sex workers are often invoked as nameless, voiceless, placeless victims, in memory of past injustices. The remembering and calls for justice are important, but the conversation must not stop there. We need to move away from positioning ourselves as advocates for, and saviours of, some disempowered sister-Other and instead facilitate a process that centres the voices of sex workers themselves. Otherwise we risk reproducing the discourses of colonialism that constitute Indigenous women as without agency.

Bringing Them to Light: Emergence of a Discourse Related to the Missing Women

Jiwani and Young (2006) argue that historically entrenched stereotypes about women, indigeneity, and sex trade work confer multiple degenerate status to the missing women from Vancouver's Downtown Eastside and continue to situate them at the margins. They suggest that media representations of the missing women serve to naturalize particular women's susceptibility to violence, blaming the women themselves for the violence they encounter. Pratt (2005) similarly states that Indigenous women are rendered as outside the public life of cities and outside the realm of law and rights. Despite Indigenous people's overrepresentation among the missing women, the issue of indigeneity remained a side-note in media coverage (Jiwani and Young 2006). As England (2004) contends, representations of Indigenous women in the Downtown Eastside oscillated between invisibility and hypervisibility: invisible as victims of violence and hypervisible as deviant bodies. In recent years, violence against Indigenous women has become more visible in mainstream media, yet little has changed. It can be argued that the violence itself has become hypervisible, but that it does not count as real violence, because Indigenous women are seen as less than human, as unworthy of response; violence is normalized and assumed to be part of the everydayness of Indigenous spaces. The violent reconstruction of Indigenous identities as inherently savage – more than racialized and sexualized, but categorically Other, within the broad discourse of Western identity – is rendered invisible through its naturalization.

Of course, violence against Indigenous sex workers is not unique to the Downtown Eastside of Vancouver. Indigenous women working in the sex trade have been murdered in Edmonton, Winnipeg, and other cities across Canada. The roots of this violence can be seen in Canadian newspapers from the nineteenth century, which indicate a widespread conflation of Indigenous woman and prostitute, and an accompanying belief that when Indigenous women encountered violence, they got what they deserved and were not worthy of police intervention (Carter 1993). These attitudes are alive today. As noted by the commissioner in the inquiry into the murder of Helen Betty Osbourne in The Pas, Manitoba, the violence of the offenders was justified by their assumptions that Aboriginal women are promiscuous and have no human value beyond the sexual gratification of men (Razack 2000). Razack contends that such assumptions also appear to be operating when police fail to respond to the disappearance of Aboriginal women, as their presumed involvement in prostitution is reason enough for inaction. Harris (1991) further notes that representations of Indigenous women are marked by strategic silences, which strip them of their agency and silence them as victims. Indeed, old colonial stereotypes are alive and well in the images of Indigenous women we see in the media and mainstream Canadian culture.

Knowledge of Sex Work Involvement: Gaps, Invisibility, and Silence

The hypervisibility of violent acts and the invisibility of sex workers themselves go hand in hand, contributing to the lack of sustained efforts to improve the quality of life for Indigenous people engaged in sex work. The lives and voices of Indigenous sex workers are obscured by discourses of victimization that, on the surface, aim to draw attention to marginalization and colonial violence but fail to provide a space for Indigenous sex workers to speak for themselves and define their own struggles.

Despite the increased awareness about violence against sex workers, we know little about the lives of Indigenous sex workers, which begs important questions: What does it mean that Indigenous people are overrepresented in the sex trade? What might a decolonizing analysis bring to discussions of sex work in Canada, beyond the polarization of debates around decriminalization and prohibition?

Anecdotal evidence from service providers and outreach workers indicates that Indigenous women are highly overrepresented in the street-level sex trade.[5] Although there are few studies on the topic, those that exist similarly indicate a high rate of Indigenous women's involvement. For example, Farley and Lynne (2005) – who take a prohibitionist stance against sex work – interviewed 100 street-based sex workers in Vancouver, a city where 1.7 percent of the population is Indigenous, and found that 52 percent of their participants were Indigenous. Another Vancouver study (Currie 2000) estimated that 70 percent of street-level sex workers in the Downtown Eastside were Indigenous women. What is not clear, however, is how many Indigenous women work in other sectors of the trade, including the indoor industry.

Another significant gap in the research and literature is regarding sex work in rural areas, including reserve communities and smaller towns and cities. Research conducted in five rural communities in British Columbia found that formal and informal sex work was happening in private homes, cars, outside, and in motels, through exchanges of sex for transportation and accommodation, drugs and alcohol, and clothing and money (Justice Institute of British Columbia 2006). Study participants, who were mainly service providers, adults with a history of involvement in sex work, and youth, stated that the primary barrier to addressing the health and safety needs of sex workers was the inability of community leaders and politicians to admit that sex work was occurring in their communities.

Conflating Issues: Youth, Sexual Exploitation, and Human Trafficking

As I have argued elsewhere (Hunt 2010), Indigenous sex work has been conflated with sexual exploitation, domestic trafficking, intergenerational violence, and the disappearance or abduction of Indigenous girls and women. Interestingly, and problematically, girls and women are talked about together, as though they are a single category, which echoes colonial views of Indigenous people as children in need of paternalistic surveillance and control. Although some research, such as that by Kingsley and Mark (2000), themselves Indigenous women who identify as having been sexually exploited, has provided some insight into the needs of Indigenous young people who have been exploited, the same has not been done with adult sex workers. Many adult sex workers first became involved as youth, which undoubtedly has implications for their adult sex-working experiences; however, a nuanced exploration of this issue has yet to be initiated. Instead, children, youth, and women are conjoined as victims, and their varying degrees of agency and choice remain unexamined.

Many Indigenous women experience sexual violence, among other forms of violence, on a daily basis. Yet efforts to raise awareness about sexual violence have conflated sex work with other forms of victimization. As previously mentioned, my own work on this issue emerged from an awareness of the normalized violence faced by Indigenous children, youth, and adults, as well as the shame and silence associated with sexual abuse. Sex work is indeed situated within the broader context of colonial violence, but in the conflation of sexual violence and sex work, critical and nuanced discussions have been neglected.

In recent years, "human trafficking" has become a growing discourse among academics and other experts concerned with Indigenous girls and women (Sethi 2007; Sikka 2009). In 2009, the Assembly of Manitoba Chiefs, which represents First Nations people in the province, initiated a human trafficking campaign focused on stopping the sexual exploitation of First Nations people. The campaign material indicates that approximately four hundred children and youth are being sexually exploited on the streets of Winnipeg each year. Although the campaign groups women and children together as potential victims of trafficking, no information is provided regarding the context of adult sex work in Winnipeg generally or regarding the distinctions between situations for youth and adults specifically.

Supporting Sex Workers: Responses from Indigenous Organizations

Given the overrepresentation of Indigenous women in sex work, it is surprising that sex work remains a largely unexplored issue within Indigenous communities. It is also surprising that sex workers' rights organizations include little Indigenous representation. In both sex work advocacy and Indigenous movements, the voices and diverse experiences of Indigenous sex workers too often go unheard. Of the few Indigenous voices to have taken up the issue of Indigenous sex work, the ones most often listened to are those who position all sex workers as victims of colonial violence. For example, the Aboriginal Women's Action Network (AWAN) in Vancouver has taken a prohibitionist position, arguing that sex work is inherently violent and that greater legislation is needed to stop sexual demand for women's and children's bodies (Aboriginal Women's Action Network 2007). Further, it claims to speak on behalf of Indigenous women from both urban and reserve communities across the country (for more information on AWAN, see http://www.awanbc.ca).

Across the country in Toronto, and in opposition to AWAN's prohibitionist stance, the Native Youth Sexual Health Network (NYSHN) and Maggie's: Toronto Sex Workers Action Project, Canada's oldest sex-worker-run organization, have partnered in an effort to support Indigenous sex workers through an Aboriginal Sex Worker Outreach and Education Project (see http://www. nativeyouthsexualhealth.com and http://maggiestoronto.ca). This is Canada's first program by and for Indigenous people that centres on a harm-reduction and sex workers' rights framework and is located in the broader struggle for Indigenous rights, self-determination, and sovereignty (Maynard 2010; van der Meulen, Yee, and Durisin 2010). Indigenous organizations like the NYSHN are beginning the important work of centralizing the voices of Indigenous people in talking about issues of sexuality, sex work, and decolonizing our bodies. Sex workers are particularly vulnerable members of our communities, and we must act as allies by working with and alongside them, listening to their voices and responding to their needs. We must also assume that we, meaning Indigenous people and communities, necessarily comprise past and present sex workers, rather than furthering the gap between a perceived "us" and "them."

At a national level, the Native Women's Association of Canada (NWAC) has argued for decriminalizing sex workers themselves and criminalizing, instead, those who profit from their work, including johns and pimps, while taking a stance that prostitution is inherently exploitative – evidenced by their use of the term "sexual exploitation" rather than "sex work" or "prostitution" in a statement released during 2011 (Women's Coalition for the Abolition of Prostitution 2011). However, NWAC recently passed a resolution at its annual general meeting in support of harm-reduction approaches that both support sex workers where they are at and recognize that violence is a result of stigma and discrimination rather than inherent to sex work itself, demonstrating a possible shift in its position (NWAC 2011). The final report from NWAC's Sisters in Spirit Initiative, a national study of more than a hundred pages focusing on the lives of missing and murdered Indigenous women and girls, dedicated only half a page to the issue of sex work, claiming that it was not a factor in these women's disappearances (NWAC 2010). The Assembly of First Nations (AFN) – the body that represents First Nations people at a national level, including constitutional issues with the federal government – has not concerned itself with sex work. Although this may be due, in part, to the issue of gendered disparity within the organization, as only one woman is presently serving on the eleven-member AFN executive committee, even the AFN's Council of Women does not include sex work in the list of key issues that it addresses. It is important to note that efforts to address sex work generally assume that all sex workers are female and that those who "exploit" or profit from them are male, failing to deal with the involvement of Indigenous men, boys, two-spirit, and transgender people in the trade. As an Indigenous person, I argue that we need to examine what lies at the heart of our inability to support our community members engaged in sex work. Further, we must strengthen our capacity to include this issue among all the other issues of marginalization in our communities.

The rights of Indigenous sex workers will become visible only if we decolonize dominant conceptualizations of sex work and Indigenous women's position within its various sectors. As Indigenous people, we have long experienced being spoken for, misrepresented, and silenced by dominant discourses about Indians and Others. Why, then, are we continuing to reproduce these conceptualizations in our own communities? We must advance new frameworks for addressing violence, while at the same time we must undo colonial notions that Indigenous women lack the ability to make decisions for themselves. Further, we must reconcile the reality that Indigenous people continue to engage in sex work within the context of colonial violence in Canada. As a result of our inability to tackle these issues, Indigenous sex workers, their voices, and their humanity are rendered silent. The hypervisibility of the stereotypical sexualized

Sarah Hunt

and racialized victim stands in stark contrast to the invisibility and silence around sex work itself.

Decolonizing Sex Work: Recommended Approaches

In order to address the current and ongoing needs of Indigenous people in the sex trade, I suggest that we must begin by humanizing sex workers as part of the broader Indigenous movements of regeneration and reclamation of our rights. To this end, I recommend the following approaches, which draw on broad efforts to strengthen Indigenous communities rather than situating the struggle purely within discourses on violence against women. These approaches are intended as a starting place, as each community must develop its own specific strategies to deal with unique issues faced by sex workers local to that context.

Embracing Sex Workers as Members of Our Indigenous Communities

Yee (2009) argues that reducing stigma and humanizing sex workers must start within Indigenous communities. Focusing on traditional teachings, such as respect, acceptance, and the principle "all our relations," will begin to increase inclusion of sex workers in broader community healing and cultural practice. Indigenous leaders and organizations must look at their role in marginalizing the voices of sex workers and seriously consider the ways in which they can be embraced rather than shamed and silenced. Many Indigenous people have internalized the attitudes about our sexuality taught to us through residential schools and generations of dehumanization under the Indian Act. Indeed, it is difficult to untangle ideas about sexuality that have been, and continue to be, projected onto us from those that we ourselves believe. However, this deconstruction is a necessary part of decolonization. Movements to reclaim and remake Indigenous practices must include examinations of sexuality on both individual and collective levels. Talking openly about sexuality and instilling a sense of pride and empowerment in ourselves and our children are integral to decolonizing the bodies of all Indigenous people, including sex workers of all genders. The inclusion of sex workers in broader Indigenous revitalization and self-determination movements is integral to the recommendations that follow.

Meeting Sex Workers' Basic Needs

Many Indigenous sex workers are concentrated in street-level work where they may have fewer resources and lower quality of life than their counterparts in other sectors. Poverty, homelessness, addiction, violence, intergenerational abuse, and other vulnerabilities that are rooted in our colonialist history must be addressed in an effort to improve the lives of Indigenous sex workers. Poor quality of life is prevalent in many Indigenous communities, which can contribute to the level of choice Indigenous people can exercise about whether or not to engage in sex work. This is not only an urban reality. For example, people in northern and isolated communities who lack transportation may exchange sex for a ride into a nearby town. Some argue that these conditions have led Indigenous women – as well as men and transgender people – to enter sex work without "real choice." Although we must focus on the inequities that put Indigenous women in positions where trading sex becomes one of few options, we must simultaneously acknowledge the agency of Indigenous people. Indeed, addressing the basic needs of sex workers, and all Indigenous people, must be at the centre of any approach to decolonizing sex work.

Multiplicity of Indigenous Cultural Practices and Beliefs

Looking to Indigenous teachings, we must work within our own communities to determine the best ways to support people in the sex trade. This means accepting a multiplicity of approaches based on relationships among people, communities, and traditions rather than creating one "right" way forward. Indigenous people have always had their own unique traditions and localized strategies, which have been more effective and meaningful in speaking to local inequities than mainstream or government-imposed strategies. The challenge here is that some Indigenous people find their community leaders to be disapproving of efforts to support sex workers. Shifting the power in our communities might mean not including official leadership (such as the chief and council) and, instead, starting a dialogue among unpaid supporters, natural helpers, elders, and others. This work entails identifying individuals who are willing to listen to the needs and experiences of sex workers and who can act as allies and advocates. If possible, distinct cultural teachings and principles should be identified by elders and healers to guide local efforts to discuss sex work in a meaningful and respectful way. We can strive to be guided by our own intellectual traditions, which are embedded in Indigenous oral traditions: "Understanding who we are as indigenous peoples, and the ways of thinking that make us indigenous, ought to provide the foundation for how we learn to navigate our way in the dominant culture" (Turner 2004, 66).

Supporting a Rights-Based Approach

Indigenous people have a complex relationship to international human rights discourses because these have been defined and determined by powerful state actors rather than being based on Indigenous worldviews and principles. However, international human rights provide broad standards that are useful in advocating for a baseline set of conditions to which each individual is entitled. These basic human rights include the right to be free from violence, forced labour, and child abuse, as well as the right to freedom of mobility. This means that individuals who are forced into sex work have the right to protection and assistance in exiting from it. It also means that those who choose sex work have the right to protection from violence. These state-guaranteed protections are clearly not being upheld in many jurisdictions. Indigenous communities may also have their own concept of rights, which can be incorporated into broader developments of a rights-based approach.

Acknowledging Agency and Voice

Currently, depictions of Indigenous sex workers as helpless victims contribute to a social context in which many of them are denied agency and voice, yet agency and voice are imperative in rehumanizing people who work in the sex trade. Agency involves the ability to make decisions for yourself, to be considered as a person with choices rather than having those choices determined for you by another individual or state actor. Indigenous views of agency can be quite different from European or Canadian concepts. For example, some Indigenous traditions recognize that all living things have an inherent agentic ability, including rocks, the land, trees, and animals. These Indigenous conceptions of agency are being fostered in revitalization movements and must include recognition of the agency of all members of our communities, including sex workers. Listening to the voices, experiences, and needs of sex workers requires allies to step back and unlearn the stereotypes and assumptions we carry. The voices of sex workers must be at the centre of efforts to improve safety, increase choice and agency, and humanize their experiences within the context of our communities and families.

Supporting Freedom of Mobility

In an effort to reduce violence against women in broader society as well as in Indigenous communities, women are often told to stay home, not wear provocative clothing, keep out of trouble, and not put themselves in dangerous positions (Lonsway and Fitzgerald 1994; Canadian Resource Centre for Victims of Crime 2009; Patterson 2011). This rhetoric serves to blame women for the violence they endure. Restricting Indigenous people's mobility has also been a central component of colonialism, through the creation of reserves, mandatory residential schools, and efforts to restrict land and resource use. The rights of

Indigenous peoples have been depicted as fixed in the past, at the point of contact with settlers, and any changes in our traditions have been seen as moves toward inauthenticity. Anishinabek legal scholar Borrows (2009) argues that mobility is a fundamental aspect of asserting our rights as Indigenous people. Portrayals of Indigenous peoples as nomadic or less attached to land and territory (due to their concepts of property ownership and land use) have been part of denying their rights to their lands. Recognition of the right to mobility includes individual and collective rights to resist forced relocation, such as has been the case for some First Nations in Canada, as well as the right to move freely. It is in this spirit of asserting Indigenous mobility that sex workers must be encouraged and supported in moving between and within community spaces. This may include efforts to ensure equal access to health care, ceremonial spaces, and family gatherings in urban and rural areas, as well as safe movement between and among rural and urban communities.

Controlling Our Own Bodies

As discussed above, Indigenous women's bodies have been violated through colonization. This has involved the control of our bodies by the state and by a number of other powerful decision-makers who think they know what is best for us. The Canadian government has used various means to control Indigenous bodies, including forced sterilization for some residential school students (Haig-Brown 1988; Chrisjohn, Young, and Maraun 2006). Those who want to prohibit and outlaw sex work are part of a movement to control the bodies of sex workers, which I see as a continuation of our colonial legacy. As with all Indigenous people, sex workers must be free to make decisions about their own bodies, including making money through sexual acts.

Community Change, Beyond Legal Response

Indigenous people know that we cannot rely on the Canadian legal system to protect our communities and ourselves. The Canadian nation-state was accomplished through the establishment of the Canadian legal system, which wholeheartedly ignored Indigenous law and sovereignty. Law, regarded by the West as an instrument of civilization, was also the West's most vital and effective instrument of empire during its colonization of Indigenous peoples (Williams 1990). Fighting for recognition and protection solely through Canadian law is inherently limited given the colonial history and ongoing power of law. Debates around decriminalization and prohibition are focused on a legal system that is inherently oppressive to Indigenous people, as the dismissal of Indigenous sovereignty and Indigenous law depends upon the perpetuation of "the myth of

Sarah Hunt

inferiority" (Borrows 2010, 17) of Indigenous peoples and their failure to count as legitimate subjects. Laws against murder and violence fail to prevent the death and violation of Indigenous people of all ages and genders because we are not valued within the dominant culture that created and maintains the legal system. Although decriminalization may have an impact on the ability of sex workers to seek police protection, Indigenous women's relationship with Canadian law will continue to frame their relationship to justice. Therefore, decolonizing sex work must go beyond debates about decriminalization, as legal responses can go only so far in providing justice and safety for Indigenous sex workers.

Conclusion

My motivation and inspiration for this work is two-fold: first, the steadfast resistance and memory of the determination of my ancestors, who have gone before me; and second, the strength, health, and brilliance of the generations yet to come. We need to look forward and back simultaneously, walking and speaking in both memory and anticipation of the lives yet to be lived. The voices of sex workers must be heard in efforts to improve their safety and reduce their vulnerability. Both Indigenous and non-Indigenous allies must look into their own hearts and ask themselves how their views and experiences might affect their feelings about sex work and their ability to be effective allies.

Twenty years ago, when I attended that Women's Memorial March on Valentine's Day in Vancouver's Downtown Eastside, community members were struggling to get the media, justice officials, and the general public to acknowledge systemic violence against women. And though today the dominant image of the Downtown Eastside is that of an Indigenous sex worker, current media and police attention has not translated into changes in the lives of Indigenous people in the sex trade.

Indeed, Indigenous sex workers' lives remain largely invisible, and many issues remain underexplored: sex work in rural communities and on reserves must be acknowledged and better understood; the role of reserve geographies and power relations inherent in band governance should be considered in connection with sex work in these communities; and efforts should be made to assess the ability of service providers to meet Indigenous sex workers' needs and to better integrate Indigenous perspectives and analyses of colonialism in front-line organizations. Further, intergenerational involvement in sex work will affect our future generations, and we must consider the implications for all aspects of community growth and revitalization. On a broad level, we must seek to better understand how issues of housing, poverty, trauma, and systematic racism/sexism/homophobia/colonialism shape the choices facing sex workers and their ability to assert individual agency. Measures must be taken to improve safety for all Indigenous people, but particularly those who are at heightened risk of violence, such as sex workers, children, youth, women, and two-spirit people. The links between interpersonal violence and systemic colonial violence, both ideological and material, must be examined in relation to sex work. Additionally, the voices and experiences of sex workers must be recognized along with their particular histories, which could include victimization (such as childhood sexual abuse), while respecting their decisions, agency, and resilience. We have a long way to go in reconfiguring approaches that increase safety in the lives of Indigenous sex workers. Let's make sure to put the voices, needs, and rights of sex workers themselves at the centre of this movement.

Notes

1   From first contact with Europeans to the present day, the English language has contained many ever-changing names for us, including Indigenous, Aboriginal, Native, First Nations, and Indian. In recent years, critical Indigenous scholars in Canada and abroad have begun using the term "Indigenous" rather than "Aboriginal" when referring to the broad grouping of First Nations (government-designated status Indians), non-status, Métis, and Inuit peoples of Canada, as well as for first peoples internationally. The use of "Aboriginal" and "Indian," neither of which were created by Indigenous people ourselves, was perpetuated by the state. As a Kwakwaka'wakw scholar, I align my work with that of other Indigenous people who wish to link the local experiences of first peoples in Canada with others around the world, asserting the shared primacy of our relationship to the lands of our ancestors as well as the international quality of our political movements. I primarily use the term "Indigenous" in this chapter but also employ "First Nations" to talk specifically about federally recognized Indian bands and status Indians.

2   Said critiques Orientalism as a constellation of false assumptions underlying Western attitudes toward racialized Others, particularly Eastern peoples. He argues that racist images of Others are rooted in Eurocentric prejudice and have served as an implicit justification for European imperialism and colonialism.

3   Attendance at these federally mandated schools was optional at first, but a 1920 revision to the Indian Act made it a requirement for all status Indian children. The purpose of the schools was to assimilate Indigenous children into white society, in efforts to get rid of "the Indian problem" (Haig-Brown 1988).

4   "Aboriginal" is the term used in this government research, meaning individuals who self-identify as having First Nations, Métis, or Inuit ancestry.

5   Indigenous men, transgender, and two-spirit people are also present in street-level work, but, again, the numbers are unclear, and little research has been done in this area.

References

Aboriginal Women's Action Network. 2007. Statement opposing legalized prostitution and total decriminalization of prostitution. 6 December.

Acoose, J. 1995. *Iskwewak-Kah 'Ki Yaw Ni Wahkomakanak: Neither Indian princesses nor easy squaws.* Toronto: Women's Press.

Alfred, T. 2005. *Wasáse: Indigenous pathways of action and freedom*. Peterborough: Broadview Press.

Allen, P.G. 1992. *Sacred hoop: Recovering the feminine in American Indian traditions*. 2nd ed. Boston: Beacon Press.

Borrows, J. 2009. Physical philosophy: Mobility and the future of Indigenous rights. In *Indigenous peoples and the law: Comparative and critical perspectives*, ed. B. Richardson, I. Shin, and K. McNeil, 403-20. Portland: Hart.

–. 2010. *Canada's Indigenous constitution*. Toronto: University of Toronto Press.

Brant, B. 1994. *Writing as witness: Essays and talk*. Toronto: Women's Press.

Brennan, S. 2011. Violent victimization of Aboriginal women in the Canadian provinces, 2009. *Juristat* (Statistics Canada, Canadian Centre for Justice Statistics) 85-002-X (17 May). http://www.statcan.gc.ca/pub/85-002-x/2011001/article/11439-eng.pdf.

Brzozowski, J.A., A. Taylor-Butts, and S. Johnson. 2006. Victimization and offending among the Aboriginal population in Canada. *Juristat* (Statistics Canada, Canadian Centre for Justice Statistics) 85-002-XIE 26, 3.

Cameron, S. 2010. *On the farm: Robert William Pickton and the tragic story of Vancouver's missing women*. Toronto: Knopf Canada.

Campbell, M. 1973. *Half-breed*. Toronto: McClelland and Stewart.

Canadian Resource Centre for Victims of Crime. 2009. Victim blaming. Canadian Resource Centre for Victims of Crime, Ottawa. http://crcvc.ca/docs/victim_blaming.pdf.

Carter, S. 1993. Categories and terrains of exclusion: Constructing the 'Indian woman' in the early settlement era in Western Canada. *Great Plains Quarterly* 13: 147-61.

Chrisjohn, R.D., S.L. Young, and M. Maraun. 2006. *The circle game: Shadows and substance in the Indian residential school experience in Canada*. Penticton: Theytus Books.

Chrystos. 1988. *Not vanishing*. Vancouver: Press Gang.

–. 1995. *Fire power*. Vancouver: Press Gang.

Corntassel, J. 2008. Toward sustainable self-determination: Rethinking the contemporary Indigenous-rights discourse. *Alternatives* 33: 105-32.

Coulthard, G. 2007. Subjects of empire: Indigenous peoples and the 'politics of recognition' in Canada. *Contemporary Political Theory* 6, 4: 437-60.

Currie, S. 2000. Assessing the violence against street involved women in the Downtown Eastside/Strathcona Community. Report for the Ministry of Women's Equality, Province of British Columbia.

Dumont, M. 1996. *A really good brown girl*. London: Brick Books.

England, J. 2004. Disciplining subjectivity and space: Representation, film and its material effects. *Antipode* 36, 2: 295-321.

Farley, M., and J. Lynne. 2005. Prostitution of Indigenous women: Sex inequality and the colonization of Canada's First Nations women. *Fourth World Journal* 6, 1: 1-29.

Francis, D. 1992. *The imaginary Indian: The image of the Indian in Canadian culture*. Vancouver: Arsenal Pulp Press.

Haig-Brown, C. 1988. *Resistance and renewal: Surviving the Indian residential school*. Vancouver: Tillicum Library.

Harris, D.W. 1991. Colonizing Mohawk women: Representations of women in the mainstream media. *Resources for Feminist Research* 20, 1-2: 15-20.

Health Canada. 2000. *The health of Aboriginal women*. Ottawa: Health Canada, Women's Health Bureau.

Hunt, S. 2010. Colonial roots, contemporary risk factors: A cautionary exploration of the domestic trafficking of Aboriginal women and girls in British Columbia, Canada. *Alliance News* 33: 27-31.

Indian Act [Repealed], R.S.C. 1985, c. 32 (1st Supp.), ss. 20, 109-13.

Jiwani, Y., and M.L. Young. 2006. Missing and murdered women: Reproducing marginality in news discourse. *Canadian Journal of Communication* 31, 4: 895-917.

Justice Institute of British Columbia. 2006. *Violence in the lives of sexually exploited youth and adult sex workers in BC: Research report.* New Westminster: Justice Institute of BC, Centre for Leadership and Community Learning,

Kingsley, C., and M. Mark. 2000. *Sacred lives: Canadian Aboriginal children and youth speak out about sexual exploitation.* Vancouver: Save the Children Canada.

Lonsway, K.A., and L.F. Fitzgerald. 1994. Rape myths: In review. *Psychology of Women Quarterly* 18: 133-64.

Maracle, L. 1996. *I am woman: A Native perspective on sociology and feminism.* Vancouver: Press Gang.

Maynard, R. 2010. Sex work, migration and anti-trafficking: Interviews with Nandita Sharma and Jessica Yee. *Briar Patch* 39, 4: 28-31.

Moss, W., and E. Gardner-O'Toole. 1991. *Aboriginal people: History of discriminatory laws.* BP-175E. Ottawa: Parliamentary Research Branch, Library of Parliament.

NWAC (Native Women's Association of Canada). 2010. *What their stories tell us: Research findings from the Sisters in Spirit Initiative.* Ottawa: Native Women's Association of Canada.

–. 2011. AGM sex trade resolution "In support of Aboriginal Sex Workers Harm Reduction," 08-05-2011. E-mailed statement.

Patterson, J. 2011. Sex assault still somehow women's fault. *Victoria Times Colonist,* 1 April. http://www2.canada.com/victoriatimescolonist/.

Peters, E.J. 1998. Subversive spaces: First Nations women and the city. *Environment and Planning D: Society and Space* 16: 665-85.

Pratt, G. 2005. Abandoned women and spaces of the exception. *Antipode* 37, 5: 1053-78.

Razack, S. 2000. Gendered racial violence and specialized justice: The murder of Pamela George. *Canadian Journal of Law and Society* 15, 2: 91-130.

RCAP (Royal Commission on Aboriginal Peoples). 1996. *Report of the Royal Commission on Aboriginal Peoples.* Vol. 4, *Perspectives and realities.* Ottawa: Canada Communication Group.

Said, E. 1978. *Orientalism.* New York: Vintage Books.

Sethi, A. 2007. Domestic sex trafficking of Aboriginal girls in Canada; Issues and implications. *First Peoples Child and Family Review* 3, 3: 57-71.

Sikka, A. 2009. Trafficking of Aboriginal women and girls in Canada. Aboriginal Policy Research Series, Institute on Governance.

Smith, A. 2005. *Conquest: Sexual violence and American Indian genocide.* Cambridge: South End Press.

Turner, D. 2004. Perceiving the world differently. In *Intercultural dispute resolution in Aboriginal contexts,* ed. C. Bell and D. Kahane, 57-69. Vancouver: UBC Press.

van der Meulen, E., J. Yee, and E. Durisin. 2010. Violence against Indigenous sex workers: Combatting the effects of criminalization and colonialism in Canada. *Research for Sex Work* 12: 35-37.

Williams, R. 1990. *The American Indian in Western legal thought: The discourses of conquest.* New York: Oxford University Press.

Women's Coalition for the Abolition of Prostitution. 2011. Prostitution poses a fundamental threat to women's security. The solution: Decriminalize women and criminalize the demand. News release. Toronto, 16 June. http://vancouver.mediacoop.ca/.

Yee, J. 2009. Supporting Aboriginal sex workers' struggles. *Canadian Dimension* 43, 1: 45-47.

7

Transitioning Out of Sex Work: Exploring Sex Workers' Experiences and Perspectives

TUULIA LAW

For many sex workers and sex work researchers, the topic of transitioning out of the industry is highly contentious and politically loaded. This contention is derived, in part, from court-mandated exit programs and prohibitionist feminist efforts to "save" sex workers, particularly those who are street-based, by helping them leave the industry. Since much of the existing literature focuses on the exiting strategies of the most marginalized and smallest sector of the sex industry, street-based sex workers (see Mansson and Hedin 1999; Woodman 2000; McIntyre 2002; Brown et al. 2006; Canada 2006; DeRiviere 2006; McNaughton and Sanders 2007; Oselin 2009; Ward and Roe-Sepowitz 2009), the term "exit" positions the sex industry as something that needs to be escaped, thus overshadowing the diverse labour arrangements and experiences of sex workers. However, if sex work is indeed a form of labour, as I and other authors in this collection contend, it needs to be situated as part of the trajectory of one's working life. Because of this, I use the more neutral term "transition" to describe the journey from the sex industry to mainstream work.

Taking a sex-work-as-labour perspective to examine the process through which sex workers shift into other forms of work differs significantly from the approach of most of the literature, as does looking at the experiences of sex workers who work in off-street locations. This chapter, then, focuses on the labour transitions of indoor sex workers, including escorts, dominatrices, and massage parlour attendants, who are criminalized through their labour activities. This perspective has been developed through a qualitative study with ten women from Toronto and Montreal who have transitioned out, or begun transitioning out, of full-time sex work and into mainstream jobs during the last five years. The women's ages ranged from twenty-eight to fifty-two, and all had left the industry between one and three times over a span of three to twenty-three years. Their class backgrounds ranged from working to upper-middle class, and one identified as a racialized woman. The majority were university educated, and all had worked in a variety of sex industry sectors and establishments.[1] Drawing on quotes from their interviews, this chapter will discuss the women's decision-making processes, the skills and strategies they used, and the challenges and changes they faced in entering the mainstream job market. Although they were dealing with stigma and discrimination because of their work in the sex industry, they were able to integrate into the mainstream labour market with grace and success, albeit with some ambivalence.

The Transition

Participants' reasons for transitioning out of sex work can be categorized as physical, emotional, and situational, or an intersecting combination of the three. The most common physical reasons included injury, weight gain, and illness. For example, Alana's most recent transition *"came about ... literally by accident ... I broke my wrist and I really couldn't work with a broken wrist."* Unable to exercise following her injury, Alana continued to stay out of sex work because of the weight she had gained.

Whereas some studies identified "burnout" (Rickard 2001; McNaughton and Sanders 2007; Sanders 2007) and love (Mansson and Hedin 1999; Manopaiboon et al. 2003; Sanders 2007) as reasons for leaving the sex industry, my participants also identified depression as an emotional reason for doing so. For Lisa, depression that coincided with other life changes compelled her to leave sex work a second time, whereas Leila was happy to quit escorting when she got married; she returned to it after her divorce. Participants in this study insisted that burnout was neither unmanageable nor specific to sex work but was compounded by stigma and its consequences; Rosie described the psychological toll of *"a life of secrecy,"* whereas Julie's first transition was precipitated by *"terrible shame"* about her involvement in sex work.

Situational reasons for transitioning included the pursuit of a new career or educational path, moving to a new city, and poor labour conditions. The first time Lisa left was to have a child, a situation echoed in the literature (Mansson and Hedin 1999; McIntyre 2002; Hedin and Mansson 2004; McNaughton and Sanders 2007). Violence or fear of violence have been identified by several scholars as reasons for leaving sex work (Mansson and Hedin 1999; McIntyre

2002; Hotaling et al. 2004; McNaughton and Sanders 2007), but only Vivian's transition was precipitated by a bad experience:

> I was working in a massage parlour on and off for a few years, and ... I was doing blow jobs. I took like a six-month break ... and then when I got back into it I decided that the only way I could sort of like, do it again and last more long-term was to not do blow jobs ... [An old client] came with certain expectations and then when he realized, you know, that like, it wasn't gonna happen, he got very angry ... It was really scary ... I yelled, and you know, told him to fuck off ... I went home, and then I was scheduled to go back the next day ... I just was so fearful, I couldn't really do it. So then I left, and stopped.

Although Vivian was not physically attacked, the situation violated her boundaries and disrupted her sense of control over her work, causing her to leave the industry.

Several participants left for a combination of physical, emotional, and situational reasons. For example, Sara described her transition as a cumulative shifting of goals and opportunities: "I had some savings, I had the house. [My partner was] pro-sex-worker, but ... they were very concerned that their family would find out ... I had to tone it down and ultimately decided that I should get another kind of job. One day I lost my black book. My wallet was stolen. Suddenly it was an opportunity to quit." Anik described her decision to leave as "not having my heart at work because I'm in love," combined with the fact that sex work "wasn't a real career for me, and now I should move on to my real career." Interestingly, and in contrast to common assumptions as well as the literature (see Brewis and Linstead 2000; Rickard 2001; Escoffier 2007), none of the participants stopped sex work because they felt they were too old to continue. Sara, for example, did not start escorting until she was thirty-five, and she still works occasionally at age fifty-two.

Most participants transitioned out of sex work and returned (sometimes into different sectors) at least twice, whereas others never left despite transitioning into mainstream jobs and careers alongside their sex work. After Alana quit due to burnout from working for an escort agency, she "started missing it, and then I went into it differently" by returning only part-time. Alternatively, it was the money that compelled Leila, Julie, Rosie, and Vivian to return to sex work.

Several of the women reduced their overall hours of availability for sex work while they took on other jobs. Some also found that maintaining relationships with their regular clients prolonged their transition. Jill stated, "It would have *been a gross absence in my life if you know, this group of people with whom I had – albeit within professional parameters – with whom I had intimate relationships, for them suddenly to be gone. I mean that would be like losing a whole whack of friends at once.*" Similarly, Anik was reluctant to relinquish her two regulars, whom she keeps in addition to working four days per week in a mainstream job. Although she and Jill do not share the same goal – Anik is *"about to do my last call,"* whereas Jill *"wouldn't leave. I think I would feel a loss in terms of connections, community, sense of self"* – both are on parallel work trajectories, with their mainstream jobs now taking up the majority of their time. Indeed, although participants' transitions out of sex work were not direct or linear, they were not disorganized. In this respect, their experiences differed from those described in the literature, where sex workers haphazardly shuttled between the sex industry and mainstream work (see McIntyre 2002; McNaughton and Sanders 2007; Sanders 2007). Instead, participants' transitions were steeped with intention and shaped by strategy as they responded to changing needs, events, and opportunities.

Although most participants were able to draw on their friendship and familial networks when they needed emotional or financial support, their complicated decisions to transition were not always met with understanding. This was true even for Leila, the only participant who had completely disclosed her work to her family. Instead of recognizing that her decision to transition was complex and involved many emotions, her family assumed that she would be singularly relieved about no longer doing sex work. Anticipating a similar response, Anik did not talk much about her transition: *"I just assume that my friends who are not in this business just think, 'Oh my god, you don't have to put up with ugly people that sweat any more, and you miss that?'"* Julie summarized participants' awareness of the popularity of such stigmatic perceptions: *"The powers that be make the right decision always leaving."*

The Strategies

Stigma was a central factor in many of the decisions involved in the women's transitions, in particular whether, and to whom, to disclose their sex work. This meant that they had to strategize about how to rearticulate their sex work skills in order to utilize them in subsequent mainstream jobs.

Participants identified the following skills as transferable to the mainstream labour market: money management, human resources management, entrepreneurship, communication skills, hospitality, therapy/counselling, listening skills, networking, teamwork, conflict resolution, advertising, maintaining a website, marketing, stress management, organizing and scheduling, self-motivation, adaptability, creative problem solving, long-term planning, strategy, assertiveness, maintaining boundaries, negotiation, diplomacy, self-confidence, reading body language/assessing people, and self-care (see also Chapter 2 in this volume). Studies that view "exiting" as trauma recovery (Mansson and Hedin 1999; McIntyre 2002; Hedin and Mansson 2004; DeRiviere 2006; Oselin 2009; Ward and Roe-Sepowitz 2009) do not consider sex work to be a form of labour and therefore do not recognize the valuable skills that people learn in the industry. Indeed, as Sara insisted, *"It's the same skill set as any kind of business."* No matter what kind of job participants got outside of the industry, they found the communication and interpersonal skills developed in sex work to be very useful. This is a pronounced contrast to Woodman (2000) and Rabinovitch (2004), who portrayed former sex workers as floundering in mainstream jobs.

Despite the transferability of the skills they had learned, most of the women did not feel comfortable listing them on their resumés or curricula vitae (CVs), because of concerns about stigma associated with work in the sex industry. However, Alana included sex work on her CV because, *"I thought, 'What looks better, having a big two-, three-year gap on my resume?' or saying 'Here, I worked for this company and I did this.'"* At the same time, Alana *"had a little fun with it"* and *"really couched it in all the kinda [human resources] speak ... You know, 'ensured repeat business' ... 'de-escalated issues.'"* Jill also included sex work on her resumé because, as she said, *"Apart from some very part-time work I'd done, say, through sex worker organizations, I had nothing else on my resumé, including very little formal education ... So, my resumé clearly suggests that I've been a sex worker."* By including it on their resumés, both Alana and Jill bravely argued for the legitimacy of sex work as job experience. For Alana, this was a kind of "test" for her potential employers, particularly those in the harm-reduction and nonprofit sectors; she explains, *"In theory, they're pro-sex-work or whatever, so it's like fine, put your money where your fucking mouth is, right?"*

Other participants managed to avoid gaps in mainstream work experience by euphemistically describing the skills they had acquired in sex work or by focusing on other experiences. After a few years of graduate school, Julie felt that gaps in her CV were no longer an issue *"because I have enough [other] things."* Others strategically emphasized certain types of work or slightly embellished their experiences. For example, as Bertha explains, *"An informal education session that I did in my basement would turn into more of a public education session."* Similarly, Lisa *"didn't differentiate between volunteer work and paid work. And just, you know, fluffed it up a little bit."* Creating a CV was not stressful for everyone, however. Having started relatively late in the sex industry, at age twenty-seven and thirty-five respectively, both Rosie and Sara had held main-stream jobs previously, as well as simultaneously to and interspersed with sex work. As Sara said, *"I had a lot of credentials already, so it wasn't a problem."*

Challenges and Changes

The difficulties of formulating CVs and looking for mainstream work were accompanied by three interrelated areas of challenge and change: money, lifestyle, and schedule. As many studies indicated (Rickard 2001; McIntyre 2002; Manopaiboon et al. 2003; Murphy and Venkatesh 2006; McNaughton and Sanders 2007; Sanders 2007), the first and foremost challenge was money. As Bertha said, *"I made a shitload of money [in sex work]. I knew ... that I would never see money like that again."* Closely related to money is the lifestyle it affords. Most participants had to cut back their spending: Vivian and Bertha missed shopping; Jill had to take fewer taxis; and Leila had to drastically reduce the amount of money she spent on rent, travel, and food. Participants' difficulty in changing their lifestyle varied and was not necessarily related to the amount of money they had made as sex workers but rather to their money management skills.

Certainly, not all the lifestyle changes had to do with money. Anik had enjoyed getting dressed up for work in the sex industry, but now that she has a mainstream job, she must make a concerted effort to dress up: *"You find occasions to wear a pretty dress and pretty shoes and go out. You have to make it happen."* Safety and security also presented challenges for some of the women, but in paradoxical ways. For example, Jill identified an increase in mental and emotional security: *"I hadn't realized that I was living with this sort of low-grade, constant anxiety, not just around physical safety, but also around legal safety. And it wasn't until I stopped advertising and was only seeing regulars where they were super-long-term regulars, I didn't and still don't have any concerns around safety ... I actually felt this shift in – almost felt like a bodily shift ... a relaxation."* By contrast, Alana suffered a decrease in financial security: *"Security ... is wrapped up with money, but also just the knowledge of where is my next job coming from. Is it going to last? ... So there's always this kind of, am I going to have to go back [to sex work] or what? You know, it's waiting for the other shoe to drop, always."* Although participants acknowledged that sex work does not provide a consistent income, they were keenly aware of the precariousness of the mainstream labour market and the growing proportion of temporary and part-time work (Vosko 2000; Westcott, Baird, and Cooper 2006; Ilcan 2009). Compared to unstable mainstream jobs, sex work can be seen as a more secure source of income because its hours are not fixed, and there is no impending contract expiration.

For some, the relatively rigid schedule of mainstream work proved to be a significant challenge. After years of working late into the night, both Alana and Bertha found it particularly difficult to get up early. Participants also found they had less free time overall because they were working more hours than they had previously. Where Rosie missed having time for herself, Vivian found that she was *"seeing [her] friends less because I had less free time because I'm working more."* Despite these challenges, the women managed to secure mainstream jobs that, in many cases, they found just as satisfying as sex work.

The Mainstream

The women in this study had transitioned from the sex industry into one of three sectors of the mainstream labour market: health and social services, the service industry, and academia. Perhaps unsurprisingly, their sex work history was most often considered valid employment experience in the health and social service sector. Of the five women who found positions in this sector, four are currently at sex worker organizations, and one is in a health clinic. Both Lisa and Anik started as interns or volunteers at the sex worker organizations where they are now employed.

Rosie and Sara are employed in what can be termed as the service industry: Rosie is learning massage therapy, a passion she discovered through erotic massage, whereas Sara was hired by a former client to staff his art gallery. Others have transitioned to graduate school and academic work: Bertha works part-time for a community organization in addition to going to school, whereas Julie and Vivian have both held teaching and research positions at universities.

Although stigma constituted a significant challenge to finding gainful employment, participants also encountered other kinds of discrimination in the mainstream labour market that sometimes affected the course of their transitions. Rosie, for example, had not experienced racism during her sex work at a massage parlour and escort agency but did encounter it at an office job:

> *I was the only non-white person in that whole building who wasn't handling food ... It made me feel weird. The people there were really not nice people. One advertising executive in my division, she was always calling me Zahra, and I'm like, "My name's not Zahra." I had to tell her several times, and I knew she*

was just doing it to be insulting, and I was like "I don't need to be insulted at work ... You don't need to treat me like that." I didn't feel like I was getting any recognition, I didn't see that there was any room for me to move up, so I was like, "Why am I doing this?"

After about a month, Rosie had *"had it with that"* and returned to sex work.

Other participants experienced sexual and gendered harassment in their mainstream employment. For example, Julie was harassed while *"working at [a fast food chain] for a summer. I was sexually harassed by the owner and that ended that."* She also encountered harassment when she was teaching: *"I had a student come into my office, a young man ... He was sitting very close to me, and he felt like it was okay to touch my leg ... I've had a lot of different clients and I've certainly worked in some 'seedy' locations in my time, but my clients today really won't touch me without being like, 'Is it okay to touch?' They're quite respectful of my boundaries ... In many cases I feel more powerful and in control as a [sex] worker than I do as an instructor."*

Julie's experiences of sexual harassment speak to the ubiquity of sexism in the mainstream workforce, as does Rosie's experience with racism. However, neither these incidents, nor stigma, nor the limitations of job availability in the mainstream labour market discouraged them. Instead, though acknowledging that mainstream work may be *"not as fun"* (Bertha), that the pay is *"a fucking joke"* (Alana), and that when *"you're applying for jobs, you wanna get hired just like you want the men to choose you"* (Vivian), many participants retained the sense of autonomy they had fostered in sex work and felt empowered to resist or change jobs. As Jill said, *"I'm not going to put up with any shit."*

Conclusion

Although not direct or linear, these women's transitions out of sex work have been shaped by strategy, social location, and changing needs. Because they made progress toward mainstream goals, such as school or career advancements, while working in the sex industry either continuously or sporadically, their transitions can be seen as complex journeys that involve multiple parallel trajectories. These women's stories also suggest that working in the sex industry can be a positive experience that teaches useful, transferable skills. Thus, while it is important to understand the intersecting impacts of stigma and discrimination, it is equally important to emphasize that though these factors may limit chances or choices in the transition out of sex work, they do not dictate them.

Tuulia Law

Note

1 Leila, Anik, and Bertha had worked as escorts; Lisa, Rosie, and Julie had worked in escorting and erotic massage; Vivian had worked in erotic massage; Sara had been an escort and a dominatrix; and Alana and Jill had worked as escorts as well as on the street. Most participants had also worked in other sectors of the industry, both independently and for agencies.

References

Brewis, J., and S. Linstead. 2000. The worst thing is the screwing: Context and career in sex work. *Gender, Work and Organization* 7, 3: 168-80.

Brown, J., N. Higgitt, C. Miller, S. Wingert, M. Williams, and L. Morrissette. 2006. Challenges faced by women working in the inner city sex trade. *Canadian Journal of Urban Research* 15, 1: 36-53.

Canada. 2006. *The challenge of change: A study of Canada's criminal prostitution laws: Report of the Standing Committee on Justice and Human Rights*. Ottawa: House of Commons.

DeRiviere, L. 2006. A human capital methodology for estimating the lifelong personal costs of young women leaving the sex trade. *Feminist Economics* 12, 3: 367-402.

Escoffier, J. 2007. Porn star/stripper/escort: Economic and sexual dynamics in a sex work career. *Journal of Homosexuality* 53, 1-2: 173-200.

Hedin, U., and H.A. Mansson. 2004. The importance of supportive relationships among women leaving prostitution. *Journal of Trauma Practice* 2, 3-4: 223-37.

Hotaling, N., A. Burris, B.J. Johnson, Y.M. Bird, and K.A. Melbye. 2004. Been there done that: SAGE, a peer leadership model among prostitution survivors. *Journal of Trauma Practice* 2, 3: 255-65.

Ilcan, S. 2009. Privatizing responsibility: Public sector reform under neoliberal government. *Canadian Review of Sociology* 46, 3: 207-34.

Manopaiboon, C., R.E. Bunnell, P.H. Kilmarx, S. Chaikummao, K. Limpakarnjanarat, S. Supawitkul, M.E. St. Louis, and T.D. Mastro. 2003. Leaving sex work: Barriers, facilitating factors and consequences for female sex workers in Northern Thailand. *AIDS Care* 15, 1: 39-52.

Mansson, H.A., and U. Hedin. 1999. Breaking the Matthew effect – on women leaving prostitution. *International Journal of Social Welfare* 8: 67-77.

McIntyre, S. 2002. *Strolling away*. Ottawa: Department of Justice Canada, Research and Statistics Division.

McNaughton, C.C., and T. Sanders. 2007. Housing and transitional phases out of 'disordered' lives: The case of leaving homelessness and street sex work. *Housing Studies* 22, 6: 885-900.

Murphy, A.K., and S.A. Venkatesh. 2006. Vice careers: The changing contours of sex work in New York City. *Qualitative Sociology* 29: 129-54.

Oselin, S.S. 2009. Leaving the streets: Transformation of prostitute identity within the Prostitution Rehabilitation Program. *Deviant Behaviour* 30: 379-406.

Rabinovitch, J. 2004. PEERS. *Journal of Trauma Practice* 2, 3: 239-53.

Rickard, W. 2001. "Been there, seen it, done it, I've got the T-shirt": British sex workers reflect on jobs, hopes, the future and retirement. *Feminist Review* 67: 111-32.

Sanders, T. 2007. Becoming an ex-sex worker: Making transitions out of a deviant career. *Feminist Criminology* 2, 1: 74-95.

Vosko, L.F. 2000. *Temporary work: The gendered rise of a precarious employment relationship*. Toronto: University of Toronto Press.

Ward, A., and D. Roe-Sepowitz. 2009. Assessing the effectiveness of a trauma-oriented approach to treating prostituted women in a prison and a community exiting program. *Journal of Aggression, Maltreatment and Trauma* 18: 293-312.

Westcott, M., M. Baird. and R. Cooper. 2006. Re-working work: Dependency and choice in the employment relationship. *Labour and Industry* 17, 1: 5-17.

Woodman, S. 2000. Mentorship and the experiential voice: Transitioning from sex work to mainstream employment. Masters' thesis, Royal Roads University.

Organizing and Social Change

PART 2 OF THIS COLLECTION highlights the historical unfolding of the contemporary sex workers' rights movement in Canada and sex workers' organizing against not only poor working conditions in the industry, but also misperceptions about the work itself. Jenn Clamen, Kara Gillies, and Trish Salah's (Chapter 8) round-table discussion opens this part of the book by highlighting both the challenges and successes of sex workers' and allies' attempts to build bridges with national labour associations and to redefine prostitution as a form of sexual labour on the national stage. We then shift to three chapters that focus on organizing and activist experiences in specific geographies. Joyce Arthur, Susan Davis, and Esther Shannon (Chapter 9) present an in-depth look at Vancouver's sex workers' rights movement as they foreground the voices of current and former workers who have been integral to the city's activist community. Moving from west to east, Anna-Louise Crago and Jenn Clamen (Chapter 10) recount the history of sex work organizing in Montreal from the early 1900s to the present day, locating the city's historical red-light district in an important prism through which to understand the genesis of its bilingual, multi-racial, and multi-gendered sex work activist community. Then to the Maritimes where Gayle MacDonald, Leslie Ann Jeffrey, Karolyn Martin, and Rene Ross (Chapter 11) focus on micro-level policies and practices of Halifax's sex worker organization, addressing zoning restrictions, the recent court case to decriminalize prostitution in Ontario, and the challenge of working from a harm-reduction philosophy under a federal Conservative government.

Part 2 also explores some of the tensions and challenges within the sex workers' rights movement, in particular sex workers' relationship to feminist anti-prostitution activism, a topic examined in detail by Jane Doe (Chapter 12). Exploring discourses of victimization in the violence against women sector, Doe draws on her personal experiences as an anti-violence activist to explore the similarities between the ways in which women who have been sexually assaulted and women who are sex workers are defined through the law and their sexuality. Jacqueline Lewis, Frances M. Shaver, and Eleanor Maticka-Tyndale (Chapter 13) conclude this part of *Selling Sex* by discussing a challenge that sex workers and activists have identified as a key barrier to the advancement of sex workers' rights – the ongoing misperceptions about, and stigmatization of, sex work.

8

Working for Change:
Sex Workers in the Union Struggle

JENN CLAMEN, KARA GILLIES, AND TRISH SALAH

Since the late 1970s, sex workers have challenged the social stigma attached to their work, lobbied for decriminalization, and increasingly advanced an analysis of their work as legitimate labour. This movement has gained ground in the last fifteen years as sex workers have formed local, national, and transnational organizations. With this growth has come an increased focus on labour rights and organizing, including efforts to gain support from the broader labour movement and established trade unions. In the early 2000s, several factors coalesced to put sex work on the agenda of Canada's largest public service union, the Canadian Union of Public Employees (CUPE). When CUPE passed a resolution in 2001 supporting decriminalization, a fragile alliance between the union and sex workers was born (Gillies and Clamen 2004).

In a casual and frank round-table discussion, Trish Salah, former member of CUPE's National Pink Triangle Committee, and Kara Gillies and Jenn Clamen, founders of the Canadian Guild for Erotic Labour, reminisce on the challenges, experiences, and successes in the attempt to gain public support from Canada's largest union.

The Big Meet

Jenn Clamen: I remember meeting both of you at a bar in Toronto's queer neighbourhood that has become one of my favourite spots to do dirty-elbow activism with my heroes. I was very new to the activist scene in Canada in 2002 and was lucky to have connected with you, Kara, who had been active since the early '90s. Having spent the previous two years under the wing of Ana Lopes, organizing with the International Union of Sex Workers (IUSW) in London, UK, meeting other sex work activists in Canada with a labour focus was reinforcing. The IUSW had solidified a branch (what was then called the London Entertainment and Sex Workers Branch) within one of the UK's largest unions, the GMB. While harm-reduction frameworks in London offered a much-needed person-centred approach and some really effective work around violence prevention, the labour framework of the IUSW at the time felt like a sigh of relief; it addressed sex industry working conditions, including violence, through the optic of labour protections. It also insisted on sex worker leadership. Internationally, there were other labour unions that had accepted sex workers by that time; for example, the Argentinean sex workers' rights organization, AMMAR (http://www.ammar.org.ar/.), was a member of the country's trade-union federation the CTA, and the Lusty Lady (http://www.lustyladysf.com/), a peep show in the United States, was organized by the Exotic Dancers' Union, an affiliate of the Service Employees International Union.

Kara Gillies: While the IUSW was working on developing a labour focus and strategy in the UK, here in Canada, sex workers were also moving the discussion onto the labour front. The Canadian sex workers' rights movement had previously pursued decriminalization largely (but certainly not solely) from a general human rights perspective, arguing that the criminal laws exposed us to incarceration, violence, and other subjugations. It was in the late 1990s and early 2000s that many of us started to realize that many of the injustices we faced, such as income insecurity, poor work conditions (including exposure to violence), and discriminatory employment practices, were clear violations of our basic labour rights. This gap was really not surprising, given that most people outside the sex trade did not think of sex work as a form of work, but rather as a social problem or personal dysfunction.

My own interest in addressing sex work through a labour lens was influenced by some of my activist and advocacy activities at the time. In 1999 and 2000, I curated a couple of sex-work-focused events for Toronto's Mayworks: Festival of Working People and the Arts, which I believe helped introduce some activists in organized labour to sex work issues. I then went on to host a sex workers' radio program and was struck by the interest participants and listeners had in issues that I came to recognize as occupational health and safety concerns.

Meanwhile, throughout the late 1990s and early 2000s, police and immigration enforcement officers were increasingly targeting migrant sex workers. These campaigns were spun as "anti-trafficking" initiatives as opposed to the anti-immigration law-and-order enterprises they clearly were. At the United Nations, an anti-trafficking protocol was in development as part of a broader convention countering organized crime (United Nations 2000, 2003), and in Canada, anti-trafficking provisions were introduced through the new *Immigration and Refugee Protection Act* (2001). In Canada and across the globe, sex workers, both local and migrant, were insistent that these anti-trafficking measures were counter-productive and that most abuses migrant sex workers face would be more effectively addressed through providing legal means for workers to enter and stay in destination countries, and for migrant workers, including undocumented workers, to be protected under labour standards. Interestingly, while on the one hand, the Canadian state was embracing anti-trafficking initiatives, on the other hand, they hadn't signed on to the *International Convention on the Protection of the Rights of All Migrant Workers and Members of Their Families* (United Nations 1990). To me, this clearly illustrated that migrant workers' welfare was not the state's real priority. In response, I became involved in the creation of an advocacy group for migrant sex workers in the Toronto area, which highlighted the importance of labour and immigration rights for workers' well-being.

Trish Salah: My entry into sex work activism was through the work I was doing as a trans activist in the late 1990s, when much of the important political work going on was led by trans sex workers (see also Chapter 4 in this volume). Trans sex workers and their allies developed front-line peer-run drop-ins and social services for street-based and poor trans people, like the High Risk Project in Vancouver, Meal Trans in Toronto, and Action Santé Travesti(e)s/Transsexuel(le)s du Québec. Trans sex workers challenged the criminalization of sex work and of drug use, and violence against prisoners. They documented institutional violence against trans people, created transsexual/transgender cultural spaces like the Counting Past 2 Festival, and challenged transphobia in the women's anti-violence movement, the queer community, and academic feminism (see Forrester et al. 2002). It was clear that trans advocacy that did not centrally address sex workers' rights would likely do more harm than good, and it seemed to me that unions might be a viable place to do some useful work.

At the time, I was a teaching assistant at York University in Toronto. In my local, CUPE 3903, many members were active in feminist, anti-oppression, queer as well as anti-globalization, anti-imperialist, anti-poverty groups and movements. The local seemed like a hospitable and well-resourced site to do trans activist work. CUPE 3903 was on the leftist edge of the Canadian labour movement. And yet, while there had been some equality gains for lesbian and gay workers in the broader Canadian labour movement, trans and bisexual workers were not being well represented by their unions.

The unions knew this because a small number of trans and bi unionists had been agitating for better representation for some time. In response, the umbrella organization for Canadian and international unions, as well as provincial federations of labour and regional labour councils, called the Canadian Labour Congress (CLC), organized a series of community consults. During that process some of us stressed the importance of unions being accountable not only to their workers but to those trans people who were unable to secure employment, let alone unionized employment, because of transphobia or the criminalization of sex work (see also Chapter 4 in this volume). Among trans activists in Toronto there was some ad hoc organizing to try to ensure greater inclusivity in who was surveyed by the unions and to foreground the need to act in solidarity with trans people who do sex work.

Within local 3903 we began to work actively on trans rights and sex worker rights. One way in which we began that work was to send members and resolutions to CUPE's 2001 national convention.[1] One of these resolutions, number 189, would be the start of a long process. It read,

WHEREAS THE CLC Solidarity and Pride Conference identified outreach to and solidarity with lesbian, gay, bisexual and transgender community activists as a pressing need; and

WHEREAS at the transgender/transsexual community consultation conducted by the CLC, transsexual and transgender activists requested CLC and affiliate solidarity with transsexual and transgender sex workers and sex worker activists; and

WHEREAS transsexual and transgender sex workers and activists have been at the forefront of the struggle for transsexual and transgender rights in Canada; and

WHEREAS transsexual and transgender sex workers are subject to extremely unsafe and violent working conditions as a result of the criminalization of sex work; and

WHEREAS sex workers and sex worker advocates are calling for the decriminalization of sex work in Canada;

THEREFORE BE IT RESOLVED that CUPE National take the lead within the CLC and its affiliates to work in solidarity with transsexual, transgender and non-trans sex workers to end the criminalization of sex work in Canada; and

Jenn Clamen, Kara Gillies, and Trish Salah

BE IT FURTHER RESOLVED that CUPE adopt a convention resolution calling for the decriminalization of sex work in Canada. (CUPE 2001)

Kara: When I first heard about this resolution, I was absolutely ecstatic! To have a major union call for decriminalization was a groundbreaking step, both because of CUPE's potential power in support of law reform and because having a union address sex work helped position us as workers, and our issues as labour matters.

Trish: It committed CUPE, at least in principle, to recognizing sex work as important to trans communities and activism, to working with sex workers and activists on decriminalization, and to showing leadership with the CLC in fighting for decriminalization. It also acknowledged that the CLC's own process of trans community consultation mandated them to do this work. On the downside, it perhaps over-identified struggles for sex workers' rights with trans advocacy in a way that was contested by some within CUPE.

Kara: Another downside was the foregrounding of violence against sex workers, which, while a serious concern, is often used to advance paternalistic narratives and policies that undermine sex workers' rights and detract from progressive organizing, which in turn often results in further oppression. And, as we later witnessed, the conflation of sex work with violence against women became fodder for anti-sex-work rhetoric and positions within certain parts of organized labour.

Trish: Resolution 189 was adopted, as was a resolution creating seats for trans workers on the National Pink Triangle Committee, CUPE's equity committee for lesbian, gay, and bisexual workers, which I then joined. Later that year, Kara and sex work activist Mirha Soleil Ross spoke on a panel that I organized on sex work as labour. Some (but not enough) union folks turned up. Fred Hahn, then president of CUPE local 2191 and an activist on CUPE's National Pink Triangle Committee, was one. In November 2002, Fred and I got in touch with you, Jenn, as the Canadian representative of the International Union of Sex Workers.

Jenn: Yes, you wanted to know more about how the IUSW was successful at having sex work recognized within the union in the UK, as well as details about the highly successful certification drive and what possible steps we could take in Canada. You mentioned that CUPE was interested in organizing around sex work issues, but it was still unclear what that could look like.

Kara: A key question was whether unionization was a good option and if it would even be possible in a Canadian context. We spent some time exploring potential forms of labour support for sex workers and considering how well – or poorly – these might meet the diverse needs of sex workers across a spectrum of social locations, geography, and sex work sectors. Our first priority was considering sex workers' varied preferences: like working people in general, some sex workers prefer to be self-employed, some prefer to work as freelancers, and still others like to have a formal employer who is responsible for the business end of things (see also Chapter 17 in this volume). However, they still face the same typically substandard work conditions and usually lack formal verbal or written contracts; and even if they have contracts, under criminalization these are basically unenforceable. We wanted sex worker labour rights mobilization to be inclusive of these workers. Workplace issues, relationships, and needs vary accordingly, and any attempt to advance labour rights needs to be inclusive of all these contexts. However, some people have questioned the applicability of labour laws and organizing to street-based sex work, for example. Simply because a worksite is "non-standard" doesn't preclude the possibility of establishing effective labour protections. Indeed, bike couriers have successfully organized in Quebec.

Trish: It's important for unions and labour organizers to recognize the diversity of labour arrangements and worksites in the sex industry; a model that might work well in a massage parlour might or might not translate well to street-based work or outcall escorting. Also, in Canada, most unions only organize workers who are considered formal employees. So-called autonomous workers who are not affiliated with (or at least not recognized as being affiliated with) a single employer or worksite are deemed not eligible to unionize.

Kara: These limitations to unionization are exacerbated by the criminalization of sex work management (through the procuring law) and worksites (through the bawdy-house law). In essence, anyone who manages or has "influence" over someone selling sexual services is subject to serious criminal sanction. Not surprisingly, then, many managers insist that their workers are freelancers in an attempt to protect themselves from criminal charges. However, this lowers their legal responsibilities to their workers while eliminating unionization as an option.

Jenn: Some sex workers are in, and frequently seek out, more formal employer-employee relationships, where one is employed by, or employs, an agency or individual to look after the business end of things, including protection. Normally, workers in this type of workplace can organize a union drive because under provincial labour acts their employee-employer relationships are recognized as such. However, with the criminalization of prostitution-related activities, worker-management relationships in the sex industry are viewed as criminal, which means that anyone in a "manager" position is not considered an employer, but rather an exploiter, under the Canadian Criminal Code. Needless to say, this makes unionizing difficult since most unions will not organize autonomous workers, and there isn't a formal employer-employee relationship.

Kara: There are also other aspects of sex work management that need to be considered. For example, sex workers themselves, both on and off street, often hire people for protection, as drivers and to seek out clients. As a result, sex workers both manage others and are managed in the business. All of these working relationships are criminalized and therefore not recognized under labour law.

Jenn: This means that in Canada we would need to take a different approach from that of the IUSW, because in the UK, the GMB was able to organize autonomous workers. So independent sex workers both on and off the street were able to join the same union branch as sex workers who worked in pornography, escort agencies, or dance clubs. We agreed that sex work labour organizing in Canada would have to focus more on gaining support through the unions' political bodies and less on organizing sex workers into their own union locals.

Birthing the Canadian Guild for Erotic Labour

Kara: In addition to initiating ongoing dialogue between sex worker activists and CUPE, our initial "big meet" also sparked further discussions between you and me, Jenn, about various other forms of labour organizing and mobilization outside of formal unionization.

Jenn: Yes – you and I had been strategizing about formalizing a Canadian branch of the IUSW. But the desire to address labour rights for sex workers beyond unionization led instead to the birth of the Canadian Guild for Erotic Labour (CGEL), which we launched in 2003 (King 2004; Gall 2012). CGEL's mission was to establish, promote, and uphold sex workers' labour rights. Our guiding principles recognized all forms of sex work as legitimate work and that sex trade workers be entitled to the same basic human and labour rights as other working people.

These rights include the decriminalization of all aspects of sex work and the right to be free from state regulations that are more repressive than those imposed on other workers and businesses, whether through criminal law, municipal bylaws, or other mechanisms. We also demanded basic workers' rights for sex workers, including the right to work independently, collectively, or for third parties. This broke down further into the right to work as independent contractors (with recognized contracts-for-service), employees (with recognized contracts-of-service), or as self-employed workers. With that, of course, comes the right to form and join professional associations, the right to unionization and collective bargaining, and fair and equitable income taxation.

Kara: We also highlighted the right to travel and cross borders and the right of all migrant workers, including undocumented workers, to labour protections and fair practices. In practice, we wanted to assist sex workers in negotiating fair work practices and conditions with employers – for example, earnings, hiring/termination procedures, scheduling, grievance procedures, physical condition of work venue and equipment, as well as upholding workers' rights when contracts or employment laws are violated.

Of course, when prostitution is criminalized, it is close to impossible to enforce labour laws. However, there are many municipalities in Canada that regulate sex work businesses through bylaws such as licensing and zoning (see also Chapter 20 in this volume). The tricky bit is that cities can't acknowledge that the businesses they are regulating offer prostitution services, because the criminalization of prostitution places its regulation solely in the hands of the federal government. As a result, all parties involved pretend that sex work is not taking place; for example, escort services are "dating" services, and massage parlours provide "relaxation rubdowns." We figured we could take advantage of this wilful ignorance to promote labour rights and standards – after all, if nobody, including the local government, is going to acknowledge that prostitution is occurring, then criminalization would not be as big a barrier to accessing labour protections.

Jenn: In fact, one of the reasons we chose the term "erotic labour" instead of "sex work" in our name and communications was to facilitate our engagement with sex workers in these pseudo-legal sectors without outing, and consequently putting at legal risk, the sex work aspects of their business.

Sex Work and CUPE: A Short-Lived Affair

Trish: I believe it was in 2004 that we, CUPE's National Pink Triangle Committee, invited you, the Canadian Guild for Erotic Labour, to help us in our efforts to further our internal education. We wanted to advance the sex workers' rights material we were working on for CUPE Pride Campaigns. Within the Pink Triangle Committee there was nervousness about whether we should be working on sex worker solidarity. It seemed largely to do with feeling like it was new territory, that we were not equipped to do the work well. There was an interest in getting more education on the sex workers' rights movements and decriminalization. There was also a need to address and debunk representations of sex work (as violence against women and as trafficking).

Kara: Jenn and I went to Ottawa to meet with the Pink Triangle Committee and present on these issues. We spent a lot of time addressing some initial conceptualizations that had been outlined in a draft CUPE background paper on sex work (CUPE 2004). It was to be their first public document on sex work that would serve as the basis for their solidarity with sex workers. However, it was problematic for several reasons.

Jenn: Firstly, the background paper positioned prostitution as distinct from other forms of sex work and assumed a level of inherent exploitation rather than considering the impact of criminalization and resulting stigma and discrimination. It also promoted, and hence privileged, indoor sex work without recognizing the need to protect the rights and safety of those working outdoors.

Kara: The paper also reflected what we quickly came to realize was CUPE's rationale for supporting sex workers – namely, that we are a marginalized social group who could potentially benefit from CUPE's historical commitment to supporting equity-seeking communities. While on one level this was a laudable stance, it was also both surprising and disappointing. We were not requesting union solidarity to advance a generic "whores are people too" perspective. We were seeking union recognition of sex work as labour, and union support for our rights as workers – more of a "whores are *workers* too" perspective, if you will!

Jenn: While the paper did acknowledge the link between sex work and union issues, it was in the context of upholding union rights for the social service workers who provide front-line services to sex workers, not for sex workers themselves. The most telling statement in the draft background paper that should have, perhaps, rung the alarm for us was, "CUPE is not seeking to organize sex workers." While they rightfully recognized that getting union representation was unlikely for sex workers given that sex work is criminalized, they made little mention of actually combating criminalization in the hopes that sex workers could one day unionize and protect their labour rights.

Trish: CUPE's commitment to recognizing sex work as labour, and sex workers as workers, should have been the basis for that paper, but a significant portion of CUPE's membership are involved in administering the criminalization of sex work (for example, police and social service locals), and some of the language in the paper reflects that. At the same time, that language also reflected arguments made within CUPE that a) CUPE's membership includes sex workers, and b) that sex work experience was a bona fide credential for some social service worker positions that CUPE organizes. In any case, your presentations to the Pink Triangle Committee went over very well, and people learned a lot that day. Outside of the committee meetings, the discussions at national and provincial conventions and conferences were having ripple effects, both positive and negative. One strong supportive voice was that of Wayne Lucas, president of CUPE Newfoundland and Labrador, who went on public record as supporting decriminalization and unionization for sex workers (Vaccaro 2005).

Kara: This was also during preparation for the CUPE's Pink Triangle Pride Campaign, which included a poster depicting a brick wall with all sorts of LGBT-friendly messages. In the bottom corner of the poster was the tag "Decriminalize Prostitution." Resolution 189 had been passed, but members were still up in arms about support for prostitutes.

Trish: The poster was an attempt by the National Pink Triangle Committee to start mobilizing around the issue with CUPE's national membership, one that made the tactical decision to associate sex workers' rights with Pride. In retrospect, that might have been another step in the wrong direction. Certainly, some folks, perhaps on the other equality committees, and at the national office, were getting antsy. I think that the shit hit the fan precisely when things seemed to be taking a huge step forward.

Jenn: Wayne Lucas's comment and the poster led to an invitation to CGEL from CUPE Newfoundland and Labrador, to speak to CUPE members in the province;

it served as a great opportunity to engage with and mobilize a broader group of unionists (Davis 2004; Lakritz 2004; Vaccaro 2004). Our priority for this talk was to convince the membership that sex workers had a place in unions. With trepidation, and not knowing what to expect, we went. The experience turned out to be hopeful in some ways. The people we spoke to grasped the links between workers in the sex industry and other forms of labour; I pressed the importance and privilege of having one's work recognized as labour and the dangers of working with little to no labour protection and no recourse. As soon as I finished presenting, one of the members stood up to proclaim, "I hate lesbians, I hate prostitutes, but you, you *are* my sister." I tell this story so often, because, despite the obvious issue I took with his deep hatred, I was touched by his ability to transcend these differences in the name of labour rights. It really drove home for me why I had been interested in labour politics for sex workers from the start: within the union locals, workers' issues, and in this, access to the rights that protect one's place in a system of capitalism that drives one's ability to access the world – health, safety, and personal integrity – trumped personal morals. Other people in the room named their moral hesitation with other types of labour (for example, pharmaceutical companies, prison guards, etc.), yet stressed the importance of rights associated with work and earning wages. There was a real appreciation for the dangers that come with working without protection and while at risk. While the membership present was fraught with stereotypes, prejudices, and misconceptions about sex work that would obviously require education campaigns, they voiced their agreement that sex workers are workers too and deserve recognition and protection of their labour rights.

Kara: If only we could have replicated that dialogue across the country! Unfortunately, divergent opinions and strong reactions among CUPE members seemed to grow at an exponential rate, and the media fanned the flames with salacious and frequently contemptuous commentaries.

Trish: A week prior to the 2004 national Equality Committee meetings, and after the meeting in Newfoundland, a letter was sent by the acting director of CUPE's Equality Branch to the Pink Triangle Committee indicating the national office had decided that the decriminalization campaign did not fit with the union's strategic directions. We responded by demonstrating how the campaign *did* fit within our strategic directions, and we raised questions about the appropriateness of the national office dictating the meaning and method of the Equality Committee's work. At another meeting the national president, Paul

Moist, intimated that leading a campaign for the decriminalization of sex work should be limited to CUPE raising the level of public discussion on sex work. Of course, we challenged him on that at the time.

Kara: The message CGEL received was not as direct. We were advised by the president and Equality Committee that CUPE's inability to organize autonomous workers meant that they were not our most effective partners, and they suggested we would be better off working with the Canadian Labour Congress. This came as a total surprise, since we were not focusing on unionization. Further, the Pink Triangle Committee had committed to an ongoing collaboration with CGEL and had promised that sex work issues were a top priority. The only prior whisper of trouble had been when CUPE's Women's Committee exhibited resistance to the support for decriminalization and had attempted to block progress within the Equality Branch, which housed both the Women's and Pink Triangle Committees. We had been assured that the issue was resolved, and we certainly had been led to believe that the national office was on board!

Trish: As a committee, we attempted to do damage control on what was happening, but those efforts were unsuccessful. At that point, those of us who believed our work could only happen in partnership with sex workers, and who understood sex work as work, had been effectively outmanoeuvred within the union. I think that was the work, not only of the Women's Committee, but also of the president's office and members of the Equality Branch.

When I resigned from the Pink Triangle Committee in 2005, I argued that while important, education is not, in itself, a campaign for decriminalization. It is also necessary to work with other unions, with national and provincial political parties, with LGBT community groups, and most importantly, with sex workers' rights organizations to mobilize for significant legal, social, and political reform. I also argued that we would not succeed in raising the level of public discussion on sex work if we did not work with sex workers, respect their activism and their expertise. In fact, we would do more harm than good.

Passing the Buck: Sex Work Issues Get Blocked

Trish: The 2001 CUPE resolution had mandated CUPE to show leadership within the CLC to work on a campaign for decriminalization. However, that language was basically employed by the president's office, in a way directly counter to its intent and implication, to defer responsibility for a decriminalization campaign to the CLC.

Kara: In and of itself, this did not necessarily pose an insurmountable problem, given that the CLC had also passed an earlier resolution to develop policies supportive of sex workers.

Trish: Yes, at the June 2002 CLC convention, a resolution calling on unions to act in solidarity with sex workers had been passed. At that time, the discussion of sex work was linked to the then recent murder of Faye Urry, a transsexual woman and sex worker in Prince George, British Columbia, in the same month that Robert Pickton was arrested. The convention took place in Vancouver, where sex work was being associated with a specific kind of targeted violence, as well as with police inaction in relation to massive numbers of missing and murdered women. Those contexts both shaped the rhetoric and enabled the passage of the resolution:

> WHEREAS sex trade workers are subject to extremely unsafe working condi-
> tions; and
> WHEREAS because of criminalization, sex workers are unable to seek formal
> measures of protection; and
> WHEREAS the Canadian labour movement has long fought for social and
> legal supports for workers;
> THEREFORE BE IT RESOLVED that the CLC through the Solidarity and Pride
> working group and the women's committee, consult within labour and the
> community to develop policies that provide supportive measures for sex
> trade workers.

Jenn: On one hand, the resolution did not link sex work with trans rights in the same manner as the 2001 CUPE resolution, and so it mandated a commitment to a broader constituency of sex workers. However, its language was ambiguous, weak even, and wasn't strong or specific enough in mandating sex worker consultation or specifying that sex workers must be respected as the experts about sex work.

Trish: It's more common, although problematic, to assign expertise to prohibitionist feminists, cops, and social service workers administering shelters and "exit" programs. Again, this is particularly pertinent, given that CLC affiliates, like CUPE, organize and represent people working in the social service sector and, in some provinces, the police.

Jenn: This meant that unless the CLC committed to working with CGEL and other sex workers, we were taking a step back in terms of addressing sex workers' rights within this labour movement.

Trish: Initially, we tried to bring forward a much better resolution, one that explicitly framed sex work as labour and which committed the CLC to specific actions in solidarity with sex workers. Instead, the resolution that passed was a poor compromise arrived at after much politicking. Before a resolution can be voted on at convention, it first needs to be submitted to, and approved by, a Convention Resolutions Committee. These committees have a great deal of power to set the agenda for which resolutions are brought forward to the membership to vote on. They can promote, combine, rewrite, and/or bury resolutions in ways that set the terms of debate for the convention. Further, although the Resolutions Committee is technically at arm's length from the union leadership, there is considerable overlap in who sits on both committees. The other major limitation of convention is that if you don't have union representation, you don't have a voice, let alone a vote, in discussions that profoundly impact you.

Jenn: Because sex workers are not a represented group within the CLC, we had to rely on various internal committees to bring the issues forward. In the end, the CLC Women's Committee was ambivalent (if not hostile) around sex work issues. Indeed, they were a mirror image of the prohibitionist feminist movement outside of union walls.

Kara: When we attempted to connect with the CLC's Women's Committee to continue the work, we were advised that they were not consulting with sex workers or sex workers' organizations, because they perceived us as biased. Instead, the Women's Committee wanted to form their own opinions and consolidate their own positions. Yes, we are biased! It is our lives, work, rights, and worth they are discussing! This act of exclusion spoke volumes about their disregard of not only sex work, but of women working in the sex trades.

Jenn: There was a real disconnect between actual workers, like those who attended our meeting in Newfoundland, and the committee debates. This is a replica of the disconnect we often see between anti-sex-work/prohibitionist feminists and those who work on the ground with people working in the sex industry or who are themselves sex workers. It was just as disappointing to see sex workers' rights and lives being treated as a theoretical debate at the level of union organizing as it was to witness it within the most visible parts of the women's movement.

Lessons Learned and Possibilities for Future Union Organizing

Trish: Reading between the lines, and reflecting on my own experience, it seems that a number of factors were at play that worked to remove sex workers' rights from the union agenda. For one, pushing for sex workers' rights in terms of CUPE's obligations to transsexual and transgender workers may have been a strategic error. That claim was responsive to trans prostitutes' criticism of more liberal forms of trans advocacy that simply pursued human rights and hate crimes reforms, and was what got us to the table in the first place, but it may have been useful to start building solidarity more broadly from the beginning.

Jenn: While getting sex work onto the agenda was a significant advance, it seems that the initial association of sex work with sexuality and gender issues framed sex work as a broad social issue for CUPE. Aside from specific instances, they never seemed to be able to move forward to position sex work as a labour issue.

Kara: CUPE's lack of ability to connect sex work issues and union issues consistently undermined a commitment to a labour analysis and any real solidarity. The threads of moralism and victim narratives woven into their early discourse were picked up by the Women's Committee. Even those actors and groups who did not adhere to this perspective appear to have been cowed into compliance or at least into silence. It was, and continues to be, very distressing, especially given that anti-sex-work/prohibitionist feminist thought is actually the minority feminist voice in Canada – yet it gets the most air time. Many people within and outside unions are made to believe that if they support sex work, they are supporting the exploitation of women, when in fact it is the exclusion of sex workers from labour organizing and the ongoing denial of our rights that are most destructive.

Trish: That obviously has to do with the pervasiveness of the victim discourse and of active work being done to silence and restigmatize sex workers by prohibitionist feminists and others (see also Chapter 14 in this volume).

Jenn: It also had to do with a failure on the part of unions to have an analysis of labour that engages with differing conditions – and definitions – of work, in this case, work that is criminalized. While those conditions may interact with social difference (for example, class, race, sexuality, and gender), unions still need to address sex work in terms that do not reduce it down to identity-based equality-seeking issues.

Trish: Ultimately, I believe opposition to working for sex workers' rights within CUPE and the CLC was mobilized by influential and organized union women and men who took a prohibitionist feminist stance. Within CUPE, this opposition was convenient for the national president's office, which seemed increasingly eager to move the issue over to the Women's Committee and then on to the CLC. Despite convention resolutions, like 189 that directed CUPE to show leadership on sex work issues, the national executive and union feminists who opposed both transsexual women's and sex workers' rights succeeded in quashing the initiative – I flag both here because that opposition seemed both transphobic and anti-sex-worker.

I recently spoke to Joanne Martin (in February 2011), a senior staffer who recently retired from CUPE and who spent some time supporting the work of the National Pink Triangle Committee. She described the 2006 International Lesbian and Gay Human Rights Conference held in Montreal, at which CUPE delegates pushed for a statement of solidarity with sex workers. Joanne suggests that within CUPE, the Pink Triangle Committee has kept the issue of sex workers' labour rights on the agenda with "sporadic attempts to move forward in terms of educating new members of the committee." She also suggested that the National Pink Triangle Committee has continued to press for a meeting with the Women's Committee, which remains conflicted at best on the question of sex worker solidarity.

Kara: This leaves open the possibility of sex workers once again seeking support from unions. It is also possible that as union memberships continue to decline, and as work in general becomes increasingly precarious, informal, and otherwise non-standard, traditional trade unions will need to explore new and innovative organizing methods and structures. This might lead them to reach out to groups of workers – including sex workers – who have previously been excluded from organized labour.

Jenn Clamen, Kara Gillies, and Trish Salah

Note

1   The national convention is one "representative body" where representatives of union locals come together annually and debate the policies and practices of the national union, in parliamentary style. Resolutions are brought forward, debated, defeated, or adopted. The National Equality Committees are another set of representative bodies and are comprised of members elected at the convention.

References

CUPE (Canadian Union of Public Employees). 2001. Twentieth Biennial Convention Proceedings. November 19-23, 2001. Vancouver, British Columbia.

–. 2004. Background paper: Sex work, why it's a union issue. http://cupe.ca/.

Davis, G. 2004. Unionizing the 'oldest profession.' *Western Star* (Corner Brook, AB), 15 September, P6.

Forrester, M., J.L. Hamilton, V. Namaste, and M. Soleil Ross. 2002. Statement for social service agencies and transsexual/transgendered organizations on service delivery to transsexual and transvestite prostitutes. *ConStellation* 7, 1: 22-25.

Gall, G. 2012. *An agency of their own: Sex worker unionizing.* Winchester, UK: Zero Books.

Gillies, K., and J. Clamen. 2004. When sex works: A call for worker solidarity. *Workers' Voice* 2, 5: 10-12.

Immigration and Refugee Protection Act, S.C. 2001, c. 27.

King, M. 2004. Sex-trade workers seek labour representation. *Montreal Gazette,* 9 October, A7.

Lakritz, N. 2004. Hooker union: Lunacy run amok. *Calgary Herald,* 14 October, A20.

United Nations. 1990. *International Convention on the Protection of the Rights of All Migrant Workers and Members of Their Families.* UN Doc. A/RES/45.158. http://www2. ohchr.org/.

–. 2000. *United Nations Convention against Transnational Organized Crime.* http://www.unodc. org/documents/treaties/UNTOC/Publications/TOC%20Convention/TOCebook-e.pdf.

–. 2003. *Protocol to Prevent, Suppress and Punish Trafficking in Persons, especially Women and Children, Supplementing the United Nations Convention against Transnational Organized Crime.* G.A. Res. 25, annex 2, U.N. GAOR, 55th Sess., Supp. No. 49, at 60, U.N. Doc. A/55/49 (Vol. 1).

Vaccaro, Anthony. 2004. C.U.P.E. hailed for stance on social issues. *St. John's Telegram,* 21 September, A4.

9

Overcoming Challenges:
Vancouver's Sex Worker Movement

JOYCE ARTHUR, SUSAN DAVIS, AND ESTHER SHANNON

For thousands of years, the Coast Salish peoples have flourished in the land that is now Vancouver. We would like to acknowledge and honour the three Coast Salish nations whose land this is: Squamish Nation, Musqueam Nation, and Tsleil-Waututh Nation.

Vancouver's earliest sex workers were strong, resourceful women who played a key role in the birth and growth of the city, beginning in the 1870s. For a full century, they enjoyed relatively safe and peaceful times, especially working in supper clubs after the 1920s. Although attempts to eradicate the sex industry occurred sporadically, they did not begin in earnest until the 1970s. One supper club frequented by sex workers, the Penthouse, was raided and shut down by police in 1975, resulting in the quick emergence of a visible street-level trade; the first recorded murder of a sex worker in Vancouver took place that same year (Lowman 2000). For the next decade, sex workers plied their trade in Vancouver's vibrant West End district, but a neighbourhood campaign against them culminated in the 1984 "West End injunction" – a BC Supreme Court decision that forced them to migrate into Vancouver's Downtown Eastside, the most poverty-stricken area of the city (Ross and Hamilton 2007-11). After 1985, coinciding with passage of the "communicating" provision (section 213 of the Criminal Code) and Vancouver's increasing enforcement of city bylaws that pushed sex workers into isolated areas, the disappearance and mortality rates of Vancouver sex workers skyrocketed (Davis and Bowen 2008).[1] The dangers that resulted from legal reforms and prohibitionist campaigns gave rise to a dynamic sex workers' rights movement in British Columbia, one that is unique in Canada because of its diverse and collaborative nature. This chapter describes the evolution of Vancouver's sex workers' rights movement by chronicling the sex-worker-run organizations that have formed in the face of social and legal adversity since the early 1980s. Highlighted below are the narratives of the current and former sex workers and allies who played an instrumental role in this little-known history.

Outreach and Empowerment: Sex Worker Organizing from the 1980s to the 1990s

Vancouver's diverse sex worker movement began to organize community-based initiatives in the 1980s, such as founding sex worker support groups, safe workspaces, and harm-reduction programs, as well as engaging in labour and community organizing, dialogues with police and government, public education campaigns, and activism. Members of the movement also gained momentum and confidence by attending several key conferences in the 1980s and 1990s that enabled them to benefit from the experiences of other movements and activists around the world.

One of the first sex worker groups to form in Vancouver was the Alliance for the Safety of Prostitutes (ASP) in the early eighties. Founded by Sally deQuatros and Marie Arrington, the group organized against both violence and the 1985 communicating law. It also produced bad trick sheets for every sex work stroll in the area. The ASP disbanded around 1986, and Arrington soon founded a new group called POWER, which took over the collection of bad date information; however, it too closed down in 1990.

Another early sex worker group began in a church in Vancouver's Mount Pleasant district in 1984 – the WISH Drop-In Centre for young men and women. It later became a centre for women only, providing limited services and respite to sex workers. However, armed with the newly forged communicating law, which prevented sex workers from arranging dates with clients in public, police and residents of the area exerted considerable push-back, and WISH was forced to move its services into the Downtown Eastside in 1987. The demand for its services grew from less than a dozen women a night coming in for coffee to over a hundred women attending the centre each day for meals, showers, and clothing, and to participate in programs. Today, WISH continues to offer street-based sex workers a safe, non-judgmental place of respite from their daily work on the street (WISH, n.d.).

Despite the work of WISH, there was still an overall shortage of services and supports for people involved in the sex industry. In the early 1990s, a group of sex workers and their allies met in a one-bedroom apartment in Vancouver's West End to found the PACE Society. Led by Paige Latin and others, it became a major centre of sex worker community development and rights organizing. Today, the PACE Society continues to provide a safe gathering place for sex workers while also offering peer counselling services (PACE 2005). Some of the sex workers who once accessed PACE's services have remained active in the organization, such as the current executive director, Kerry Porth, who explained her involvement with PACE as follows: *"I first came to PACE Society as a client when I was ready to get off of drugs and out of sex work. PACE ... supported me during the first couple of years of my recovery and exiting process, and being around PACE really helped me in processing my experiences as a sex worker. I started working at PACE in February of 2006 as an office manager, the same week I took my last dose of methadone. There aren't many employment opportunities where you are supported through a thirty-day detox!"*

Other sex workers found that PACE empowered them personally and inspired them to start making a difference in the lives of "survival sex workers."[2] Susan Davis, for example, became an activist in the BC Coalition of Experiential Communities and is dedicated to labour organizing for sex workers, in addition to continuing her twenty-five-year calling as a sex worker:

> *Once I discovered PACE and started working on the board [of directors] and on the policy development workshops and all those things, I began to really see where we could make a difference, and how if we were organized enough, we could actually make an impact. For me as a sex worker, it's been all over the map. I've worked on the street, I've been in prison, I've had people try to kill me, I've been on private planes making thousands of dollars for doing basically nothing. But the movement has definitely shown me a way to bring stability for everybody, so you don't have to assume that sex work is going to be dangerous. I guess that's the hardest part for me, is that people always say, "You should know better than to be a sex worker because it's dangerous!" Well, the movement has given me the fight to say, "No, that's not reasonable." Other industries are dangerous and enjoy human rights, so why are we excluded? For me it's just been empowering.*

Jamie Lee Hamilton, a transsexual sex worker and activist who began street work in Vancouver during the late 1970s, also recognized the lack of safe venues for women to work. After being pushed into the Mount Pleasant district due to the 1984 West End injunction that banned sex workers from the West End, Hamilton became concerned when some of her fellow workers began to go missing. In her words, she took an *"almost motherly interest"* in them, first becoming an activist with the ASP and participating in its meetings and marches, then supplying fellow workers with food and other basic needs after another worker was found dead in 1991. Eventually, she opened Grandma's House in 1997, a safe place for street workers to drop by and warm up, have a coffee, and use the computer (see also Chapter 15 in this volume). When reports surfaced of a serial killer preying on sex workers, Hamilton began allowing women to use Grandma's House as a safe place to entertain their clients. But after an undercover sting operation by police in 2000, Hamilton was arrested and charged with keeping a common bawdy-house (Harris 2010). She managed to obtain some outside help to launch a constitutional challenge, and the charges were eventually dropped.

Other members of the sex workers' right movement, such as exotic dancers, were also advocating for the labour rights and safety of sex workers in the 1980s and 1990s. Seeing discrimination in pay rates across the city's strip clubs, exotic dancer Jacquie Carstensen spearheaded an initiative to unite dancers and organize efforts to create a dancers' association or union. In the late 1980s, club owners and managers had collectively drawn up a list of dancers and agreed on the price that clubs would pay each one. Carstensen was furious because she had worked hard to create elaborate theme shows with props, yet Vancouver clubs would pay her only fifty dollars per show. As she explained,

> There was a lot of positive momentum and support from the agents and even some of the club managers who did what they could to support my allegations of "price fixing." My lawyer told me that this would be grounds for a class-action lawsuit. I coordinated a local Vancouver dancers' meeting, secretly through word of mouth, for fear of backlash from the clubs and agents. The turnout was quite large. A lawyer explained everything and how we could stand up for our rights through a united front. Besides trying to initiate a class-action lawsuit, it was also suggested that we stage a "strike" against the Vancouver clubs and that nobody work for a day, or even better, the entire week.

Unfortunately, strong forces opposed the unionization of dancers, and the effort was stopped in its tracks because of gang-style intimidation tactics against dancers and their agents, including threats of blacklisting and loss of livelihood. It was *"very scary"* for Carstensen and everyone else:

I eventually felt the backlash of trying to stand up for our rights and ended up having to work gigs outside of Vancouver and even back east. I learned that manipulation and intimidation controlled most of the dancers into conforming and accepting whatever they were given. But I've always believed in free enterprise and the right of entrepreneurial dancers to dictate what our individual show prices should be based on experience, entertainment quality, dance abilities, and theme shows. So I ended up creating my own career path, rather than having to conform to the typical job requirements that dictate my monetary value. Erotic dancing has taught me how to deal with every type of personality and not to be quick to judge anyone.

Strength from Adversity: The Twenty-First Century

In 2002, a serial killer was arrested and charged with the murders of twenty-seven women, most of whom were Aboriginal survival sex workers who had gone missing from the Downtown Eastside starting in the 1980s.[3] During those twenty years, sex workers, their support workers, and family members had pressured the police to investigate the disappearances and warned that Vancouver had a serial killer (Cameron 2010). Even though the RCMP had information pointing to the primary suspect by mid-1999 (Kines 2010), he was not arrested until three years later, enabling him to kill at least another dozen women. The killer was ultimately tried and convicted for only six murders in 2007. It took three years, until December 2010, for the provincial government to launch the Missing Women Commission of Inquiry to investigate police errors and wrongdoing in the case. As this collection goes to press, the Commission's report has been submitted to government, yet in the eyes of many the inquiry was a complete failure because it excluded the voices of Aboriginal and sex-working women and did not support community participation, among other problems (see Bennett et al. 2012).

The hopelessness and anger that many felt over the inadequate response of government and police led to the first Women's Memorial March in 1991. Held on every Valentine's Day since – and attended by thousands in recent years and led by Aboriginal women – the march both honours and demands justice for the missing and murdered women. Although it acknowledges the ever "increasing deaths of many vulnerable women" (Women's Memorial March 2011), the march's organizing committee, which is a mix of Aboriginal and non-Aboriginal women, does not identify the missing women as former sex workers, because it believes that sex work is foreign to Aboriginal cultures and a harmful effect of colonization (see Chapter 6 in this volume). Vancouver sex

Joyce Arthur, Susan Davis, and Esther Shannon

workers try to respect this stance, despite its underlying prohibitionist position against their work.

Prohibitionist feminists became increasingly active in Vancouver during the mid-2000s. The groundswell was led by Vancouver Rape Relief and Women's Shelter and later joined by the Aboriginal Women's Action Network (AWAN), along with a number of Christian-based groups and a few smaller associations run by individuals close to Rape Relief, such as the Asian Women Coalition for Ending Prostitution (AWCEP) and Exploited Voices Now Educating (EVE). Representatives of these prohibitionist organizations often speak together at anti-prostitution forums and conferences where pro-decriminalization and sex workers' rights advocates are unwelcome and even aggressively attacked. As Esther Shannon of FIRST (Feminists Advocating for Rights and Equality for Sex Workers) puts it,

> I think the level of anger that some have in the anti-decriminalization camp is really damaging people. What makes it worse is that we actually have so much in common. We are all concerned about women, violence, the lack of access to health services and social services. But these groups have absolutely no interest whatsoever in recognizing any common ground. Instead, there's this repetitive and extreme anger at public events, where if you're sitting on a panel, you're going to be denounced. They're going to stand up and yell at you about how you are abusing Aboriginal women, how you are pimping Aboriginal women. That in itself is damaging, and so is the feeling that we cannot get anywhere on what we hold in common.

Jennifer Allan, of Jen's Kitchen, an outreach service for survival sex workers, noted,

> The missing and murdered First Nations women and survival sex workers are now a huge thing in Canada. But now the two sides are colliding with each other instead of coming alongside each other and joining hands. I hear a lot in First Nations communities about how they're against prostitution because it represents colonialism and colonization. It really breaks my heart to see two groups doing that instead of working alongside each other, because our women are dying. But instead they bicker with each other. And now First Nations groups are running off and inventing abolitionist organizations with Rape Relief.

The legal case surrounding the missing and murdered women, along with prohibitionist campaigns led by Rape Relief, fostered the founding of several new sex worker groups and allied organizations, who began to forge links together in favour of decriminalization. This solidarity created a stronger and deeper movement in the twenty-first century, marked by increasing involvement from BC Aboriginal activists, four of whom co-signed a statement in support of Aboriginal sex worker rights (Native Youth Sexual Health Network 2011).

A significant ally to sex workers since its founding in 2000, Pivot Legal Society is a human rights organization that strategically uses the law to "address the root causes of poverty and social exclusion" (Pivot, n.d.) and to advance the interests of marginalized people living in the Downtown Eastside – including sex workers. A firm advocate of decriminalization, Pivot (2004, 2006) has produced noteworthy and influential research reports and recommendations for social and legislative reform grounded in its extensive community-based studies with local sex workers. In 2007, it launched a constitutional challenge to Canada's prostitution laws on behalf of a group of current and former sex workers from the Downtown Eastside (SWUAV – Sex Workers United against Violence), and Sheri Kiselbach, a former sex worker and PACE's violence prevention coordinator. A BC Supreme Court judge initially ruled that the plaintiffs lacked standing because they were not directly affected by the laws, claiming that only an individual who is a current sex worker could raise a Charter challenge. Although this decision was overturned by the BC Court of Appeal in 2010, the federal government appealed to the Supreme Court of Canada, which heard arguments in January 2012 (Hiltz 2012). In the fall of 2012, the Supreme Court ruled that the group should be granted public interest standing, allowing the constitutional challenge to proceed.

The first sex-worker-run group to form in the twenty-first century was PEERS Vancouver, a non-profit group that empowered, educated, and supported sex workers looking to transition out of the industry. It was co-founded in 2001 by former sex worker Amanda Bonella and community ally Shelly Woodman (formerly of PEERS Victoria, which was founded in 1995 and continues to operate) (Bonella, n.d.). Until it closed in 2011 due to funding cuts, PEERS Vancouver offered programs such as counselling, life skills, and bridging to employment assistance. Ty Mistry, then executive director of PEERS Vancouver, noted that *"a large percentage of [survival] sex workers did not have the choice of entry. Many are coerced and kept through violence, poverty, prejudice, and a lack of other options. Recovery from sex work is hard. This industry can brand the psyche of the person with its stigma. At PEERS, we know what it takes for an individual to get out and stay out of the trade. We know because we ourselves have done it."*

Jennifer Allan is a young Aboriginal woman who began doing sex work in northern BC when she was eighteen. She later moved to Calgary, where she worked on the street and began doing outreach to other survival sex workers before moving to the west coast around 2001. She states,

> I ended up in Vancouver's Downtown Eastside ... and heard about the missing women because my mom told me. She was all fearful because I was down there. That case just opened my eyes, as the person responsible was just arrested and that made me want to fight for those people's rights even more. We need to do something! We can no longer turn our backs, because people are dying on the streets. So I came here and got involved with PACE. I got hired right away as a youth peer support worker. I went to jails and I worked with sexually exploited youth who are incarcerated.

Allan went on to found Jen's Kitchen in 2004, a service that fast became essential to Vancouver's street workers. An advocacy, outreach, and food relief service for women and their children (Wasson 2009), Jen's Kitchen provides dinners, food hampers, clean needles, condoms, and safe places for women to detox from drug use. The service is run on a volunteer basis, with donations and no government funding. In addition, Allan runs a twenty-four-hour crisis line to help women in need, liaises with police to hold them accountable for their treatment of sex workers, and lectures at universities and colleges about Canada's missing and murdered women. Her courageous daily advocacy on behalf of survival sex workers' right to belong in society has probably saved lives and is an inspiration to Vancouver's sex worker movement:

> I know what it's like to stand on the street corner and starve and have to turn tricks to eat. I knew that sometimes I'd have to sneak into agencies and pretend to fit the criteria there so I could eat. I remember what it's like to have to go to other agencies and participate in their strict religious beliefs in order to eat. I wanted something where we could give people healthy food and there was none of this other stuff attached to it. So I just started making sandwiches, and we would walk down the street and hand them out to the women working. I also didn't want to see people entering the survival sex trade who didn't need to be there and didn't want to be there. And I wanted to lower the amount of bad dates. If you give people their basic needs, there's no need for them to work on the street to eat. In a lot of the missing women cases, the women were out there just for their basic needs. If you start giving them their basic needs, you also give them choice.

Safety and a supportive community are pressing needs for many sex workers. In 2001, an exotic dancer named Annie Temple who wanted to create a safe Internet site for dancers, began NakedTruth.ca with the aim of challenging misconceptions, providing a space for support and information sharing among industry members, and educating patrons about appropriate behaviour in show lounges. The site grew quickly and became a central network for exotic dancers in British Columbia and across Canada. News reporters and media outlets noticed the site, and Temple soon became a spokesperson for exotic dancers' rights. She also expanded her advocacy to include all sex industry workers by collaborating with the BC Coalition of Experiential Communities (discussed below) and leading sex work organizers such as Raven Bowen, Susan Davis, and Matthew Taylor.

When a colleague and friend was diagnosed with terminal cancer in 2004, Temple organized a fundraiser and birthday party with help from the NakedTruth.ca community. Using volunteers to coordinate a silent auction and donate striptease performances, the Exotic Dancers for Cancer fundraiser was a rousing success (*Vancouver Province* 2007). Jocelyne Sioui gave a touching speech, thanking Annie and the others for making her "immortal like Elvis." She died in November of 2004. Exotic Dancers for Cancer became an annual fundraiser in her memory, inspiring a sister event in Victoria, British Columbia.

NakedTruth.ca has also led the way in proudly celebrating the work and accomplishments of sex workers, thumbing its collective nose at stigma related to prostitution and exotic dancing. Temple and other website members organized Canada's first-ever adult entertainment awards, which debuted in Vancouver in 2010. The goal of the awards is to celebrate the positive aspects of the adult entertainment industry and to promote the best, most ethical, and most favoured adult entertainment industry members, businesses, and supporters. Members of NakedTruth.ca nominate and vote for their favourites from diverse categories spanning the adult entertainment industry – from stripping and pornography, to media and advocacy, to support services for survival sex workers – with proud winners honoured at a gala event each June (Thomas 2010; Smith 2011).

Another of Vancouver's highly influential and media-savvy sex worker groups is the BC Coalition of Experiential Communities – originally called the BC Coalition of Experiential Women (BCCEW). The BCCEW arose out of two regional meetings of women from the sex industry held in 2002 and 2004, and it works toward the elimination of oppressive systems that create harm within the industry. Its membership has decades of combined experience in advocacy, research, service delivery, and management, as well as in all facets of the sex industry (BCCEC 2007). Some of its members have founded, operated, or significantly contributed to a number of other sex worker organizations in the province.

In 2003, women from the BCCEW held a forum in which they called for a twenty-four-hour mobile support service for sex workers, where women could have access to food, supplies, support, showers, and respite. A partnership was struck between the WISH Drop-In Centre and the PACE Society to implement the Mobile Access Project (MAP). Its goals included decreasing violence against street workers, contributing significantly to harm reduction, and giving jobs to women exiting the sex industry. The MAP van took to the streets in March 2004, and despite periodic challenges with funding, it has been a reliable source of support for Vancouver sex workers ever since (Gibson et al. 2006). Indeed, it provides resources to between forty and fifty sex workers per night, receives up to 90 percent of the bad date reports made, and distributes two hundred bad date sheets each month. Sex workers consider MAP to be an essential service and an effective tool for reducing the potential for violence on the street.

These and other successful initiatives led by the women of BCCEW were the impetus for the formation of the BC Coalition of Experiential Men, which merged with the BCCEW to become the more inclusive BC Coalition of Experiential Communities. This was soon followed by HUSTLE: Men on the Move, a group for male sex workers founded in 2007 by former sex workers Matthew Taylor and Don Presland. HUSTLE offers front-line support services to male and transgendered survival sex workers, and to street youth at risk of exploitation (Taylor 2008-09). Before founding HUSTLE, Taylor and Presland saw that male sex workers were struggling with many of the same issues as women workers, but existing support services were all targeted toward women, making male sex workers feel invisible (see also Chapter 2 in this volume). As Matthew Taylor, program director of HUSTLE, explained,

> One young man said to me, "Hustling is what I do, but it is not who I am."
> The truth of this statement resonates with me still. The reality is that for many
> young men involved in the sex industry, their identities are determined by
> necessity, experience, and circumstance – much of which can change from
> moment to moment, hour to hour, and day to day depending on the constant
> ebb and flow of basic daily needs and personal survival. Add to this a shame-
> based society that still sees sex as taboo and imposes labels serving only to
> further stigmatize these young men, it is little wonder they prefer to remain
> invisible. Throughout our process of self-discovery, it became clear that the
> majority of supports and services offered for sex workers in the community were

constructed through a female lens, and only effective to a point. We recognized
the need for front-line supports specific to men involved in sex work.

By Sex Workers, for Sex Workers: Taking Control of Our Future

Sex workers initiated several projects in the 2000s that involved building partnerships with community groups, universities, police, and government, as well
as projects that built capacity within the sex worker movement and empowered
and educated workers. Some of these initiatives included the following:

- Policy development workshops were led by the PACE Society in 2005 to
  give emerging leaders the tools to communicate respectfully with each other
  and to engage constructively with non-sex-working communities.
  Participants also developed best-practice documents for researchers who
  conduct studies involving sex workers (Bowen and PACE Society 2005).
- The History of Sex Work Project began in 2004 to research the role of sex
  workers in Vancouver's founding and growth, as well as why working conditions had become so dangerous. The aim was to build community partnerships and improve workers' safety, stability, and self-determination. Simon
  Fraser University offered resources and support, and public libraries and
  museums – including the Vancouver Police Museum – were positive and
  helpful, graciously sharing their historical archives (SFU 2007).
- The BC Coalition of Experiential Communities (BCCEC) led a province-
  wide series of consultations with sex workers in 2006 to discuss issues
  around violence and sex trafficking. This led to the BCCEC hosting a satellite
  session on sex work, trafficking, and harm reduction at the Seventeenth
  Annual International Harm Reduction Conference in Vancouver (IHRA
  2006) and the subsequent release of BCCEC's "From the Curb" research
  paper on violence and domestic trafficking (Bowen 2006).
- Living in Community, a two-year city-wide initiative (2006-07), brought
  together sex workers, groups of residents, business associations, and community policing centres. They produced an action plan and recommendations for increasing the health and safety of all community members and
  fostering positive change, such as putting male, female, and transgender
  sex workers at the forefront of the communications campaign (Living in
  Community 2007).
- Developing Capacity for Change was a 2007 BCCEC initiative to explore
  cooperative business models as a way to generate alternative sources of income for sex workers, to increase health and safety, and to build community

capacity. The project led to two comprehensive reports that laid out plans to increase the safety for all sex workers in the current environment, but that could also serve as a template for working in a decriminalized context (Davis and Bowen 2007b; BCCEC 2010).

- Trade Secrets is a comprehensive best-practices guide created by Vancouver sex workers in a collaborative process. The guide's aim is to empower all sex workers by helping them work safely and successfully in all aspects of their work (BCCEC 2009).

Vancouver sex workers' efforts to involve the community and police in constructive solutions bore fruit in 2008 with the formation of the Sex Industry Worker Safety Action Group (SIWSAG 2009). This advisory body is composed of representatives from sex worker organizations and community groups, and from the Vancouver Police Department; it also includes some legal experts. The group commissioned research and a subsequent report about incidences of trafficking related to the 2010 Winter Olympics to be held in Vancouver (Bowen and Shannon 2009). The report echoed a Global Alliance against Traffic in Women document that argued, "an increase of trafficking in persons into forced prostitution does not occur around sporting events" (GAATW 2009, n.p.). Warning that ill-informed assumptions about sex trafficking and the Olympics may actually endanger sex workers, SIWSAG's report focused on the real concern: that Games-related street closures and the planned security risked displacing sex workers into more dangerous and isolated areas (see also Chapter 16 in this volume).

Another of SIWSAG's key accomplishments has been to improve working relationships between the police and sex workers while still making sure that police are held accountable for sex workers' safety. Holding police answerable is an aspect of sex worker organizing in Vancouver that continues to be critically important, especially from the perspective of survival sex workers. As Jennifer Allan recalls, *"The [police] called me a couple of years ago, and at the time they were giving Christmas donations to Jen's Kitchen to give to the women. One of the female detectives sat me down and said, 'Can you please stop going around saying that we're responsible for the missing women? Because we're not.' And I simply said to them, 'No, you are responsible for them.' After that they quit giving Christmas gifts to Jen's Kitchen. And that was okay, because I'm more about integrity. No matter how much shampoo you give me, it's not going to shut me up."*

Although relations between law enforcement and street-based sex workers remain tenuous, indoor sex workers in Vancouver rarely seem to worry about police interference. Scarlett Lake, a former sex worker and exotic dancer who is now the madam of Scarlett's House, her own escort agency, explains, *"I never really got the feeling that there were forces actively out there looking for people working, certainly [not] out of their homes. There wasn't anybody running around trying to catch you, and I think that's terrific. Maybe it's just a West Coast, more open-minded kind of feeling amongst the populace. I think that has contributed greatly to the way that we're able to sit around and talk about sex work, and not feel like we're looking over our shoulders the whole time."*

Meanwhile, the knowledge and experience that sex workers gained through their self-led initiatives spurred the creation of the West Coast Cooperative of Sex Industry Professionals (WCCSIP) in 2008. Its goal was to form Canada's first sex worker cooperative whose membership would guide all decisions. Members hammered out governance policies, decision-making procedures, terms of reference, membership criteria, a code of conduct, and conflict management procedures, producing a fifty-one-page report that reflected their vision as a community (Davis and Bowen 2007a). One of the most controversial enterprises proposed was the co-op brothel. Since street sex workers in Vancouver face the highest risk of violence (Lowman 2000), their biggest concern was to be safe at work and to be able to control their working conditions. The proposed solution was a cooperatively run rooms-for-rent space that would qualify as a body rub parlour or steam bath (terms for business licences in Vancouver). With such a licence, a cooperative brothel would provide a legal place for prostitution to occur and potentially save the lives of workers facing danger on the street. Unfortunately, a misinformation campaign about the purpose and intent of the enterprise led to widespread opposition to the idea and even death threats against the project coordinator.

Although some feminists – often called radical feminists – hold a prohibitionist stance on prostitution, many other feminists are strong allies of the sex workers' rights movement and argue in support of decriminalization (see also Chapter 11 in this volume). The divide between feminist factions appears to be particularly evident in Vancouver. In 2007, a representative of the prohibitionist group Rape Relief complained to a local newspaper that a recent story sympathetic to decriminalization of sex work did not "seriously consider feminist perspectives on prostitution" (FIRST 2007b, n.p.). The suggestion that all feminists are opposed to decriminalization inspired the founding of FIRST (2007a), a coalition of feminists who advocate for decriminalization and the rights of sex workers. Feminist activist Esther Shannon wrote a rebuttal letter to the paper and collected signatures from Melanie Conn and seventy other feminists, including founding members Joyce Arthur, Raven Bowen, Daniele Hurley, Tamara O'Doherty, and Katrina Pacey. Published in the *Georgia Straight* on 20 September

2007, the letter became the group's first act of advocacy (FIRST 2007b). Esther Shannon of FIRST describes her changing ideas about sex work:

> I came into the movement as a radical feminist who had a very stereotypic view of sex workers and sex work. I thought of it as something that was male exploitation of women. But feminism believes that oppressed women have the right to organize around their oppression and that they are the best people to analyze their oppression. So as a feminist who recognized that feminists should be allies to women who are oppressed, I came to feel that I needed to respect this movement and become an ally. I can't really own the identity of "radical feminist" myself any more, because radical feminism has so disgraced itself on the sex work issue.

Through its advocacy and e-mail listserv, FIRST has been instrumental in bringing together sex worker groups and their allies across Canada to work in solidarity and share news and strategies. In this way, FIRST embodies the vibrancy of Vancouver's sex worker movement, one that other Canadian sex worker groups often look to for support or connection. However, FIRST has no outside funding and operates successfully on *"less than a shoestring,"* in the words of one member. Some sex worker organizers believe that the *lack* of government funding may have actually freed Vancouver's sex worker movement to boldly demand real change in the community. Susan Davis of BCCEC and SIWSAG observed, *"When you're not under the thumb [of government], scared of losing your funding, there is no controlling you. I remember during the Living in Community project and on various committees, especially the police committee and the Sex Industry Worker Safety Action Group, they were afraid of me. They were terrified when I showed up there and started screaming. Because I had no reason not to. Or going to the police board and yelling at them for a while. I must have done that ten times."* Scarlett Lake pointed out that, *"essentially, sex workers are fighting our activist work by sex work. We're taking a portion of that and saying we don't need welfare, we don't need a grant, we don't need anyone's endorsement. We're just going to go out there and say what we think and feel and try and move things around."*

Because sex work itself is so diverse, it stands to reason that a successful sex worker movement must also be diverse and must reflect the needs of people with many different experiences and realities, while respecting all of them. Matthew Taylor notes that the Vancouver sex workers' rights movement is a good example of this diversity: *"If my experience in sex work has taught me anything, it is this: There is no one reality that can adequately define or represent men in sex work. Rather, there are many realities out there for the men, both young and old, who are involved in the industry. No doubt, at the end of the day, there is common ground between all of us – the element of survival. It is the difference in the method and motivation of why men sell their bodies for money that results in them working 'under the radar.'"* And Kerry Porth, executive director of PACE Society, states, *"Sex work activism in Vancouver is populated by an amazing group of smart, powerful, unique, and fierce individuals, and there is so much respect for one another. I have found real friendship and am proud to be part of this movement."*

Conclusion

There's no doubt that the tragedy of the missing and murdered women galvanized Vancouver's sex worker movement. Sex workers' rage and grief were channelled into dedicated efforts to put a human face on their fallen sisters and to protect those still working the street. In the words of Jamie Lee Hamilton, a transsexual sex worker and activist, *"Vancouver had the largest and most tragic example of violence against the sex trade, with dozens of women going missing, being murdered, and so little being done about it."* By educating themselves and the public about the harms of prostitution laws, Vancouver's sex workers steered the Canadian movement as a whole toward decriminalization as a necessary first step in addressing the violence and abuse. As Hamilton articulated, *"I feel Vancouver was 'ground zero' of the [sex worker] movement in Canada and was a frontier for getting the issues on the table and in the press."*

Over the past thirty years, more than twenty sex worker rights groups have formed, linking together Vancouver sex workers and their allies. Almost all these groups still exist today, and none function in isolation from each other – rather, they constitute a loosely knit coalition of groups who support and respect each other and who act in solidarity to achieve common aims. They are united by many issues: ensuring the safety and dignity of survival sex workers; supporting evidence-based research that respects sex workers' voices; holding law enforcement accountable; educating the public about sex work and the harm of prostitution laws; countering prohibitionist campaigns and propaganda; and last but not least, celebrating their achievements.

Acknowledgments
The authors would like to thank the following activists for their contributions to this chapter: Jennifer Allan, Amanda Bonella, Raven Bowen, Jacquie Carstensen, Kate Gibson, Jamie Lee Hamilton, Scarlett Lake, Ty Mistry, Tamara O'Doherty, Katrina Pacey, Kerry Porth, Mary Shearman, Matthew Taylor, and Annie Temple.

Notes

All quotes in this article were obtained by interviewing the speakers in February 2011 by e-mail, phone, or in person. All web links were accessed in July 2012.

1   For more on Vancouver's early sex work history, see Francis (2009) and Ross (2009).
2   We define "survival sex workers" as those who, because of poverty and life circumstances, sell sex in order to meet their basic needs for food, rent, clothes, drugs, or alcohol. They generally work on the street and may experience poor health, a lack of housing, or difficulties managing substance use.
3   To honour and respect Vancouver sex workers, the serial killer is not named in this chapter.

References

BCCEC (BC Coalition of Experiential Communities). 2007. Background. 13 December. http://bccec.wordpress.com/.

–. 2009. Trade Secrets: Health and safety in the sex industry. http://tradesecretsguide.blogspot.com.

–. 2010. *Opening the doors: Building transparency and accountability in the sex industry.* http://www.wccsip.ca/doc/Opening the Doors.pdf.

Bennett, D., D. Eby, K. Govender, and K. Pacey. 2012. Blueprint for an inquiry: Learning from the failures of the Missing Women Commission of Inquiry. BC Civil Liberties Association, West Coast Women's Legal Education and Action Fund, Pivot Legal Society, Vancouver. http://www.westcoastleaf.org.

Bonella, A. n.d. Herstory. http://peersvancouver.blogspot.ca/.

Bowen, R. (BCCEC). 2006. From the curb: Sex workers' perspectives on violence and domestic trafficking. BC Coalition of Experiential Women. March. http://bccec.files.wordpress.com/2010/01/final-report-violence_and_domestic_trafficking_bccew.pdf.

Bowen, R., and PACE Society. 2005. Research ethics: A guide for community organizations. http://bccec.files.wordpress.com/2007/12/community_research_-guidelines_feb2006_draft_.pdf.

Bowen, R., and E. Shannon (SIWSAG). 2009. *Human trafficking, sex work safety and the 2010 games.* http://vancouver.ca/police/assets/pdf/reports-policies/report-human-trafficking-2010-games.pdf.

Cameron, S. 2010. *On the farm: Robert William Pickton and the tragic story of Vancouver's missing women.* Toronto: Knopf Canada.

Davis, S., and R. Bowen. 2007a. Developing capacity for change: Cooperative development exploration report. BC Coalition of Experiential Communities. http://bccec.files.wordpress.com/2008/02/developing_capacity_for_change_coop_development_report.pdf.

–. 2007b. Labor on the margins: Sex industry safety and stabilization. http://bccec.files.wordpress.com/2008/02/labor_on_the_margins.pdf.

–. 2008. Leading the way: Strategic planning toward sex worker cooperative development. BC Coalition of Experiential Communities. January. http://bccec.files.wordpress.com/2008/03/leading_the_way.pdf.

FIRST. 2007a. Feminists advocating for rights and equality for sex workers. http://www.firstadvocates.org/.

–. 2007b. Many feminists want the sex trade decriminalized. *Georgia Straight.* 20 September. http://www.straight.com.

Francis, D. 2009. *Red light neon: A history of Vancouver's sex trade.* Vancouver: Subway Books.

GAATW (Global Alliance against Traffic in Women). 2009. Trafficking in persons and the 2010 Olympics: Briefing paper. February, http://bccec.files.wordpress.com/2009/04/gaatw_2010olympics1.pdf.

Gibson, K., R. Bowen, P. Janssen, and P. Spittal (WISH). 2006. Evaluation of the Mobile Access Project (MAP). 31 May. http://www.vancouveragreement.ca/wp-content/uploads/2006_EvaluationofMobileAccessProject.pdf.

Harris, M. 2010. The unrepentant whore. *The Walrus*. June. http://www.walrusmagazine.ca/.

Hiltz, Robert. 2012. Supreme Court to decide whether B.C. sex workers can mount Charter challenge. *Vancouver Sun*, 19 January. http://www.canada.com/news/.

IHRA (International Harm Reduction Association). 2006. Vancouver 2006 – International Conference on the Reduction of Drug Related Harm. http://www.ihra.net/.

Kines, L. 2010. Report cites RCMP, VPD failure in Pickton case. *Vancouver Sun*, 18 August. http://www2.canada.com/.

Living in Community. 2007. Living in Community: Balancing perspectives on Vancouver's sex industry. Action Plan. http://www.livingincommunity.ca/docs/living_in_comm_web.pdf.

Lowman, J. 2000. Violence and the outlaw status of (street) prostitution in Canada. *Violence against Women* 6, 9 (September): 987-1011. http://www.hawaii.edu/hivandaids/Violence_and_the_Outlaw_Status_of_Street_Prostitution_in_Canada.pdf.

Native Youth Sexual Health Network. 2011. Indigenous peoples in the sex trade – speaking for ourselves. 9 June. (Notes). http://www.facebook.com.

PACE Society. 2005. Education: Clearing the path. http://www3.telus.net/.

PEERS Victoria. 2011. PEERS Victoria Resource Society. http://www.peers.bc.ca/.

Pivot Legal Society. 2004. Voices for dignity: A call to end the harms caused by Canada's sex trade laws. http://www.pivotlegal.org/.

–. 2006. Beyond decriminalization: Sex-work, human rights and a new framework for law reform. http://www.pivotlegal.org/.

–. n.d. What we do. http://www.pivotlegal.org/.

Ross, B. 2009. *Burlesque west: Showgirls, sex, and sin in postwar Vancouver*. Toronto: University of Toronto Press.

Ross, B., and J.L. Hamilton. 2007-11. The expulsion of sex workers from Vancouver's West End, 1975-1985: A cautionary tale. West End Sex Work Memorial Project. http://westendsexworkhistory.com/.

SFU (Simon Fraser University). 2007. *The History of Sex Work: Vancouver*. http://www.sfu.ca/content/dam/sfu/continuing-studies/forms-docs/cep/History_SexWork_final.pdf.

SIWSAG (Sex Industry Worker Safety Action Group). 2009. Collaborative action group connects Vancouver police, sex industry workers and community organizations to address the safety concerns of sex workers. http://vancouver.ca/police/assets/pdf/brochures/siwsag-overview.pdf.

Smith, C. 2011. Videos: The Naked Truth Adult Entertainment Awards. *Georgia Straight*, 10 June. http://www.straight.com/.

Taylor, M. 2008-09. HUSTLE: Men on the Move Outreach and Support Service, phase II. http://www.bccec.files.wordpress.com/.

Thomas, S. 2010. City hosts Canada's first adult awards. *Vancouver Courier*, 14 May. http://www.canada.com/.

Vancouver Province. 2007. Shirts dropped, $6,000 raised. 5 March. http://www.canada.com/.

Wasson, J. 2009. Jen's Kitchen – serving up sandwiches and humanity to survival sex workers. Blue Planet Green Living. 29 September. http://www.blueplanetgreenliving.com/.

WISH Drop-In Centre Society. n.d. Our history. http://wish-vancouver.net/.

Women's Memorial March. 2011. *Feb 14th annual Womens Memorial March: About*. http://womensmemorialmarch.wordpress.com/.

10

Né dans le Redlight:
The Sex Workers' Movement in Montreal

ANNA-LOUISE CRAGO AND JENN CLAMEN

In many parts of the world, brothel-districts and neighbourhoods where a large number of sex workers are assembled – whether due to ghettoizing discrimination, law enforcement patterns, or the lure of favourable working conditions, convenience, or company – have served as some of the most fertile grounds of resistance (see Jenkins 2000; Associacion de Trabajadoras Autonomas 2002; Swendeman et al. 2004). The sex workers' movement in Montreal similarly arose largely out of the streets of what was the largest sex work area, affectionately called le Redlight: it has reflected many elements of its bilingual, multi-racial, and multi-gendered culture, usually proclaiming itself in the colourful and unrepentant language of the street, the bars, and prison.[1]

This chapter will present pivotal moments that shaped the movement and will highlight the challenges, strategies, and framing of important issues that developed.[2] Though the movement has always included sex workers from other parts of both the city and the industry, the chapter will trace how attempts to resist and adapt to repression and displacement have been inextricably tied to the history of le Redlight. The area that spans out from where Saint-Catherine meets the Main is, in fact, a crucial prism through which to understand the genesis and emergence of formal sex worker organizing, and the ways in which leadership from street sex workers and a concern with street issues have remained at its core.[3]

History of Sex Work in Montreal

Sex work in Montreal has a unique historical context. For the better part of the last century, the city's tacit tolerance of prostitution made its unofficial sex work area internationally famous by outlasting every other such zone in a major city on the continent, including the famed Storyville district in New Orleans (Proulx 1997). In 1910, in the first documented instance of sex worker organizing, a Jewish American prostitute by the name of Maimie Pinzer (Pinzer 1977, xxxv) opened an apartment in the Redlight district to allow prostitutes, whom she considered "proud, dignified, autonomous women," to come together, rest, and socialize. By 1924, the district occupied a large part of the downtown core and was reputed to have three hundred brothels and two thousand street-walkers (Proulx 1997). With the exception of sporadic crackdowns propelled by moral entrepreneurs or politicians that alternately targeted brothels, the street, or sometimes both, prostitution was allowed to thrive, largely through a highly organized and routinized system of police payoffs (Myers 1996). By 1944, under pressure from the military, which feared the spread of venereal disease, the city briefly shut down the brothels in the Redlight district (Lacasse 1991). Although they re-emerged in 1954, they would be shut down for good following a public inquiry into police corruption and payoffs by brothels. Evicted brothel workers were displaced to the street and clubs, where they worked in far less safe conditions (ibid.). During the run-up to Expo '67, a number of politicians made their careers on campaigns to "clean up" the clubs in the Redlight (Proulx 1997). New bylaws and measures forcing venues to close displaced women who sold sex, including trans women, moving them from the clubs to the street (see Podmore 1999; Namaste 2002).

By the 1970s and early '80s, the rise of Quebec biker gangs in the Redlight introduced a period of relative tolerance for sex workers on the street (Crago 1999). With the criminalization of prostitution-related activities through the Criminal Code, reprieve from repression, literally, came at a price for women. The extortion system that followed was two-tiered: In collusion with the police, biker gangs ran a protection racket between Saint-Urbain and Saint-Hubert. Sex workers paid a weekly "protection" fee if they wanted to work in the area. In exchange, the bikers paid the police to leave the women alone (ibid.). When women who paid their fee were arrested, they contacted a biker-owned restaurant on Saint-Catherine Street and would be released the next day (ibid.). This "protective" form of tolerance allowed sex workers to experience strength in numbers, visibility, and a small measure of inclusion. Black, white, and Aboriginal women, as well as those of mixed heritages, lined Saint-Catherine,

Anna-Louise Crago and Jenn Clamen

openly leaning against cars in a neighbourhood that was becoming renowned as a destination for its nightlife and in particular, its prostitutes, strippers, discos, motorcycles, and hot dogs (ibid.). According to Miss Pat, a black sex worker who worked the street for three decades, "Those were fun times, there was a lot of sisterhood and a lot of looking out for each other. We lived together. We did everything together" (quoted in ibid., 22). However, neither the bikers' nor the police's extortion rackets truly protected sex workers from violence – whether from attackers, or boyfriends, or, by the 1980s, from increasing targeting by pimps (ibid.).

Recriminalizing the Street

The memory, and for some the experience, of a period of mostly tolerated sex work stood in stark contrast to the waves of repression that would replace it. Although bikers continued to operate protection rackets on the Main in the second half of the 1980s, they were unable to halt a tide of police repression against sex work that took a new shape. Sex worker organizing in Montreal emerged in direct response to the crackdowns and the many layers of violence they left in their wake.

An important turning point for sex workers across the country occurred in 1985. A new bill sought to amend the Criminal Code of Canada in order to remove "street prostitutes and their customers from downtown neighbour-hoods" (La boîte à qu'on-se-voir 1994; see also the Introduction in this volume). The passage of Bill C-49 replaced "solicitation" with the gender-neutral offence of "communicating for the purposes of prostitution," casting the net of crim-inalization over a much broader set of activities while also criminalizing clients and male sex workers (Jeffrey 2004). Penalties now consisted of a fine between $500 and $2000, as well as the possibility of a prison sentence and a criminal record.

Police in Montreal implemented Bill C-49 through a series of large-scale raids against sex workers in the Redlight (Larsen 1996). Montreal maintained gender quotas for arrests under "communicating." Though these were partly met by arresting customers, police arrested more male sex workers than in any other Canadian city (ibid.). Nonetheless, of the 652 charges laid in 1986, 80 percent were against sex-working women (ibid.). Although the rates of arrest decreased over the next five years, sex workers in the Redlight were specifically targeted in a concerted effort to "clean out" the Main between 1987 and 1988 (La boîte à qu'on-se-voir 1994, 17; Gemme, Payment, and Malenfant 1989). A report commissioned by the Ministry of Justice hypothesized that these systematic police raids may actually have been a strategy timed to influence the parliamentary review of the law (La boîte à qu'on-se-voir 1994). Indeed, there was widespread support among police and from many politicians for retaining increased powers to arrest sex workers and clients (ibid.).

According to a 1989 federal Ministry of Justice evaluation of Bill C-49, Montreal sex workers reported an increase in violence since the law's implementation, which police denied (Gemme, Payment, and Malenfant 1989). A feminist group in Montreal, the Association for the Safety of Prostitutes, noted that the discrepancy was due to the fact that sex workers were not reporting violent incidents to the police (Beaulieu 1986). A later evaluation commissioned by the Ministry of Justice in 1994 found that the repression of sex workers and their clients in Montreal under the communicating law had "contributed to creating a climate of violence" by isolating the workers, impeding their negotiations with clients, and most importantly, creating a pretext for police abuse and violence (La boîte à qu'on-se-voir 1994, 24).

By the late 1980s, many sex workers on the Main had been arrested multiple times, a factor that often led to long sentences. One transsexual sex worker from the Redlight recounts, "After [Bill C-49], I began to get arrested often for communication. Very quickly, in 1987, I began getting longer and longer sentences" (quoted in Gobeil 2003, 18). As a result, many began leaving the area to evade arrest and police harassment. In 1987, 80 percent of street sex workers in the city worked in the Redlight: approximately four hundred women and trans people, often working together in groups of six to eight on a corner. By 1994, only 50 percent of street sex workers worked in the area, and they did so in smaller groups or often alone (La boîte à qu'on-se-voir 1994).

By the early 1990s, police repression in the Redlight had steadily pushed sex workers into the traditionally white francophone working-class residential Centre-Sud neighbourhood to the east, adding to the numbers of trans, women, and male sex workers who had lived and worked in the area for decades. In the late 1980s, Centre-Sud had begun to gentrify, hemmed in by the increasingly upscale Gay Village to the south and the Plateau to the north. In response to the increased presence of sex workers, Centre-Sud's non-sex-worker residents declared "a war on prostitution" in 1991, and their organization vowed to patrol the streets to chase sex workers away: "If the citizens of the Centre-Sud neighborhood want to get rid of the prostitutes and pushers that soil their streets, their parks and their school yards, they must take control of their territory and defend it" (Pelchat 1991, n.p.). Sex workers recounted stories of people throwing boiling water and rocks at suspected sex workers in 1991. Two years later, in 1993, residents of Centre-Sud and neighbouring Hochelaga-Maisonneuve once

Anna-Louise Crago and Jenn Clamen

again organized to displace women, including trans women, sex workers, and drug users, through assaults and threats (Bérubé 1993; Namaste 2000; Ross and Charlebois 2005). A local newspaper reported that a hundred residents assaulted suspected prostitutes and vandalized a building during what it dubbed a "hooker hunt." The paper quoted a sex worker as saying, "Every woman walking alone right now could be beaten because they think she's a prostitute" (*Montreal Mirror* 1993, n.p.). Many of the attacks carried an additional racist element, and in some instances black sex workers were specifically targeted (see Namaste 2000). Such racist hostility may have contributed, along with linguistic divisions, to the fact that a disproportionate number of the sex workers who chose to remain in the Redlight, despite heavy policing, were black or Aboriginal.

The 1980s to mid-1990s also marked the time when Montreal was hit hardest by the HIV epidemic. Sex workers, much like other communities considered at risk, faced discrimination linked to their perceived role in causing and spreading the virus (Irvine 1998-99; Mensah 2003). Many trans sex workers cared, often militantly, for those who became sick and died in their midst as colleagues, peer-educators, and caretakers (Namaste 2000). Some of these efforts became formally organized when transsexual sex workers founded Action Santé Travesti(e)s/Transsexuel(le)s du Québec (ASTTeQ) in 1998 (ASTTeQ 2011). The increasing public discourse on sex work and HIV led a female stripper and trans woman street sex worker to found l'Association Québécoise des Travailleuses et Travailleurs du Sexe (AQTTS) in 1992 (Thiboutot 1999). Not long afterward, the AQTTS joined a committee on sex work and HIV struck by Montreal's Centre for AIDS Prevention. This important partnership between sex workers, public health officials, and researchers led to the formation of Montreal's first sex workers' organization, in 1995: Stella, l'amie de Maimie (Stella, Maimie's friend) (Gendron and Hankins 1995). Stella was tasked with doing HIV prevention in the sex worker community and involving sex workers in its efforts. Its English mission statement was "Making Space for Working Women." In French it was somewhat more ambitiously militant, *"Travailler en santé, sécurité et avec dignité"* (Working in health, safety, and with dignity). The organization's name referred to Maimie Pinzer and a woman named Stella, whom Maimie deemed the smartest and most beautiful prostitute in Montreal (Pinzer 1977).

Stella opened its doors as a small drop-in space in the Redlight for sex workers "who live or work as women." At the time, women, transsexual women, and transvestites worked together on the same streets and in some cases, in the bars on the Main and Ontario Street in Centre-Sud. Initially, Stella offered hot showers, food, and condoms as well as a place to rest and to put on makeup or talk. It also compiled a list of violent attackers. Despite Stella's avoidance of outright political positioning, its activities proved contentious; the group was evicted by its first landlord within months of opening (Charlebois 2005b). Next, the federal government refused to give Stella a charity number, because *not* forcing women to leave sex work was in itself too political – a position the government maintained until it finally accorded the group charitable status in 1998.

"Whose Streets? Our Streets!": Formal Organizing Takes Off

The mid-1990s marked the beginning of a wave of sex workers' formal mobilizing against police repression and the constant negative effects of criminalization. In 1996, Montreal was host to Quand le sexe travaille ... /When Sex Works ..., a large conference on sex work. The conference featured panels with sex workers, vice cops, city politicians, and researchers. At its close, a coalition of eight community groups and experts issued a declaration and press release in favour of decriminalization (Coalition to Decriminalize Adult Prostitution 1996). Perhaps most importantly, sex workers who presented at the conference established a new political action group: La Coalition pour les droits des travailleuses et travailleurs du sexe, or the Coalition for short.

Stella hosted the Coalition's first meeting of about ten people, where it was decided that the group would include male, female, and trans sex workers. As a new organization dependent on funders' support, Stella could not lead the activist charge; it offered instead to support the Coalition logistically and behind the scenes. The Coalition's second meeting at an anti-poverty centre attracted a crowd of close to fifty people, almost all of whom were sex workers from the street – a large number were trans – and a few representatives of supportive community groups.

In 1997, the Coalition organized its first action, a private vigil in memory of a woman who worked on the streets downtown and had been murdered. In a second action, street-based sex workers distributed pamphlets during the city's large outdoor Montreal Jazz Festival, requesting passersby to call city hall to denounce the annual wave of arrests of sex workers and street people that systematically preceded the festival. That same summer, the Coalition made its first decisive step into the spotlight with a masked protest in front of city hall, demanding that sex workers be included on a newly struck City Committee on Street Prostitution. The Coalition elected a transsexual sex worker as its spokesperson; a former injection drug user and tireless advocate on behalf of sex workers who were drug users, she had survived several stabbings and bullets,

Anna-Louise Crago and Jenn Clamen

and was well known and respected in the street community. Approximately thirty sex workers and friends gathered in front of city hall, wearing plastic imitation Carnival masks for the occasion. In the end, street sex workers from the Coalition were invited to sit on the committee, and along with the first spokesperson, a black trans street worker and a white woman street worker later joined its ranks. This set an important standard for sex worker representation and was influential in the committee's recommendations.

During the summer of 1998, as repression continued and working conditions deteriorated, sex workers demonstrated on many occasions to demand the right to work in decent conditions on the street. This early leadership of street workers and the focus on street concerns are important in understanding the movement's later rejection of language such as "women in survival sex," "survival sex workers," and "experiential women." These terms for defining sex workers on the street or who use drugs are associated with an anglophone social work gaze and tend to project a vision of street conditions as fixed and immoveable, and of women on the street or using drugs as incapable of individually or collectively changing them. This was incompatible with the Montreal struggle, implicit in which was the challenge to survive, but beyond that, to live.

On 22 June 1998, the Coalition organized a street prostitute occupation of city hall in response to unrelenting raids in the Redlight. Under the slogan "Since you won't let us work in our work place, we will work in yours," about forty sex workers and friends – many from the world of the street – occupied the front steps and demanded decriminalization. Coalition members strung red garlands and lanterns over the entrance to city hall and added red dye to the water of the large city fountain.

Police repression was equally affecting sex workers on the increasingly crowded Ontario Street and surrounding Centre-Sud. In August of 1998, a number of trans prostitutes called media attention by posing topless (and maskless), announcing a strike and castigating Quebec's largest union, the Confédération des Syndicats Nationaux (CSN), for its lack of support. The women held signs that read "Prostitute on strike for a fair salary" and "I demand the right to be different, I'm drawing attention to myself so that people leave me the hell alone!"

The Coalition capped off the summer by attacking police repression as a labour rights issue. In celebration of Labour Day, it invited the media to attend as it presented the Quebec labour minister, Louise Harel, with a human-sized cake – containing an older stripper. The Coalition prepared a manifesto for the event that addressed the labour issues faced by escorts, strippers, and masseuses but paid particular attention to those encountered by workers on the street who lacked safe affordable spaces to take their clients: these included police repression, violence, and the safety and fire risks in the tourist-rooms and *piaules*.[4] This was one of Montreal's first actions to address working conditions in all areas of the sex industry.

Most sex workers (and allies) wore masks during the first Coalition demonstration. By 1998, a number of them had stopped covering their faces, and in the case of one action described below, none did. The issue of whether to mask remained contentious over the next few years in the Coalition. Those who felt they couldn't come out resented what they saw as a lack of solidarity on the part of those who chose to bare their faces (and sometimes their breasts). Conversely, others felt that sex workers would not be humanized as long as they could not be seen.

In the late 1990s, a meeting occurred between police, merchants, and developers in the Redlight, where the business owners complained that the presence of prostitutes and "drunk Indians" was a hindrance to business. Police suggested that if merchants sent them a petition, they would have the mandate to clean up the neighbourhood. The merchants followed through with this plan, as did the police (Crago 2000). Indeed, sex workers and street people who were charged with prostitution-related offences and who were subject to pre-trial and release conditions on being in public (called *quadrilatères*) were rendered de facto subject to imprisonment if they were found in the Redlight, or often, the whole of downtown. Given that criminal "communicating" charges could be hard to prove in court, the police began increasingly to rely on another tactic to remove people from the area (Saint-Jean 2005). Antiquated or little-known municipal provisions (such as "spitting on the sidewalk" and "taking up more than one space on a bench") were dusted off and zealously enforced against sex workers and homeless Aboriginal people (ibid.). Some individuals accumulated tens of thousands of dollars in fines over a few months. Unpaid, they became warrants for immediate imprisonment.[5]

Meanwhile, Stella had hit a turning point in 1999. One of its co-founders, a stripper and sex worker activist, was hired as its director, and its credibility as a service provider was mounting, two developments that allowed increasing room for advocacy and for Stella to declare itself as an organization "by and for sex workers." Sex workers staffed its newly expanded outreach team and were thus well connected on the ground. This, along with institutional resources, allowed Stella to introduce new activist strategies into the movement. In 2000, with the support of a pro bono lawyer, Stella began a collective defence of sex workers who were discriminatorily ticketed for infractions against municipal

Anna-Louise Crago and Jenn Clamen

bylaws (Saint-Jean 2005). Stella's class-action case came before the courts in 2001. The Crown offered to drop all charges against the plaintiffs in exchange for dropping the case. Although most accepted these terms, one woman persisted in bringing the case forward in hopes that the practice would stop. The Crown, however, dropped the charges against her, making it impossible for the case against social profiling to be heard (Stella 2001; Saint-Jean 2005).

The Beginning of a Backlash

The political mandate to repress sex work in the late 1990s gave police increasing power over workers. When sex workers managed to evade police, they would often be caught and charged the next time they were seen in public, doing things as innocuous as buying milk or visiting their mothers (Crago 1999). Women were taken on "starlight tours" during the winter: in freezing temperatures, they would be picked up in police cars and dropped off at the top of the mountain or down by the water and left with no shoes (Crago 1998). A number of police officers threatened sex workers with arrest if they did not provide them with sexual services (Crago 1999). When the city announced its community policing strategy under the banner of "Community Policing: A Police Force That Is Close to Its Citizens!" the Coalition responded with a very popular poster campaign that skewered the slogan by placing it above the image of a police officer forcing a woman to give him a blow job. Along the bottom it read "Sex Workers Denounce Sexual Violence."

Widespread tolerance of and indifference to violence against sex workers had long been a systemic problem in Montreal. Police rarely investigated violent attacks against sex workers, who themselves rarely reported what they lived or saw, fearing it would place them in greater danger, either from attackers or from police (ibid.). This became poignantly clear when three sex workers in the Coalition were violently attacked during a short period. In one of these cases, after using the sexual assault kit to collect evidence from the worker, police interrogated her about her outstanding prostitution warrants while she lay on a hospital bed. In the second of these cases, of a woman who survived being stabbed seventeen times, the police did not open a file or start an investigation: instead, the officers who came to the scene simply listed the occurrence under a section called "notes of the night." The level at which the criminalization of prostitution rendered violence both invisible and sex workers' own fault came to stark light when the sex worker who survived the stabbings applied for victim's compensation. The government agency responsible for victim's compensation, Indemnisation des victimes d'actes criminels (IVAC), refused her claim on the grounds that she was a prostitute, and in their view, she was at "gross fault" for what had occurred (Cartier 2005). Stella retained the assistance of a pro bono lawyer to appeal the decision. IVAC subsequently changed its decision and specified that the woman was at gross fault, not for being a prostitute, but for being an *older* and experienced prostitute who should have known "the risks" she had chosen. The sex worker appealed the decision to the administrative courts, and in 2000, she won and was financially compensated, though her welfare payments were suspended as a result. For Stella and the Coalition, these experiences underscored fighting against criminalization as one of the most direct ways to break through the impunity fuelling violence against sex workers.

Projet Pilote: Backlash in Action

The visibility of sex worker actions brought increasing attention to the human costs of criminalization and repression. In 1999, this incited the City Committee on Street Prostitution to propose a suspension of enforcement of federal sex work laws or "dejudiciarize" sex work (Sansfaçon 1999). A pilot project was initiated in the areas with the largest concentration of street prostitution. Instead of repressing sex work, a community worker and police officer would respond to complaints from residents, including sex workers, mediate tensions due to disturbances, and take action against violence. If successful, the pilot project would be extended to the entire city (ibid.).

A backlash from politicians and residents' groups emerged no sooner than the project was announced. Stories abounded in the media and at residents' meetings that described sex workers as soliciting children in schoolyards, offering to pay children to touch them, and washing their own genitalia in drinking fountains (Stella 2005). A transsexual sex worker, who had lived her whole life in the neighbourhood and worked its streets since her early teens, decided to organize an action. Under the name les Maries-Madeleines, and with Stella and the Coalition's support, forty sex workers led a peaceful action to rename a park on the corner of Ontario Street the Marie-Madeleine Park. The underlying message was a plea to the neighbourhood not to "throw the first stone." Unimpressed, residents yelled insults and threw tomatoes at the assembled sex workers as they raised their Marie-Madeleine replica of a city sign onto the signpost.

City hall waited nine months before holding its first community consultations on the pilot project in March of 2000. An angry crowd of hundreds attended the first meeting (Ross and Charlebois 2005). When a homelessness activist

Anna-Louise Crago and Jenn Clamen

spoke at the microphone in favour of the project, he was punched. A man with a baseball bat stood in the speakers' line, threatening to "take care of the prostitution problem" himself. People yelled and threatened the sex workers who had attended (Charlebois 2005a). The second community consultation fared no better and had to be relocated after a bomb threat; it was moved to the chapel of a Catholic church, where it was hoped no violent attacks would occur (Ross and Charlebois 2005).

In the interim, the windows at Stella were shattered, and a dead bird was left on the doorstep. Stella and Coalition members received personal death threats (Charlebois 2005a). Strangers left messages on Stella's answering machine in which they named the children of Stella employees; those responsible for the threats were never discovered. The attacks on sex workers created new alliances. For example, when a residents' association held a march on 11 June 2000, demanding a crackdown on sex workers and clients, it was met with a counter-march organized by the recently created Association against the Criminalization of Poverty, composed of street youth, sex workers, and anti-poverty activists. The latter decried gentrification for violently displacing marginalized people in the city.

Not long after the mayor quashed the pilot project, the police initiated a major and highly publicized clampdown against clients in Centre-Sud. In essence, the initiative was a miniature replica of what is now known as the Swedish Model (see also Chapter 15 in this volume), meant to appease those who opposed prostitution while casting sex workers as victims needing to be saved. Sex workers reported to Stella that numbers of clients in the area were diminishing. As a result of this, they themselves were having to become less discriminating, accepting clients who were drunk or aggressive, or whom they would normally have refused. During the three-month period following the crackdown, Stella documented a three-fold rise in violent attacks and a five-fold increase in attacks with a deadly weapon (Crago 2008).

The logic of the police plan to target clients had another crucial flaw. Had sex workers truly been on the street because of client demand, perhaps they would have disappeared once the clients did. Instead, some workers were more visible to residents since they had to wait longer for a client, whereas others moved into smaller streets or farther east into the Hochelaga-Maisonneuve neighbourhood. Under unabating pressure from residents' groups, the police turned again to arresting women, including trans women. Whereas the city had reported 38 arrests for solicitation in 2001 (Nepton 2005), it reported over 400 in 2002 and 600 in 2003 (Cauchy 2004). In 2003, responding to the daily aggression she was facing, a trans sex worker named Claudia, who had organized the Marie-Madeleine action, collected 720 signatures on a statement she read to a local city council meeting:

> We are citizens and/or sex workers, and/or drug users,
> and we can be on Ontario Street where:
> We have the right to go out without ID.
> We have the right to socialize.
> We have the right to sit on a public bench.
> We have the right to be in a park before 11 pm.
> We have the right to take a cigarette break.
> We have the right to eat a slice of pizza.
> We have the right to dress sexy.
> We have the right to dress as women.
> Without constantly having to provide ID, without being followed, without being ticketed, without being harassed with headlights, without being threatened, without being addressed in a vulgar manner, without being treated like trash.

Despite the organizing efforts of sex workers and allies, following the end of the pilot project, the city was no longer open to hearing what sex workers had to say. When Stella was forced to relocate its offices in 2002, it chose to follow many of the sex workers and move to Centre-Sud.

Painting the Town Red

Following the violent backlash against the pilot project, Montreal's sex workers' movement became increasingly outward looking as it searched for more allies. As the majority of workers were women, Stella first approached the Fédération des Femmes du Québec (FFQ), Quebec's largest network of women's groups. Stella was met with resistance from the majority of women's groups, who refused to take a stance in favour of decriminalization (Charlebois 2005b). The Coalition chose not to join the FFQ discussions as many members felt that the FFQ excluded trans women and male sex workers, and didn't engage with poor or street women's struggles. Stella remained within the FFQ in order to strategically maintain a sex worker voice in the organization. In this spirit, for the World March of Women in 2000, Stella painted a two-storey mural of a target on the side of its building; this featured a sex worker who stood pinned to the target with chains and arrows. The words "criminalization," "laws," "hatred," and "prejudice" also figured in the design. As part of the march, sex workers lined the street, balconies, and windows, standing behind mock prison bars or proudly on cement blocks with a black band across their eyes to represent how they often appeared in the media. A three-storey banner read "We don't want our sisters, our mothers, our daughters, friends, our girlfriends, our lovers in prison" (ibid.).[6] This was one of a number of actions that would rightfully earn sex workers a seat at the table, albeit small, within feminist debates in Quebec.

Throughout this time, the sex workers' movement continued to count on strong support from homeless, drug users' rights, prisoners' rights, and trans rights' organizers. A number of activists from these communities participated directly in the Coalition, and conversely, a number of sex workers were also leaders in those movements. In an example of such intersections, in 2003, a wall on the border of the Redlight would become the site of a mural by the Living Monument Project – an ad hoc activist group made up of approximately forty people, most of whom had worked or lived on the street and almost all of whom were Aboriginal. Together, they organized and painted a three-storey mural as a memorial to the sex workers in Vancouver, many of them Aboriginal, who at the time were considered missing but were later found to have been murdered (see also Chapter 6 in this volume).

In the early 2000s, as Stella was able to hire more outreach workers to service the various sex work milieus and as the Coalition gained more visibility, actions increasingly targeted issues faced by sex workers in differing areas of the sex industry. For example, the Coalition was attracting the participation of a number of escorts and porn actors who were part of Montreal's web-porn boom. It also tapped into a new set of allies, including young people in the overlapping anglophone and francophone radical queer scenes. Young queers, some of whom were sex workers, became some of the staunchest supporters of the marches for 17 December, the International Day to End Violence against Sex Workers.

In 2003 and 2004, the Coalition organized two sex worker festivals called Turn Up the Heat! which were funded through its popular Red Light Night fundraisers. These festivals gave increasing visibility to a diversity of sex workers' issues. They were also a vehicle for visits from sex workers abroad, many of whom inspired Montreal actions and strategies. Notably, Karina Bravo of the Ecuadorian sex workers' union came to the 2003 festival to speak of the brothel strikes across the province of Machala. She convinced many Montreal sex workers of the need to stop wearing masks and called for solidarity from Western sex workers against the rise of a new anti-trafficking rhetoric that infantilized sex workers in and from the global South in order to repress them. The discourses and actions that have developed in Montreal were directly influenced by a number of these exchanges with sex workers in other parts of the world.

Interfacing with Institutions

Sex worker organizing in Montreal took on a different tone from 2002 onward. During this period, Stella was gaining more institutional support, which led to its growth and a shift toward strategies that involved interfacing with institutions such as Parliament, universities, and the police. Though some spontaneity and freedom of action were lost, the resulting interventions were ultimately more sustainable and allowed for more long-term strategies. Simultaneously, the Coalition petered out, resurfacing sporadically as a number of Coalition organizers began working at Stella. Stella's infrastructure allowed it to intervene in institutional processes around law reform, such as the parliamentary Subcommittee on Solicitation Laws Review (SSLR), between 2002 and 2006. In Montreal, Coalition members presented at the SSLR hearings, following which the subcommittee members went to Stella to meet with over forty sex workers.

During this time, in 2005, in collaboration with a professor and staff members from the Université du Québec à Montréal, Stella organized the Forum XXX, an international meeting of 250 sex workers from across Canada as well as from Argentina, Australia, France, India, Israel, New Zealand, South Africa, Sweden, Thailand, and the United States (Stella 2006). The Forum XXX focused on learning from each other's community-building strategies and celebrating the ten-year anniversaries of three sex workers' rights organizations: Stella in Canada, Cabiria in France, and the Durbar Mahila Samanwaya Committee in India. Despite the success of the Forum XXX, this moment underscored the challenges of being a Quebec movement organizing primarily in French with a dearth of North American francophone texts, networks, or nearby sex worker groups.

Important institutional inroads were made locally during this time. After many years of sensitizing police, Stella was able to find a few police officers who were willing to take sex workers' reports of violence without arresting them on sex-work-related warrants, arresting their clients, or busting their brothels or agencies (unless the latter were the source of the violence). This development, along with the growing refusal among sex workers to accept the discourse that violence is a part of their job, resulted in a surge in the number of women approaching Stella to go forward to police. In 2004, Stella supported four women who testified against a serial attacker of sex workers. By 2010, sex workers had come forward in the cases of three separate alleged serial attackers who were on trial in Montreal.

Surviving the Prohibitionist Feminist Attack

In Quebec, prohibitionist feminists have attacked sex worker organizing, specifically singling out both the Coalition and Stella. One means of doing this has been through a series of newspaper op-eds, or opinion pieces. One such piece by a male academic questioned Stella's right to exist and accused the sex workers at Stella of being "allies of the traffickers of women and children" (Poulin 2004, n.p.). Provincial government feminists were barely more supportive. In 2002, the Québec Council on the Status of Women issued a report that purported not to "take sides" but in actuality presented a biased and sensationalist view of sex work, decrying that Montreal had become the "Bangkok of the West" (Conseil du statut de la femme 2002, 17). In 2010, it officially took a prohibitionist position, a move that was criticized by a number of other feminist and human rights advocates (Montpetit 2010).

During the lead-up to the Forum XXX, prohibitionists focused their attacks and attempted to shut down sex workers' meetings. They lodged public complaints against the university for hosting the event and tried to get the forum evicted days before its start date (Toupin 2009). They also lodged complaints with Stella's funders and sent out a press release denouncing the allocation of funds for the event. On the day of the forum's opening press conference, prohibitionist anti-prostitution activists held a counter press conference to unveil their new group: the Concertation des luttes contre l'exploitation sexuelle (CLES) (CLES 2005).

Perhaps their most distressing show of force occurred in December of 2008 when sex workers were appearing in court to testify against a man they accused of raping them. In collaboration with one of the women, Stella organized a rally on the courtroom steps to support them before they entered court. Alongside written messages from sex workers across the world, slogans included "We believe you," "Courage," and "Stop the Violence." Members of CLES arrived and counter-demonstrated, handing out flyers that denounced all prostitution as violence.

Conclusion

Organizing for sex workers' rights in Montreal has changed over the past twenty years: many types of informal organizing became formalized; actions began to target conditions for workers across the industry; ad hoc demonstrations and events were often substituted for more bureaucratized interfacing with institutions; and sex workers' visibility and legitimacy have grown. Nonetheless, the leadership of street sex workers and the focus on street issues that emerged with the Coalition have remained entrenched through Stella, in part because of its regular contact with the street through outreach work.

As for the Redlight, in 2010, the city announced its plan to develop highrises over the remaining blocks where some sex workers continue to work. Ironically, many of the small businesses that had asked the police to empty the Redlight area in the late 1990s are among those slated to be expropriated and demolished by the city. At the time of writing, famous working bars such as the Peter's and the Alouette have shut down, and most of the tourist-rooms have stopped offering hourly rates. The Bolero, where a number of sex workers who were drug users lived and worked, was raided and closed, and the women were dispersed. Cleopatra's, an iconic establishment with a strip club downstairs and a trans bar upstairs, led a long fight against expropriation and won, in large part due to the advocacy of various artists, members of trans communities, and sex work activists.

Only a few female and trans sex workers remain in and around what is left of le Redlight. For many more, though, it continues to be a significant locale: a place where thousands have worked; a place where too many lost their lives to violence, to AIDS, to overdoses; a place of resilient survival and colourful defiance; and a place that birthed a movement.

Notes

1 The chapter's title, which translates as "born in the Redlight," refers to this area.
2 This chapter is based primarily on our own personal experiences and discussions in which we participated during the course of our sex worker organizing in Montreal: Jenn since 2002 and Anna-Louise beginning as a street sex worker in 1996. Where possible, we have tried to triangulate these experiences with data from a number of sources including archival documents, interviews, and academic publications. We have deliberately removed specific reference to the names of people involved. Principally this is because collective actions are often reduced to the stories of individual participants, particularly those who could afford to be "out." We felt that naming could overshadow those who couldn't be named. We preferred to focus on presenting a layered narrative of collective action instead.
3 Montreal has a long and storied history of sex workers engaging in both individual and collective acts of resistance. However, we have chosen to examine when these became formally organized through sustained collective action and strategy.
4 Street sex workers see many of their clients in what are known as "tourist-rooms." Also known as "siesta" rooms, they are found in cheap hotels and are rented for one or two hours. Piaules are generally apartments where drugs are sold and consumed (crack houses or shooting galleries); for a small fee, many women on the street bring their clients to a piaule.

5 Though municipal infractions remain a tactic for racial and social displacement, they are less in use since the Quebec government passed a law prohibiting incarceration for unpaid tickets.

6 This phrase was borrowed from the 1975 action by sex workers in Lyon, France, who occupied the St-Nizier church: "On ne veut plus nos soeurs, nos mères, nos filles, nos amies, nos blondes, nos amoures en prison!"

References

Associacion de Trabajadoras Autonomas 22 de Junio. 2002. *Memorias vivas: Nuestra organización, nuestras vidas*. Machala: Associacion 22 de Junio.

ASTTeQ. 2011. Historique d'ASTTeQ. http://cactusmontreal.org/.

Beaulieu, Carole. 1986. Une prostituée vaut-elle plus qu'une statistique. *La Vie en Rose* 39 (October): 14-15.

Bérubé, A. 1993. Les prostituées chassées!!! *Journal de Montréal*, 22 June, 1.

Cartier, C. 2005. Contraventions et IVAC. Special prison issue, *ConStellation* 18.

Cauchy, C. 2004. La carotte et le bâton pour contrer la prostitution de rue. *Le Devoir* (Montreal), 20 May, A2.

Charlebois, M.C. 2005a. Je me souviens du projet-pilote. Special tenth-year issue, *ConStellation* (Spring): 94.

–. 2005b. Rétrospective Montréal: 1995-2005. Special tenth-year issue, *ConStellation* (Spring): 112-30.

CLES. 2005. Pour un monde libéré de la prostitution. News release. 19 May. http://sisyphe.org/.

Coalition to Decriminalize Adult Prostitution. 1996. Position statement. http://www.walnet.org/.

Conseil du statut de la femme. 2002. *La prostitution: Profession ou exploitation? Une réflexion à poursuivre*. Synthèse No. 202-04-I. Quebec, Canada. http://www.csf.gouv.qc.ca/.

Crago, A.L. 1998. Squeegee: La criminalization des jeunes de la rue. Report for the Ville de Montréal.

–. 1999. Things that change, things that stay the same. Interview with Miss Pat. *Le festival du 8e art: Le travail du sexe*. Livret de la Coalition pour les droits des travailleuses et travailleurs du sexe. 21-23.

–. 2000. *Red light don't burn bright*. Montreal: Self-produced.

–. 2008. *Our lives matter: Sex workers unite for health and rights*. New York: Open Society Foundation.

Gemme, R., N. Payment, and L. Malenfant. 1989. *Street prostitution: Assessing the impact of the law, Montreal*. Ottawa: Department of Justice.

Gendron, S., and C. Hankins. 1995. *Prostitution et VIH au Québec: Bilan des connaissances*. Montreal: Direction de la Santé Publique.

Gobeil, D. 2003. 25 ans de prostitution et 2 ans de prison. Special prison issue, *ConStellation* 18.

Irvine, M. 1998-99. From social evil to public health menace: The justifications and implications of strict approaches to prostitutes in the HIV epidemic. *Berkeley Journal of Sociology* 43: 63-96.

Jeffrey, L. 2004. Prostitution as public nuisance: Prostitution policy in Canada. In *The politics of prostitution: Women's movements, democratic states and the globalization of sex commerce*, ed. J. Outshoorn, 83-102. New York: Cambridge University Press.

Jenkins, C. 2000. *Female sex worker HIV-prevention projects: Lessons learnt from Papua New Guinea, Bangladesh and India*. Geneva: UNAIDS.

La boîte à qu'on-se-voir. 1994. *Étude sur les violences envers les prostituées à Montréal: Rapport technique no TR1996-17F*. Ottawa: Ministère de la Justice du Canada.

Lacasse, D. 1991. La prostitution feminine à Montréal, 1945-70. PhD thesis, Université d'Ottawa.

Larsen, E.N. 1996. The effect of different police enforcement policies on the control of street prostitution. *Canadian Public Policy* 22, 1: 40-55.

Mensah, M.N. 2003. *Ni vues ni connues? Femmes, VIH et médias.* Montreal: Remue-ménage.

Montpetit, C. 2010. Prostitution: Le Conseil du statut de la femme essuie des critiques. *Le Devoir* (Montreal), 3 November.

Montreal Mirror. 1993. Hooker hunt, 24 June-1 July.

Myers, T. 1996. Criminal women and bad girls: Regulation and punishment in Montreal, 1890-1930. PhD diss., McGill University.

Namaste, V. 2000. *Invisible lives: The erasure of transsexual and transgendered people.* Chicago: University of Chicago Press.

–. 2002. Les grandes de la gaffe: L'histoire de la prostitution transexuelle et travestie à Montréal. Special issue, *ConStellation* 7, 1: 18-20.

Nepton, N. 2005. Quand revitalisation rime avec répression. *Cybersolidaires.* http://cyber solidaires.typepad.com/.

Pelchat, M. 1991. Le Centre-sud déclare la guerre à la drogue et à la prostitution. *La Presse,* 9 September.

Pinzer, M. 1977. *The Maimie papers: Letters from an ex-prostitute.* Edited by R. Rosen and S. Davidson. Bloomington: Indiana University Press.

Podmore, J.A. 1999. St-Lawrence Blvd as 'third city': Gender place and difference along Montreal's 'Main.' PhD thesis, McGill University.

Poulin, R. 2004. La prostitution, un "droit des femmes"? *Le Devoir* (Montreal), 13 September.

Proulx, D. 1997. *Le red light de Montréal.* Montreal: VLB Éditeur.

Ross, M.M., and M.C. Charlebois. 2005. Chronologie pour démêler une somber histoire: Le projet-pilote d'alternative à la judiciarisation de la prostitution de rue. Special tenth-year issue, *ConStellation* (Spring): 90-91.

Saint-Jean, M.N. 2005. Défense collective. Special tenth-year issue, *ConStellation* (Spring): 87.

Sansfaçon, D. 1999. *Rapport du Comité montréalais sur la prostitution de rue et la prostitution juvénile.* Montreal: Ville de Montréal.

Stella. 2001. Une victoire bordélique! Some victory. News release. 31 October.

–. 2005. Anecdotes stelliennes. Special tenth-year issue, *ConStellation* (Spring): 20-23.

–. 2006. *Les actes du Forum XXX.* Montreal: Stella.

Swendeman, B.T., I. Basu, S. Jana, M.J. Rotheram-Borus, S.J. Lee, P.A. Newman, and R.E. Weiss. 2004. Evidence for the efficacy of the Sonogachi Project in improving condom use and community empowerment among sex workers: Results from a cohort-control study. Paper presented at International Aids Conference, Bangkok, 11-16 July.

Thiboutot, C. 1999. Les travailleuses du sexe sont-elles politically correctes? *ConStellation* 4, 3.

Toupin, L. 2009. La légitimité incertaine des travailleuses du sexe dans le mouvement des femmes au Québec. *Revue internationale des études québécoises* 12, 1: 109-27.

11

Stepping All Over the Stones: Negotiating Feminism and Harm Reduction in Halifax

GAYLE MacDONALD, LESLIE ANN JEFFREY, KAROLYN MARTIN, AND RENE ROSS

> Viewing sex work as work rather than sexual exploitation or moral debauchery enables political approaches that recognize and support sex workers as rights-bearing political and social agents rather than objects of intervention and control. It also allows policy responses that are more likely to address sex workers' concerns and a politics based on solidarity rather than saving.
>
> – Jeffrey and MacDonald (2006, 11)

The best practices of organizations that deal with sex workers, such as Stepping Stone in Halifax, tend to embrace the holistic nature of what it is to live in contradiction. The embodied contradiction of sex work is that it is at once emancipatory and exploitative, agentic and constrained. For example, the sex worker herself is not in violation of law, but "acting like one" is.[1] The sex worker represents the imagined repository of our fantasy/self-loathing related to sexuality, of our collective pleasure/displeasure with the sexual act, and of our misguided morality. As a parody of our sexual (mis)understandings, she embodies the victim, the wilful agent, the "fallen" woman, and a target for hostility. Outreach organizations like Stepping Stone seek to move beyond moralistic politics and try to negotiate a more nuanced and complex response to sex work based on sex workers' own experiences. Stepping Stone can provide peer support, assistance to leave a violent situation, help to access stable housing, and support for transitioning to more self-sufficiency or out of the work itself. At the same time, the organization fights against the violence and stigma directed at sex workers and supports their rights. That is, it addresses both the problems within sex work and the problems of how society views sex work. This complexity in its positions arises from the fact that it is based in sex workers' own experiences. As Rene Ross, Stepping Stone's executive director, explained, *"For Stepping Stone, the key is to deliver programs, services, and options based on what sex workers want and need, based on their own experience, while respecting and protecting their self-determination. Our values come from the work we do. They come from listening to each other, as hard as that can be at times, especially when considering the extent that sex workers are criminalized."* In doing so, Stepping Stone engages in a complicated dance with feminist theory, women's organizations, police, and government. Although this dance is familiar to many sex worker organizations, Stepping Stone's position as the only sex worker outreach organization in the Atlantic region intensifies these struggles and offers us the ability to draw insights into how it challenges common (mis)understandings about sex work.

Sex work in the Maritimes differs little from sex work elsewhere in Canada, but organizing for sex workers' rights faces distinct challenges in the "periphery" of the country. This chapter will explore how Stepping Stone navigates its way through tensions within the feminist community between conceptualizations of sex work as harm and sex work as work. It will further consider the difficulties of working within and against the laws around sex work, and the challenges of applying a harm-reduction approach under the current federal Conservative government. This discussion takes place within the turbulent climate of the East Coast of Canada, a region marked by economic struggle but also a spirit of community support. Nova Scotia, like the other Maritime provinces, has a smaller population and weaker economy than elsewhere in the country. Often viewed as traditionalist and conservative, Maritime culture reflects a pragmatism rooted in the need to avoid risk in a precarious economy and divisiveness within a small population. There is also a long history of cooperative movements and a sense of community solidarity. Although rapid modernization, particularly in urban areas, has led to a new dynamism, the effects of recent downturns in the global economy, the general rise of social conservatism and economic neoliberalism, and the continuing strength of rural and religious conservatism are reflected in current political and social discourse. It is in this context that Stepping Stone seeks to negotiate support for sex workers. This chapter serves as a conversation between two academics, a graduate student, and the executive director of Stepping Stone about the meaning and significance of an organization dedicated to support, to advocate for, and to listen to sex workers in increasingly intolerant and economically precarious times.

Stepping Stone: Sex Worker Outreach in an East Coast City

Stepping Stone is the "only organization in the Maritimes that deals with street life and sex work from a specifically harm-reduction model" (Stepping Stone 2008, n.p.). It "strongly believes that all individuals have the right to self-determination," and it endeavours to assist workers "in making safe and positive life choices" rather than attempting to stop sex work (ibid.). The organization is located in a small house in the downtown core and hosts a drop-in centre, visits from community partners such as health workers and legal aid, peer counselling, educational workshops, and recreational activities. It works with female, male, and transgendered sex workers, and many of its staff are former sex workers themselves. It incorporates ongoing harm-reduction practices such as passing out bad date lists and harm reduction supplies, and it gives workshops about sex worker safety.[2] The staff also provides court support and referral to services, including housing. Four times a week staff members engage in street outreach to make contact with and provide condoms, food, and support to sex workers on the street or working out of their homes (ibid.). Rene Ross, the current executive director of Stepping Stone, outlines the organization's mandate and the evolution of its relationship with the wider community: *Stepping Stone is an organization that provides crucial supports to sex workers at crucial times in their lives. We provide rights-based options that are rooted in harm reduction, choice, and self-determination. We are an organization that listens to sex workers and strives to advocate for policies that are based in their realities. It is these policies, we find, that are best in protecting the health and safety of this highly marginalized population.*

Stepping Stone was born out of feminist concern over the rising rates of violence against sex workers in Halifax. In the late 1980s, a group of Halifax women banded together through the Elizabeth Fry Society to establish the organization, which has, against all odds, managed to keep its doors open for over two decades. During this time, Stepping Stone has expanded its mandate beyond providing services to demanding better treatment for sex workers and legal changes supportive of their rights. It straddles the line between focusing on outreach and rights-based advocacy. Its clientele is mainly drawn from the street-based trade, and many would fall under the category of "survival sex workers," those who exercise less control over their working and life conditions. However, a number of clients have experience in a variety of sex work sectors, and some have become outspoken advocates of sex workers' rights. The organization's board is mainly drawn from the non-sex-working community, but as noted above, the staff includes former sex workers. Thus, though Stepping Stone's structure seems to place it within the outreach tradition, this is balanced with a rights-based advocacy strategy. For example, on 17 December 2010, the International Day to End Violence against Sex Workers, it held its first Red Umbrella event – a public coming together of sex workers and advocates that had not been previously seen on the East Coast. Stepping Stone also recently launched a pointed ad campaign challenging the stereotypes of sex workers. It also regularly issues press releases calling for changes to the justice system and the need for decriminalization, and it speaks out against the arrests of sex workers and the violence and stigma they face.

However, maintaining funding and community support means that Stepping Stone walks a delicate line between service provision and advocacy; it is viewed as too radical by some, particularly the local community, and not radical enough by others, particularly those within the national and international sex workers' rights movement. Stepping Stone is constantly challenged on positions and policies because it doesn't fit into an easily distinguishable framework and because it subscribes to multiple schools of thought regarding sex work. But as an organization, however, it never loses sight of its primary purpose: to contribute to the health and safety of sex workers through supportive programs and community education, and to encourage the public to see sex workers as people first.

Dance Steps: Feminist Theory and Politics

When theorizing about sex work, Ross and other staff members are hesitant to draw on feminist theories. Ross has consistently questioned what it means for her to be a feminist because of the debates surrounding sex work, debates in which common ground is a rarity. Feminists are engaged in contentious debates regarding the reasons why people engage in sex work and the ways that it affects women (for example, MacKinnon 1989; LeMoncheck 1997; Jeffrey and MacDonald 2006; Bernstein 2007).[3] The interpretation of sex work is highly contested, particularly between the polarized perspectives of radical feminists, who support prohibition, and sex-radical feminists, who support decriminalization (Jeffrey and MacDonald 2006; see also the Introduction in this volume).[4] Both of these feminist ideologies have greatly influenced organizations that work directly with sex workers and are related to the ways in which harm-reduction strategies have been applied. Although the reality is that these two ideological positions are not clear-cut (Ditmore 2006), we will polarize the debate for the purposes of this chapter. It is truly far more complex, "with debates over choice, freedom, violence, and resistance occurring as much among sex workers themselves as within the feminist movement (which also includes sex workers)" (Jeffrey and MacDonald 2006, 64).

The Debate
Sex work advocacy groups, along with their pro-sex feminist allies, understand sex work as a form of labour that is distinguishable from other varieties of low-status employment, in part by virtue of its better pay (Bernstein 2007). Sex-radicals argue not only for economic justice "but also for the decriminalization and social legitimation of sex work" (ibid., 167). They protest the blanket perspectives, often proposed by radical feminists, that claim that all sex workers are physically coerced into their work, that all sex workers are forced into it by life circumstances, or that they are all "victims of an internalized patriarchy that has convinced them that theirs is a freely chosen life, not without risks, but with the promise of greater financial reward and independence than other jobs demanding the same hours, level of training, or education" (LeMoncheck 1997, 136). Sex-radical feminists consider feminists who fail to see anything other than degradation in sex work to be the "natural allies of a sexual conservatism that condemns the anonymous, recreational, pleasure-seeking sex in sex work" (ibid., 114). From a sex-radical viewpoint, sex workers are considered to be creative and emancipated women who subvert gender roles within the current patriarchal, capitalist framework that structures much of our social lives (Pendleton 1997; Jeffrey and MacDonald 2006). Sex-radicals regard the sex industry as having the ability to redefine women's sexuality in their own terms and to end the stigma associated with "combining female sexual pleasure and recreational sex" (LeMoncheck 1997, 137). Whereas radical feminists often accuse sex-radicals of being celebratory of sexual liberation without contextualizing the constraints of gender, class, race, ability, and other factors that structure social life, many sex-radical accounts see sex work as a terrain of struggle but also one that presents the potential for change and for the reclamation of power to determine meaning (Chapkis 1997; Jeffrey and MacDonald 2006).

When asked about how Stepping Stone reacts to feminist theory, Ross replied, "*Well I think that depends on the theory. We reject the theories that see sex workers as only victims with no self-determination ... [or] theories that paint all experiences of sex workers with the same brush. Overall though, it's hard to define exactly where an agency such as Stepping Stone 'fits' in regards to the women's movement and the stream of feminism that I thought I understood. I don't get it.*" Again, Ross explicitly stated that when it comes to sex work, many feminists *"don't get it"* and instead impose their own interpretations of the work onto the experiences of sex workers. To qualify this statement, she explained,

> *We all agree that men should not influence women's policy. We all agree that First Nations and Aboriginal people should direct and influence First Nations and Aboriginal policy ... We all agree that if you want to know how your health care system is treating patients, you listen to patients. Why is it that, when it comes to sex workers being at the table and having a say, you will see the attitude of "Oh no, not the prostitutes. We know what's best for them." You know what I think it comes down to? Sex. It comes down to fucking sex. I can't think of any other difference between me and the women in the sex industry except for how we make a living.*

This powerful statement explicates what may be one of the most pivotal problems in the feminist debate on sex work: it comes down to sex. Feminists, especially postcolonial, anti-racist, and queer/trans/lesbian feminists, have fought to have their voices heard in every aspect of mainstream feminism (Johnson 2005). It is no longer acceptable for feminists to speak about women's lives as if there were one common experience among all people who identify as women. Why, then, are the voices of sex workers so hard to hear? Why is it inconceivable that autonomous adults know what's best for them and their lives? Although some recent gains have been made, mainstream feminism "has yet to make major moves beyond analyzing how sex work oppresses women, to theorizing how feminism reproduces oppression of sex workers, and how incorporating sex worker feminism results in richer analyses of gender oppression" (Nagle 1997, 1).

Stepping Stone has managed to avoid, at least in the local milieu, the divisions between feminist organizations that have made sex work politics difficult in other parts of Canada. Again, Ross contextualized Stepping Stone's position in Halifax:

> *I worked for feminist organizations and groups before Stepping Stone, and I know that the tension between sex worker organizations and women's groups is much more prevalent than it is here in Nova Scotia. From a local perspective, there is a growing partnership, but in other cities this is certainly not the case. We have heard of other groups who are like Stepping Stone who have had their annual general meetings protested. Even we at Stepping Stone, when we did an ad campaign, were the targets of a hate mail campaign by women's and religious groups in Vancouver. It was wild.*

Ross's statements reflect the divergent discourses around sex work. Feminists who work for NGOs and other community agencies are not immune to the general stereotypes that exist throughout the academic world that figure sex workers as either exploited victims who need rescuing or agentic subjects who can actually write policy on their work themselves. Stepping Stone, like other outreach agencies, is developing a politics that both champions sex workers as agents and recognizes the barriers that they face.

Critiques of Dichotomous Approaches to Sex Work

There are ways to move beyond these dichotomous approaches to sex work that more closely reflect Stepping Stone's realities. Shrage (1989), for example, by-passes the traditional arguments regarding the psyche of women who engage in sex work, and its moral and political effects, tackling instead the myths and beliefs that are deeply ingrained in attitudes that are oppressive to women. In doing so, Shrage (ibid., 352) suggests that the "wrongness" of prostitution "is not that it violates deeply entrenched social conventions-ideals of feminine purity," but rather, as it currently exists, that prostitution represents other problematic cultural assumptions, such as the concepts of male dominance, female purity, and inherent sex drives, which "serve to legitimate women's social subordination." In the current sociopolitical context of Western society, Shrage says that sex workers must subvert "the beliefs which currently structure commercial sex in our society" – notably, those beliefs that oppress women (ibid., 359). She writes that "the female prostitute would need to assume the role not of a sexual subordinate but of a sexual equal or superior" who has the authority to determine her services, working conditions, and price (ibid.). LeMoncheck (1997, 137) also warns against failing to examine the "ideological milieu" in which sex work is performed and believes that sex work contains "both liberating and oppressive elements."

These arguments represent a more nuanced perspective that views women's sexuality "both as a function of male dominance and as a function of women's sexual liberation under those same conditions" (ibid., 11). A variety of power dynamics, professional arrangements, and individual experiences are present in sex work, and thus a multifaceted perspective is necessary in order to account for these complexities (Weitzer 2009). This is as true in the Maritimes as it is in larger, economically more robust areas of Canada. Although many assume that sex work in have-not areas of Canada such as the Maritimes is all about poverty, "pimping," and drugs, Ross points out that the majority of Stepping Stone clients are not known to have pimps and that drugs are not the drivers of sex work that they are assumed to be. Street-based workers in the Maritimes often point out that money is a key attraction of their work, but they also appreciate the flex-ibility and independence that it gives them (see Jeffrey and MacDonald 2006, 19-61). They object, however, to the violence they experience and the way they are treated by the law. And, as in other areas of Canada, the vast majority of the trade takes place off-street, with workers who are far from marginalized or desperate, but who struggle with the oppressive weight of the criminal laws. Thus, for Stepping Stone, as for many advocates across Canada, challenging the oppressive dynamics within sex work in Canada has meant, to a large degree, challenging the legal conditions under which sex work takes place.

Stepping on Toes: Negotiating with and against the Law

Stepping Stone's attentiveness to sex workers' experience has led it, as an organ-ization, to focus not on the "problem of prostitution" but on the conditions under which sex work occurs. This has meant a shift in focus away from clients and to the ways in which sex workers are treated by the law and police. Ross outlined her experience of listening and learning:

> *There are things I believe now that I did not when I started. I never thought I'd say "Leave the johns alone." But when you actually talk with sex workers who are out there, when you read the bad date reports, there is a correlation between crackdowns on clients and the violence faced by sex workers ... I can't explain why, when [police] do the sweeps on clients, why they always pick up the ones who are not necessarily violent, [the ones] who are out to get a date while their wife is at bingo ... But I can explain why the violent [clients] are taking women out of the city – they are fleeing the police and taking the women to secluded areas where no one will hear their screams. That's what's happening.*

However, there is strong support in Halifax for measures targeted at the clients of sex workers, including from some women's organizations. Following Manitoba's lead, the Nova Scotia government even proposed amendments to the Motor Vehicles Act in 2000, which would have enabled municipalities to pass bylaws allowing for the seizure of clients' vehicles used in the commission of prostitution-related offences (Jeffrey and MacDonald 2006). The bill failed only because of concerns over legal extra-constitutionality and downloading of responsibilities onto cash-strapped municipalities. Further, in the early 2000s, Nova Scotia adopted the use of John Schools to "re-educate" and "rehabilitate" clients who are charged with prostitution-related offences but who wish to avoid the court system. The clients pay a fine and attend a one-day session in which they are educated about the "negative impact" of the sex trade. Although the funds raised are supposed to support education for sex workers, called the Jane School, the money can be difficult to access for those who do not wish to exit the trade or who have never used Stepping Stone's support services (Nova Scotia Justice Correctional Services 2010).

The preference for targeting clients has only increased in recent years along with concerns over trafficking, discussions of the Swedish, or Nordic, Model, which criminalizes only the clients, and with the *Bedford* decision in Ontario that has potentially opened the door to partial decriminalization of sex work (see also Chapter 15 in this volume). The targeting of clients appears to be a middle-ground for feminists who do not want to appear to condemn sex workers but who still oppose the industry itself. However, the end result is still damaging and dangerous for sex workers.

Although arrests of clients have climbed proportionally over the years, sex workers still experience the negative effects of the law. The Halifax police force has been active in suppressing the trade both indoors and outdoors since the 1980s, so much so that only one exotic dance club now operates in a city of nearly 400,000 people (the largest city in the Maritime provinces).[5] In 2009, fifty-eight people were arrested for prostitution-related charges and sixty-five in 2010 (Halifax Regional Police 2011). Sex workers report that they have often been harassed by police, told to move along, or charged with offences such as jaywalking to get them off the streets (Jeffrey and MacDonald 2006). In recent years, police have come under increasing pressure to "do something" about street-level prostitution in light of overall concerns regarding crime in Halifax, which was recently ranked as one of the ten most dangerous cities in Canada and the crime capital of Eastern Canada (Lunau 2008).

In this environment, sex workers remain a target of the law. Indeed, across Canada, this more "even-handed" approach (Kong and AuCoin 2008, 11) that targets clients still results in a gender imbalance in arrests insofar as female sex workers are most likely to be convicted and most likely to be charged multiple times, with the end result that they receive harsher sentences overall. Sex workers are most likely to face prison time and probation, whereas clients tend to be fined or face punishments such as restitution, suspended charges, and loss of a driver's licence (Duschene 1997; Kong and AuCoin 2008). The Halifax John School gives clients the option to avoid court proceedings altogether, but Halifax sex workers face increasingly harsh sentencing.

A major battle for Stepping Stone and sex workers in Halifax has been the use of "release conditions" or "boundaries" for arrested sex workers that restrict their access to particular geographic locations. Release conditions have been a popular and highly problematic mechanism for punishing sex workers. Breach of conditions leads to more serious punishment than the original charge of communicating, and yet the geographical areas from which women are banned often include outreach services such as the methadone clinic and Stepping Stone itself. By October 2008, the number of sex workers charged with breach of conditions for that year had already risen to seventy-five, compared to thirty-two in all of 2006 (Chapin 2008). In 2009, Stepping Stone launched a Facebook page titled "Halifax Sex Workers without Boundaries" to raise public awareness of the negative impacts of these measures. In regards to boundaries, Ross explained, *"Boundaries are automatic now. The first thing they turn to [is section] 213 [of the Criminal Code], you're on boundaries. Also, there has never been a male charged under boundaries. And there's never been a john placed on boundaries to my knowledge."* Ross surmised that the bias toward placing female rather than male workers on conditions results from the fact that the male stroll is away from residential areas, so there are fewer complaints that typically drive arrests. But in some of the neighbourhoods where women work, said Ross, *"There are residents ... that do nothing but call in day-in and day-out about that woman who is sitting on the wall at the end of the street."* Ross explained, *"The complaints are part of the cycle of criminalization. And it is driven by residents' complaints, which is why all of our communication campaigns need to target the residents. [The courts] think that the whole purpose is to break the whole cycle of going out onto the street. The courts say that boundaries are harm-reduction principles, but are they?"*

The problems with boundaries, arrests of sex workers and their clients, and other police practices that make street sex workers' lives more dangerous have strained the relationship between Stepping Stone and police. Recent attacks on and murders of sex workers have sometimes pushed this relationship to the breaking point. Ross recounted that negotiations with law enforcement have meant bringing legal expertise into the boardroom: *"We have a lawyer on our board. One of her first duties as a board member was to accompany me to my second trip to the interrogation room. A police officer was trying to get me to share confidential information about a program user at the time. But of course, legal advice is also essential when we look at the boundaries placed on program users."*

Stepping Stone has also used board membership to mediate relations with the police service. Despite the potentially antagonistic relationship with police, Stepping Stone has decided to walk a fine line between cooperation and resistance by inviting a trusted member of the force onto the board. Only in this manner can the organization see its way clear to both fulfill its mandate to protect sex workers from violence (which requires police cooperation) and to communicate its concerns to police about their mode of operation. But, as Ross noted, the relationship is constantly renegotiated:

I have a great amount of trust in [the officer on the board], and she genuinely cares about the program users. Due to some recent experiences with police officers "on the beat," however, and because the women are so criminalized if they come up, [the police] can't come in unless they get a subpoena. We have a cop on our board in case anything happens to the women. She helps us to follow proper procedure in reporting, and she is helping us to look at ways to improve our relationship with the cops. We work very closely with the women and see the effects that criminalization has on them. We see the pain it engenders. The relationship with the cops is probably the toughest relationship I have ever been in, and I admit, it needs work.

Although Stepping Stone's approach reflects Maritime pragmatism and the need to maintain relationships in a small community, this has not meant abandoning its efforts for broader social and political change. In negotiating a "middle way" in its relationship with police, as in its relationship with feminism, Stepping Stone draws on its roots in another contested approach – harm reduction – and in doing so once again challenges understandings of the practice.

Harm Reduction: Extant Policy or Active Practice?

Karoll (2010, 268) notes, "Harm reduction is any program or policy designed to decrease harmful health, social, or economic consequences of substance use while not insisting upon abstinence. Thus its primary goal is to reduce or minimize harmful consequences associated with active or ongoing substance use." Harm reduction has traditionally been seen as a way around the divisive politics of contentious issues such as substance use and sex work. By focusing on reducing harm rather than on the rightness or wrongness of a particular activity, harm-reduction approaches allow organizations to undertake outreach and receive support without necessarily triggering a moral debate. Harm-reduction strategies have been adopted by many sex worker organizations that engage in peer education, safer sex programs, and anti-violence activities. Stepping Stone employs similar tactics including street outreach, provision of safer sex materials, bad date lists, anonymous STI testing, peer support, and workshops on health and legal issues. Harm reduction has been criticized, however, for being aimed exclusively at those who are most at risk (from, for example, HIV/AIDS or substance use) rather than being the basis for building a broader movement for sex workers; sex workers are not equally at risk and do not necessarily share the same daily struggles (Rogers and Ruefli 2004; Cusick 2006). Harm reduction can, as a top-down strategy, be co-opted as well. As noted above, the courts have presented boundaries and conditions of bail as harm-reduction measures. Once again, however, Stepping Stone moves beyond the traditional focus of harm reduction, using it as a base from which to build support for the broader, and more progressive, principle of putting people in charge of their own lives. As Ross explained,

What harm reduction means is putting people in control of their own lives. So, in addition to reducing harm, I believe that harm reduction is about giving power to the people that policies and programs are aimed at helping ... and it is also very realistic. I think that it is the best approach in working with marginalized populations where violence, or health, et cetera et cetera, are prominent ... It is not just about "reducing harm"; it is [about] that, but it's so much more ... When you look at our core philosophies, we believe in self-determination, and we are a user-directed organization whereby we listen to sex workers, and we tailor our programs and services based on what they need and their realities, which is really important.

Expanding on the principles of harm reduction in a way that emphasizes self-determination enables Stepping Stone to walk the tightrope between acting as a rights-based advocacy group and appealing to funders for support of outreach activities. This balancing act has become more complicated with the current federal government's positioning on harm reduction. Under the Conservative Party, Canada has seen a dramatic change in harm-reduction policies; within its rhetoric, harm reduction is equated with drug addicts having an easy time of it. To that end, the needle exchange and supervised injection site located in Vancouver's Downtown Eastside is under attack by Ottawa in an attempt to shut it down. In this context, AIDS service organizations and needle exchange programs across the country collectively gasped in horror as they realized that public funding for these types of programs was in grave danger. As a result, many tried to frame their "asks" of government in decidedly different terms, ones that would garner support for their (mainly health) programs but not raise the ire of right-wing and conservative interests that continued to express disdain for those who use substances. As a result, organizations such as Stepping Stone have had to tread carefully in appealing to notions such as harm reduction when trying to access government funding. But, as Ross pointed out, this balancing

Gayle MacDonald, Leslie Ann Jeffrey, Karolyn Martin, and Rene Ross act is also one that the organization performs when working with feminist funders:

> I have been told that if we apply for funding and mention [harm reduction] our chances would not be that great. You have to walk such a tightrope when applying for funding under a harm-reduction model ... or any model for that matter. We never seem to fit anywhere. For instance, what do you do when your funding application – from a "feminist" funder – states you cannot have men in your leadership roles? We work with male and trans sex workers. They influence our policy as do female sex workers. Our board chair is a man. We have men on staff who, like the other staff, are integral to the organization. Now, here is this grant application. It has been months since the program you are running, that actually helps people, has seen money; you could be shut down, hundreds of marginalized people depend on you. What would you do?

Ironically, government cutbacks have served to renew the bond between the feminist community and Stepping Stone. According to Ross,

> So, we went to Status of Women, and even other women's organizations said, "You will get this money for sure" because it wasn't a lot of money we were asking for, fifty thousand dollars, so maybe twenty-five thousand from each [the Homelessness Initiative and Status of Women]. But Stepping Stone did not get that funding from Status of Women Canada. Thing is, most of the women's groups in the province didn't either. But the positive thing that came out of that is that all the women's groups are now lobbying to get together, and Stepping Stone is now a part of that. So, a letter that has just gone to all the Members of Parliament, where it says what is not going to happen to women's services in Nova Scotia – there is a bulletin there that says so many sex workers are not going to get housing and opportunity for meaningful employment, which means that there is no talk about exit out of the sex trade.

For Stepping Stone, then, harm reduction has been a springboard for collective action and for challenging the path of both feminism and harm reduction itself.

Conclusion

Harm reduction and feminism are far more like uneasy lovers than committed partners. Sometimes they "sleep with each other," recognizing that as monies for non-profits shrink, all feminists must band together to gather state funds. Necessity is the mother of political partnership, it would seem. However, most days, the sparring is most visible; for most feminists, sex workers represent the embodied contraction about which we wrote earlier in this chapter. One would think that harm reductionists and feminists should be committed partners; most feminists would easily argue that they have no wish to see women harmed in any situation. But there's the rub – the argument becomes a matter of victimization versus agency. If the sex worker is a victim and requires rescuing, feminists of most stripes are on board. If, however, she is refusing to leave the trade, much like the substance user who refuses to stop using, the sympathy of many feminists seems to vanish. There are exceptions: both harm-reduction policies and feminist theory are based on models of empowerment, both are rooted in the premise that the personal is political, and both contend that getting the user (in the case of harm reduction) or the woman/sex worker (in the case of feminism) to a place of self-actualization and placing the tools of self-esteem and health in their hands will result in a more just, safer, and healthier life for both groups. However, there are also some interesting differences. Harm reduction is about protection from further harm and taking people where you find them, while dealing with unrealistic goals such as the elimination of substance abuse. Agencies such as Stepping Stone practise precisely these principles; taking sex workers where you find them and offering the protections and safety necessary to continue their work.

Both harm reduction and feminism can be useful approaches for supporting women on the street. One way they do so is by endeavouring to increase sex workers' self-esteem. Although harm reduction doesn't attempt to eliminate substance abuse, it can help if addicted people become empowered enough to realize that addiction may not be the best path to self-care. In a similar way, sex-radical feminism doesn't work well to eliminate all violence against sex workers, but it can help if sex workers reach a level of self-confidence to refuse undesirable clients and to help in the writing of policy that better reflects their needs and interests. However, some fundamental differences between harm reduction and feminism are also prevalent. Whereas harm reduction assumes that dysfunctional behaviour may never change, some branches of feminism, particularly radical feminism, often hope to eliminate dysfunction.

The paradigms, theories, and approaches do a dance, back and forth, silent and salient, passive and active. The dancing is due to the context itself, as our conversation with Stepping Stone attests; one minute it's about funding, the next minute court-mandated boundaries are at issue. Either way, Stepping Stone

Gayle MacDonald, Leslie Ann Jeffrey, Karolyn Martin, and Rene Ross survives and thrives through the contradictions and challenges presented by feminism, funding, policies, and public reaction.

Acknowledgments
The authors are grateful to Jocelyne Tranquilla, who wrote an original draft of this essay, and to Christina O'Neill for her careful editing and additional research when needed.

Notes
1 This distinction in law is one that is familiar to Canadians: for many years, homosexuality was presented in the Criminal Code under the same logic – to be a homosexual was not against the law, but to act like one was.
2 Stepping Stone does not provide needles, as the local needle exchange is right up the street.
3 Although sex work also involves men and transgendered individuals, this essay is limited to women.
4 Sex-radical feminism is also sometimes called pro-sex or sex-positive feminism.
5 This figure includes the sister city to Halifax, Dartmouth, and the surrounding area.

References

Bernstein, E. 2007. *Temporarily yours: Intimacy, authenticity and the commerce of sex*. Chicago: University of Chicago Press.

Chapin, A. 2008. Sex workers' rights. *The Coast* (Halifax), 23 October. http://www.thecoast.ca/.

Chapkis, W. 1997. *Live sex acts: Women performing erotic labor*. New York: Routledge.

Cusick, L. 2006. Widening the harm reduction agenda: From drug use to sex work. *International Journal of Drug Policy* 17, 1: 3-11.

Ditmore, M.H. 2006. Feminism. In *Encyclopedia of prostitution and sex work*, ed. M.H. Ditmore, 154-60. Westport, CT: Greenwood Press.

Duschene, D. 1997. Street prostitution in Canada. *Juristat* 17, 2: 1-13.

Halifax Regional Police. 2011. Staff report. Board of Police Commissioners. January.

Jeffrey, L., and G. MacDonald. 2006. *Sex workers in the Maritimes talk back*. Vancouver: UBC Press.

Johnson, R. 2005. Feminism, law, inclusion: Intersectionality in action. In *Feminism, law, inclusion: Intersectionality in action*, ed. G. MacDonald, R. Osborne, and C.C. Smith, 21-37. Toronto: Sumach Press.

Karoll, R.B. 2010. Applying social work approaches, harm reduction, and practical wisdom to better serve those with alcohol and drug use disorders. *Journal of Social Work* 10: 263-81.

Kong, R., and K. AuCoin. 2008. Female offenders in Canada. *Juristat* 28, 1: 1-23. http://www.statcan.gc.ca/pub/85-002-x/85-002-x2008001-eng.pdf.

LeMoncheck, L. 1997. *Loose women, lecherous men: A feminist philosophy of sex*. New York: Oxford University Press.

Lunau, K. 2008. How Halifax just made it into the 10 most dangerous cities. *Macleans.ca*, 17 March. http://www.macleans.ca.

MacKinnon, C. 1989. *Toward a feminist theory of the state*. Cambridge, MA: Harvard University Press.

Nagle, J., ed. 1997. *Whores and other feminists*. New York: Routledge.

Nova Scotia Justice Correctional Services. 2010. Prostitution education program. http://www.gov.ns.ca/just/corrections/_docs/pep_000.pdf.

Pendleton, E. 1997. Queering heterosexuality. In *Whores and other feminists,* ed. J. Nagle, 73-87. New York: Routledge.

Rogers, S., and T. Ruefli. 2004. Does harm reduction programming make a difference in highly marginalised, at-risk drug users? *Harm Reduction Journal* 1, 7: 1-7.

Shrage, L. 1989. Should feminists oppose prostitution? *Ethics* 99, 2: 347-61.

Stepping Stone. 2008. About Stepping Stone. http://www.steppingstonens.ca/.

Weitzer, R. 2009. Sociology of sex work. *Annual Review of Sociology* 35: 213-34.

12

Are Feminists Leaving Women Behind? The Casting of Sexually Assaulted and Sex-Working Women

JANE DOE

I sometimes wonder what was the turning point for me in the development of my feminism. How did I evolve into a pro-sex-work anti-censorship feminist and ally? Was it the influence of my parents' passionate trade unionism? The love and admiration for close friends who worked in massage parlours during the 1970s? Was it my coming of age at a time when women were suddenly free to (among other things) fuck for joy and with joy? Was it the battles feminists fought then, with joy and fucking hard, for access to abortions? The ones for the human rights of lesbians, gays and queers, pay equity, child care, and maternity benefits? The work to address the racism and colonialism of our feminisms – with which we struggle still – along with the rights of transgendered and transsexual women and men? Was it the struggle by and for equality rights for disabled women, psychiatrized women, Aboriginal, immigrant, racialized, Islamic, and Jewish women, and their right to define their issues, challenge ours (white and mainstream) as oppressive, and to delineate the very terms and language we should use to speak of them and to them? Was it the ongoing battle to name and address violence against women as an equality issue? Certainly all of these subjects are connected, and it should follow, then, logically and politically, that the equality and rights to self-autonomy for women who engage in sex work and especially prostitution are equally connected.

Instead, there is a divide that places some feminists in support of the decriminalization of prostitution legislation and the equality rights of women who are sex workers, and others who support an anti-sex-work prohibitionist position that equates prostitution with violence against women, especially sexual assault.

Then there is a third group, a majority (I believe) who are undecided about the debate, certain that criminalizing women is not a feminist objective, but hesitant to enter the discussion, fearful of censure, unclear about the issues, too busy, and with little or no access to sex work theory, research, reality, and practice.

In this chapter, I hope to provide some of that through research drawn from interviews that identify the similar ways in which sex-working and sexually assaulted women, though distinct, are each understood and treated as victims. I will provide an examination of existing legislation that criminalizes and otherwise negatively affects sex-working and sexually assaulted women by denying them agency, choice, and action. I will also investigate harmful police practices and policies as well as historical constructs of female sexuality that classify women as damaged and defiled as a result of the crime committed against them (sexual assault) or through the occupation in which they engage (sex work). Throughout the chapter, I will address current practices in academic-embedded feminism and in community-based women's anti-violence sectors that affirm and legitimate oppressive criminal justice responses to both groups of women, even when we think they do not.

It is my intention to present alternative thought and analysis through a personal/political narrative based in my locations as an active sex worker ally and an expert in sexual assault. The content is designed to take us away from broken narratives, to build new ones, and to encourage meaningful dialogue by examining the ways in which all women can be negatively defined through the whore stigma (Pheterson 1993; Jackson and Brents 2010) and then purportedly rescued or saved/redeemed via criminal justice and other social systems (Agustin 2007).

My understanding of sex workers is that they form a politicized and feminist sector dealing with the goals, barriers, and internal issues faced by all progressive movements seeking to end state control and discrimination. As with feminists or women generally, sex workers are not a homogeneous group. Class and race influence strongly, separating women from each other demographically, economically, culturally, and otherwise.[1] A large factor in my support for sex workers' equality rights is the similar manner in which sex-working and sexually assaulted women are cast.

Broadly, both groups rely on anonymity to avoid the labelling (branding) of social stigmas such as fallen woman, slut, and whore (Schur 1984). Each group – sexually assaulted and sex working – is defined by popular constructs of women as victims, which fuel legal, academic, media, religious, and Hollywood stereotypes (Projansky 2001; Kamir 2006). The actions of both groups are highly regulated by the state through the police and result in fear-based

Jane Doe

warnings that require "good" women to regulate their lives and the public space they occupy in order to avoid rape. Current communicating and bawdy-house legislation prevents sex-working women from being in most public or private spaces, and it denies them their freedom of movement and safety. Both groups are immediately rendered bad or fallen and are criminalized when they transgress or are blamed for the crime they have experienced.[2] Both groups are pathologized as traumatized and unable to overcome the real or perceived hardships they have suffered. The crimes that have been committed against them, or the work in which they engage, are mediated, defined, judged, counselled, taught, or written about for them, to them, and despite them.

In 2005, I collaborated in research that would make some of these connections, focusing on moral constructions of female sexuality as the defining theme (Currie and Gillies 2006; see also Chapter 17 in this volume). The final report examined the manner and the degree to which the Canadian state exercises control over women through certain laws and policies intended to offer protection to those who have experienced sexual assault or who work in the sex trade.[3] With permission, I include some of my research here, taken from the concluding section of the unpublished report.

Back to the Future

In 1998, after an eleven-year court battle, I won a civil suit against the Toronto police force in which it was found guilty of negligence and gender discrimination – or breach of my equality rights – in its investigation of my rape (*Jane Doe v. Board of Commissioners of Police for the Municipality of Metropolitan Toronto* 1998; see also Doe 2004). Since then I have worked as a writer, lecturer, researcher, policy analyst, activist, consultant, and organizer in many things rape – and there are way too many. I approach the subject from an equality or human rights position and analysis. I am forever a feminist and work hard to practise within an intersectional framework that integrates gender with race, colonialism, ability, sexuality, and the resulting matrix of individual and group identities.

I publish and lecture under my court-ordered pseudonym Jane Doe and thought it relevant to do so here because the stigma attached to the use of the real names for women who are sexually assaulted (Doe 2009) – the shaming and blaming, and the danger – is also experienced by women who are sex workers, although they get to have much more interesting and expressive aliases.

In 1986, in the early days of my work – and my rape – I turned naturally for support to the women's movement of which I was, and am, a part. I received it in huge amounts and different forms, for which I am forever grateful. Sometimes, however, it was more than I wanted, or not what I wanted, or given to me in ways that made me feel as if I had no agency of my own. I was pathologized by all the institutional groups I dealt with – police, the courts, the media, and medical institutions – it wasn't like that with anti-violence and other VAW (violence against women) sector women, but at times it approached it and sometimes felt worse. The problem for me in the 1980s, which I could not articulate then, was that I experienced an often singular focus on my rape trauma (of which there was plenty). This focus, however, was in disregard of my ability to take action around what had happened to me, and it came from women I saw as my allies.

Since then, and during the past decade, I have had the opportunity to work closely with a Toronto sex workers' rights organization, Maggie's: Toronto Sex Workers Action Project, whose members have consulted with me on projects I have initiated (Griffiths 1999), on whose board of directors I have sat, on whose behalf (as well as my own) I have deputed to parliamentary subcommittees and police homicide and sexual assault squads, and with whom I have organized forums to address some of the issues presented here.[4] As a woman who has been raped, and often leads with this identity, I have never experienced any distancing as a "rape victim" or inappropriate care taking from the sex worker community – just a solidarity and sense of community, a seat at a banquet of feminist politics, joy, drama, comfort, activism, and generosity that Maggie's and other sex worker agencies have shared with me.

How to explain the difference? Why would I feel more at home in one sector and more a visiting relative in the other? Has radical feminism left some women behind?

The institutionalization of women's anti-violence services, especially VAW shelters and community-based rape/sexual assault centres, has become a subject of feminist research and debate (Bonisteel and Green 2005; Beres, Crow, and Gotell 2009).

There has been a commodification of services (and politics) in many rape crisis and sexual assault centres that privileges state, social work, and medical regulatory requirements of service delivery. They are conveyed by the singular framing of the women involved (increasingly adults who experienced childhood sexual abuse) as traumatized victims, often in need of help and medical intervention versus information, support, and advocacy (Bonisteel and Green 2005; Beres, Crow, and Gotell 2009). As Yaros (forthcoming), the director of a rape crisis centre, writes,

Too many of us continue to get lost in the overwhelming task of providing services to help individual women cope with the distress caused by their experiences of sexual assault, without the advocacy piece. Some of us drop the advocacy piece for the funding; some of us do it for legitimacy, credibility and recognition; some of us do it because, as women, we feel powerless to confront a system that does not allow for the reality of women's lived experiences, a system that at its most humane provides for a medical model response while women continue to be raped, murdered, assaulted and exploited. We end up contributing, in spite of ourselves, to the maintenance of the status quo.

The same positioning and models (social work, legal, and medical) are applied to sex workers, often in the form of remedial and exit programs. Community-based rape crisis/sexual assault agencies that tout progressive sex work policies on their websites do not enact them in meaningful ways or publicly ally with pro-sex-work groups. Some are openly prohibitionist in their policies and in print. All can be seen to collude and even benefit from regulatory and "law and order" practices of policing regarding sexual assault and sex work. Yet they would be shocked to hear me say so.

I am not speaking of all feminist agencies and positions, but the contradictions are in keeping with the fractures in feminism, where, for example, the Toronto Women's Bookstore carried pornography even while I witnessed other feminist groups march down Yonge Street, declaring that strip clubs exploited the women who worked in them. And, of course, they weren't talking about unfair labour practices, which would have been helpful. They were moralizing. Judging. Defining women's experiences for them and defining them as exploited but only in the guise of taking care of them – rescuing them.

Bound by Law

In the collaborative research I reference in this essay, we rejected the common characterization of sexually assaulted or sex-working women as fundamentally damaged and in need of protection. Instead, we applied a framework that centres their individual and collective agency.

We did not use the discourse of victimization ("rape victim," "prostituted woman," or "rape/prostitution survivor"), and avoided imposing a victimology analysis on women's experiences. Our philosophy necessitates an understanding of sex work as labour, although unquestionably, women who are sex workers are subject to sexual assault and other violence, especially given the criminalization and stigma under which they must live and work (Jeffrey and MacDonald 2006; Lewis and Shaver 2011).

We employed a qualitative research method designed to elicit rich personal accounts of women's own experiences and perceptions. In-depth interviews were conducted in five Canadian provinces with twelve women who had experienced sexual assault and fifteen who had worked in the sex trade. An additional ten sex-working women participated in focus group discussions. In all cases, a diversity of race, class, ability, and other social locations was represented. Another nineteen interviews were held with health care workers, law enforcement officers, and advocates in community and hospital-based sexual assault centres, for a total of fifty-six participants.

Our analysis of women's experiences exposed a pattern: The examined policies exerted control over women and could also cause, promote, or condone outright violence against the very women they purported to protect. The existing procuring law prevents adult women and their professional associates from establishing appropriate security measures and protocols that would afford them safety in their work in the sex trade. Similarly, women's community and individual attempts to develop proper and effective public safety practices such as postering and organized political action regarding sexual assault are open to criminalization.

It is well established that the majority of violence against women takes place in private and is perpetrated by men known to the women they abuse. Police rape warnings and the sexual assault evidence kit (SAEK), or rape kit, negate this reality by focusing solely on the rarer – and sensational – "stranger rape." At the same time, the procuring law jeopardizes sex-working women's safety in the personal realm and hinders access to general protections against violence by intimate male partners by reducing their relationships to "pimp-ho" stereotypes.

Our research provides compelling evidence that women experience the examined policies as oppressive, either because of the controlling impact on their lives and bodies or because of the fear, instability, or violence they can provoke. Our findings indicate that the policies are often intended more to advance law-and-order agendas than to protect or aid women.

Kit and KARE, or Who Cares?

The overriding purpose of the SAEK is the collection of forensic evidence for use in criminal proceedings and certainly not to prevent or examine the root cause of the violent crime women experience. Women working in prostitution also report that violence against them is considered only if it is linked to police or political agendas, such as the targeted prosecution of alleged procurers or so-called traffickers. In both cases, women's humanity and agency are debased, their beings literally reduced to physical crime sites that are cordoned off, plucked, processed, and picked over for use by the criminal system. The administration of the SAEK usually involves the probing of intimate body parts (vagina, anus, mouth), the pulling of hair, the snapping of photographs, clipping of nails, drawing of blood, and collecting of undergarments and past sexual, medical, and criminal histories, all geared toward gathering DNA and other evidence that is considered more reliable and genuine than women's own testimonies. In multiple jurisdictions, law enforcement programs have addressed unsolved and largely uninvestigated murders of women working as prostitutes by creating data banks in which sex workers can register their DNA in the form of hair and swab samples, as well as photographs and other personal information.

As is the case with sexually assaulted women, the gallop to forensic technology as a police crime-fighting tool negatively affects sex-working women. Project KARE is an investigational unit of the RCMP created in 2002 to "examine the deaths of several High Risk Missing Persons who were found in rural areas surrounding the city of Edmonton" (Project KARE, n.d.). Two officers assigned to the project agreed to take Gillies, Currie, and me on their regular ride around – they were interviewing women who are street-based sex workers in order to compile an official database containing their identifying information.

On a warm April evening, we drove around for nearly an hour until the officers spotted a woman they thought they recognized and pulled up beside her in their unmarked tinted-window SUV. They greeted her in a friendly manner, identified themselves as police officers, and asked if she were familiar with Project KARE. She said no. One officer explained their mission with assurances that they were not about to arrest or criminally interrogate her and asked if she was willing to participate. He assured her that she could stop the process whenever she chose and that it would not take long. She said yes. The officers took turns asking her a series of personal questions including her age, address, place of birth, marital and parental status, mother's maiden name, preferred drug use, HIV status, and work (sexual) practices. While we remained in the van, one officer jumped out and asked her to pluck a hair from her head for a DNA sample. He then grabbed his camera and took her photo along with a few shots of her tattoos, for which she had to remove some of her clothing. The woman was visibly uncomfortable, but the officers pushed ahead, increasing their pace of questioning. It was only when she firmly declined further cooperation that they stopped and asked her to sign a consent form. The police thanked her, and she walked back into the night.

In both the SAEK and Project KARE, women are classified as victims or villains, or both. Physical material taken from the bodies of women to compile the SAEK produces the necessary evidence to support their stories as victims of rape or to reveal them as liars. DNA evidence determines if there will be a police investigation and is used to assist the Crown in presenting its case – if it gets that far.[5] With Project KARE, the gathered information is used to assist the police to identify women working as prostitutes who are murdered. If an arrest is made in that murder, the information becomes central to the Crown's case. Further, in the instances of both sexual assault and sex work, women are requested/required by police to sign consent forms indicating their willingness to participate in the collection of DNA and other bodily evidence. It was our observation, supported by first-person accounts of conflict and power imbalances between police and women whom we interviewed, that the nature of the consent given does not meet the social or legal standard of what would constitute truly informed consent (Doe forthcoming).

When feminists support the use of the SAEK or Project KARE without knowledge of their intent and efficacy, they reinforce a criminal justice system that does not function in the best interest of the women involved and instead criminalizes their behaviour.

A Warning about Warnings

Women's narratives reveal many shared or parallel experiences of sexual assault and prostitution policies, which in turn reflect and support the academic discourse about public and private women. An example of this is the practice of warnings. At the turn of the nineteenth century, media, social, and religious organizations colluded to issue multiple warnings to "keep your girls at home" (Valverde 1991). Ostensibly designed to protect good women, these warnings encouraged an atmosphere of moral panic that focused on women who worked in prostitution. A "Warnings to Girls" published in 1914 by the Social Service Council of Canada capitalized on the misconception of the social evil of prostitution and the women who ran brothels: "Do not loiter in public places, and remember that there are women as well as men in strange cities or traveling by train who are watching for chances to decoy the innocent. They have many traps such as pretending to be in a faint, or wishing to be taken home; claiming to know you or to represent some society for the protection of strangers etc." (quoted in Valverde 1991, 98).

Despite the passage of nearly a century, such infantilization of adult women informs current police warnings around stranger rape and continues to serve a similar goal of controlling women's access to, and use of, public space.[6] The linkage of sexual violation to a public space allows us to define the woman who is wilfully outside of a marital or normative relationship as "public" or "bad." As such, she can be perceived as common property to men at large. Conversely, good women stay home; they are not prostitutes and are thus afforded protection through warnings. However, any necessary or chosen forays into public space make them available to penalty by the (public) stranger rapist.[7] Women's failure to comply with the warning casts suspicion on the value they place on their own virtue, making them complicit in their own rapes.

For women working in the sex trade, the rules of engagement embedded in warnings are very hard not to break. Sex workers, especially prostitutes, are seen as public women who are sexually available and therefore undeserving of equal protection. At the same time, the criminalization of common work activities negates personal relationships and forbids female sex workers a private identity. Not only is there a conceptual notion of a public-private divide, it is entrenched in the law.

At Risk and Risky Women

Women navigate their lives with the understanding that they can be at risk of rape. Indeed, social agencies, especially police, exaggerate this danger specific to public risk. Once raped, women are simultaneously cast as victims and as contributing to the risk of other women if they do not report their rape. Prostitution laws are an exemplar of this at risk/risky tension. Procuring laws serve to protect women from the perceived evil and risk of prostitution – namely, that of the "pimp." Once "fallen," however, the same women are seen as putting the safety and value of other women (and indeed, entire neighbourhoods) at risk by their actions and are subject to criminal laws that govern their behaviour (Bruckert forthcoming; see also Chapter 13 in this volume).

It would appear that we are still reluctant to deal with female sexuality outside of simplistic good girl/bad girl dichotomies. Sexually assaulted and sex-working women have a foot in each, and there is an element of victimhood or risk in both groups. There is no room for sexually assaulted or sex-working women to behave outside of these paradigms – no room for intelligent, active,

happy women who are seen to have experience outside of consensual, monogamous, heterosexual, and preferably married norms. They are, instead, bound
by law. Women's own lived experiences, observations, and analyses do not match
the state's interpretations and remedies; it is not surprising that women experience the purported protectionist policies under examination as controlling and
restricting of their activities and choices.

The fallout of this state protectionism affects all women. When equality-
seeking women in academia and VAW sectors are not aware of the nature and
the extent of the damage inflicted by existing laws on sex-working and/or
sexually assaulted women, our negligence must be challenged. When we sit on
state or police committees in what we know are vain attempts to address their
negligence, or when we partner with religious organizations to address prostitution, or we counsel the women we work with to enter systems that do not operate
in their best interest, our collusion, conscious or not, supports the oppression
of all women.

Police Culture, Sexual Assault, and Sex Work

Since 1998, I have been researching and assessing the policing of sexual assault,
the policies that govern it, and the training that officers receive to investigate
the crime (Doe, Dale, and Bain 2010). In 2006, the Toronto Police Service Board
(TPSB) employed Beverly Bain and me to attend, observe, and review the curriculum at the two-week Sexual Assault and Child Abuse (SACA) training
program. The SACA program is mandatory for all detectives tasked with investigating sexual assault.[8] Sexist and racist stereotypes and language permeated
the training content, and we found evidence of adherence to rape mythology,
especially the notion of false allegations. We also observed and documented
the absence of a gendered analysis specific to adult women, the lack of an anti-
racist analysis and philosophy, the use of gender-neutral and re-victimizing
language, and the uniform lack of opportunity for questions, discussion, and
interactive learning methods. Racist depictions of immigrant women, the overwhelming use of images of black men (in baseball caps) as examples of rapists,
jokes about Al Qaeda, and the understanding of rape as sexual gratification
were also documented.

When the police trainers presented their SACA module on sex work and
the Toronto Service's Special Victims Unit, which is mandated to investigate the
sexual assault of sex workers, their sole focus was youth and children. The session began with an outdated police training video featuring three teenage

prostitutes, bad girls who had run away, or lost girls who were forgotten, all of whom were read as deviant. One died of AIDS and another was beaten to death by a "trick," or "john." The mythical pimp was portrayed as a black man with flashy clothes. The third girl escaped and entered an exit program but could never live happily, because she was forever after traumatized by her sex work.

The SACA course content then turned to the subject of exit or diversion programs for sex workers who had been criminally charged. A young woman who was once a teenage prostitute addressed the class of police officers. She was employed by SOS, a Toronto-based agency affiliated with the police and designed to work with street prostitutes. Her presentation was compelling as she was a good speaker who quickly brought her audience of burly cops to tears. Her story was essentially an updated version of the training video we had just watched, and it included a long piece about how fabulous the police were to her and the benefits of the exit program she had entered. Interestingly, she was a graduate of a counsellor advocate program where I once taught; the program is feminist-based and proclaims a pro-sex-worker position. But, by naming her authority as a graduate of the program, with its feminist focus, and weaving it into her position of "If I can get out of that horror, you can too!" she aligned herself with anti-sex-work prohibitionist feminists and religious groups.

Despite some improvements in the investigation of sexual assault against sex workers in Toronto, the concerns espoused by the Special Victims Unit do not hide its bottom line – that it, and the police generally, continues to support the law-and-order position regarding prostitution when, ironically, the police are best positioned to speak to the laws' negative consequences for women. The same is true for sexual assault legislation and protocols that do not work in women's best interests; police who investigate those crimes acknowledge the failure to report and the abysmal conviction rate.

Our report and assessment of the SACA training program included recommendations for improvements. These were presented to the police and generally stated the imperatives that the training should be redesigned within a gendered anti-racist analysis and must focus on adult women. Additionally, the training should be delivered by professional adult educators with expertise in the subject of sexual assault, not by untrained police officers. To date, we have not been informed of any actions taken in response to our recommendations. The continued participation of feminist anti-violence workers on police or state-led committees to address violent crime and sex work can be seen as a factor in depoliticizing feminist anti-violence work in favour of social service, medical, and other state models.

What's a Good Feminist to Do?

This chapter holds that both sex workers and women who have been sexually assaulted are similarly cast as sexually damaged or defiled and that this commonality is reflected in state policies of protection, even though sex work and sexual assault are independent areas of policy and experience. This linkage has been based on a concept of shared victimhood, specifically an assault on women's sexuality, which is constructed as an assault on their entire personhood.

Legal, social work, and medical models of service categorize sex workers and women who have been sexually assaulted as victims or survivors. Such labels assign a lack of agency and activity to sex-working and sexually assaulted women. The training and culture of police rape investigation presumes that the women who experience sexual assault are to be observed. This preoccupation with women's sexual behaviour is also central to investigations involving sex work.

Radical, and increasingly other, feminist practice also categorizes raped women as victims/survivors and more recently as "thrivers" requiring assistance, but it seldom equivocates in the classification of "prostituted women" as broken and without agency. This is borne out in feminist positions that support the use of the SAEK and the criminalization of sex work in the presumed interest of women's well-being, but without their direction and input.

Feminist counselling, shelters, information centres, and a whole array of legal, health, educational, and material aid for women who experience violence are critical, and the work of feminists to provide them is laudable. The same cannot be said, however, for services for sex workers, especially for women working in prostitution. Whereas the "deviant" label has largely shifted to that of "victim" in social and other programs, there is still a sense of sex workers' deviance, inclusive of the risk their occupation is seen to project to other women. Many feminists have joined and champion exit programs and prohibitionist politics as solutions for these "victims."

What Exit?

Exit programs are about rescuing and rehabilitating sex workers, and are not an assessment of what women want – which absolutely can, but does not necessarily, include transitioning out of the sex trade (see also Chapter 7 in this volume). The programs are not structured to allow women to exercise their own agency or choice in the matter or the work to which they are directed through the program, which is often limited to gender-stratified, low-waged occupations in word processing, food service, and the garment industry.[9] Exit programs aren't about working with women to see what they want, but are instead another arm of criminal justice that has been rolled into social work practice.

The police enforce criminal law against sex workers with the argument that sex workers must hit rock bottom in jail, where they will then be safe so that they can be sent to an exit program. The development of exit programs in multiple jurisdictions in Canada was based on the recognition that criminalization of prostitution alone was not enough – there needed to be a system that would reprogram women while they were in custody via a court order. Women are arrested under current laws and are given the option of attending an exit program or facing criminal charges and possible incarceration. Which would you choose?

In Agustin's (2005, 96) article on feminist responses to migrant sex workers, the limits and political costs of a rescue and rehabilitation approach to services for women are precisely articulated: "Services, as essential as they are, will not change the underlying sexist system and, when state-funded, may even give the illusion of government benevolence. Instead of demanding greater freedom for women, such an orientation risks complicity in feeding the police and courts additional information and augmenting their power to check, constrain, stigmatize and criminalize women. Licking our wounds and those of other women may offer some comfort but it implies retreat – called 'return' (a euphemism for expulsion), 'rehabilitation' (euphemism for confinement and forced conformity) and 'warning' to other women that they had better stay home." Although the author is talking about sex work in a transnational context, the same analysis can easily be applied to state-run services and programs for sex workers domestically, as well as for women who have been sexually assaulted.

Obviously, there are differences between the "prostitute" and the "rape victim." There are multiple laws and policies that cast sex-working women as criminals, whereas raped women are cast first as victims and then later as lying or traumatized (depending on the outcome of the police investigation).[10] But the sexual nature of the act in which one has chosen to engage and the act committed against the other is a common ground. The sexual character of both acts and the sexist quality of patriarchy organize a good/bad morality-based understanding of the women involved as sexually defiled, virtuously suspect, and without agency, choice, or activity of their own.

My interviews and direct work experience, however, reveal an entirely different picture; women are vibrant and reflective, and they have a political understanding of the crime committed against them or the criminalizing of their actions – in spite of the state and individual oppressions they may have faced. The victim/survivor/thriver hierarchy does not allow for their acumen, joyfulness, and capacity. Sex-working and sexually assaulted women are cast and treated as damaged *because* of views of their sexuality as defiled and are thereby "sexed classed" within the larger group known as "women."

Sexed classed women continue to wear and bear certain historical constructs of female sexuality once placed on a broad base of women. Legal, religious, and medical traditions have constructed female sexuality itself as unbridled or submissive, thereby undeserving of and unresponsive to basic rights such as voting, property ownership, reproductive and economic control, and so on. Although equality has been established in some of these areas, in some places (for some women), we continue to equate women's behaviour with female sexuality. How individuals or groups of women behave their sexuality will then determine their status and safety, publicly and privately.

Sexed classed women and the degree to which they are Othered within the broader group of women are highly informed by sexualized notions of race, ability, and class. Racialized and colonized women are fetishized by racist practices and stereotypes. Even within the two categories of sexual assault victim and sex worker, the raped black woman is treated differently from the white sex-working woman. Ableist prejudices contribute to the higher rate of sexual assault against women with disabilities and their exclusion from most sex work (Odette forthcoming). Aboriginal women in both groups experience a higher degree of violence, including murder. Working-class women and women who live in poverty continue to be seen as sexually irresponsible.

Part of many "good" women's defence or response to paternalistic and protectionist policies is to support them – in order not to be (further) sexed classed themselves. The traditional family beliefs that no man whom they know would rape or respectfully and consciously buy sex, and the construction of the evil pimp and the rapist as the stranger, are instances of such denial. The adherence to criminal justice law-and-order policies as solutions, the self-censuring of their movements, and the denial of their own sexual nature and freedom are further examples. And possibly, that effect is more deliberate, more traditional than we like to think. The patriarchal state neutralizes the risk and threat that female sexuality is seen to represent. Laws and policies work toward this end when they are grounded in stereotypical notions of female sexuality that classify women as damaged victims. Although raped and sex-working women are the obvious targets, the fallout of such state protectionism affects all women.

Conclusion

A few months ago, I was gifted with a copy of Pheterson's (1996) collection of essays titled *The Prostitution Prism*. The author writes of the whore stigma as the lens or prism through which all female sexuality is viewed, understood, and graded. She positions such characterizations of female sexuality as "an official and traditional mechanism of social control inextricable from issues as diverse as migration, health care, sexual violence, autonomy, employment and freedom of speech" (ibid., back cover). Her essays challenge us to identify individually and socially with whore constructs of all women that underpin our institutions and perpetuate sexist, racist, and other oppressive stereotypes. I wept and my heart leapt as I read the book, wondering "Where has this been? Why haven't I seen it before?" as I wrote "I love you" in the margins.

I was a little less thrilled to read that Pheterson had explored territory very similar to mine and coined the term "sex classed" over a decade ago to represent all women affected by the whore stigma. Less thrilled because her seminal work did not surface in literature reviews on sex work/prostitution or female sexuality. Less thrilled because my own work could have been so much stronger, and the theory of all North American feminists examining these issues could be clearer and more informed because of Pheterson's contributions and those of others. If only we knew about them. This speaks to the importance of the emergence of critical and feminist theoretical approaches that offer a framework from which to think about equality and sex work – not as mutually exclusive, but necessarily integrated – and the failure of North American feminist legal, academic, and other researchers and agencies to fund, access, and utilize it. The challenge is to do so, to lay down the ideological and morality-based beliefs and systems that buttress our criminal justice system and other of our institutions. The rewards for equality-seeking women and men will be enormous.

Acknowledgments
I wish to acknowledge and appreciate the support and contributions of Kara Gillies and Jenn Clamen in writing this piece.

Notes
1 Sex-working men also face separations, challenges, and criminalization, which require more research and learning. They are, however (and as with the sexual assault of men versus women), located in differing social, historic, and cultural contexts. The current discussion is specific to adult biological cis and transgendered women.
2 Legislation that criminalizes female sex workers is outlined in the Introduction in this volume. Raped women are threatened and charged criminally when they retract their reports or are seen as not cooperating with the police investigation.

3   This research project was supported through a grant from the Status of Women Independent Research Fund. Due to Conservative government cuts to that fund, it remains unpublished.

4   I coordinated two provincial forums, "What Works for Sex Workers" Part 1, in 2010, and Part 2, in 2012, convened by Maggie's. They were designed to allow sex-working women the opportunity to inform VAW and other community organizations of their requirements when accessing those agencies.

5   The conviction rate for sexual assault cases that do make it to court hovers between 1 and 5 percent nationally. This includes reports unfounded or not cleared by the police (Johnson forthcoming).

6   For example, women are told the following: don't open the windows, don't take shortcuts, don't use underground parking, don't use the parks, don't take the bus, don't leave your drink unattended, don't work late at the university, don't go out, and so forth.

7   The majority of rapes/sexual assaults are committed by men who are well known to the women involved (Statistics Canada 2006).

8   We presented the executive summary of our assessment of the training to the TPSB in February 2007.

9   The Durbar Mahila Samanwaya Committee (DMSC) in West Bengal, India (www.durbar.org) and the Thai Empower Foundation (www.empowerfoundation.org), both well-established sex-worker-run groups, organized campaigns to protest state programs to rehabilitate sex workers into low-paid piecework in their country's garment industry.

10 In Toronto, the Sexual Assault Squad of the Sex Crimes Unit refers to women whom it believes to have filed false allegations as "Alligators." It has also been disclosed that alligator stickers adorn(ed) police computers as tallies to indicate how many "false allegations" have been uncovered.

References

Agustin, L. 2005. Migrants in the mistress's house: Other voices in the "trafficking" debate. *Social Politics: International Studies in Gender, State and Society* 12, 1: 96-117.

–. 2007. *Sex at the margins: Migration, labour markets and the rescue industry.* London: Zed Books.

Beres, M.A., B. Crow, and L. Gotell. 2009. The perils of institutionalization in neoliberal times: Results of a national survey of Canadian sexual assault and rape crisis centres. *Canadian Journal of Sociology* 34, 1: 135-63.

Bonisteel, M., and L. Green. 2005. Implications of the shrinking space for feminist antiviolence advocacy. Paper presented at Twelfth Biennial Canadian Social Welfare Policy Conference, Fredericton. 16-18 June. http://awcca.ca.

Bruckert, C. Forthcoming. Rethinking the prostitution debates: Transcending structural stigma in systemic responses to sex work. *Canadian Journal of Criminology and Criminal Justice.*

Currie, N., and K. Gillies. 2006. Bound by law: How Canada's protectionist public policies in the areas of both rape and prostitution limit women's choices, agency and activities. Unpublished report. Status of Women Canada.

Doe, J. 2004. *The story of Jane Doe: A book about rape.* Toronto: Vintage Canada.

–. 2009. What's in a name? Who benefits from the publication ban in sexual assault trials? In *Lessons from the identity trail: Anonymity, privacy and identity in a networked society,* ed. I. Kerr, V. Steeves, and C. Lucock, 265-81. New York: Oxford University Press.

–. Forthcoming (October 2012). Who benefits from the sexual assault evidence kit? In *Sexual assault in Canada: Law, legal practice and women's activism,* ed. E. Sheehy. Ottawa: University of Ottawa Press.

Doe, J., A. Dale, and B. Bain. 2010. A new chapter in feminist organizing: The sexual assault audit steering committee. *Canadian Woman Studies* 28, 1: 6-14.

Griffiths, J. 1999. *Review of the investigation of sexual assaults: Toronto Police Service.* Toronto: Toronto Audit Services. http://www.walnet.org/jane_doe/griffiths-991025.pdf.

Jackson, C., and B. Brents. 2010. Why decriminalizing sex work is good for all women. *Ms Magazine,* 1 November. http://msmagazine.com/.

Jeffrey, L.A., and G. MacDonald. 2006. *Sex workers in the Maritimes talk back.* Vancouver: UBC Press.

Johnson, H. Forthcoming (October 2012). Limits of a criminal justice response: Trends in police and court processing of sexual assault. In *Sexual assault in Canada: Law, legal practice and women's activism,* ed. E. Sheehy. Ottawa: University of Ottawa Press.

Kamir, O. 2006. *Framed: Women in law and film.* Durham: Duke University Press.

Lewis, J., and F.M. Shaver. 2011. The regulation of adult sex work and its impact on the safety, security and well-being of people working in the sex industry in Canada. In *Global perspectives on prostitution and sex trafficking: Europe, Latin America, North America, and global,* ed. R.L. Dalla, L.M. Baker, J. DeFrain, and C. Williamson. Lanham, MD: Lexington Books.

Odette, F. Forthcoming (October 2012). Sexual assault and disabled women ten years after Jane Doe. In *Sexual assault in Canada: Law, legal practice and women's activism,* ed. E. Sheehy. Ottawa: University of Ottawa Press.

Pheterson G. 1993. *The whore stigma: Female dishonour and male unworthiness.* Durham: Duke University Press.

–. 1996. *The prostitution prism.* Amsterdam: Amsterdam University Press.

Projansky, S. 2001. *Watching rape: Film and television in postfeminist culture.* New York: New York University Press.

Project KARE. n.d. Project KARE. http://www.kare.ca/.

Schur, E. 1984. *Labeling women deviant: Gender, stigma and social control.* New York: Random House.

Statistics Canada. 2006. *2006 census.* Ottawa: Government of Canada. http://www12.statcan.gc.ca.

Valverde, M. 1991. *The age of light, soap, and water: Moral reform in English Canada, 1885-1925.* Canadian social history series. Toronto: McClelland and Stewart.

Yaros, D. Forthcoming (October 2012). Where has all the anger gone? In *Sexual assault in Canada: Law, legal practice and women's activism,* ed. E. Sheehy. Ottawa: University of Ottawa Press.

Case Cited

Jane Doe v. Board of Commissioners of Police for the Municipality of Metropolitan Toronto (1998), 39 O.R. (3d) 487 (Ont. Ct. G.D.).

13

Going 'round Again:
The Persistence of Prostitution-Related Stigma

JACQUELINE LEWIS, FRANCES M. SHAVER, AND ELEANOR MATICKA-TYNDALE

> As a social process, stigma operates by producing and
> reproducing social structures of power, hierarchy, class, and exclusion
> and by transforming difference into social inequality.
>
> – Tempalski et al. (2007, 1252)

Although sex work is a lawful revenue-generating activity in Canada, the stigmatization and marginalization of the sex industry and people working in it is pervasive. Even in settings where sex work has been decriminalized such as New Zealand (Jordan 2005; Abel and Fitzgerald 2010) and parts of Australia (Jeffreys and Sullivan 2009; Jeffreys, Mathews, and Thomas 2010), stigmatization and marginalization persist. The perpetuation of negative perceptions of the sex industry and people working in it is often grounded in an incomplete and misleading portrait of sex work that ultimately threatens the health, safety, well-being, and rights of workers. In this chapter we explore how the stigmatization of sex workers in Canada interferes with their ability to attain full citizenship rights and the recognition of their work as labour even in the face of progressive legislative change.

Erving Goffman (1963) is credited with drawing the concept of stigma to the attention of academics and non-academics alike (see also Chapter 19 in this volume). According to Goffman (ibid., 3), stigma "refers to an attribute that is deeply discrediting," one that is interpreted as a symptom of an underlying moral failing and/or a failure to live up to an agreed-upon social norm or value.

It affects how an individual is viewed and treated by other members of society and is often used to justify prejudicial treatment or marginalization by family and friends, employers and co-workers, health care professionals, government workers, and policy makers. It also results in the self-denigration among many who are stigmatized. In an effort to enhance the explanatory power of Goffman's conception of stigma, Parker and Aggleton recently combined Goffman's work on stigma with Foucault's (1978) work on "the cultural production of difference in the service of power" (Parker and Aggleton 2003, 17). This combined model produces a better understanding of how stigmatization serves to maintain entrenched differentials in power (that is, to maintain the status quo). They argue that we need to examine the role of power structures in the application of stigma, whereby the mark of significant difference, or stigmatization, is used to draw distinctions between groups of people and to insert them into structures of power. Thus, those individuals perceived to be aligned with culturally preferred norms are deemed worthy and afforded full rights and powers of citizenship. Those who resist or challenge such alignment are culturally defined as deviant and therefore deemed unworthy. Parker and Aggleton (ibid., 17, emphasis added) note, "Stigma and stigmatization function, quite literally, at the point of intersection between *culture, power* and *difference* – and it is only by exploring the relationships between these different categories that it becomes possible to understand stigma and stigmatization not merely as an isolated phenomenon, or expressions of individual attitudes or cultural values, but as central to the constitution of social order." It is this conceptualization of stigma that we will apply to sex work and sex workers.

Harm and Stigma

Research on sex work, including our own (STAR 2004, 2006; Lewis et al. 2005; Shaver 2005; Lewis 2010; Lewis and Shaver 2011; Shaver, Lewis, and Maticka-Tyndale 2011), has illustrated the impact of stigma and its management on a diverse array of workers' lives (street-based, escorts, masseuses, dancers, men, women, and transgender sex workers).[1] As Jeffrey and MacDonald (2006, 127) point out, "Stigmatizing attitudes that paint sex workers as backward, victims, uneducated, addicted, and whores ... contribute to the climate of violence and marginalization that sex workers face." For sex workers, stigma plays a persistent role in their everyday reality. It is felt at the individual level on the job in response to the daily treatment they experience from customers and the public. Stigma is manifested at the structural level in the reflection and reinforcement of stigmatizing notions in the policies and practices of governments and social institutions that control aspects of sex work. It is the persistence and pervasiveness of this stigma – across time and social spheres, and in the face of evidence that refutes the assumptions and beliefs upon which it is based – that serve to maintain workers' marginalization and to justify their continued discriminatory treatment. Even when progressive policy change is on the brink of being implemented, efforts to maintain or reinforce the status quo and the established social order regarding the position of sex workers in society are readily apparent.

On 28 September 2010, the Ontario Superior Court judgment by Justice Himel quashed several sections of the Canadian Criminal Code that apply to sex work (*Bedford v. Canada* 2010). Her ruling highlighted the many efforts aimed at keeping sex workers "in their place" and officially recognized the harms associated with some of the prostitution-related sections of the Criminal Code: the role that stigma, marginalization, and discrimination play in the continued victimization of sex workers and the denial of their Charter rights (see also Chapter 15 in this volume). The harm-reduction and rights-based discourse echoed in Justice Himel's judgment adds powerful support to the worker, activist, and academic voices that have long been calling for policy change.

Concerns with Canadian prostitution laws, including the harm they cause people working in the sex industry, have been repeatedly voiced by witnesses who have appeared before government committees struck on the issue since the 1980s (see also Chapter 14 in this volume). It was the most recent of these, the Subcommittee on Solicitation Laws Review (SSLR) hearings, that offered the greatest hope for change because, for the first time, sex workers were officially invited as witnesses and were included as members of research teams to testify about the effects of Canadian law and policy on their lives (SSLR 2006). If workers' voices were finally heard, if the damage resulting from the silencing of this segment of the population were made evident, if the harms tied to the current prohibitionist policy were clear (such as the Pickton murders, which were the impetus for the SSLR hearings), then perhaps the government would be forced to enact harm-reduction-oriented policy change. However, before the SSLR could finalize and release its report, the federal Liberal government was defeated by the Conservative Party of Canada in the 23 January 2006 federal election. This party change likely influenced both the subcommittee's final report and the subsequent failure of the Canadian government to enact policy change.

After the 2006 election, the SSLR was reconstituted to include more members from the Conservative Party and fewer members from the Opposition parties.

The result of this change was readily apparent in its final report. The report failed "to call for amendments to the *Criminal Code* provisions which have been demonstrated to increase the health and safety threats faced by sex workers" (Mar and Betteridge 2007, 15). One of the few points receiving unanimous agreement among subcommittee members and across parties was that "the status quo was not acceptable" (SSLR 2006, 86).[2] Although on the surface this acknowledgment sounded promising, the discourse used to detail this conclusion is problematic due to its reliance on concepts such as "preventing prostitution," "exploitation," and "harm to communities." Despite views from members of all three Opposition parties (Liberal, New Democratic, and Bloc Québécois) that "sexual activities between consenting adults that do not harm others ... should not be prohibited by the state" (ibid., 90), the framing of what needs to be done contained in the unanimous points of agreement reinforced the continued use of criminal law to control sex work, as well as the division between "us" and "them." The division – between the members of "decent" society and those who are seen to be a threat to the moral order – reinforces and maintains the stigmatization of sex workers and their position on the margins of society. This limits their access to power and their ability to resist or challenge traditional cultural attitudes such as those reflected in the position of the Conservative Party members of the SSLR: "The Conservatives do not believe it is possible for the state to create isolated conditions in which the consensual provision of sex in exchange for money does not harm others ... All prostitution has a social cost, and ... any effort by the state to decriminalize prostitution would impoverish all Canadians – and Canadian women in particular – by signaling that the commodification and invasive exploitation of a woman's body is acceptable" (ibid.).

Since the release of this report, as was the case of prior government reports, little has been done to improve the situation for people working in the sex industry. Instead, the report simply reinscribed prostitution as the exploitation of persons (particularly women and children) and the supposed relationship between prostitution and a variety of social harms.

We saw something similar occurring shortly after the announcement of Justice Himel's Ontario Superior Court judgment about the constitutionality of sections of the Criminal Code. An overview of media coverage reveals government efforts to provide alternative constructions of sex work and sex workers to those detailed in the judgment – constructions that reinforce mainstream cultural (mis)understandings of sex work and echo common rationales used to support the structural inequality experienced by workers. Representatives of Ottawa spoke out against the ruling and made their plans to appeal the decision. It is here that we see issues tied to culture, power, and difference in action (Parker and Aggleton 2003). For example, federal justice minister Rob Nicholson asserted, "It is the government's prerogative to decide how best to protect prostitutes and the communities in which they ply their trade. 'The Government is very concerned about the [Ontario] Superior Court's decision'" (quoted in Makin 2010). In contrast to the empirical evidence that Justice Himel detailed in her judgment (*Bedford v. Canada* 2010), the discourse used by the government continues to reinforce the acceptability of the victimization and murder of sex workers. Of particular interest here is the language that was used and the cultural values cited in an effort to challenge a significant threat to existing cultural understandings of sex work. Prostitution is presented as harmful "because it is [seen to be] immoral and offensive and therefore threatening to moral order and the stability of Canadian society" (Lewis 2000a, 209; 2010).

In opposition to calls for rights and harm reduction for workers, what was heard from Conservative politicians leading up to the Ontario Court of Appeal hearing on 23 November 2010 were claims of the harms that would result if the decision were not overturned. The harms were framed as threats to the wall that separates and isolates sex work and sex workers from "respectable society" and that prevents the infiltration of the sex industry and its associated harms (such as drugs, violence, and exploitation) into communities. These claims served to elevate public concern and to reinforce the continued stigmatization of prostitution. Newspapers headlined federal positions in the following ways: "Tory MP Sees 'the Nation as the Pimp' If Prostitution Ruling Stands" (Taber 2010); "Ontario About to Become Hooker Hub, Feds Warn" (Tibbetts 2010). Echoing the Conservative government conclusions in the SSLR report, Crown lawyer Michael Morris noted in his arguments to extend the stay past 23 November 2010 that Himel's "decision will create profound and immediate consequences upon communities, neighbourhoods and women engaged in prostitution" (quoted in Nguyen 2010a). Government lawyers argued that the decision would result in "irreparable harms to the public interest" (Tibbetts 2010). The Government of Ontario warned that the ruling could spark "vigilantism by residents who will begin to see an increase of street prostitution – and other illegal activities associated with it – move into their neighbourhoods" (Nguyen 2010b). The general message was summed up by Prime Minister Stephen Harper: "The government's position is very clear. There are laws on the books. The government supports those laws. The government is in court to encourage the court to uphold those laws ... We believe that the prostitution trade is bad for society. That's a strong view held by our government and I think by most Canadians" (quoted in Nguyen 2010c).

Jacqueline Lewis, Frances M. Shaver, and Eleanor Maticka-Tyndale

Harper's comment restates the party stance regarding prostitution, a stance taken on other controversial social issues (such as marijuana policy and supervised injection sites). The Conservative Party has consistently positioned itself as the party that supports the status quo – the social order that reinforces the divide between Canadians. This divide affords full citizenship rights and powers to those on one side while denying or limiting those rights and powers to those on the other. It is achieved by creating and reinforcing a particular culture of "knowledge" that privileges a pseudo-science founded on a moral ideology that ignores evidence grounded in research that follows scientific methods (Weitzer 2010). Thus, evidence demonstrating harm to the health, well-being, and civil liberties caused by marijuana prohibitions (Senate Special Committee on Illegal Drugs 2002) and evidence of the benefits of supervised injection sites in eliminating overdose deaths and reducing injection-related transmission of HIV and hepatitis C (Broadhead et al. 2002; Elliott 2008) are ignored. With respect to prostitution, rather than attending to the evidence of the harm resulting from the Criminal Code statutes and the arguments for harm-reduction policy presented before the SSLR and all preceding commissions as well as in *Bedford v. Canada,* the Conservative government continues to base its support of the existing policy on opinion grounded in a morality-based discourse of harm. Similar to Lewis's (2000a, 204) examination of the discourse surrounding the push for the lap-dancing ban in Ontario, following Justice Himel's judgment, we see the government using a discourse designed to "elevate latent public fears and concerns regarding the threat posed by sex workers to public morality, health, safety and way of life." The use of such discourse, however, is in direct contrast with the Vienna Declaration of Human Rights, which states that policy "should be based on evidence, not ideology" (United Nations 1993).

The rationale provided for the continued prohibition of prostitution and the maintenance of the status quo is one we have heard repeatedly. Under the guise of protecting the family, women, children, neighbourhoods, the good of society, and even sex workers themselves, we are told it is necessary to maintain a prohibition on sex-work-related activities. This position rationalizes laws that perpetuate the harm experienced by sex workers as necessary for the protection of those very workers as well as of society in general. It privileges one segment of the population and vilifies another. In the case of the motion to stay the judgment of Justice Himel, the arguments made by the attorney general of Canada privilege a claimed public interest that involves protecting the public (and sex workers) from anticipated harms that are expected to result from changes to the Criminal Code (*Bedford v. Canada (Attorney General)* 2010).

The well-documented and life-threatening actual harms that result from criminal laws are given, at best, only minor consideration.

The ideology reflected in various court documents, such as the attorney general's factum in *Bedford v. Canada,* and media statements by government officials, such as those cited above, frame the harm experienced by sex workers in a particular way and reassure the public that something is being done, that existing laws are working, and that the government knows best how to deal with this "problem." The numerous government commissions add to the illusion that Ottawa is taking action – despite the scant attention paid to their conclusions and recommendations. By diverting the focus from the harms caused to sex workers by criminal laws, the status quo is maintained.

Destigmatizing Sex Work and Sex Workers

Given the degree and persistence of stigma surrounding sex workers' lives, the challenge is how to reduce it. The literature suggests that attitudinal change is difficult to achieve (Bobo, Kluegel, and Smith 1997) and that there are limits to stigma reduction (Stryker 1980). However, there is hope! There is a history of disenfranchised groups (such as the disabilities rights, women's rights, civil rights, gay rights, and rights for people living with HIV/AIDS movements) working to support and empower their members and advocate for change (Gussow and Tracy 1968; Murray 1984; Lewis 2000b; Brown, Mcintyre, and Trujillo 2003). In terms of people who work in the sex industry, since the emergence of the Canadian Organization for the Rights of Prostitutes in 1983 and of Maggie's: Toronto Sex Workers Action Project in 1986, a growing number of grassroots community organizations and activists have been challenging cultural conceptions of sex work, sex workers, and the laws used to control their work and lives. These include Stella in Montreal, PEERS in Vancouver and Victoria, PACE in Vancouver, DERA and POWER in Ottawa, and Stepping Stone in Halifax. Such efforts have been supplemented by various research and policy groups (Canadian HIV/AIDS Legal Network and STAR; see also Pivot 2004, 2006). Education of the public to counter common myths and assumptions about people working in the sex industry as a strategy to reduce stigmatization has been adopted as a core objective of FIRST (Feminists Advocating for Rights and Equality for Sex Workers), a recently formed group (see also Chapter 9 in this volume). In late 2010, FIRST released its inaugural public service announcement on television and the Internet (FIRST, n.d.) wherein it countered the stereotype that sex workers are profoundly and inherently different from "ordinary" people.

Jacqueline Lewis, Frances M. Shaver, and Eleanor Maticka-Tyndale

Parker and Aggleton argue that, in addition to grassroots efforts for change, structural changes in the form of evidence-based policy reforms that focus on harm reduction and human rights are essential. This requires a government that privileges empirical evidence, even when it runs counter to party ideology; it also requires protecting the rights of all citizens, including the most marginalized. Whether we are looking at the institutionalization of gay marriage, the legalization of marijuana, the recognition of minority group rights (for women, gays, people of colour, and people who are mentally or physically challenged), or the decriminalization of prostitution, policy change – especially policy that fosters equality and rights for all – can facilitate attitudinal and behavioural change and lessen stigma.[3] According to Parker and Aggleton (2003, 22), "Judicial and policy interventions in many settings have shown real effectiveness in impeding the worst impact of ... stigmatization and discrimination." Governments can create a package to stimulate change, engaging directly with disenfranchised communities to design and implement educational initiatives that supplement grassroots campaigns. In addition, although "we cannot ask [or expect] people to be totally free of the biases imbedded in the cultural cleavages that exist in ... society" (Pescosoldio et al. 2007, 438), we should at least be able to look to the government to set an example regarding issues of social justice – rather than watching it persistently reinforce injustices. In this regard, governments should also institute policy that prohibits people from acting on their prejudices through ensuring that there are penalties available and imposed for the mistreatment and/or violation of the rights of all citizens (Parker and Aggleton 2003; Pescosoldio et al. 2007).

In short, in order to avoid going "round again" – using stigma to justify and perpetuate the division between "decent" folks and "prostitutes," and to maintain the status quo – it is imperative that the government commit to basing law and policy on empirical evidence, taking a social justice stance toward the sex industry, and actively promoting the development of a more evidence-based understanding of the people who work in it. Such changes will counteract the ideology-based thinking that contributes to stigmatization and will advance social justice and citizen rights for all Canadians. Although these commitments require political courage on the part of the government, a March 2011 Ekos survey suggests that such change may actually be in line with the attitudes and opinions of most Canadians. The poll revealed that the Canadian public prefers a government whose policies are based on scientific evidence, rather than tradition and ideology (Graves 2011). In a pluralistic society such as ours, public policy cannot be built on pseudo-science founded on a particular type of moral ideology; it can be developed only through emphasizing both justice and science, and by creating conditions where diversity is recognized, respected, and protected.

Notes

1 All the transgender sex workers in our own work were male-to-female (MTF). They present themselves as women and most live full-time as women. They may or may not have had sex reassignment surgery.
2 The subcommittee's unanimous recommendations were as follows: the commercial sexual exploitation of minors and trafficking in persons are unacceptable; the status quo for prostituted persons in Canada is unacceptable; criminal laws pertaining to prostitution are unequally applied in Canada; there is an urgent need for education campaigns and programs; and there is a need for further research and data collection (SSLR 2006, 85-87).
3 An example of this is "See Change," a recent initiative by the Irish government to destigmatize mental illness. In emphasizing the importance of the program, the Irish minister of disability and mental health stated, "Stigma has no place in Irish society today. It damages people's lives and can be deeply hurtful and isolating, and is one of the most significant problems encountered by people with mental health problems" (Minister Moloney 2010).

References

Abel, G., and L. Fitzgerald. 2010. Decriminalisation and stigma. In *Taking the crime out of sex work: New Zealand sex workers' fight for decriminalization,* ed. G. Abel, L. Fitzgerald, and C. Healy with A. Taylor, 239-58. Bristol: Policy Press.

Bobo, L., J.R. Kluegel, and R.A Smith. 1997. Laissez faire racism: The crystallization of a "kinder, gentler" anti-black ideology. In *Racial attitudes in the 1990s: Continuity and change,* ed. S.A. Tuch and J.K. Martin, 15-44. Greenwood, CT: Praeger.

Broadhead, R.S., T.H. Kerr, J.C. Grund, and F.L. Altice. 2002. Safer injection facilities in North America: Their place in public policy and health initiatives. *Journal of Drug Issues* 2, 1: 329-56.

Brown, L., K. Mcintyre, and L. Trujillo. 2003. Stigma: What have we learned? *AIDS Education and Prevention* 15, 1: 49-69.

Criminal Code, R.S.C. 1985, c. C-46.

Elliott, R. 2008. Adrift from the moorings of good public policy – ignoring evidence and human rights. *International Journal of Drug Policy* 19: 229-30.

FIRST (Feminists Advocating for Rights and Equality for Sex Workers). n.d. http://www.firstadvocates.org.

Foucault, M. 1978. *The history of sexuality.* Vol. 1, *An introduction.* New York: Vintage Books.

Goffman, E. 1963. *Stigma: Notes on the management of spoiled identity.* New York: Simon and Schuster.

Graves, F. 2011. Power and knowledge: Shifting public perspectives. Presented to the Walter Gordon Symposium on Public Policy, Massey College and the School of Public Policy and Governance, University of Toronto, 22-23 March. http://www.waltergordonsymposium.com/wp-content/uploads/2010/12/Walter-Gordon-Symposium-in-Public-Policy-March-23-2011.pdf.

Gussow, Z., and G.S. Tracy. 1968. Status, ideology, and adaptation to stigmatized illness: A study of leprosy. *Human Organization* 27, 4: 316-25.

Jeffrey, L.A., and G. MacDonald. 2006. *Work, stigma, and resistance: Sex workers in the Maritimes talk back.* Vancouver: UBC Press.

Jacqueline Lewis, Frances M. Shaver, and Eleanor Maticka-Tyndale

Jeffreys, E., K. Mathews, and A. Thomas. 2010. HIV criminalization and sex work in Australia. *Reproductive Health Matters* 18, 35: 129-36.

Jeffreys, L.A., and B. Sullivan. 2009. Canadian sex work policy for the 21st century: Enhancing rights and safety, lessons from Australia. *Canadian Political Science Review* 3, 1: 57-76.

Jordan, J. 2005. *The sex industry in New Zealand: A literature review.* Wellington, New Zealand: Ministry of Justice.

Lewis, J. 2000a. Controlling lap dancing: Law, morality and sex work. In *Sex as work, prostitution, pornography and the sex industry,* ed. Ronald Weitzer, 203-16. New York: Routledge.

–. 2000b. Managing deviant identities: HIV and social support networks. *Health and Canadian Society* 6, 1: 111-30.

–. 2010. Shifting the focus: Restorative justice and sex work. *Canadian Journal of Criminology and Criminal Justice* 52, 3: 285-302.

Lewis, J., E. Maticka-Tyndale, F.M. Shaver, and H. Schramm. 2005. Managing risk and safety on the job: The experiences of Canadian sex workers. Special issue, *Journal of Psychology and Human Sexuality* 17, 1-2: 147-67.

Lewis, J., and F.M. Shaver. 2011. The regulation of adult sex work and its impact on the safety, security and well-being of people working in the sex industry in Canada. In *Global perspectives on prostitution and sex trafficking: Europe, Latin America, North America, and global,* ed. R.L. Dalla, L.M. Baker, J. DeFrain, and C. Williamson, 237-53. Lanham, MD: Lexington Books.

Makin, K. 2010. Judge decriminalizes prostitution in Ontario, but Ottawa mulls appeal. *Toronto Globe and Mail,* 28 September. http://www.theglobeandmail.com/.

Mar, L., and G. Betteridge. 2007. Subcommittee fails to recommend legal reforms needed to promote human rights of sex workers. *HIV/AIDS: Policy and Law Review* 12, 1 (May): 15-17.

Minister Moloney launches national stigma reduction campaign 'See Change.' 2010. An Roinn Sláinte agus Leanai/Department of Health and Children. News release. 15 April. http://www.dohc.ie/.

Murray, S.O. 1984. *Social theory, homosexuality realities.* Gai Saber monograph 3. New York: Gay Academic Union.

Nguyen, L. 2010a. Ont. judge to rule on landmark prostitution decision. *Vancouver Sun,* 1 December. http://www.vancouversun.com/.

–. 2010b. Lawyers plead with court not to pass prostitution law before appeal. *Canada.com,* 23 November. http://www.canada.com/.

–. 2010c. Prostitution laws to stay in place in Ontario. *Canada.com,* 2 December. http://www.canada.com/.

Parker, R., and P. Aggleton. 2003. HIV and AIDS-related stigma and discrimination: A conceptual framework and implications for action. *Social Science and Medicine* 57: 13-24.

Pescosoldio, B.A., J.K. Martin, A. Lang, and S. Olafsdottir. 2007. Rethinking theoretical approaches to stigma: A framework integrating normative influences on stigma (FINIS). *Social Science and Medicine* 67: 431-40.

Pivot (Pivot Legal Society). 2004. Voices for dignity: A call to end the harms caused by Canada's sex trade laws. Pivot Legal Society, Vancouver. http://www.pivotlegal.org/pivot-points/publications/voices-for-dignity.

–. 2006. Beyond decriminalization: Sex work, human rights and a new framework for law reform. Pivot Legal Society, Vancouver. http://www.povnet.org/.

Senate Special Committee on Illegal Drugs. 2002. *Our Position for a Canadian public policy.* Ottawa: Senate of Canada. http://www2.parl.gc.ca.

Shaver, F.M. 2005. Sex work policy: An integrated approach. Invited presentation to the House of Commons Subcommittee on Solicitation Laws (SSLR), Ottawa.

Shaver, F.M., J. Lewis, and E. Maticka-Tyndale. 2011. Rising to the challenge: Addressing the concerns of people working in the sex industry. *Canadian Review of Sociology* 48, 1: 47-64.

SSLR (Subcommittee on Solicitation Laws of the Standing Committee on Justice and Human Rights). 2006. *The challenge of change: A study of Canada's criminal prostitution laws.* Ottawa: House of Commons. http://www2.parl.gc.ca.

STAR (Sex Trade Advocacy and Research). 2004. Exotic dancing in Ontario: Health and safety. STAR, Windsor. http://www.uwindsor.ca/star.

–. 2006. Safety, security and the well-being of sex workers: A report submitted to the House of Commons Subcommittee on Solicitation Laws (SSLR). STAR, Windsor. http://www.uwindsor.ca/star.

Stryker, S. 1980. *Symbolic interaction.* Menlo Park: Benjamin/Cummings.

Taber, J. 2010. Tory MP sees 'the nation as the pimp' if prostitution ruling stands. *Toronto Globe and Mail,* 29 September. http://www.theglobeandmail.com/.

Tempalski, B., R. Friedman, M. Keem, H. Cooper, and S.R. Friedman. 2007. NIMBY localism and national inequitable exclusion alliances: The case of syringe exchange programs in the United States. *Geoforum* 38: 1250-63.

Tibbetts, J. 2010. Ontario about to become hooker hub, feds warn. *Canada.com,* 17 November. http://www.canada.com/.

United Nations. 1993. The *Vienna Declaration.* http://www.viennadeclaration.com.

Weitzer, R. 2010. The mythology of prostitution: Advocacy research and public policy. *Sex Research and Social Policy* 7: 15-29.

Cases Cited

Bedford v. Canada, 2010 ONSC 4264.

Bedford v. Canada (Attorney General), 2010 ONCA 814.

The Politics of Regulation

PART 3 CONCLUDES THE COLLECTION with a broad overview of the political context for prostitution and sex work in Canada. Authors consider policies at the federal, provincial, and municipal levels to examine the inherent contradictions in Canada's prostitution laws as well as the ways in which sex workers have been cast in discourse and political narratives on prostitution. To open this part of the book, Michael Goodyear and Cheryl Auger (Chapter 14) consider how key actors and witnesses in the federal Subcommittee on Solicitation Laws Review framed their discourses as one of victim, deviant, or work and whether sex workers' own narratives influenced the discussion. John Lowman (Chapter 15) further examines discourse in policy processes as he analyzes expert witness testimonies based on prohibitionist and victim-paradigm hyperbole in the 2010 Ontario Superior Court ruling of the constitutional validity of the Criminal Code.

Annalee Lepp (Chapter 16) expands upon the critical analyses put forth in Chapters 14 and 15 to include considerations of race and ethnicity in her discussion of trafficking policy, mythology, and controversies in the lead-up to the 2010 Winter Olympic and Paralympic Games in British Columbia. Exploring how laws and policies that are purported to protect sex workers can instead produce the conditions for harm, Kara Gillies (Chapter 17) draws on interviews with sex workers from four provinces to examine the consequences of the criminalization of sex industry managers, which is based largely on myths surrounding the "pimp." Building on Gillies's contribution, Steven Bittle (Chapter 18) critically examines state responses to youth prostitution in Canada, which are rooted in the language of sexual abuse and exploitation. He demonstrates how current responses are constitutive of a hegemonic process that aims to "rescue" and "protect" young women engaged in sex work.

The final two chapters turn their attention from federal and provincial policies to the politics of regulation within municipal jurisdictions. Chris Bruckert and Stacey Hannem (Chapter 19) present empirical research about police abuse of power in Ottawa and expose the ways in which those in authority actualize stigma and discrimination through direct violence and harassment, in particular against street-based sex workers. Emily van der Meulen and Mariana Valverde (Chapter 20) conclude the collection with a consideration of Canada's complex and convoluted municipal licensing and zoning regulations, a critical issue for the sex industry on the cusp of partial decriminalization.

14

Regulating Women's Sexuality: Social Movements and Internal Exclusion

MICHAEL GOODYEAR AND CHERYL AUGER

Democratic governance implies accountability, power sharing, and consultation, subject to interjurisdictional distribution of authority, political ideologies, the power exercised by governing parties, and that which social actors can access and leverage. Governments make policy decisions as proxies for popular will, and in the absence of consensus, they act as brokers between opposing views, which are often polarized in moral matters. Young described participatory democracy as extending beyond suffrage to access deliberative processes by which citizens make claims and express opinions, and the right to express that opinion and be heard. Overcoming external exclusion to reach the deliberative table is a necessary but not sufficient condition for equitable democracy, since one must also overcome "internal exclusion" (Young 2000, 53), whereby invisibility effectively masks the grievances of groups already disadvantaged by power inequity, further entrenching injustice. The disadvantaged require effective representation because such groups' experiences are "so different from others' that their views are discounted" (ibid., 55).

Governments seek stakeholder input to policy processes through consultation, but actors also lobby power centres directly, or indirectly through media, opinion leaders, or demonstrations. The relative power of stakeholders depends on numbers, organization, resources, skills, homogeneity of objectives, links to political parties and power brokers, and congruence with prevailing ideologies and discourses. Resource mobilization theory argues that established interest groups have low-cost access to levers of power, whereas emerging social movements must pay higher costs to win polity seats (Jenkins 1983).

Rationally, actors who are directly affected by policy should be privileged as opposed to those whose interest lies in opinion. In practice, negatively privileged actors (Weber 1947) are marginalized or made invisible but may gain power through alliances with positively privileged power brokers (Gamson 1990) or by organizing, although such strategies are not without their own problems (Mathieu 2003).

States are presumed to minimize intrusion into private lives and freedoms, and to bear the burden of proof when declaring interest, yet "the main determinants of criminalization continue to be *political opportunism* and *power*, both linked to the prevailing political culture of the country" (Ashworth 2006, 52, emphasis added). In moral law the state's role has become contentious (Valverde 1999), and the contemporary landscape is mapped by milestones such as the Wolfenden Report in the United Kingdom (Wolfenden 1957), separation of state and bedroom in Canada (Trudeau 1967), *Lawrence v. Texas* (2003) in the United States, and other legal decisions on morality, community standards, and indecency. These collectively represent retreat by the state from encompassing private adult consensual behaviour within criminal law, yet the increasing social control of sex work remains an anomaly within this framework.

While broadly interrogating the representation of sex worker engagement and participation in the policy agenda and process, this chapter specifically examines to what degree Canadian sex workers were able to leverage power, were consulted, or played any effective role in policy in the 2005 Subcommittee on Solicitation Laws Review (SSLR), by examining how they were constructed in that process. At the time of the SSLR, the organization of sex workers was greater than in earlier policy engagements (Fraser 1985), which theoretically would place them in a stronger position to have their voices recognized and heard. This chapter examines how the SSLR process reflects Young's internal exclusion theory as an explanation for the limitations of resource mobilization in explaining social movements.

A constructionist approach to social problems – namely, how processes are constructed by social actors (Giddens 1976) – is used in examining the SSLR. In this tradition, the emphasis is not so much on objective conditions as the process by which such conditions are constructed and reconstructed by a variety of actors and meanings attached to them, which determine whether they are considered normative or deviant (Goffman 1963). An exploration of the "how" and the "why" of ongoing processes informs our understanding of how the sex workers' movement in Canada continues to fall short of achieving its political goals.

The report, minutes, and testimony of the SSLR were analyzed with framing discourse analysis (Goffman 1974). In addition, media reports were examined and a number of stakeholders interviewed by one of the authors (Cheryl Auger) during 2010 to expand on and clarify the texts. The various frames or discourses that arose during the process – deviant, victim, and work – are examined in terms of their meanings and how they have been used to exclude sex workers from influencing policy. We argue for a more inclusionary process in resolving the current dilemma.

Sex Worker Mobilization as a Social Movement

Historically, sex workers are absent from sex work debates (Mathieu 2003), being constructed as deviant, health or moral threats, or passive victims (Bell 1994). In these constructions by other actors, they are assumed to be unable to exercise voice or agency, needing guidance from their betters in other social worlds (Allwood 2008). Pheterson (1989, 3) states, "Never have prostitutes been legitimised as spokespersons or self determining agents," and McLaren (1995, 552) observes, "Nobody apparently thought to ask what prostitutes felt. As a subject group, marginalised and despised, they were voiceless." This absence from the policy table is contested by sex workers and their allies.

Although the obstacles to organization are considerable (Mathieu 2003), including stigma (Goffman 1963) and criminality, sex workers' rights movements appeared in the West in the 1970s (Weitzer 1991), gaining momentum during the 1980s in response to the HIV/AIDS epidemic (Delacoste and Alexander 1998). Resurgence of fears of "contagious" sex workers funded sex work research, whereas sex workers, concerned for their survival, developed resistance to new prejudices through reversing historical discourses and contesting the construction of their work as a social problem (Lichtenstein 1999), whether by agents of social control, morality, or health (Jenness 1993). These factors fuelled alliances with health groups and academics that were to prove powerful since funding and alliances both enabled and legitimized these movements.

Further visibility emerged with the creation of a cultural record of sex workers' voices, sometimes amplified by privileged others with closer ties to power centres, such as *Sex Work* (Delacoste and Alexander 1988), *A Vindication of the Rights of Whores* (Pheterson 1989), and *Whores in History* (Roberts 1992). These helped meld a necessary collective identity (Melucci 1996) over the space of about twenty years and should have provided sex workers with a legitimate policy seat, but the proliferation of oppressive legislation, despite some small progressive movements, demonstrates a disjuncture between increasing visibility and engagement on contested terrains and the ability to influence the policy agenda.

A number of factors affect the interaction between social movement organizations (Zald and McCarthy 1987) and the policy process to disempower them. Weitzer (1991) used resource mobilization theory to describe the collective resistance of deviant liberation movements, suggesting that deficiencies of moral, material, and human resources accounted for the failure to achieve objectives. Jenness (1990), examining the actions and claims making of a sex workers' group, suggested that though not achieving its political goals, it had successfully engaged the process of social construction of sex work as a social problem, demonstrating that contrary to historical discourses it could be relocated within a discourse of work, choice, and rights. Mathieu (2003) observed that sex workers are traditionally excluded from debates, due to coding or representation that denies them the ability to express opinions. Whether they are portrayed as criminals, delinquents, or passive victims, and despite inherent inconsistencies in these often simultaneously expressed images, the effect is a convergent politic of exclusion. This politic is in turn contested by emergent social movements in a politic of inclusion, challenging their representation, claiming moral agency, and, by seeking legitimization as workers, positioning themselves as actors who contest the state's role in determining their status. The success of social movements should not be measured solely in terms of formal politics of engagement and policy change, but also by the relocation of discourse in informal processes that facilitate policy change.

Despite increasing experience and availability of communication tools, the situation of sex workers' movements has not improved, requiring examination of emergent social movement and social change ideas that resource mobilization tends to marginalize (Canel 1997). Although the objectives of movements differ with time and with cultural and political contexts, there are generally two intersecting goals – legitimization and legalization. The former seeks acceptance and normalization from the margins toward the mainstream, the latter a diminution of state constraints. These intersect since changes in knowledge and attitudes are necessary to enable political change, and political change that reduces criminality signifies increased acceptability because crime is a social construction.

Canadian Prostitution Policy and the Solicitation Subcommittee

Following codification of criminal law in 1892, Canadian prostitution laws remained largely unchanged over seventy years (McLaren 1986; see also the

Michael Goodyear and Cheryl Auger

Introduction in this volume). Many aspects, but not the act, of prostitution were criminalized, including third-party involvement, use of premises (bawdy-houses), and solicitation, which situated prostitutes, the poor, and the homeless as undesirable vagrants. In 1970, the Royal Commission on the Status of Women recommended repeal of the vagrancy laws (SOW 1970). No reference to sex worker input was made, but the report and subsequent reconstruction of prostitution laws in 1972 opened a new era of debate including a series of consultations such as the Fraser Committee (Fraser 1985). Other opportunities for formal public engagement with the policy agenda included appearances and submissions before legislative committees, municipalities, and courts. During this time, there were periodic changes to solicitation ("communicating") laws as well as underage involvement and, more recently, trafficking of human beings for the purposes of sexual exploitation. Public attention focused on visible street sex work and the conflict between sex workers' rights and safety, on the one hand, and neighbourhoods that felt threatened, on the other. Meanwhile, migration of sex workers and the presence of "foreign-looking" sex workers on the streets revived moral panics, and crusades centred on a perceived nexus with trafficking, which have proven to be a powerful force creating demand for stronger involvement of the state in suppressing the domestic sex trade.

Concern over missing and murdered women in Vancouver during the 1990s and suggestions that authorities were not responding, because the women were alleged to be sex workers (see Chapter 9 in this volume) led to a parliamentary subcommittee (SSLR) being struck in 2003 to review solicitation laws and the safety of street-based sex workers. Eventually, it addressed all criminal provisions related to adult prostitution, meeting with some three hundred interested parties in 2005 (House of Commons 2005) and reporting in 2006 (SSLR 2006). Sex workers could testify in camera and were assured of parliamentary privilege (John Maloney, SSLR chair, 29 March 2005, in House of Commons 2005).[1]

Initial reaction from the sex work community was mixed. Some thought that the SSLR constituted an important opportunity (Pacey 2010), whereas others, frustrated by past experiences, considered a boycott (Clamen 2010), stating that sex workers were excluded at the outset (*Montreal Mirror* 2007) and that any discussion should come from the grievances of workers themselves. However, the final subcommittee report states that it heard from approximately a hundred people involved in sex work (SSLR 2006).

Although the opportunities to make submissions had been advertised, witnesses stated that they were initially unaware of this. The breadth of submissions was wide, covering moral convictions, people's lived realities, and empirical research. In contrast to judicial proceedings, the report provided no description as to how evidence was assessed and weighed. Among the issues raised by the inconclusive and partisan report is how the various constituencies, particularly sex workers, were represented. The majority opposition on the subcommittee sided with the more liberal views of prior inquiries, whereas the minority governing Conservative Party report supported the dominant oppression discourse (ibid.; see also Chapter 13 in this volume). Reactions reflected previously held views together with a good deal of frustration by activists that despite consensus on the unacceptability of the status quo, it would clearly remain entrenched (Canadian HIV/AIDS Legal Network 2007), which was confirmed by the subsequent government response.

Although sex workers and organizations appear in the appendix as having contributed to the process, there was a general feeling that their specific grievances were not reflected in the report. The responses to the report largely dealt with outcomes; our concern is with process.

Constructions of Sex Work

Whereas earlier policy processes literally excluded sex workers, intentionally or unintentionally, the SSLR reveals a process of metaphoric exclusion. Policy making involves conflicts of meaning, not only between opposing actors but in terms of competition for attention in a finite political arena. Successful actors are those who sufficiently enlarge the scope of their issue and frame it to emphasize its importance to the state, its degree of support, and the political capital to be associated with its realization. Much attention has been paid to the way in which debates on sex work are framed (Outshoorn 2004; Goodyear and Weitzer 2011), but less attention has been paid to the way that actors themselves are represented by other actors and by the policy process.

Although many themes were identified, consistent with the contested nature of sex work, three key frames by which sex workers were constructed by various actors emerged: the deviant, victim, and work frames respectively, providing a heuristic for understanding the process and outcome of the SSLR. The deviant and victim frames were often expressed simultaneously, and they form a discourse of exclusion, whereas the work frame was a distinct discourse of inclusion. Thus, two frames constructed sex workers as illegitimate actors, but a third frame constructed them as competent actors, entitled to contribute to the process, and experts on their own profession.

Actors using the deviant frame emphasized perceived connections between sex work, crime, trafficking, drugs, child abuse, and public order, advocating a criminal justice response. In the victim frame, sex work was depicted in terms

Michael Goodyear and Cheryl Auger

of violence, trafficking, poverty, and absence of choice or agency, advocating a combined criminal-social response, including sanctions against clients and third parties, and diverting sex workers into exit strategies. Frequent reference was made to the Swedish policy of criminalizing clients while rehabilitating sex workers, labelling it as a model (see also Chapter 15 in this volume). The work frame, used by a majority of witnesses, associated sex work with economic activity and market forces, advocating a non-criminal regulated environment, emphasizing the existence of sufficient generic law to void any necessity for specific criminal provisions and the need for policy to be based on the lived realities of sex workers' lives.

The exclusion discourse was numerically smallest, but it was more powerful, despite a general acknowledgment that sex work represented an economic activity and that social inequalities contributed to the problems faced by sex workers. We suggest that this dominance drew on historical views of crime, deviance, sin, and gendered sexuality, utilizing strong archetypal imagery such as "the social evil" and the place of sex workers on the margins of society. These images worked not only to dehumanize and "other" sex workers, but to undermine their legitimacy as witnesses and experts, contributing to reinscribing stigma, prejudice, and discrimination, potentially further escalating the cycle of violence.

Since authority and tradition were incompatible with the view of sex workers as social or political agents within legitimate society, denying their voices at the policy process and diverting their grievances regarding safety and violence into discussions of law and order, public safety, and morality meant that they were continually forced to legitimize their right to speak.

Deviant Frame

The deviant frame has the longest history, reflecting deep-seated views on controlling female sexuality and the construction of sex workers as vectors of contagion who attract other vices such as organized crime and drugs (Walkowitz 1992; McLaren 1995). Advanced predominantly by witnesses speaking on behalf of police, religious leaders, and community spokespersons, this frame portrays society as the victim (Detective Page, Toronto, 15 March) and the state as the protector. Some witnesses emphasized the nexus with morality (Reverend Tse, Christian Social Action, 15 March), and others suggested that the threat to society arose from the sex workers' lifestyle and moral failings, which set them apart from the community and hence from social citizenship (Sergeant Dugal, Ottawa, 6 April). In this construction, a distinction is made between "citizens" and "prostitutes," who were not welcome in the Canadian community; Councillor Ceci (Calgary, 31 March) illustrated this approach by stating that "citizens want prostitution out of their community." This representation of the Other was reinforced by distinguishing good sex from sex work.

The policy response advocated greater penalties, depicting law and justice as tools to abolish prostitution (Janet Epp, Evangelical Fellowship, 2 February), dispose of clients (Detective Page, Toronto, 15 March), help and protect sex workers (Cristina Basualdo, Neighbourhood Patrol, Edmonton, 31 March), and facilitate solving homicides – sex workers being envisioned as future corpses in a "discourse of disposal" (Lowman 2000). These depictions all contrasted sharply with sex workers' own accounts.

Victim Frame

Although framing sex workers as victims is a more recent approach than depicting them as deviants, it is becoming increasingly dominant as was the case here. A number of women's groups at the hearings constructed sex workers as a threat (for instance, to gender equality) but did not consider them responsible since they were mere agents of patriarchal hegemony, requiring saving. This power inequality worldview constructs sex workers as victims of male violence and exploitation, rendering them paradigms of gender inequity.

The harms attributed to sex work were extensive: as Beverley McAleese of Streetlight Support Services (15 March) argued, "It's about child exploitation, post-traumatic stress disorder, and poverty. It's about lack of choice, unresolved childhood trauma, addiction, desperation, and violence against women. It's about housing crises, human trafficking, and organized crime. It's about broken homes and shattered dreams." This reflected the experiences of those who dealt with people in crisis, in which violence was essentialized. Indeed, sex work was the "ultimate violence" (Eckberg, adviser on prostitution to the Swedish government, 4 May), being constructed as both instrumental (male clients, third parties) and symbolic (imbalances of power, male desire and entitlement). This threat to gender equality was considered extensive by witnesses such as Lee Lakeman, Association of Sexual Assault Centres (30 May), who said, "No equality-seeking women's group at the provincial, regional, or pan-Canadian level calls for or agrees with the complete decriminalization of prostitution, either domestic or international. That should draw your attention to the equality issues at stake."

Claims of reward or empowerment by sex workers were negated, and violence (conflating symbolic and instrumental meanings) was depicted as voiding choice and consent, since "the very concept of consent is a form of violence and

Michael Goodyear and Cheryl Auger

exploitation" (Yolande Geadah, feminist author, 7 February), making any distinction between voluntary and coerced sex work irrelevant (Richard Poulin, sociologist, February 9), and excluding any insight, agency, or voice on the part of the sex worker.

Some police witnesses also used the victim frame, describing sex workers as forced or *feeling* forced into prostitution, shifting the criminal justice response to clients and third parties, and envisaging the law as an exit tool. For example, Deputy Chief Le Pard, Vancouver (30 March), argued that arresting sex workers was a means of rescuing them and that the threat of criminal proceedings was a lever to encourage exiting.

Both deviant and victim frames were used simultaneously without acknowledging any contradiction. Evangelical and conservative women's groups, describing the harms, included "the prostitutes themselves, the clients, their families" (Gwendolyn Landolt, REAL Women, 14 February), constructing sex workers as *both* victims of inequality and threats to equality, suggesting that agency was a fluid concept depending on the position being taken at the time. The agencyless sex worker was emphasized by the use of "prostituted" as opposed to "prostitute" to highlight the status as object, not subject.

A powerful driver in this frame was the conflation of sex work with trafficking, arguing that demand for sex fuelled trafficking and must be suppressed: "The dominant characteristic of prostitution, as currently practiced, is the globalization of procuring and sexual trafficking" (Yolande Geadah, feminist author, 7 February), neither involving consent. Danielle Shaw, Salvation Army (16 February), stated, "There are important similarities between people affected by trafficking and those engaged in domestic prostitution, ... The commercial sexual exploitation has similar effects on the physical, emotional, and spiritual health of both groups of people." In addition, sex work as non-heteronormative sex outside the bonds of marriage was stated to be both morally and spiritually bad sex.

Women in the sex trade were depicted as non-autonomous beings, dependent on men and incapable of making good decisions. Their perceived inability to see what was right was explained by police witnesses: "The difficulty is that a lot of times we have to rely on the evidence of somebody who has been involved in sex trade work. That witness is akin to a battered spouse ... You're dealing very much with people who have been brainwashed ... There's no other way to describe it" (Sergeant Dugal, Ottawa, 6 April). Not engaging the criminal justice system was seen as a failing, both deviance and victimization. Workers were seen as victims of both men and substance use – "too drugged out ... alcoholic

... couldn't keep a doctor's appointment if they wanted to ... We should try to help them" (Gwendolyn Landolt, REAL Women, 14 February). Such help was envisaged as "reintegration" (Richard Poulin, sociologist, 9 February).

The policy response to this frame was generally the Swedish approach, which was claimed to create equality without further victimization of women. However, those emphasizing the hybrid deviant-victim frame wanted to maintain criminalization of workers as a way of "helping" them. Decriminalization constituted degradation of women and fuelling trafficking (Catherine Williams-Jones, New Opportunities for Women, 18 May).

Work Frame

The most recent construction of sex work, the work frame, arose from the collective resistance manifested in social movements, relocating sex work as an economic and labour activity. It differs from previous frames by the inclusion of sex workers' experiences and perspectives, rather than objective projections. This frame was expressed by sex workers, allies, academics, and associated organizations.

Raven Bowen, of the sex worker rights organization PACE (29 March), stated, "We want this subcommittee to adopt as a basic principle that whatever discussion happens around this, you include the individuals most affected by the issue in the creation of its solution. That means that individuals living with criminal charges and individuals currently criminalized must be central to any discussion or any decisions made on this issue." Witnesses were concerned that, due to the efforts of the exclusion frames, the subcommittee's attention was being deflected from work safety and the effects of the law to morality and the abolition of sex work. Anastasia Kusyk, Sex Workers Alliance of Toronto (15 March), argued that "sex workers in general across the nation feel that this subcommittee is inappropriate, because for the last 10 to 15 years the majority of us have been working to advance law reform as well as study it ... It's not about how I feel and how the laws affect me, how they impact on my life ... I'm tired of the politicians, the lawmakers, the police, the doctors, the lawyers, and even the ministers deciding how I feel."

Witnesses acknowledged many of the problems identified within the deviant-victim frames but placed these within a context of exercising or resisting power and exercising agency within structural constraints. Maggie de Vries, sister of a murdered woman (16 February), asserted, "They're making that choice out of a whole range of choices and I just don't see why they shouldn't have the right to do that." Sex workers identified forced rehabilitation as just another form of victimization, suggesting that being provided with tools for self-help was more empowering and that alternatives to sex work such as dependency on the welfare state or minimum wage were not very attractive and certainly not liberating (Valerie Scott, Sex Professionals of Canada [SPOC], 9 March) compared to "sex work ... a viable and legitimate profession" (Amy X, SPOC, 15 March).

Rather than essentializing violence within sex work, sex workers and allies took a structuralist approach, centring the harms within the criminal law. John Lowman, criminologist (21 February), stated that "criminal law has exposed women at the bottom end of the sex trade – mostly those involved in survival sex – to great risk, and in a variety of ways. They've been forced into commercial districts. The areas of street prostitution have expanded through the use of things like area restrictions on bail and probation orders ... It's more and more difficult for people to look after each other."

One sex worker (Amy X, SPOC, 15 March) described the lack of protection: "I have been raped and abused ... I have chosen not to report any of these crimes. I will continue not to report them to police if I experience any more bad dates, because I know I will be shamed, and I will be investigated. I know I can be countercharged. Your laws have forced me to stay silent." This shifted violence to the state, both symbolically and instrumentally, in the nature of police violence. Anna-Louise Crago, Coalition for the Rights of Sex Workers (16 March), argued that "criminalization of our lives, of our work, of our families is a form of violence." Even in the absence of overt violence, police attitudes were described as contemptuous (Darlène Palmer, Cactus, Montreal, 16 March; Rene Ross, Stepping Stone, 17 March).

The policy response here was decriminalization as a harm-reduction and labour rights process. The Swedish approach, citing Swedish sex workers' experiences (Jennifer Clamen, Coalition for the Rights of Sex Workers, 30 May), was described as simply another form of criminalization that also victimizes sex workers. Elizabeth Hudson, author (17 March), explained that "each move made by federal, provincial, or civil governments to punish and/or humiliate the johns has, in effect, only punished the street sex trade worker, purposely and continually leaving them with fewer options." Witnesses did not accept the "protective" function of the criminal law provisions, pointing to the existence of generic laws. Maurganne Mooney, Aboriginal Legal Services (15 March), stated, "When a husband beats up his wife, he's not charged with being a husband; he's charged with what he did." Within this frame, witnesses felt that the onus of proof lay with them to change the status quo and traditional views of prostitution.

Sex workers already faced effective external exclusion due to stigma and criminality (Mensah 2010) but exercised sufficient collective resistance to ensure at least a presence, although they were underrepresented relative to the centrality of the issue to them and had considerable reservations. Sandra Laframboise, former worker (29 March), noted, "I want to ensure that I will not be subject to any reprisals ... I want to ensure that anything I say will not be used against me at my job," and Raigen D'Angelo, who identified as a former "professional sex provider" (29 March), stated, "I'm disappointed to see that all people who work in the industry are not here and that they have not been asked to participate." Similarly, Shawna Hohendorf, Kindred House (31 March), pointed out, "I see none of my women here ... They do feel marginalized ... They don't come out of their area, because this building would not be welcoming to them, nor would they feel comfortable here."

Witnesses were defensive, stating that they were "part of this society. We are voters, we are workers, and above all, we are human" (Jennifer Clamen, Coalition for the Rights of Sex Workers, 30 May). Anna-Louise Crago, Coalition for the Rights of Sex Workers (16 March), commented,

> I find it heart-wrenching year after year to sit here and remind you that we're human, remind you that we're citizens, and remind you that we're residents ... It does not diminish our humanity that we have to remind you that we're humans and that sex workers are workers, and that they're deserving of human rights ... It's your humanity that is diminished by the lack of courage and justice in your hearts. You have to stand up and do something very brave, which is to stand up for sex workers and their rights as workers and as human beings, because violence is not intrinsic to the sex trade.

Sex workers objected to the way in which they were represented. Cherry Kingsley, Canadian National Coalition of Experiential Women (14 February), remarked, "I really wish people would stop representing us that way ... It's part of what has perpetuated our not having the right to speak for ourselves or to communicate on our own behalf. It's perpetuated this stigma, this shame, this stereotype, and our lack of ability to participate as community members – we aren't able to communicate, we aren't able to make decisions for ourselves, people literally have to intervene, and we just shouldn't even speak, really."

They described the effective silencing of their voices, whether on the street or in policy, as disempowering. Although they had the most to say about their living and working conditions, the debate was diverted from this subject, "hijacked," as Elizabeth Hudson (17 March) put it, into areas from which sex workers felt excluded "by community associations, by police associations, by other organizations ... Sex trade workers themselves are terribly under-represented."

Role of the Subcommittee

Subcommittee members reflected their party's views. The Conservative member, Art Hanger, who dissented from the final report, was committed to the deviant frame, noting that moral dimensions were underrepresented (23 March) while dismissing links between law, violence, and the murder of sex workers (16 March). Sex workers were depicted as deviant Others whose lifestyle resulted in their misfortunes and as criminals who should be actively excluded from any dialogue (31 March), privileging community concerns.

The centre and left parties (Liberal, New Democratic Party [NDP], and Bloc Québécois) suspended moral judgment, focusing on harm reduction. They demonstrated willingness to listen (Hedy Fry, Liberal, 1 April) and accepted sex work as an economic activity while attempting to strike a balance between competing demands. One committee debate dealt with whether sex workers were part of the community or were excluded (29 March). Some members felt that the Charter of Rights and Freedoms mandated inclusion of minorities, the marginalized, and the dispossessed (Hedy Fry, Liberal, 29 March). As Hedy Fry (1 April) suggested, "It's really important that we hear from everyone in- volved. The women who work within the sex trade need to have their voices heard. These are women who are very much marginalized in society. They have been devalued completely in society. The only way to find out from them what will work and will not work and how they see themselves is to give them some respect and a voice. No one has cared about that." Members also challenged witnesses regarding discrepancies between their testimony and that of sex workers, showing awareness of the role of myths, stereotypes (Libby Davies, NDP, 23 March), stigma, and depersonalization (Hedy Fry, Liberal, 16 February). Despite this, no clear consensus or recommendation emerged. The perpetuity of the status quo, though deemed "unacceptable" was inevitable, and with it the exclusion frame, within which emerged the confounding issues of underage sex work and trafficking.

An analysis of the SSLR process reveals a conflict of meanings reflecting deeply held beliefs and representations, independently of empiricism and the realities of the lives of those affected. It demonstrates how the meaning of sex work is embedded in wider symbolic meanings, both informing and informed by a matrix of discourses, including control of female sexuality, gender rela- tions, power, race, class, and contested public space. Although there was align- ment between political ideology and discourses, this cannot be generalized since these frequently transcend party lines in the dialectic between law and order, morality, and protectionism, on the one hand, and individual freedoms, on the other. This construction of invisibility has been previously noted (Marques 2006; Ivy 2010). The Fraser Committee (Fraser 1985) included a few sex workers and organizations, but although their numbers were much greater in the SSLR process, they continued to remain largely invisible. Rather than deal with sex workers' central issue, their lives and safety, much of the discussion was based on the criminal corollaries that problematize sex work (Wagenaar 2006; Daalder 2007), leaving sex workers struggling to recentre the debate.

Origins and Relationships between Frames

The deviant frame is informed and sustained by neoliberal "governmentality" and its regulation of marginality (Foucault 1991; Garland 1997; Pollack 2010) predicated on the rational actor and rational choice theory, eschewing structuralist approaches. Criminal law contributes to the construction of the Other, reinforcing existing stigma. Young (1994) argues that punishing the disadvantaged further reinforces that process of exclusion by emphasizing the distinction between "deviant" and "normal," a discourse still informed by the construct of vagrancy. It reconstructs the sex worker "from a whole and usual person to a tainted, discredited one" (Goffman 1963, 4), from normal to Other, a process that "reproduces social stratifications and hence is profoundly implicated in processes that legitimate marginalization at the same time as they become the justification for discrimination, sanction, neglect, and the denial of fundamental rights, including the right to protection and criminal justice redress" (Bruckert and Chabot 2010, 79). Once the Other is depersonalized and "morally invisible" (Bauman 2000), abuse of him or her may appear justifiable in the absence of normative moral inhibitions. The combination of law and stigma has been effective in "disappearing" (Sudbury 2005, xxvi) even those who are not disadvantaged from roles as social actors overtly engaging the policy process. This chapter demonstrates how both internal and external exclusion operated through the deviant frame to limit sex workers' access to processes that could improve their condition.

In the victim frame, sex workers are an iconic symbol of a battle over patriarchal hegemony and gender relations. As in the deviant frame, they are constructed as an object incapable of seeing the harm done to them, requiring rescuing by their betters. The depiction of sex workers as mere victims of male desire and violence who must be saved has been described as a reinscription of patriarchy (Lindberg and Berg 2010), implying that women cannot be responsible for their own sexuality. This conflicts with arguments over women's right

Michael Goodyear and Cheryl Auger

to control their own bodies, and it risks co opting feminist interests into systems of governance (Scoular and O'Neill 2008).

Whether as deviant or victim, sex workers are effectively excluded from consideration in higher policy debates and thus from social citizenship. These two frames are equally products of advanced liberalism, focusing on identities at the expense of the structural factors that create them (ibid.). The political reasoning behind the ascendancy of the victim frame is one in which experiences of victimization are conflated with the individual's status and agency, a frame that is essentially paternalistic, predicated on protection and saving (Phoenix 2008). The dual roles of deviant and victim have been reconciled through the concept of responsibilization (Scoular and O'Neill 2008). Responsible social citizenship requires conforming to the normative; for sex workers, this elides any distinction between voluntary or involuntary work, which separated these frames.

State social inclusion is more properly described as selective inclusion. By constructing sex work outside of normative inclusive citizenship, responsibilization demands that victims recognize and accept their constructed status. This division of roles is expressed in terms of exit strategies and mandatory rehabilitation. Individuals who accept victimhood, conform to normative citizenry, and reject impugned behaviour (exit the sex trade) are included, whereas persistence or refusal to embrace victimhood constitute deviance, exclusion, and a necessity for punishment for their own good. This relocates the centrality of the justice response on those who do not exit voluntarily and in turn infantilizes the sex worker who refuses to be rescued. This strategy both isolates individuals from the structural factors that contribute to their status while simultaneously reifying the latter.

Both deviant and victim frames are examples of "identity thinking," which equates the individual with certain undesirable qualities (Scoular and O'Neill 2008) in sharp distinction from a holistic politic of inclusion and social justice that recognizes sex workers' agency and the choices they make, even under conditions that they did not choose (Giddens 1984). Although both are frames of exclusion, when understood this way, the victim frame increasingly converges with the deviant by advocating criminal law as a means of controlling responsible citizenship, further entrenching the dichotomies that divide and oppress women.

Social Movements

Resource mobilization remains a necessary but not sufficient condition for achieving social change by social movement organizations. As with neoliberal governance, it assumes a rational actor model de-emphasizing structurally based approaches and macro-level interactions (Giddens 1984) and is relatively ahistorical. Social movements' acquisition and utilization of resources need to be considered within their cultural context and in the light of their construction by more dominant discourses. For example, in the Netherlands, funding alone did not translate into shaping political process, and in New Zealand, sex workers were constructed as partners of government, giving them not only resources but legitimacy at negotiating tables that enabled them to construct a reverse discourse and achieve policy change (Laverack and Whipple 2010).

The SSLR constitutes formal political engagement, but social movements engage at informal and formal levels, which exhibit reciprocity. The outcome suggests that further formal engagement is unlikely to significantly shift the status quo without addressing wider public perceptions through informal mechanisms. Traditional discourses are malleable, not immutable (Outshoorn 2001). Sex worker participation was not fruitless. Sex workers constituted a counter-voice to traditional symbols and positioned their voices within the official record, introducing the concept that they are the true experts on their own lives (Jennifer Clamen, Coalition for the Rights of Sex Workers, 16 March), bringing new knowledge and perspectives to the policy debate. Most valuable of all, they gained experience in policy process.

Conclusion

Forward movement requires adoption of a true social inclusion politic that is not predicated on normative responsibilization but recognizes that all citizens are entitled to a voice and engages the necessity of de-othering. Including sex workers does not imply exclusion of other interest groups; problem solving involves inclusion of all actors in a way that fosters collaboration, respect, and negotiation. There *are* real issues in the way that communities react to sex workers, about whom they know little. We need to move beyond adversarial forms of democracy, which are entrenched in problematic dichotomies that caricaturize experiences, to look at the real issues of life and to work for *all* members of the community (Scoular and O'Neill 2008). Finally, alternative venues are available to sex workers, who can mobilize resources outside of traditional policy processes by fighting state oppression on their own terms in the courts, as is being currently pursued.

Michael Goodyear and Cheryl Auger

Note

1   Subsequent citations of witnesses and members of the subcommittee refer to the published proceedings (House of Commons 2005).

References

Allwood, G. 2008. The construction of prostitutes and clients in French policy debates. In *Demanding sex: Critical reflections on the regulation of prostitution*, ed. V. Munro and M. della Giusta, 67-81. Aldershot: Ashgate.

Ashworth, A. 2006. *Principles of criminal law*. Oxford: Oxford University Press.

Bauman, Z. 2000. *Modernity and the Holocaust*. Ithaca: Cornell University Press.

Bell, S. 1994. *Reading, writing and rewriting the prostitute body*. Bloomington: Indiana University Press.

Bruckert, C., and F. Chabot. 2010. *Challenges: Ottawa area sex workers speak out*. Ottawa: POWER.

Canadian HIV/AIDS Legal Network. 2007. Not up to the challenge of change: An analysis of the report of the Subcommittee on Solicitation Laws. Toronto. http://www.aidslaw.ca/publications/interfaces/downloadFile.php?ref=975.

Canel, E. 1997. New social movement theory and resource mobilization theory: The need for integration. In *Community power and grassroots democracy*, eds. M. Kaufman and H. Dilla Alfonso, 189-221. Ottawa: International Development Research Centre.

Clamen, J. 2010. Interview by Cheryl Auger, Montreal, 30 September. Tape recording.

Daalder, A. 2007. *Prostitution in the Netherlands since the lifting of the brothel ban*. The Hague: Netherlands Ministry of Justice.

Delacoste, F., and P. Alexander. 1998. *Sex work: Writings by women in the sex industry*. 2nd ed. San Francisco: Cleis Press.

Foucault, M. 1991. Governmentality. In *The Foucault effect: Studies in governmentality*, ed. G. Burchell, C. Gordon, and P. Miller, 87-104. Chicago: University of Chicago Press.

Fraser, P. 1985. *Report of the Special Committee on Pornography and Prostitution: Pornography and prostitution in Canada*. Ottawa: Government of Canada.

Gamson, W. 1990. *The strategy of social protest*. 2nd ed. Belmont: Wadsworth.

Garland, D. 1997. 'Governmentality,' and the problem of crime: Foucault, criminology, sociology. *Theoretical Criminology* 1, 2: 173-214.

Giddens, A. 1976. *New rules of the sociological method*. New York: Basic Books.

–. 1984. *The constitution of society: Outline of the theory of structuration*. Berkeley: University of California Press.

Goffman, E. 1963. *Stigma: Notes on the management of spoiled identity*. Englewood Cliffs: Prentice-Hall.

–. 1974. *Frame analysis: An essay on the organization of experience*. New York: Harper and Row.

Goodyear, M., and R. Weitzer. 2011. International trends in the control of sexual services. In *Policing pleasure: Sex work, policy and the state in global perspective*, ed. S. Dewey and P. Kelly, 16-30. New York: New York University Press.

House of Commons. 2005. Subcommittee on Solicitation Laws (SSLR). Meetings. http://www2.parl.gc.ca/.

Ivy, S. 2010. The (in)visibility of sex workers: A politics of the flesh. Mary McDonald Essay, BC Civil Liberties Association. http://bccla.org/wp-content/uploads/2012/03/2010-Ivy-Essay-Comp-Sex-Workers.pdf.

Jenkins, J. 1983. Resource mobilization theory and the study of social movements. *Annual Review of Sociology* 9: 527-53.

Jenness, V. 1990. From sex as sin to sex as work: COYOTE and the re-organization of prostitution as a social problem. *Social Problems* 37, 3: 403-20.

–. 1993. *Making it work: The prostitute's rights movement in perspective.* Hawthorne: Aldine de Gruyter.

Laverack, G., and A. Whipple. 2010. The sirens' song of empowerment: A case study of health promotion and the New Zealand Prostitutes Collective. *Global Health Promotion* 17, 1: 33-38.

Lichtenstein, B. 1999. Reframing "Eve" in the AIDS era: The pursuit of legitimacy by New Zealand sex workers. In *Sexuality and culture.* Vol. 2, *Sex work and sex workers,* ed. B. Dank and R. Refinetti, 37-59. New Brunswick, NJ: Transaction.

Lindberg, C., and M. Berg. 2010. Skrota sexköpslagen för kvinnornas skull [Scrap the sex purchase law of the women's movement]. *Expressen,* 21 July. http://www.expressen.se/debatt/debatt-skrota-sexkopslagen-for-kvinnornas-skull/.

Lowman, J. 2000. Violence and the outlaw status of (street) prostitution in Canada. *Violence against Women* 6, 9: 987-1011.

Marques, O. 2006. Governing female sexuality: Prostitution, problematic associations and the Subcommittee on Solicitation Laws. Master's thesis, Department of Sociology and Anthropology, University of Windsor.

Mathieu, L. 2003. The emergence and uncertain outcomes of prostitutes' social movements. *European Journal of Women's Studies* 10, 1: 29-50.

McLaren, J. 1986. Chasing the social evil: Moral fervour and the evolution of Canada's laws, 1867-1917. *Canadian Journal of Law and Society* 1: 125-65.

–. 1995. Recalculating the wages of sin: The social and legal construction of prostitution, 1850-1920. *Manitoba Law Journal* 1: 524-55.

Melucci, A. 1996. *Challenging codes: Collective action in the information age.* Cambridge: Cambridge University Press.

Mensah, M. 2010. L'idée de communauté et l'action collective des travailleuses du sexe [The idea of community and collective action among sex workers]. In *Mais oui c'est du travail! Penser le travail du sexe au delà de la victimisation* [Of course it's work! Thinking about sex work beyond victimization], by Colette Parent, Christine Bruckert, Patrice Corriveau, Maria Nengeh Mensah, and Louise Toupin, 79-106. Quebec City: Presses de l'Université du Québec.

Montreal Mirror. 2007. Safety last. 4-10 January. http://www.montrealmirror.com/.

Outshoorn, J. 2001. Debating prostitution in Parliament: A feminist analysis. *European Journal of Women's Studies* 8, 4: 472-90.

–, ed. 2004. *The politics of prostitution: Women's movements, democratic states and the globalisation of sex commerce.* Cambridge: Cambridge University Press.

Pacey, K. 2010. Interview by Cheryl Auger, Vancouver, 20 April. Tape recording.

Pheterson, G., ed. 1989. *A vindication of the rights of whores.* Seattle: Seal Press.

Phoenix, J. 2008. Be helped or else! Economic exploitation, male violence and prostitution policy in the UK. In *Demanding sex: Critical reflections on the regulation of prostitution,* ed. V. Munro and M. della Giusta, 35-50. Aldershot: Ashgate.

Pollack, S. 2010. Labelling clients 'risky': Social work and the neo-liberal welfare state. *British Journal of Social Work* 40, 4: 1263-78.

Roberts, N. 1992. *Whores in history: Prostitution in Western history.* London: Harper Collins.

Scoular, J., and M. O'Neill. 2008. Legal incursions into supply/demand: Criminalising and responsibilising the buyers and sellers of sex in the UK. In *Demanding sex: Critical reflections on the regulation of prostitution,* ed. V. Munro and M. della Giusta, 13-33. Aldershot: Ashgate.

SOW. 1970. *Report of the Royal Commission on the Status of Women in Canada.* Ottawa: Government of Canada.

Michael Goodyear and Cheryl Auger

SSLR. 2006. *Standing Committee on Justice and Human Rights. Sixth report: The challenge of change. A study of Canada's prostitution laws.* Ottawa: Government of Canada. http://www.parl.gc.ca/content/hoc/Committee/391/JUST/Reports/RP2599932/justrp06/sslrrp06-e.pdf.

Sudbury, J. 2005. *Global lockdown: Race, gender, and the prison industrial complex.* New York: Routledge.

Trudeau, P. 1967. Omnibus Bill: 'There's no place for the state in the bedrooms of the nation.' CBC Digital Archives. 21 December. http://www.cbc.ca/.

Valverde, M. 1999. The harms of sex and the risks of breasts: Obscenity and indecency in Canadian law. *Social and Legal Studies* 8, 2: 181-97.

Wagenaar, H. 2006. Democracy and prostitution: Deliberating the legalization of brothels in the Netherlands. *Administration and Society* 38, 2: 198-235.

Walkowitz, J. 1992. *City of dreadful delight: Narratives of sexual danger in late-Victorian London.* Chicago: University of Chicago Press.

Weber, M. 1947. *The theory of social and economic organization.* Translated by T. Parsons. New York: Simon and Schuster. Originally published as *Wirtschaft und geselschaft,* 1922.

Weitzer, R. 1991. Prostitutes' rights in the United States: The failure of a movement. *Sociological Quarterly* 32, 1: 23-41.

Wolfenden, J. 1957. *Report of the Departmental Committee on Homosexual Offences and Prostitution.* London: Her Majesty's Stationery Office.

Young, I. 1994. Punishment, treatment, empowerment: Three approaches to policy for pregnant addicts. *Feminist Studies* 20, 1: 32-57.

–. 2000. *Inclusion and democracy.* New York: Oxford University Press.

Zald, M., and J. McCarthy, eds. 1987. *Social movements in an organizational society.* New Brunswick, NJ: Transaction Books.

Case Cited

Lawrence v. Texas, 539 U.S. 558 (2003). http://supreme.justia.com/cases/federal/us/539/558/case.html.

15

Crown Expert-Witness Testimony in *Bedford v. Canada:* Evidence-Based Argument or Victim-Paradigm Hyperbole?

JOHN LOWMAN

In 1999, Sweden was the first country to adopt demand-side prohibition of prostitution, with Norway and Iceland following suit in 2009.[1] Intent on abolishing prostitution, the Nordic (Raymond 2010), or Swedish, Model prohibits sex buying and procuring but does not prohibit sex selling on the grounds that prostitutes are victims of male sexual violence and exploitation, and thus should not be criminally culpable. From this perspective, prostitution *is* violence against women: "The man who commits the prostitution act on the prostituted woman ... is no different than a rapist" (Ekberg 2008, 2).

Since its adoption in Sweden, there has been an intensifying campaign to globalize demand-side prohibition. Its most vociferous advocates have travelled the world to present their position to national legislatures and other bodies whenever the opportunity arises; in 2010, their arguments wound up in a Canadian court.

When three Ontario sex workers brought an action against the Government of Canada, seeking a declaration that the bawdy-house laws (Criminal Code, s. 210), living on the avails law (section 212(1)(j)), and communicating law (section 213(1)(c)) violate their rights under the Canadian Charter of Rights and Freedoms (*Bedford v. Canada* 2010), the Crown attempted to defend the impugned legislation by adopting the prohibitionist discourse and arguing that prostitution is "inherently harmful" (Canada 2009, para. 1).[2] Among its expert witnesses were Melissa Farley and Janice Raymond from the United States, Mary Sullivan from Australia, and Richard Poulin from Canada, all of whom purport to offer an evidence-based rationale for demand-side prohibition. Although the

Ontario Superior Court clarified that its task in *Bedford v. Canada* (2010, para. 25) was to consider the constitutional arguments at issue and *not* which model of prostitution law is best, various prohibitionist truth claims were put to the test. This chapter examines several of the core claims advanced.

Given that *Bedford v. Canada* generated more than twenty-five thousand pages of evidence – including the transcripts of fifty-five witness cross-examinations, numerous government and academic research reports, newspaper articles, Hansard extracts, and more – it would not be possible for this short chapter to do justice to the entire range of prohibitionist evidence claims advanced.[3] Instead, it focuses on the claims of Crown expert witnesses Melissa Farley and Richard Poulin that

- The average age of entry into prostitution in Canada is fourteen years.
- The "vast majority" of Canadian prostitutes were sexually abused as children.
- Prostitution is inherently "violent" because of the psychological and physical harm it inflicts on "prostituted women" and the "power imbalance" it involves.

The chapter concludes with a discussion of the prohibitionist "harm elimination" philosophy in light of the Superior Court of Ontario's conclusion (*Bedford v. Canada* 2010), supported by the Court of Appeal for Ontario (*Canada (Attorney General) v. Bedford* 2012), that striking down the bawdy-house law and permitting in-call prostitution would reduce, but not necessarily eliminate, violence from prostitution in Canada.

Is Fourteen Years the Average Age of Entry into Prostitution in Canada?

In his affidavit for *Bedford v. Canada,* University of Ottawa sociologist Richard Poulin repeated the oft-made prohibitionist claim that "the average age of recruitment ... in Canada is 14 years old" (Joint Application Record, Volume 40, Tab 102, paras. 24, 28).[4] Poulin's testimony deserves scrutiny in light of the way that the majority report of the Standing Committee on the Status of Women (2007) – the only federal review of Canadian prostitution law to have recommended that Parliament adopt the Nordic model of demand-side prohibition – treated every claim he made at its hearings as established fact.[5]

Poulin's assertion about the age of entry into prostitution is a cornerstone of prohibitionist rhetoric, as it "raises the issue of free and informed consent and the 'choice' of prostitution as a profession" (Affidavit, para. 24). If a person begins to prostitute at age fourteen and then becomes entrenched, there are questions about the degree of choice he or she exercises after turning eighteen: "The 14-year-old in prostitution eventually turns 18 but she has not suddenly made a new 'vocational choice' ... Women who began prostituting as adolescents may have parts of themselves that are dissociatively compartmentalized into a much younger child's time and place" (Farley et al. 2003, 36). Treating prostitutes as if they are children makes it much easier for prohibitionists to argue that they should be saved from themselves and for demand-side prohibitionists to argue that a woman selling sex should not be culpable.

As evidence to substantiate his claim about the average age of entry, Poulin's affidavit (para. 28) provided several sources. However, under cross-examination it became clear that only one of them, McIntyre's (1999) study of sexually exploited youth, reported the average age of entry of its research participants as being fourteen. Because her sampling procedure excluded anyone who became involved in prostitution as an adult, it is not possible to derive the Canadian average age of entry into prostitution from it. Indeed, it is not possible to estimate that age from any stand-alone non-probabilistic sample.

Why did Poulin not acknowledge that in other Canadian studies entered into evidence, the average age of entry was much higher? For example, in O'Doherty's (2007) sample of off-street prostitutes, it was twenty-two, and in Benoit and Millar's (2001), it was nineteen.[6] Even for Farley et al. (2003) and Farley, Lynne, and Cotton's (2005) sample of Vancouver prostitutes, it was eighteen. As Poulin subsequently acknowledged under cross-examination, "There's no national inquiry in Canada, so nobody can have the pretence of knowing when people enter the sex trade, at what age" (Joint Application Record, Volume 43, Tab 105, question 158).

In view of the evidence before the court, it is difficult to understand why the attorney general of Canada nevertheless claimed that the average age of entry into prostitution in Canada is between fourteen and sixteen (Canada 2009, para. 49).

Were the Vast Majority of Canadian Prostitutes Sexually Abused as Children?

Farley et al. (2003, 35) claim that 55 percent to 90 percent of prostitutes report a history of child sexual abuse. Poulin claimed that "the vast majority of people in prostitution have been victims of sexual assault during childhood" (Joint Application Record, Volume 40, Tab 102, para. 37). When it comes to Western nations, again these claims are based on non-probabilistic samples of persons involved mainly in street prostitution contacted through social service agencies or on the street.[7] In the case of Canada, these commentators ignore the debate over the extent of sexual abuse among even these samples.

For example, although Poulin's affidavit cited the conclusion of the Committee on Sexual Offences against Children and Youth (CSOACY 1984) that running away from home is a pathway into youth prostitution, he neglected to apprise the court of the committee's conclusion that juvenile prostitutes are no more likely than members of the general population to have been victims of childhood sexual abuse (ibid., 1046). Although a re-examination of the committee's data showed nothing of the sort – the respondents to its Juvenile Prostitution Survey appear to have been at least twice as likely as respondents to their National Population Survey to have been victims of "unwanted sexual acts" during their childhood (Lowman 1987, 103) – the victims were still in the minority: 60 percent of the female respondents to the Juvenile Prostitution Survey and 78 percent of the males did *not* report having experienced "unwanted sexual acts" while they were under the age of eighteen.[8]

Other Canadian surveys providing data on incidence of childhood sexual abuse among prostitutes report a large range, varying from 10 percent to 90 percent (Brannigan and Fleischman 1989; Lowman 1991) – hence the disagreement over the relevance of childhood sexual abuse for identifying pathways into prostitution. Nevertheless, childhood sexual and physical abuse do appear to be important factors leading to premature home leaving, with prostitution being one of the few ways that "lumpen youth" can support themselves (Lowman 1987). Once they are on the street, selling sex becomes a solution to their situational poverty: "survival sex" par excellence. However it is equally clear that this is but one pathway into commercial sex, and one experience of prostitution. The incidence of childhood sexual abuse among persons who begin prostituting when they are adults – which may be the majority of Canadian prostitutes – is unknown.

Is Prostitution Inherently Violent?

To understand the prohibitionist argument that prostitution is inherently violent (see also Chapter 14 in this volume), the discussion turns to Crown witness definitions of "violence" and the meaning of "inherent."

To be "inherent," an attribute must be "permanent or essential," "inseparable," and "intrinsic."[9] To be "intrinsic," the attribute must constitute "the essential nature of a thing," and "not [be] dependent on external circumstances."[10]

The Crown's expert witnesses in *Bedford v. Canada* offered three concepts of violence, which they claim are ubiquitous in prostitution: power imbalance, psychological harm, and physical violence, the main evidentiary focus of the case.

Power Imbalance as Violence

Poulin defined "violence" as "the systematic relationship of power involving [one person's] domination over the other" (Joint Application Record, Volume 43, Tab 105, question 387). Under cross-examination Poulin asserted that any systematic power imbalance between adults constitutes "violence."[11] From this perspective, prostitution is an act of "domination" because the sex buyer exercises his power to pay for sex, in contrast to the sex seller, who is subordinate because she has to provide sex to receive that payment (ibid., question 300). By means of this trope, prostitution becomes inherently violent by definition. However, though many commentators argue that the power relationship in prostitution is much more complicated than this (O'Connell Davidson 1998; Chapkis 2001), if Parliament were to agree with Poulin's eccentric definition of violence, presumably all wage labour would be criminalized, not just prostitution, and perhaps heterosexual marriage too.

Psychological Harm as Violence

In defending the impugned prostitution laws, the attorney general of Canada claimed that "social science evidence from around the world demonstrates that the risks and harms flowing from prostitution are inherent to the nature of the activity itself" (Canada 2009, para. 1). A central pillar of this argument is that prostitution is inherently psychologically harmful (ibid., para. 44). Two indicators of this alleged psychological harm are the high levels of post-traumatic stress disorder (PTSD) among "prostituted women" and their desire to "escape" prostitution (Farley and Barkan 1998; Farley et al. 1998; Farley et al. 2003).

An oft-quoted source of evidence for the psychological harm caused by prostitution is that 68 percent of Farley et al.'s (2003, 56) respondents in nine countries met the authors' criteria for a diagnosis of PTSD, with the severity of their symptoms being in the same range "as treatment-seeking combat veterans, battered women seeking shelter, rape survivors, and refugees from state-organized torture."

It is one thing to argue that some women are traumatized by their experience of prostitution, but quite another to suggest that these findings demonstrate that prostitution psychologically harms everyone involved. Do Farley et al.'s sampling technique and method for measuring PTSD warrant such a generalization? To answer this question, first consider the methodological problems

John Lowman

with Farley et al's diagnosis of PTSD; I return to problems with their sampling methods later, when discussing the incidence of criminally prohibited physical violence in various prostitution venues.

Farley et al's method for diagnosing PTSD has been evaluated as incapable of generating the conclusions the authors draw from it.[12] Consider the comments of Dr. Paul Henry De Wet, the head of Forensic Psychiatry at Weskoppies Hospital, when he was asked to assess Farley et al's (1998) and Farley and Barkan's (1998) measurement of PTSD after it had been entered into evidence in a constitutional challenge of South African prostitution law (*S v. Jordan and Others* 2002).

When he learned that the diagnosis was based on a "PTSD checklist" and a twenty-three-item questionnaire that took about ten minutes to complete, De Wet commented that "PTSD simply cannot be diagnosed in this manner" (quoted in *Bedford v. Canada* Applicants' factum, para. 303). He explained that there is no internationally accepted measuring instrument and that a psychiatric examination would require approximately three hours with a patient, plus collateral corroboration that might involve interviews with family members, friends, and work colleagues. He argued that diagnosis requires use of accepted international classification systems (such as the *Diagnostic and Statistical Manual of Mental Disorders,* 4th ed., or the *International Statistical Classification of Diseases and Related Health Problems,* 10th rev. ed.) rather than a checklist of symptoms, as most of the symptoms are also associated with other disorders. Given that a variety of factors might produce the occurrence of such symptoms, he found the claim that "the trauma relates to prostitution as such difficult to accept" (De Wet 2002, para. 9). Any number of factors other than prostitution could have caused the trauma that Farley and her colleagues (Farley et al. 1998; Farley and Barkan 1998) claim to have measured. De Wet (2002, para. 24) concluded, "In the absence of proper control groups for the research and in the absence of proper diagnostic methodology I find the diagnosis of PTSD as well as the allegations in respect of its alleged causes to be wholly inappropriate."[13] Little wonder, then, that the International Society for Traumatic Stress Studies does not recommend that Farley and her colleagues' method be used for clinical diagnosis.

Of as much concern as De Wet's criticism of the PTSD diagnosis is Farley's refusal to disclose her research instruments on the grounds that their dissemination would compromise their validity.[14] How their validity would be compromised is unclear, and this strategy runs contrary to customary academic practice because it means that other researchers cannot subject her research instruments to critical scrutiny or use them to replicate her findings.[15] Consider this problem in relation to another indicator of the psychological harm attributed to prostitution – the finding that many women wish to "leave" it. This was the case with the samples in Farley et al. (2003) and Farley, Lynne, and Cotton (2005), which were drawn mostly from Vancouver's Downtown Eastside, one of the poorest city neighbourhoods in Canada and home to a large number of mentally ill persons, refugees, and street-connected Aboriginal women.

Two problems characterize the generalization of this sample into the claim that the large majority of women wish to escape prostitution. The first concerns the generalization of findings about the experiences of some of the most marginalized street prostitutes in Canada to prostitution as a whole, a problem taken up below in the discussion of physical violence. The second concerns the translation of a respondent's desire to leave prostitution – the relatively neutral term that appears to have been used on the questionnaire – into a desire to escape it, a word that better fits prohibitionist rhetoric, which treats all prostitution as sexual slavery.

Because Farley refuses to release her research instruments, it is difficult to ascertain exactly how the question about leaving was asked. The reporting of decontextualized self-administered survey questions may say as much or more about the researchers than their subjects. For example, though some people may wish to leave prostitution, they may nevertheless prefer it to the low paid "shit work" that may be their only alternative, from which prostitution represents "escape," the least bad alternative. Women choose to prostitute in social-structural conditions that are not of their own making. When the same structural circumstances limit their work options to minimum-wage manual or service work, prostitution may be their preferred option because of the relative autonomy and better pay it affords (Jeffrey and MacDonald 2006).

The window of opportunity for individuals to engage in sex work may also have something to do with their desire to move on (see Chapter 7 in this volume). As is the case in some other forms of work, the earning potential of adults who sell sex declines with age. Survey samples and communicating charge statistics indicate that the majority of street sex workers are between sixteen and twenty-six years of age (Lowman 1989, 267), in which case decreasing earning power may partly explain a person's desire to leave prostitution at some point. The same may be true of men and women working in low-paid agricultural occupations, manufacturing, and other poorly paid service jobs where work experience – time on the job – does not usually increase the rate at which they are paid. To say that people make a choice to do any of these jobs does not necessarily mean that they are "happy hookers" or happy labourers, although some of them may be.[16]

John Lowman

Given their experience of prostitution and the other problems they face – including substance addiction, grinding poverty, and the devastating effects of colonization on Aboriginal peoples – many street-involved women in Vancouver's Downtown Eastside would, no doubt, like to escape prostitution. They would probably like to escape poverty and colonialism too. In this regard, it would be hard to find anyone involved in the debate over prostitution law reform who would disagree with the idea that we should develop policies to help provide alternative ways for these women to make a living. But it would be just as hard to find anyone who believes that the current federal or British Columbia governments would be willing to fund the policy changes and programs necessary to create these opportunities, let alone understand what programs are needed.

Then there is the problem of making generalizations about prostitution on the basis of a sample of the most marginalized group of "survival sex" workers.

Criminally Prohibited Physical Violence

Given that one of the primary constitutional issues raised by *Bedford v. Canada* is whether the impugned provisions compromise a prostitute's constitutional right to security of the person, the case hinged on evidentiary claims about relative rates of Criminal Code definitions of violence in differing prostitution venues. The Crown argued that violence is a permanent or essential attribute of prostitution that is not dependent on external circumstances, such as the location in which sexual liaisons are arranged or occur. If the risk of violence is "inherent" in this actuarial sense, it would be "impossible to manage or transfer away" (Albion Research 2012).

The Crown's expert witnesses argued that prostitution involves physical victimization of prostitutes no matter where it occurs. The Ontario Court of Appeal asserted "that prostitution is inherently dangerous in virtually any circumstance" (*Canada (Attorney General) v. Bedford* 2012, para. 117). However, this does not mean that the risk is equivalent in every circumstance or is impossible to transfer away. The applicants presented evidence indicating that levels of violence differ substantially in varying sex work settings (Church 2001; Plumridge and Abel 2001; Brents and Hausbeck 2005; Sanders and Campbell 2007), in which case it is possible to mitigate the risk of violence.[17] If the court accepted the evidence that risk varies considerably, the question then became the degree to which the impugned prostitution laws materially contribute to the victimization that occurs by preventing risk mitigation. In the words of the appeal court, the fact that prostitution is "dangerous in virtually any circumstance" does not diminish "the connection between the criminal prohibitions in the three challenged provisions and the increased risk of physical harm to prostitutes" (*Canada (Attorney General) v. Bedford* 2012, para. 117). The court could reach this conclusion only by recognizing that risk does vary considerably in different forms of prostitution.

To exemplify variations in the degree of risk, the following discussion focuses on victimization surveys of Vancouver sex workers in differing venues and murder rates of sex workers in street versus off-street prostitution in British Columbia.

Victimization Surveys as an Index of Risk of Physical Violence

Given that the attorney general of Canada argued that "social science research conducted regarding prostitution should avoid making sweeping generalizations about prostitution at large" (Canada 2009, para. 10), one wonders why Canada's defence of the impugned laws was based on a series of sweeping generalizations about prostitution. For an illustration of the folly of generalizing from unrepresentative samples, consider the analysis of Vancouver prostitution in Farley et al. (2003) and Farley, Lynne, and Cotton (2005).

Farley et al. (2005, 260) acknowledge that "no study of prostitution can claim a representative or random sample, given the illegality of prostitution in most locations." However, they appear to believe that the mere acknowledgment of this sampling problem solves it, as they proceed to make sweeping generalizations on the basis of a convenience sample of what are probably the most marginalized sex workers in Vancouver. Are these generalizations warranted?

It is not possible to determine the overall population of sex workers in Vancouver from which to generate a random sample. Because street workers may also work off-street at some point, the street and off-street populations are not mutually exclusive. However, given that it is estimated that only 5 to 20 percent of Canada's prostitution trade occurs on the street, it is likely that the majority of persons working off-street never work the street, or rarely do.[18] To be representative, a sample would have to comprise at least 80 percent workers who never or have rarely worked the street. Although such a sample would still be self-selected and thus not necessarily representative of each population, it would at least enable a comparison of pathways into prostitution and the working experiences of sex workers in different venues. How does Farley et al.'s sample fare in light of this criterion?

Prostitution in Vancouver takes many forms, with the street trade comprising a relatively minor component. The largest part of the trade occurs in massage parlours, health enhancement centres, escort services, micro-brothels, and outcall or in-call services advertised by independent workers in print media and

John Lowman

via the Internet. Did Farley et al.'s sample include a cross-section of workers from these various sectors of Vancouver's commercial sex industry? No. Their study involved "brief interviews" with "100 women prostituting in or near Vancouver's Downtown Eastside," which they acknowledge is "one of the most economically destitute areas in North America" (Farley et al. 2003, 37).[19]

Not only did this sample exclude most off-street venues but it also excluded important components of the street trade, including the so-called high track, which at that time was the Richards-Seymour stroll in downtown Vancouver. High track women command much higher prices for sexual services than their counterparts in the Downtown Eastside, and they often supply the service in hotel rooms near the stroll rather than in parked cars in remote locations. High track is controlled by "professional pimps" who frown on intravenous drug use (Lowman and Fraser 1996), whereas the majority of women in the Downtown Eastside are intravenous drug users (Currie et al. 1995; Shannon et al. 2008). Women on high track refer to the Downtown Eastside as "low track," and there is little intermingling of the women from the two areas. Few Aboriginal women work high track, in contrast to Farley et al.'s mostly Downtown Eastside sample, 52 percent of whom were Aboriginal (Farley Affidavit, Joint Application Record, Volume 49, Tab 113, para. 49).

Farley, Lynne, and Cotton (2005, 260) claim to have made "every attempt to contact any woman known to be prostituting, indoors or outdoors." They assert, "We did this by asking women to tell friends who were prostituting elsewhere (e.g., in other areas or from their homes or clubs) that we would return to a certain location at a specific time the next day" (ibid.). It is difficult to see how this method constitutes "every attempt" when they did not use the much more successful strategies that other Vancouver researchers have employed to contact women in massage parlours and escort services or who work independently from apartments – most notably by developing contacts in those other venues (O'Doherty 2007, 2011; ORCHID Project 2007) or by advertising on-line for research participants (O'Doherty 2007, 2011).

Farley, Lynne, and Cotton (2005) argue that their failure to contact women working indoors was not a problem, as some of the respondents had off-street experience. However, they do not disclose what proportion had this type of experience or what it consisted of. My experience researching prostitution in Vancouver indicates that most Downtown Eastside women would know few, if any, people working in Vancouver's mid- to high-end escort services and massage parlours, which would appear to employ very few Aboriginal women (O'Doherty 2007).[20] If one is to collect information about the experiences of these populations, they need to be purposively sampled in a concerted way.

Although there clearly is some cross-over between street and off-street prostitution, many off-street sex workers have little or no street prostitution experience. For example, when O'Doherty (2007) purposively sampled mid- to high-end indoor sex workers, of the thirty-nine who responded to her survey, only five began their involvement in prostitution on the street, which is roughly what one would expect if street prostitution comprises 5 to 20 percent of the trade. To examine relative degrees of risk, the most helpful comparison of prostitution experiences would thus be between women (and men) who have mostly or all street prostitution experience with those who have none.

O'Doherty's sample ($n = 39$) provides a portrait of very different prostitution experiences and risks than those associated with street prostitution in the Downtown Eastside (O'Doherty 2007). Seventeen of her respondents had worked in massage parlours, fifteen had worked for escort services, and sixteen had worked independently, meeting clients by advertising on-line or in print media.[21] The characteristics of this sample differ markedly from samples of street-based sex workers. Only two of O'Doherty's respondents were under the age of eighteen when they started working. There were no Aboriginal women. The sample had much higher levels of educational attainment than other samples of Canadian sex workers: 90 percent had some post-secondary education, including seven women with postgraduate degrees. Overall, 63 percent had not encountered any kind of victimization while working. If we remove from the sample the five women who began working as prostitutes on the street, we find a much lower rate of victimization than in any street sample (e.g., Lowman and Fraser 1996; Cler-Cunningham and Christensen 2001). Indeed, in the roughly 270 years that the thirty-four remaining women had practised prostitution, there was just one assault by a client and five incidents where clients had made threats of some kind.[22] Is this degree of risk "unacceptable"? Compare it to the proportion of women in Currie et al.'s (1995) sample of street-connected women in Vancouver's Downtown Eastside, 48 percent of whom had been "beaten by a customer" in the six-month period prior to the survey.[23]

Although Farley, Lynne, and Cotton's (2005, 260) study did not access the off-street sector of commercial sex in Vancouver, the skewed nature of their sample did not lead them to qualify their generalization that prostitution is an "often violent economic option most often entered into by those with a lengthy history of sexual, racial and economic victimization."[24] Although this may be an apt description of prostitution in Vancouver's Downtown Eastside and some other areas, it would be premature to generalize it to the sex trade in the city as a whole without a sample designed to capture a cross-section of the entire population.

John Lowman

These methodological issues also suggest that sweeping generalizations about the incidence of PTSD on the basis of a highly skewed sample of street-involved sex workers are incautious. We need a much more inclusive sample to understand the psychological effects of sex work (Vanwesenbeeck 2005, 636). In this regard, Chudakov et al.'s (2002) findings provide an important quali-fication to other studies. Their interviews with fifty-five women working in organized brothels included screening items for post-traumatic stress disorder. They found that 17 percent met the criteria for PTSD, a much smaller propor-tion than Farley and Barkan (1998) reported. Chudakov et al. (ibid., 315) concluded, "It is important for hypothesis formation for researchers to realize the tremendous potential heterogeneity of commercial sex workers, as evidenced in the case histories presented here."

Murder Rates as an Index of Risk of Physical Violence
There can be little doubt that sex workers are primary targets of serial killers (Quinet 2011).[25] However, serial killers do not target sex workers in general; they focus on street prostitutes. For example, the Green River killer (Gary Ridgway, forty-eight convictions), the Yorkshire Ripper (Peter Sutcliffe, thirteen convictions), the Spokane killer (Robert Lee Yates, thirteen convictions), the Genesee River killer (Arthur Shawcross, ten convictions), the New York City killer (Joel Rifkin, nine convictions), and Robert Pickton (six convictions, twenty murder charges stayed, may have murdered as many as forty-nine women) focused overwhelmingly on street-involved women. They did not go to body rub parlours to find victims or even to escort services.

Despite the overwhelming evidence, Poulin took issue with murder expert Elliott Layton's evidence (Affidavit, Joint Application Record, Volume 40, Tab 102) that serial killers of sex workers mainly target street prostitutes. Arguing that the Pickton experience in Vancouver has warped perceptions of sex worker vic-timization, Poulin offered four examples of killers targeting indoor sex workers.

The first two examples concerned Patrice Alegre, whom Poulin claimed killed four sex workers indoors in France, and Austrian Jack Unterweger, who killed women in three different European jurisdictions. However, on cross-examination, Poulin was unable to provide any sources showing where these two truck drivers met or killed their victims.[26]

The third example consisted of Poulin's claim that, "in Quebec, at least 5 of the 14 women prostitutes killed in the last ten years did not work on the streets. They were incall and outcall prostitutes, meaning that they received clients in a private place, or travelled to meet clients at their homes or hotel rooms" (Joint Application Record, Volume 40, Tab 102, para. 47). When Poulin was pressed to provide evidence to substantiate this claim, his list of homicides revealed that, though the bodies of five victims had been found indoors (three in their own homes, one in a motel room, and one in a drug dealer's apartment), it did not establish where any of them initially met their assailant (Supplementary Joint Application Record, Volume 2, Tab 175H).[27]

His fourth example concerned murders of sex workers in the Netherlands. Poulin claimed that, "since 1992, there were 50 female prostituted persons killed, they were working in brothels and windows" (Joint Application Record, Volume 43, Tab 105, para. 91). However, the source he gave did not substantiate this claim: Dutch historian Lotte Van de Pol wrote, "Many victims were working in the streets, the majority of which [sic] were drug addicts; but there were also several women murdered in a brothel or 'window,' and a few of them were murdered at home by their pimp" (Affidavit, Joint Application Record, Volume 47, Tab 110, para. 64). From this description it appears that the majority of victims were street workers. As it is estimated that just 1 percent of Dutch prostitution occurs on the street (Siegel 2009, cited in Weitzer 2011), these figures provide further evidence that street-involved women are exposed to by far the greater risk of violence by clients or men posing as clients compared to in-call workers.

The foregoing commentary is not meant to suggest that women in off-street prostitution work risk free. There are records of women involved in outcall work being murdered. For example, when we created profiles of the fifty known murders of sex workers occurring in British Columbia between 1960 and 1993, we found a case where a man was charged in 1988 with the murder of an escort in Victoria. When the escort visited the accused man's apartment, he murdered her. He attempted to strangle a second escort three hours later, but she escaped and led police to him. After a psychiatric examination, he was found fit to stand trial, convicted, and given a life sentence (Lowman and Fraser 1996, 137).

One of the few murders we have found involving a person working indoors in Vancouver since 1960 occurred in 2007, when Andrew Evans killed Nicole Parisien, a thirty-three-year-old Aboriginal woman he met via an erotic services advertisement on Craigslist. Newspaper coverage indicated that Parisien was working alone in a fifth-floor apartment, where she serviced clients (*Vancouver Sun* 2007). It appears that a conflict developed during the sexual encounter that ended with the intoxicated Evans striking and strangling Parisien, whose body he dumped outside the apartment building where the alleged bawdy-house was said to have operated.

Parisien's demise is significant not only for being one of the very few examples of the murder of an in-call sex worker in Canada – albeit one who appears to have been working alone – but also for the interpretation of its significance by demand-side prohibitionist Janine Benedet, a professor in the University of British Columbia law school.

In a *Toronto Globe and Mail* opinion editorial, Benedet (2009) claimed that "supporters of the prostitution industry want us to believe that women would be safe if men's purchase of women for sex is legalized."[28] She used Evans's conviction for second-degree murder as evidence that no form of prostitution is safe, in which case Canada should follow Sweden and criminalize sex buying and pimping while decriminalizing the act of selling sex.

Benedet's opinion editorial sidestepped the Charter arguments before the Ontario Superior Court.[29] Given that the legislature has not criminalized the purchase or sale of sex, the main issue that Justice Himel considered is whether laws that criminalize activities pertaining to prostitution "materially contribute" to violence against prostitutes by putting their lives at greater risk than would be the case if they could work legally in a controlled indoor environment. To understand the variation in the degree of risk that workers in various commercial sex venues experience, the murder of an indoor sex worker, tragic though it is, needs putting into perspective.

Since 1980 in British Columbia, nearly 150 street prostitutes have gone missing or are confirmed homicide victims. The street trade is estimated to account for between 5 and 20 percent of prostitution in the province. If the risk of murder is as great in off-street locations as it is on the street, we would now be reading about the murder or disappearance of between 600 and 2,850 escort service and massage parlour workers during that period. However, we have found no murders of massage parlour workers, two murders of escorts, and one of a woman working alone in an apartment, in which case street prostitutes are somewhere between 200 to 950 times more likely to be victims of homicide than their off-street counterparts.

These murder patterns also suggest that instead of having an opportunity to become serial killers, the men who murder indoor sex workers are usually apprehended relatively quickly, unlike those who target street workers, who rarely leave tracks.

The Ontario Superior and Appeal Court Decisions

After considering twenty-five thousand pages of evidence, the Ontario Superior Court concluded that, on a balance of probabilities, the risk of violence toward prostitutes "can be reduced, although not necessarily eliminated" (*Bedford v. Canada* 2010, para. 300). From this perspective, the degree of risk of physical violence to which sex workers are exposed *is* dependent on external circumstances and is thus not "inherent" – risk does not constitute "the essential nature" of prostitution even if it is substantial, and it may not be possible to eliminate it completely. From this perspective, given that the Charter challenge focused on the effect of the impugned laws on the prostitute's right to security of the person, the question for the court became one of ascertaining whether the laws materially contribute to the physical risk that sex workers face.

After weighing the evidence, the Superior Court (ibid., para. 421) concluded that working indoors is generally safer than working on the street; the bawdy-house provisions can place prostitutes in danger by preventing them from working in a regular indoor location and gaining the safety benefits of proximity to others, security staff, closed-circuit television, and other monitoring; the living on the avails of prostitution provision can make prostitutes more susceptible to violence by preventing them from legally hiring bodyguards or drivers while working; and the communicating provision can increase the vulnerability of street prostitutes by forcing them to forego screening customers at an early and crucial stage of the transaction.

In sum, the Superior Court found that the bawdy-house, the living on the avails, and the communicating laws "individually and together, force prostitutes to choose between their liberty interest and their right to security of the persons protected under the *Canadian Charter of Rights and Freedoms* ... These laws infringe the core values protected by section 7 and that this infringement is not saved by section 1 as a reasonable limit demonstrably justified in a free and democratic society" (ibid., para. 3). Consequently, the Superior Court struck down all three sections.

The Court of Appeal for Ontario agreed unanimously that the bawdy-house law should be struck down. Instead of striking down the living on the avails law, the panel of judges agreed that its constitutional integrity would be saved by an amendment to make it apply only "in circumstances of exploitation." However, the appeal court did not reach consensus on the status of the communicating law. Two judges agreed with the Ontario Superior Court that it should be struck down, but the majority ruled that section 1 of the Charter saved it.

Although the Ontario Court of Appeal decision may be modified in various ways when it reaches the Supreme Court of Canada, these two decisions highlight some of the key issues at stake when it comes to the relative merits of the prohibitionist goal of eliminating violence by attempting to abolish prostitution versus the goal of reducing violence by upholding a prostitute's right to life, liberty, and security of the person.

Conclusion: Prohibitionist Symbolism at What Price?

The testimony of key prohibitionists Poulin and Farley in *Bedford v. Canada* reveals their tendency to design their research and shape their findings to fit their own agenda. They present argument-based evidence rather than evidence-based argument in their quest to bring the Nordic Model to Canada.

Its disputed practical effects aside, the most important aspect of demand-side prohibition in Sweden is its perceived symbolic virtue, a testament to the nation's commitment to gender equality and refusal to countenance violence against women.[30] What would be the likely consequence for the prostitute's right to life, liberty, and security of the person if Canada follows suit?

Just as we will never rid marriage or dating relationships of violence, we will never make prostitution absolutely safe either, but is that a reason to criminalize sex purchasing – or marriage, or dating? Because condoms do not absolutely guarantee safe sex, does that mean people should stop using them for safer sex? No legal regime will usher in a world devoid of risk.

The great irony of demand-side prohibition is that its goal of eliminating harm would expose prostitutes to a greater risk than they would experience if they could work in a controlled and monitored indoor environment. Their safety would be sacrificed to a political manifesto that claims that prostitution harms all women and prevents them from gaining equality with men. Women who continue to work in the sex industry would be absolved of any criminal responsibility on the grounds that they are victims of male violence, but the retention of the impugned provisions would mean that they could not work legally in a controlled and supervised environment. Who would pay the greatest price in this symbolic universe? In all likelihood, it would continue to be those who already disproportionately pay the price: women in the "survival sex" trade.

By way of example, take the experience of Grandma's House during the period in which Robert Pickton is thought to have murdered as many as forty-nine street-involved Downtown Eastside women (see also Chapter 9 in this volume).[31] Grandma's House was the headquarters of a charitable society established in 1997 by Jamie Lee Hamilton to provide services for sex workers in Vancouver's Downtown Eastside.[32]

At about the same time Grandma's House opened, fear that a serial killer was preying on the area's sex workers was growing on the street, and the Vancouver media were beginning to report the disappearance of numerous women. We now know that ten women disappeared from this area in 1997, nine in 1998, and six in 1999.[33] Fearing for their lives, some of the local women asked

Hamilton if they could bring dates to Grandma's House so that they could conduct their business safely: with other people around, they would be able to get help if a date turned bad. Hamilton agreed. In 1999, the Vancouver Police Department laid charges against Hamilton for keeping a common bawdy-house, at which point Grandma's House closed. Hamilton believes that the charges were retribution for her outspoken criticism of the local police and municipal authorities for failing to investigate the growing number of missing women.

The closure of Grandma's House forced the women who frequented it to perform sexual services elsewhere – the most likely place being in cars, one of the locations they find themselves most vulnerable. A large proportion of Downtown Eastside street-involved women are drug and/or alcohol dependent and are homeless or live in rooming houses (Currie et al. 1995). The message appears to be that the only way they can get help to prevent victimization is if they stop the legal act of selling sexual services.

Ironically, then, if demand-side prohibition were to be implemented in Canada – especially if the pattern of law enforcement since 1985 persists, whereby 93 percent of all prostitution charges are for the street offence of communicating – race, class, and gender would intersect in a way that would continue to marginalize and victimize the most vulnerable women in the survival sex trade, many of whom are Aboriginal. Meanwhile, because of the difficulty of enforcing laws against the off-street trade, the indoor trade would remain de facto legal, with most violators of bawdy-house and procuring laws facing only a small risk of prosecution.

Notes

1   As the subject of this chapter is prostitution per se, I use the term "prostitution" and "prostitute" to distinguish exchange of physical sexual services for reward from other kinds of sex work and sex worker.
2   One of the applicants was an active worker; the other two were former sex workers.
3   The complete record is posted at http://mypage.uniserve.ca/~lowman/. For a general critique of the Crown's expert witnesses, see the Applicants' factum, paras. 275-423.
4   Although Poulin claimed to have interviewed numerous women involved in prostitution in Montreal, cross-examination revealed that he has not published any articles describing the results of these interviews. Indeed, he could not produce any transcripts or quantitative data pertaining to them.
5   One important difference between a courtroom and a parliamentary committee room is that in court expert testimony is subject to the detailed scrutiny of the adversarial process. Both sides have the right to introduce expert opinion and cross-examine each other's experts. In sharp contrast, the standing committee invited only known prohibitionists to give expert evidence, thereby exhibiting a clear witness-selection bias (for further discussion, see Lowman 2011).

6 In van der Meulen's (2010) small study in Toronto, it was twenty, and in Chapter 19 in this volume, based on research conducted in Ottawa, it was twenty-two.

7 "Street prostitution" refers to commercial sexual transactions that are initially arranged in street locations that are known locally as prostitution strolls. In such areas, sex sellers wait on the side of the street for clients to approach on foot or in a vehicle.

8 The committee reached this conclusion by comparing questions that were not commensurate from the two surveys.

9 For the definitions, see WordReference.com, http://www.wordreference.com/; Dictionary.com, http://dictionary.reference.com/; and the Free Dictionary, http://www.thefreedictionary.com/.

10 Free Dictionary, http://www.thefreedictionary.com/; Your Dictionary, http://www.your dictionary.com/.

11 For details, see affidavit, paras. 25, 26, and 41, and transcript of cross-examination questions 301, 310, 311, 387, 548, and 575.

12 For a review, see *Bedford v. Canada* Applicants' factum, paras. 303-5.

13 For Farley's defence of her methodology, see her cross-examination questions 409-51.

14 Farley refused to produce them during her cross-examination in *Bedford v. Canada* until an agreement was reached that they would be distributed only to the participating attorneys and the presiding judge.

15 Farley's failure to submit her research protocols for independent research ethics review is also contrary to accepted academic practice.

16 Prohibitionist Victor Malarek (2009) borrowed the term "happy hooker" from Xaviera Hollander to misrepresent and trivialize arguments for decriminalization.

17 Also see Raphael and Shapiro (2004), which prohibitionists assert establishes that off-street prostitution may be even more violent than street prostitution. However, this study does not include massage parlours and other key in-call locations. For further commentary about methodological problems with this study, see Applicants' factum, para. 213.5.

18 This figure was not contested by any witness appearing in *Bedford v. Canada*.

19 According to the Applicants' factum in *Bedford v. Canada*, para. 298, this same bias characterizes all of Farley et al.'s (2003) samples: "It is clear from [Farley's] cross-examination that she recruited virtually all participants in the nine country study from populations of vulnerable, impoverished and disadvantaged persons."

20 Farley, Lynne, and Cotton (2005, 256) claim that Benoit and Millar's (2001, 18) research indicates that "15 percent of women in escort prostitution in Victoria, BC were First Nations although the First Nations population of Victoria has been estimated at 2 percent." However, they misrepresent Benoit and Millar's report – this is the percentage of Aboriginals in their sample as a whole, not those who had escort service experience.

21 O'Doherty asked respondents who had worked in more than one venue to recall their experiences in each venue.

22 If their average age was thirty years and their average age of entry in prostitution was twenty-two, then on average each respondent had worked for eight years.

23 Sixty-five respondents answered the question about types of violence experienced over the past six months.

24 They are similarly less than careful when citing other Vancouver research, as they fail to mention that Currie et al. (1995), Lowman and Fraser (1996), and Cler-Cunningham and Christensen (2001) all dealt with samples of women who were primarily involved in *street* prostitution.

25 In this section "murder" includes some homicides that may subsequently be classified as "manslaughter."

26 The same held for Poulin's claims about other kinds of violence. He asserted that a serial rapist in the USA assaulted women in massage parlours (Joint Application Record, Volume 40, Tab

102, para. 47), but examination of the newspaper article from which he derived this claim showed that it did not indicate where the assaults occurred.

27 Under cross-examination, Poulin claimed that, "in Quebec, since 1989, there were 38 murders of prostituted persons and lap dancers. Sixty-six percent that were killed were not working on the stroll, they were escorts, getting clients ... at their homes. They were killed by johns, by procurers, people from organized crime and by their sex partners" (Joint Application Record, Volume 43, Tab 105, para. 91). He did not provide a source for these assertions.

28 Benedet conflates supporting "the prostitution industry" and supporting a prostitute's right to life, liberty, and security of the person while he or she is working. For the reasons that O'Connell Davidson (2002) describes, it is possible to support the latter without necessarily supporting the former.

29 For her vision of how the court should have conceptualized the Charter issues, see Women's Coalition (2011).

30 For a discussion of the deep divide in feminism over the role prostitution plays in women's inequality, see Jolin (1994).

31 Pickton may have met some of his victims in other strolls.

32 This account is based on my personal communications with Hamilton.

33 These figures were compiled by then detective inspector Kim Rossmo of the Vancouver Police Department.

References

Albion Research. 2012. Risky thinking. http://www.riskythinking.com/.

Benedet, J. 2009. Legalizing the purchase of women for sex won't make them safe. *Toronto Globe and Mail*, 7 October, A17. http://www.theglobeandmail.com.

Benoit, C., and A. Millar. 2001. *Dispelling myths and understanding realities: Working conditions, health status, and exiting experiences of sex workers.* http://www.peers.bc.ca/images/DispMythsshort.pdf.

Brannigan, A., and J. Fleischman. 1989. Juvenile prostitution and mental health: Policing delinquency or treating pathology. *Canadian Journal of Law and Society* 4: 77-98.

Brents, B., and K. Hausbeck. 2005. Violence and legalized brothel prostitution in Nevada: Examining safety, risk and prostitution policy. *Journal of Interpersonal Violence* 20, 3: 270-95.

Canada. 2009. Factum of the respondent, the attorney general of Canada. *Bedford v. Canada*, 07-CV-329807PD1.

Chapkis, W. 2001. Power and control in the commercial sex industry. In *Sex for sale: Prostitution, pornography and the sex industry*, ed. R. Weitzer, 181-202. New York: Routledge.

Chudakov, B., K. Ilan, R.H. Belmaker, and J. Cwikel. 2002. The motivation and mental health of sex workers. *Journal of Sex and Marital Therapy* 28, 4: 305-15.

Church, S. 2001. Violence by clients towards female prostitutes in different work settings: A questionnaire. *British Medical Journal* 322: 524-25.

Cler-Cunningham, L., and C. Christensen. 2001. *Violence against women in Vancouver's street level sex trade and the police response.* A study funded by the Ministry of Status for Women with assistance from the BC Ministry of the Attorney General and the BC Ministry of Women's Equality. Vancouver: PACE Society.

CSOACY (Committee on Sexual Offences against Children and Youth). 1984. *Sexual offences against children and youth.* Ottawa: Department of Supply and Services.

Currie, S., N. Laliberte, S. Bird, N. Rosa, and S. Sprung. 1995. Assessing the violence against street-involved women in the Downtown Eastside/Strathcona Community. Mimeo.

John Lowman

De Wet, P.H. 2002. Supporting answering affidavit of Paul Henry De Wet. *Ellen Jordan, Louisa Johanna Francina Broodryk, Christine Louise Jacobs v. The State,* Constitutional Court of South Africa (*Bedford v. Canada,* Application Record, Volume 31, Tab 64(V).

Ekberg, G. 2008. Abolishing prostitution: The Swedish solution, an interview with Gunilla Ekberg. *Rain and Thunder: A Radical Feminist Journal of Discussion and Activism* 41 (Winter): 1-8. http://action.web.ca/home/catw/attach/R%26T_Interview_with_Gunilla_Ekberg.pdf.

Farley, M., I. Baral, M. Kiremire, and U. Sezgin. 1998. Prostitution in five countries: Violence and post-traumatic stress disorder. *Feminism and Psychology* 8, 4: 405-26.

Farley, M., and H. Barkan. 1998. Prostitution, violence against women, and posttraumatic stress disorder. *Women and Health* 27: 37-49.

Farley, M., A. Cotton, J. Lynne, S. Zumbeck, F. Spiwak, M.E. Reyes, D. Alvarez, and U. Sezgin. 2003. Prostitution and trafficking in nine countries: An update on violence and post-traumatic stress disorder. In *Prostitution, trafficking and traumatic stress,* ed. M. Farley, 33-74. Binghamton, NY: Haworth.

Farley, M., J. Lynne, and A.J. Cotton. 2005. Prostitution in Vancouver: Violence and the colonization of First Nation's women. *Transcultural Psychiatry* 42, 2: 242-71.

Jeffrey, L.A., and G. MacDonald. 2006. *Sex workers in the Maritimes talk back.* Vancouver: UBC Press.

Jolin, A. 1994. On the backs of working prostitutes: Feminist theory and prostitution policy. *Crime and Delinquency* 40, 1: 69-83.

Lowman, J. 1987. Taking young prostitutes seriously. *Canadian Review of Sociology and Anthropology* 24, 1: 99-116.

–. 1989. *Street prostitution: Assessing the impact of the law, Vancouver.* Ottawa: Department of Justice.

–. 1991. Street prostitutes in Canada: An evaluation of the Brannigan-Fleischman Opportunity Model. *Canadian Journal of Law and Society* 6: 137-64.

–. 2011. Deadly inertia: A history of constitutional challenges to Canadian prostitution law. *Beijing Law Review* 2: 33-54.

Lowman, J., and L. Fraser. 1996. *Violence against persons who prostitute: The experience in British Columbia.* Technical Report No. TR1996-14e. Ottawa: Department of Justice Canada. http://184.70.147.70/lowman_prostitution/HTML/violence/Violence_Against_Persons_Who_Prostitute.pdf.

Malarek, V. 2009. *The johns: Sex for sale and the men who buy it.* Toronto: Key Porter Books.

McIntyre, S. 1999. The youngest profession, the oldest oppression: A study of sex work. In *Child sexual abuse and adult offenders: New theory and research,* ed. C. Bagley and K. Mallick, 159-92. London: Ashgate.

O'Connell Davidson, J. 1998. *Prostitution, power and freedom.* Cambridge: Polity Press.

–. 2002. The rights and wrongs of prostitution. *Hypatia* 17, 2: 84-98.

O'Doherty, T. 2007. Off-street commercial sex: An exploratory study. Master's thesis, Simon Fraser University School of Criminology. http://184.70.147.70/lowman_prostitution/HTML/odoherty/ODoherty-thesis-final.pdf.

–. 2011. Victimization in off-street sex industry work. *Violence against Women* 20, 10: 1-20.

ORCHID Project. 2007. The Orchid Project: Outreach and research in community health initiatives and development, bi-annual update. http://www.peers.bc.ca/images/orchidupdat0407.pdf.

Plumridge, L., and G. Abel. 2001. A segmented sex industry in New Zealand: Sexual and personal safety of sex workers. *Australian and New Zealand Journal of Public Health* 25, 1: 78-83.

Quinet, K. 2011. Prostitutes as victims of serial homicide: Trends and case characteristics. *Homicide Studies* 15, 1: 74-100.

Raphael, J., and D. Shapiro. 2004. Violence in indoor and outdoor prostitution venues. *Violence against Women* 10, 1: 126-39.

Raymond. J. 2010. Trafficking, prostitution and the sex industry: The Nordic Legal Model. http://action.web.ca/.

Sanders, T., and R. Campbell. 2007. Designing out vulnerability, building in respect: Violence, safety and sex work policy. *British Journal of Sociology* 58, 1: 1-19.

Shannon, K., T. Kerr, S. Allinott, J. Chettiar, J. Shovellor, and M. Tyndall. 2008. Social and structural violence and power relations in mitigating HIV risk of drug-using women in survival sex work. *Social Science and Medicine* 66: 911-23.

Siegel, D. 2009. Human trafficking and legalized prostitution in the Netherlands. *Temida* (March): 5-16.

Standing Committee on the Status of Women. 2007. *Turning outrage into action to address trafficking for the purpose of sexual exploitation in Canada: Report of the Standing Committee on the Status of Women.* Twelfth Report of the Standing Committee on the Status of Women. Ottawa: Communication Canada. http://cmte.parl.gc.ca/content/hoc/committee/391/fewo/reports/rp2738918/feworp12/feworp12-e.pdf.

van der Meulen, E. 2010. Illegal lives, loves, and work: How the criminalization of procuring affects sex workers in Canada. *Wagadu: A Journal of Transnational Women's and Gender Studies* 8: 217-40.

Vancouver Sun. 2007. Slain woman was working in massage parlour. 31 August. http://www.canada.com/.

Vanwesenbeeck, I. 2005. Burnout among female indoor sex workers. *Archives of Sexual Behavior* 24, 6: 627-39.

Weitzer, R. 2011. *Legalizing prostitution.* New York: New York University Press.

Women's Coalition. 2011. Factum of the intervener Women's Coalition. *Bedford v. Canada,* Court File Nos. C52799 and C52814.

Cases Cited

Bedford v. Canada, 2010 ONSC 4264.

Canada (Attorney General) v. Bedford, 2012 ONCA 186.

S v. Jordan and Others, 2002 (6) SA 642 (CC); 2002 11 BCLR 1117 (CC); 2002 (1) SA 797 (T).

16

Repeat Performance? Human Trafficking and the 2010 Vancouver Winter Olympic Games

ANNALEE LEPP

In the last decade, and particularly since the UN Protocol to Prevent, Suppress, and Punish Trafficking in Persons, Especially Women and Children came into force in 2003, human trafficking has received growing international attention. National governments have sought to combat this crime against persons through the enactment of criminal laws and border security measures as well as the implementation of various policies aimed at the prosecution of traffickers, the prevention of trafficking, and the protection of trafficked persons. In addition, global alliances and non-governmental organizations (NGOs) have worked to raise awareness about the issue and to establish and coordinate service regimes to assist trafficked individuals.

Despite this range of initiatives, estimates of the number of persons trafficked into situations of sexual exploitation and forced labour on an annual basis have varied dramatically.[1] It is generally argued that compiling accurate human trafficking statistics is difficult given the clandestine character of the activity, challenges in identifying persons affected by it, and the reluctance or inability of trafficked individuals to contact authorities or NGOs, but such numerical variations are also the result of entrenched ideological differences as to what constitutes human trafficking (see Sanghera 2005; Musto 2009; Ogrodnik 2010). Notwithstanding legal definitions that specify that, except in the case of children and youth, threats, coercion, and deception are necessary components of trafficking persons into situations of forced labour and servitude (*Criminal Code* 1985, ss. 279.01-279.04; United Nations 2000, art. 3), prohibitionist forces – in the political and NGO sectors – have promoted interpretations that conflate or tend to conflate transnational and domestic human trafficking with sex work. Contrary to the idea that adult sex work constitutes an income-generating activity except under conditions of force, the former conceptualization is rooted in the notion that sex work is itself a form of coercion, violence, and exploitation.

Within this broad global context of more concerted action, greater awareness, statistical approximations, and varied understandings, international mega sporting events have, since 2004, come under increased scrutiny and have been targeted as highly fertile environments for human trafficking, particularly in the commercial sex sector. This is premised on the assertion that traffickers will capitalize on the expected spike in male demand for paid sexual services during such events by trafficking women and youth into the sex industry. Prior to and during the Vancouver Winter Olympic and Paralympic Games, held in February 2010, such arguments as they pertained to both transnational and domestic trafficking were integral to a number of highly vocal and visible NGO-sponsored public awareness and prevention campaigns.

This chapter draws on research, including sixty-one interviews, conducted by the Global Alliance against Traffic in Women (GAATW) Canada on human trafficking within the context of the 2010 Vancouver Winter Olympics.[2] It reviews existing data on the link between trafficking in persons and previous international sporting events, and it examines the assumptions and agendas that have fuelled assertions about this strong connection. In addition, some international and national NGOs have argued that the significant legislative and enforcement response to combating trafficking in persons has not been matched by critical attention to such issues as the root causes of trafficking; the complexities of irregular transnational and regional migrations into multiple labour sites, including sex work; the assistance and human rights of trafficked persons; and the potential harmful consequences of anti-trafficking interventions and campaigns on the rights and safety of marginalized, vulnerable, and stigmatized populations (see GAATW Canada 2001; Office of the High Commissioner for Human Rights 2002; Sutdhibhasilp 2002; Marshall and Thatun 2005; Sanghera 2005; GAATW 2007, 2010, 2011; West Coast LEAF 2009). Building on these critical assessments and the recommendations contained in GAATW's *Collateral Damage: The Impact of Anti-Trafficking Measures on Human Rights around the World* (2007, 8), which emphasize the importance of adopting an evidence-based approach as well as policies and practices that limit the "unacceptable side effects of anti-trafficking measures," this chapter also explores the grassroots debates around and implications of selected NGO-sponsored counter-trafficking crusades in the lead-up to the 2010 Vancouver Winter Olympic Games.

Human Trafficking and International Sporting Events: Lessons from the Past

Over the last five years, a number of studies have assessed the connection between international sporting events and an increase in human trafficking, and all have focused exclusively on the commercial sex sector. In 2007, the International Organization for Migration (IOM) released one of the first systematic analyses, entitled *Trafficking in Human Beings and the 2006 World Cup in Germany;* it reviewed available evidence on four mega sporting events and, as will be discussed below, focused on the 2004 Athens Summer Olympic Games and the 2006 FIFA World Cup in Germany (Hennig et al. 2007). Other evaluations followed, including the Calgary-based Future Group's *Faster, Higher, Stronger: Preventing Human Trafficking at the 2010 Olympics* (2007). This widely publicized document highlighted the significant risk of human trafficking during international sporting events due to "a short-term increase in demand for prostitution and other forms of sexual exploitation," and recommended the implementation of extensive counter-trafficking measures, including enforcement and border security initiatives and public awareness campaigns designed to deter "traffickers and potential commercial sex users" (ibid., 9, 17). The Vancouver-based Sex Industry Worker Safety Action Group's *Human Trafficking, Sex Work Safety and the 2010 Games* also offered an assessment of existing data and concluded that "trafficking and mega-events are not linked" (Bowen and Shannon Frontline Consulting 2009, iv). While emphasizing the need for "a broad-based public awareness campaign on trafficking in persons for sexual exploitation" (ibid., iii), the report also called for initiatives that would address critical concerns about sex worker safety, displacement, and criminalization during the Vancouver Olympics. More generally, a review of the literature on this much-debated question indicates that in the ideologically and politically charged world of anti-trafficking work, interpretations of the extant data on trafficking within the context of international sporting events have varied, and such divergent readings have served to shore up differing strategies to address not only trafficking in persons, but also sex work.

2004 Athens Summer Olympic Games

Available information on human trafficking in the context of the 2004 Athens Summer Olympic Games (13-29 August 2004) is limited. As noted by IOM researchers, in 2003, Terre Libere, an Italian-based NGO, predicted a rise in the "number of women being smuggled into Greece" in the year prior to the Olympic Games in order to satisfy an increase in demand for sexual services (Hennig et al. 2007, 12). Other reports warned that as many as twenty thousand women would be trafficked into the sex trade in Athens (Prasad and Rohner 2006a, 2); in June 2004, the BBC quoted one "leading expert in Greece" who had "information that traffickers will try to bring 2,000 extra women into the country and force them to work as prostitutes" (Galpin 2004, n.p.). However, in reviewing the available evidence contained in the Greek Ministry of Public Order's 2004 Organized Crime report as well as in the IOM database in Athens, IOM researchers concluded that there were no references to "instances of trafficking for the purpose of sexual exploitation during the 2004 Olympic Games" (Hennig et al. 2007, 12). Furthermore, with respect to the demand for paid sexual services, the executive director of a faith-based organization, Nea Zoi, Lost Coin Association for the Support and Restoration of Individuals Involved in Prostitution in Athens, testified before a US House of Representatives hearing in 2006 that extensive NGO "street work during the [Athens] Olympics yielded unexpected results. We were not meeting new victims of trafficking. Of the new faces, few were identifiable as victims of trafficking, and even fewer had entered the country recently. Our experience seemed to hold up around the city. There was no identifiable increase in prostitution around the Athens Olympics ... The Greek Union of Prostitutes even reported a decrease in demand compared to the previous year" (US House of Representatives 2006a, 18).

In its document released two years prior to the 2010 Vancouver Olympics, the Future Group (2007) countered the IOM's conclusions, citing police data from the Hellenic Ministry of Public Order, which indicated an increase in the number of trafficked persons identified in 2004 (181 individuals), up from the figures for 2003 (93 people) and 2005 (137 persons). While conceding that "there are numerous factors that can effect [sic] the number of known human trafficking victims," the Future Group (ibid., 14) strongly inferred that there was a correlation between the 95 percent increase in the number of known trafficked persons from 2003 to 2004 and the presence of the Olympic Games, and pointed to the Greek government's inadequate human trafficking prevention efforts prior to and during the event as the main cause. However, further research indicates that it is also possible that this numerical increase was the result of Greek authorities multiplying their "efforts to fight sexual exploitation" (195 Women 'Sex Slaves' 2003, n.p.) and organized crime after receiving a Tier 3 ranking in the 2002 and 2003 US State Department's Trafficking in Persons (TIP) Reports (upgraded to Tier 2 in September 2003) and Tier 2 Watch List status in the 2004 TIP Report. Differing interpretations of scanty available data aside, what can be said is that, upon the release of the Future Group report, some Canadian journalists, politicians, faith-based groups, and NGOs picked up on the stressed 95 percent increase in 2004 and recirculated the percentage as directly connected to the 2004 Athens Olympic Games (for example, at least twenty-five Canadian and mainly BC newspaper reports and other documents produced between November 2007 and February 2010 made the direct correlation). This statistical information was presented as evidence that the risk of an increase in human trafficking for the purpose of sexual exploitation during the 2010 Vancouver Winter Olympics was a significant one.

2006 FIFA World Cup in Germany

Of all the past international sporting events under review, the 2006 FIFA World Cup in Germany (9 June to 9 July 2006) received the greatest international scrutiny, media coverage, and subsequent scholarly analysis. The controversy began with the April 2005 prediction that forty thousand "foreign prostitutes" would be trafficked into the country to service male sexual demand during the event. Where the prediction originated is unclear, but the estimate quickly circulated in the international media and incited widespread attention, including two hearings before the US House of Representatives Committee on International Relations, Subcommittee on Africa, Global Human Rights and International Operations in May and June 2006 (2006a, 2006b). Also, the Coalition against Trafficking in Women sponsored an international on-line petition titled "Buying Sex Is NOT a Sport!" which was circulated between 25 January and 30 June 2006 (Buying Sex Is NOT a Sport! 2006). Much of the discussion focused not only on the anticipated massive spike in human trafficking prior to the event, but also on the German government's move in 2002 to officially legalize sex work, which for opponents of legalization automatically made the country a haven for sex trafficking (Milivojević and Pickering 2008). Although some German officials, labour unions, and sex worker organizations expressed doubts about the predicted dramatic increase, international, European Union, and NGO pressure prompted the expansion and fortification of various human trafficking prevention efforts in Germany. These included state-federal information sharing and intelligence gathering as well as border security and law enforcement measures, which involved extensive brothel and sex club raids in a number of German host cities. A coalition of women's, human rights, and faith-based groups also mobilized, launching a series of government-funded public awareness campaigns and twenty-four-hour telephone hotlines for trafficked persons and World Cup attendees (Hennig et al. 2007; Milivojević and Pickering 2008).

In a January 2007 report to the Council of the European Union's Multidisciplinary Group on Organised Crime, German officials stated that the anticipated increase in human trafficking for the purpose of prostitution had not materialized, and, in total, five cases were identified as possibly linked to the FIFA World Cup. They further stated that, though there was "an increase in the number of prostitutes ... recorded at game venues and the surrounding areas," the "police and to a large extent the special counselling services also noted that the increase in the number of punters [clients] which was forecast by some did not materialise and this was the reason why some prostitutes left before the 2006 World Cup was over" (Council of the European Union 2007, 4). In light of these developments, IOM researchers cited the concerns of some NGOs who maintained that the unfounded and unrealistic estimates that circulated prior to the event could undermine future credibility of and attention to the issue (Hennig et al. 2007).

Two reports produced prior to and during the 2006 FIFA World Cup, however, sought to expand the conversation about the connection between this tournament and trafficking. In May 2006, the European Commission's Expert Group on Trafficking in Human Beings presented a series of recommendations, many of which were echoed in the 2007 IOM report. In a cautionary note, the Expert Group (2006, 2) emphasized "the need for facts-based and differentiated information as the basis for effective policies, avoiding to feed the myths – specifically on the numbers of victims of trafficking for sexual exploitation in connection with this event – circulating in the public." The document also emphasized that a "careful distinction should be made between prostitution and trafficking" (ibid.), presumably in response to the prohibitionist position that characterized many of the pre–World Cup national and international public awareness campaigns. Finally, it stressed that "it should be kept in mind that trafficking does not happen for the purpose of sexual exploitation only, but occurs in many other unregulated segments of the labour market, such as domestic work, the construction sector, the gastronomy, agricultural work and sweat shops. Some of these sectors play an important role in connection with such major international sports events" (ibid.).

Also in 2006, a Berlin-based organization founded in 1988 that runs a shelter for Southeast Asian women, a counselling centre for migrant and trafficked women, and an anti-trafficking coordination centre circulated a statement in which it presented a number of reasons as to why the 2006 FIFA World Cup was not a conducive environment for a massive increase in transnational human trafficking for the purpose of "forced prostitution" (Prasad and Rohner 2006a). The authors maintained that, given heightened levels of security and an enhanced

Annalee Lepp

enforcement presence in host cities as well as the substantial financial invest-ment required to move women across borders, it would be too risky and not cost-effective for traffickers to set up operations for a four-week period. They went on to challenge the notion that the influx of male spectators at mega sporting events necessarily resulted in a significant rise in demand for paid sexual services; they suggested that the priority of fans was by and large to watch the tournament. Anecdotal evidence from previous hallmark events tends to support this claim (McDonald 2000; Prasad and Rohner 2006a), and similar assertions emerged in some of the expert interviews conducted by the IOM researchers (Hennig et al. 2007). However, a review of available literature sug-gests that there has been no evidence-based research conducted that has ana-lyzed the fan-bases of or measured the often-assumed high male demand for paid sexual services during international sporting events.

Prasad and Rohner (2006a) raised a number of other concerns about the various anti-trafficking campaigns and measures initiated prior to the 2006 FIFA World Cup. First, they indicated that there had been significant govern-ment investment in various national prevention measures, including public awareness campaigns, but little or no investment in enhanced support and assistance for the predicted influx of trafficked women in the form of expanded counselling services and the creation of new shelters. Second, they noted that many Berlin-based organizations that were involved in pre–World Cup anti-trafficking campaigns and were establishing government-funded hotlines had not previously been interested in the issue, leading to a suspicion that these organizations became involved in order to raise their own profiles. Third, in contrast to Tavella's (2007, 217) conclusion that "the sensationalism of inaccur-ate facts did not have a significant impact on the situation," Prasad and Rohner (2006b) emphasized that more attention to the human rights impact of counter-trafficking measures prior to and during the 2006 World Cup was needed. For example, in the name of rescuing "foreign women" from situations of sexual exploitation, police in Berlin and other host cities aggressively targeted sex workers, raided brothels (seventy-one in Berlin alone) and sex clubs, and in-tensified checks on brothels and other establishments. These raids and inter-ventions, however, yielded no evidence of trafficking. In other words, as noted by the European Commission's Expert Group on Trafficking in Human Beings (Expert Group 2006, 2-3), "all activities in connection with this or other similar events should not be misinterpreted or instrumentalised to discriminate against prostitutes or to further marginalise or stigmatise them, thus increasing their vulnerability to trafficking and other forms of violence and abuse ... All policies have to be assessed against their impact on human rights." Finally, Prasad and

Rohner (2006a) questioned the proposed enhanced gender and national profiling at German border entry points prior to the World Cup as a justifiable counter-trafficking measure, arguing that such tactics also violated human rights principles.

2010 Vancouver Winter Olympic and Paralympic Games

Similar debates about the connection between the presence of mega sporting events and an increase in human trafficking seen in Greece and Germany surfaced in the run-up to the 2010 Vancouver Winter Olympic Games. Vancouver received the bid for the Games in July 2003. Analysis of national and local print media suggests that NGO discussions about an anticipated jump in transnational and increasingly domestic trafficking for the purpose of adult and youth prostitution during this sporting event began to emerge in early June 2006 – one week before the much-scrutinized FIFA World Cup commenced in Germany (Bains 2006). As NGO and public concerns intensified in subsequent years, media reports and first-person interviews indicated that federal officials and local enforcement personnel remained cautious in making definitive predictions. Internal intelligence data and available information about the lessons learned and prevention measures implemented by previous host nations were the main reference points for strategic planning prior to the Games. In addition to tight security measures at the Canadian border, strict passport and visa requirements, and an enhanced enforcement presence in Vancouver and Whistler, which, it was suggested, would serve as deterrents to traffickers (Montgomery 2008), preparations included public education on trafficking, coordination and partnerships between federal, provincial, and service provision agencies, and the training of enforcement officers (border security, immigration, and police) and first responders in trafficking in persons indicators.

In Vancouver, however, the countdown to the 2010 Winter Olympics was marked by escalating and fierce debates about sex work, prostitution, and "sex trafficking," involving two main coalitions. The first included sex worker organizations and advocates whose primary concern was the rights, safety, and well-being of their constituents during the Games, especially in the face of traffic rerouting as well as the influx of tourists, the media, law enforcement, and security personnel into the downtown area. The other consisted of increasingly vocal prohibitionist groups whose main goal was to raise public awareness about transnational and especially domestic trafficking of Indigenous and non-Indigenous women and girls into Vancouver's sex industry, the operations of pimps and traffickers, and the extent to which male demand for paid sexual services fuelled "sex trafficking" – all of which would be exacerbated during the Olympic Games. As a number of interviewees noted, NGO discussions and associated campaigns that emerged in the pre-Olympic period tended to focus more on the long-standing and highly polarized prostitution debates than on trafficking per se. Some local sex worker activists and front-line workers went further to suggest that the intent behind the prohibitionist campaigns was less about combating and preventing trafficking and more about *"raising the hysteria about and fear around trafficking to abolish sex work as a whole"* (front-line worker).

Sex Worker Safety: Cooperative Brothel Campaign and Harm Reduction

The first major controversy erupted in November 2007, when a group of Vancouver sex workers affiliated with the BC Coalition of Experiential Communities (later named the West Coast Co-operative of Sex Industry Professionals; see also Chapter 9 in this volume) announced that, in anticipation of the 2010 Olympic Games and subject to the approval of the federal government, it intended to establish a cooperative brothel in Vancouver on an experimental basis for a two-year period. In the longer term, the group envisioned opening four more brothels as a way to provide female, male, and trans adult sex workers with a "safer working environment when the world comes to visit in 2010" (Lee 2007, A1). NGO and political supporters of the initiative maintained that it would offer one mechanism to reduce the violence experienced, particularly by street-based sex workers, address concerns about displacement "into more isolated areas" during the Games, and allow for "collaborative ownership," "a worker-controlled safe space to conduct sex work," and access to an array of support services (Arthur and O'Doherty 2007, A17). "While alarmist rhetoric continues to plague discussions on sex industry work," noted two members of FIRST, a feminist organization that works in solidarity with Vancouver sex workers, "the lack of concern for the safety and well-being of Vancouver's sex workers continues unabated. In light of the 69 missing women from the Downtown Eastside as well as the Pickton trial, this is deplorable and deeply troubling" (ibid.).

As reported in the local press, intense opposition to the brothel proposal from prohibitionist groups was immediate. Speaking at public forums and in the media, they argued that, as a decriminalization initiative, the establishment of cooperative brothels would not reduce violence and abuse in the sex industry; rather, this move would entrench and normalize prostitution and "legitimize pimps and traffickers" (Lee 2007, A1), with the attendant consequences for such groups as "Asian women ... trafficked through licensed escort agencies and massage parlours" and Indigenous women and girls who "dominate the dangerous street trade" in Vancouver and other Canadian cities (Fournier 2008, A16). In their view, a more effective alternative would be a legal crackdown on "pimps, johns, and those running unofficial prostitution rings such as massage parlours and escort agencies," and enhanced economic and social supports for "vulnerable women" (Culbert 2008, n.p.). In an effort to block the initiative, the Committee against Human Trafficking, a coalition of Vancouver prohibitionist organizations, launched a formal campaign (Delaney 2007). Asserting that, "in every city where brothels have operated openly there has been a DRAMATIC increase in human trafficking" and "child exploitation," opponents urged Canadians to contact Vancouver's mayor to register their opposition to "his stated openness to the proposal" (REED 2007, n.p.). In February 2008, federal justice minister Rob Nicholson announced that the Conservative government was "not in the business of legalizing brothels" and would not approve the initiative (Montgomery 2008, A18).

In the lead-up to and during the 2010 Olympic Games, other Vancouver-based sex worker activists and organizations also devised and implemented strategies to address sex worker safety. Some key initiatives included conducting information sessions with and distributing resource materials among constituents that focused on such issues as what to expect during the Games, the location of safe spaces and supports, legal rights in regard to interactions with media and law enforcement, tips on screening and meeting clients, and the do's and don'ts of various neighbourhoods. During the event, some organizations increased their on-street outreach efforts and extended the hours of drop-in centres; one legal society established a twenty-four-hour legal hotline and offered free legal services at the downtown courthouse. A program that conducts peer-led outreach, particularly with Asian women working in massage parlours in Vancouver and surrounding areas, distributed extra harm-reduction supplies as well as written materials for any new staff, including information about safer sex practices, STI transmission, and legal rights of sex workers and immigrant women. Finally, one organization distributed a pamphlet directed at potential clients that outlined appropriate behaviour in exotic show lounges, escort services, and on the street, as well as contact information for NGOs working with trafficked persons, should visitors encounter them.

A number of Vancouver sex worker organizations and advocates were also members of the Sex Industry Worker Safety Action Group (SIWSAG), a multi-stakeholder collaboration with local law enforcement and other service provision agencies. Such a collaborative model, it was noted in interviews, was designed to address concerns about criminalization, surveillance, and harassment of marginalized and stigmatized communities, including female, male, and trans street-based sex workers and street-involved youth prior to and during the Games. Basing their stance on the principle that coercion, violence, and exploitation are unacceptable in all sectors, including the sex industry, interview participants further emphasized that active consultations with sex workers, marginalized local populations, and front-line workers – groups attuned to everyday, on-the-ground realities in all their complexities – should be integral to the development of national and provincial anti-trafficking policies, measures, and campaigns in general and within the context of mega sporting events in particular.

Deterring Human Trafficking: Male Sexual Demand

The most visible and vocal public awareness campaigns launched prior to and during the 2010 Olympic Games focused their anti-trafficking efforts on addressing the anticipated explosion of sex tourism. The Citizens' Summit on Human Trafficking (One Is Too Many 2009, 1), a coalition of twenty-three Vancouver-based organizations and individuals, released a declaration in April 2009 that called for an end to "the sexual enslavement of women and youth." Among its various recommendations, the Citizens' Summit proposed the negotiation of an agreement "between Craigslist and the RCMP/Department of Justice" to establish "a system to monitor and track online postings back to users in the case of human trafficking investigations" (ibid., 2). It also suggested the distribution of "educational materials directed to men on the consequences of human trafficking including criminal penalties." These "could take the form of a warning card, distributed at borders alongside visitor's permits, at social gathering venues or mailed in ticket packages for Olympic events" (ibid.).

One month later, REED, a Christian-based organization, officially launched its Buying Sex Is NOT a Sport campaign. Arguing that "the demand for sexual access to the bodies of women and children fuels human trafficking," that "women and children in Metro Vancouver and Whistler are routinely coerced into the flesh trade to meet this demand," and that "a large sporting event such as the 2010 Olympics will only further exploitation through a rise in demand for paid sex," the campaign concentrated on stemming "the tide of human trafficking" by directly targeting demand (REED 2009, n.p.).

Prior to and during the Olympics, REED and its partnering groups sought to raise public awareness about these issues through community-based public and media forums, poster campaigns, T-shirts, and buttons, as well as silent direct actions outside various exotic dance clubs and at public venues.[3] Such actions, however, drew criticism from local exotic dancers. One dancer featured in the *Vancouver Courier* accused REED of "using the Games to draw attention to their anti-sex work and abolition campaigns" (Thomas 2010, 11). She argued that "spreading the message that exotic dancers in Vancouver are sex slaves" was not only "demeaning" and misleading, but also put "dancers at risk" and interfered "with their ability to make a living" (ibid.).

The pre–2010 Olympic public awareness campaign that sparked the most local controversy, however, was titled The Truth Isn't Sexy. Initiated in Vancouver during the fall of 2008 by the Salvation Army, a well-known faith-based organization, its first phase included billboard, transit shelter, and men's washroom ads, which depicted women being beaten, kicked, choked, and brutalized by pimps and traffickers with copy that read, "Suzanne: Runaway from Incest, Age 10; Prostitute 12; Imported, Abused, Enslaved, 15"; "Julia: Violent Pimp, No Freedom, 30 Men a Day, Indebted, Enslaved"; and "Amy: 14: Imported from Seoul, Sold Three Times; Abused, Indebted, Enslaved." The tag line on each ad stated, "250,000 Slaves exist in North America. 27 Million worldwide." The campaign's second phase consisted of another series of ads, which targeted the "demand side of the equation: johns." Each ad included an image of a young woman and a letter addressed to "dear john"; the women depicted were from various, but in some cases unspecified, regions of the world (Eastern Europe, the Balkans, and Canada). Each letter provided a brief first-person narrative recounting the woman's experiences of deception, abuse, or being sold by a family member/boyfriend, and of drug addiction, as well as debt bondage and violent sexual exploitation; the image and story were framed by the tag lines "i am a slave" and "save me." On one postcard, for example, a freckle-faced young woman shared her experience of being sexually abused by her step-father and her facilitated entry into the sex trade under the control of a violent pimp. Other postcards depicted the bruised faces of women from various racial backgrounds, with the statement "I am the face of sex trafficking." Designed by the Vancouver-based company Mercer Creative, the campaign, by targeting pimps, traffickers, and johns, was intended to prevent the anticipated increase in human trafficking prior to and during the Games. As Major Venerables, the public relations and development officer of the Salvation Army's BC chapter explained, it was also designed to produce a particular effect:

> I wanted it to be a campaign that was distinctive ... Yes, there is some violence to the images, but it causes people to stop and ask why is that on the billboard ... The second phase is directed at ... the johns. The photographs are non-sexual and depict the innocence of each woman or girl. The overall effect is haunting, and I believe more disturbing than the more violent

campaign. The girls depicted could be your next door neighbour, your daughter or niece – and this truly is the reality, the face of human trafficking ... The idea is if we can get them to think maybe they won't buy ... If they don't buy there will be less demand for them and we won't have a spike during the Olympics. (quoted in Lazarus 2009, n.p.)

The Salvation Army campaign generated intense criticism from Vancouver-based sex worker activists and advocacy organizations. The ads were denounced in the press and in first-person interviews as unduly "graphic," "disturbing," "misleading," and slim on concrete evidence that supported the claims about a strong connection between mega sporting events and a rise in sex trafficking (Sinoski 2009). Given the overt conflation of human trafficking and sex work, critics were offended by the fact that local sex workers had not been consulted prior to the launch of the campaign and alarmed by the way in which it cast all sex workers as slaves and exploited victims, without recognizing the diversity and complexities of their choices, lives, and experiences. Without diminishing the seriousness of trafficking in persons as "a gross violation of human rights" (BC Coalition of Experiential Communities 2008, n.p.) and strongly advocating for sex worker participation in anti-trafficking efforts, critics questioned the ads' educational value, arguing that they were designed to evoke emotional responses from the public rather than engendering an informed and meaningful understanding of the systematic causes, nature, and realities of trafficking into multiple sites and how to engage with the issue.

Concern was also expressed about the traumatizing, marginalizing, and stigmatizing effects of the "shock-and-awe" ads on local sex workers. As one interviewee emphasized, *"Having a billboard of an underage girl in her underwear being stomped on can be triggering ... It's selling sex and violence to prevent them. The posters were actually very titillating in the imagery that they used"* (SIWSAG member). Finally, sex worker activists and advocates not only argued that such public education campaigns perpetuated highly gendered and racialized as-sumptions about the Winter Olympics fan base, clients, trafficked women, and sex workers, but also maintained that the images and messages advanced could lead to increased violence against, and intensified police surveillance and ha-rassment of, street-based and indoor sex workers during the Games (FIRST 2009). Demands to end The Truth Isn't Sexy campaign went unheeded, however. In justifying the campaign, the Salvation Army maintained that it was not directed at sex workers in general, but at "people who are forced into sex slavery" (Hasiuk 2009, 7) – "innocent victims who were kidnapped and forced into prostitution" (Vancouver Sex Workers Angry 2009, n.p.). Hence, the initiative proceeded as planned, and throughout the Games, volunteers were also tasked with distributing the postcard-sized ads to both visitors and locals at various Olympic venues.

The prevalent reliance on the discourse of sexual slavery in the context of anti-trafficking campaigns and media discussions in Canada is not new, but emerged in the late 1990s when law enforcement and immigration officials conducted a series of massage parlour raids in Toronto and arrested the Thai women found in the establishments. In the ensuing years, the term "sex slaves" – with its Orientalist overtones – has been a popular term used by Canadian state officials, the media, and some NGOs to describe Southeast Asian migrant sex workers (GAATW Canada 2001; Sutdhibhasilp 2002); more recently, it has also been applied to "the Natashas" – Russian and East European migrant sex workers (Malarek 2003). The subtext of such constructions has been that sex slavery is predominantly a foreign import, facilitated by transnational organized crime gangs, from which Canada has needed to secure its borders and communities. Migrant sex workers in general and those women categorized as victims of transnational sex trafficking in particular have, however, held an ambiguous position within the national imaginary – as they have variously and often simultaneously been cast as sex slaves in need of rescue and state benevolence, as objects of suspicion and possible transgressors of immigration laws, and/or as potential pawns of a criminal justice system intent on prosecuting and punishing traffickers. They have also become central symbols in broader grassroots and political campaigns, including the prohibition of sex work, the promotion of human rights for all migrants and asylum seekers, and the intensified efforts to protect Canadian national security from "illegal" border crossers and transnational criminals. Transnational trafficked women in need of identification, interception, and rescue were invoked in the pre-Olympic anti-trafficking campaigns in Vancouver, but the "Asian women" allegedly trafficked through licensed escort agencies and massage parlours – or the young Korean girl being kicked by her trafficker on the street as depicted in one Salvation Army advertisement – remained shadowy figures. They were nameless, faceless, and voiceless victims, devoid of complex histories, agency, rights, or desires for the future.

Since 2004, the domestic trafficking of Indigenous and non-Indigenous women and girls has received growing attention in British Columbia. Hunt (2010; see also Chapter 6 in this volume) has identified multiple factors – most notably colonial violence, the root causes of exploitation, and the complicity of the Canadian state – that need to be taken into account in discussions of the trafficking of Aboriginal women and girls for the purpose of sexual exploitation, many of which were imperceptible in the billboard ads, sound bites, and silent actions that comprised many pre-Olympic anti-trafficking public awareness campaigns. Furthermore, the vulnerability and trafficking of "young innocents" – the gendered and racialized construct of the girl next door as invoked in the Salvation Army campaign – seemed to achieve greater currency in the lead-up to the Olympic Games. Hearkening back to the white slavery narratives of the turn of the twentieth century (Rosen 1982), the application of the term "human trafficking" to procuring, youth sexual exploitation, and even mobility strongly implied that sex slavery not only affects foreign or colonized Others, but has come to threaten ordinary Canadian women and girls living in rural and urban communities. In this scenario and not unlike the assumption that women at risk of being trafficked in a transnational world are better off and safer at home (and thus their rights to mobility should be restricted), the regulation of inter-provincial and intraprovincial movements and the prevention of the trafficking of young innocents prior to and during the Olympic Games, as emphasized by various NGOs, required a multi-pronged and proactive approach. This included extensive public education, hypervigilance, and access to twenty-four-hour hotlines, the specialized training of law enforcement and front-line workers, and above all, heightened surveillance on-line, in hotels, and on the streets (see MP Calls for Action 2006; Bellett 2007; Colebourn 2007).

Conclusion

In Vancouver, there was no coordinated effort at the grassroots level to address trafficking in persons prior to and during the 2010 Olympic Games. Sex worker and prohibitionist organizations were clearly ideologically and strategically divided, holding different positions on prostitution and sex work, divergent understandings of what constitutes human trafficking, and conflicting strategies of how to address both phenomena. As was the case in the lead-up to previous international sporting events, the anti-trafficking public education campaigns that emerged in Vancouver tended to rely on pre-existing agendas, unsubstantiated conjecture, harmful assumptions, and the recycling of misinformation. Organizers of these initiatives also appeared to be oblivious to the articulated needs of sex workers across the entire spectrum of the industry and the stigmatizing consequences of specific interventions. Buried beneath this unfolding narrative about sex trafficking and male sexual demand were a few muffled voices that raised the possibility of human trafficking into other labour sites in the run-up to the Olympic Games. Nor did there appear to be extensive public monitoring of or concern about the working conditions under which workers in the global South produced the dizzying array of consumer goods available at Olympic venues and on-line, based on international labour standards and the principles of ethical purchasing practices. Rather, what unfolded was predominantly a story about the highly charged and contested terrain of prostitution and sex work in Vancouver, one that did not begin or end with the 2010 Winter Olympic Games.

Notes

1 Although "sexual exploitation" is not defined in the UN Trafficking Protocol, Canada's Criminal Code (1985, s. 279.04) defines exploitation as follows: "A person exploits another person if they *(a)* cause them to provide, or offer to provide, labour or a service by engaging in conduct that, in all the circumstances, could reasonably be expected to cause the other person to believe that their safety or the safety of a person known to them would be threatened if they failed to provide, or offer to provide, the labour or service; or *(b)* cause them, by means of deception or the use or threat of force or of any other form of coercion, to have an organ or tissue removed."
2 The GAATW Canada research team consisted of Shauna Paull, Sarah Hunt, and Annalee Lepp. The research was funded by Public Safety Canada (see GAATW Canada forthcoming).
3 Twelve media forums were held in the Vancouver area, as well as in Edmonton and Toronto, between May 2009 and February 2010.

References

Arthur, J., and T. O'Doherty. 2007. A 2010 deadline for prostitution; Decriminalization and a sex worker cooperative in time for the Games would provide safety and equal rights. *Vancouver Sun,* 6 December, A17.
Bains, C. 2006. Human trafficking could be huge issue during 2010 Olympics; women's groups. *Nelson Daily News,* 2 June, 8.
BC Coalition of Experiential Communities. 2008. Salvation Army tells untruths. 16 December. http://bccec.wordpress.com/.
Bellett, G. 2007. Hotels program aimed at cutting child prostitution; Staff members are being instructed on how to spot and deal with incidents of sexual exploitation by guests. *Vancouver Sun,* 23 June, B11.
Bowen and Shannon Frontline Consulting. 2009. *Human trafficking, sex work safety and the 2010 Games: Assessments and recommendations.* Vancouver: Sex Industry Worker Safety Action Group.
Buying sex is not a sport! 2006. *Stop Trafficking!* 4, 4: 1, 7.
Colebourn, J. 2007. Video targets sex trade; Group warns about the city's dark side during Olympics. *Vancouver Province,* 24 June, A23.
Council of the European Union. 2007. *Experience report on human trafficking for the purpose of sexual exploitation and forced prostitution in connection with the 2006 football World Cup in Germany.* Brussels. 5006/1/07 REV 1.
Criminal Code, R.S.C. 1985, c. C-46.
Culbert, L. 2008. Canada needs to do more to protect women, Vancouver meeting told. *Vancouver Sun,* 3 December.
Delaney, J. 2007. 2010 Olympics could boost human trafficking. *Epoch Times* (Vancouver), 12 December, n.p.

Expert Group. 2006. Opinion of the Expert Group on Trafficking in Human Beings of the European Commission. Brussels.

FIRST. 2009. Rights not rescue: An open letter to the Salvation Army. 24 September. http://rabble.ca.

Fournier, S. 2008. Games expected to fuel 'trafficking' of prostitutes. *Vancouver Province,* 4 December, A16.

Future Group. 2007. *Faster, higher, stronger: Preventing human trafficking at the 2010 Olympics.* Calgary: Future Group.

GAATW. 2007. *Collateral damage: The impact of anti-trafficking measures on human rights around the world.* Bangkok: GAATW.

–. 2010. *Feeling good about feeling bad ... a global review of evaluation in anti-trafficking initiatives.* Bangkok: GAATW.

–. 2011. *What's the cost of a rumour? A guide to sorting out the myths and the facts about sporting events and trafficking.* Bangkok: GAATW.

GAATW Canada. 2001. *Transnational migration, trafficking in women, and human rights: The Canadian dimension.* Victoria, BC: GAATW Canada.

–. Forthcoming. *2010 Winter Games analysis on human trafficking.* Ottawa: Public Safety Canada.

Galpin, R. 2004. Fears of Athens sex slave boom. *BBC News,* 21 June.

Hasiuk, M. 2009. Pro-prostitution lobby wages war on Salvation Army; Protesters will target prayer vigils. *Vancouver Courier,* 9 September, 7.

Hennig, J., S. Craggs, F. Laczko, and F. Larsson. 2007. *Trafficking in human beings and the 2006 World Cup in Germany.* Geneva: International Organization for Migration.

Hunt, S. 2010. Colonial roots, contemporary risk factors: A cautionary exploration of the domestic trafficking of Aboriginal women and girls in British Columbia, Canada. *Alliance News* 33: 27-31.

Lazarus, E. 2009. Salvation Army renews hard-hitting sex traffic ads. *Marketer News,* 30 September.

Lee, J. 2007. Coalition pushes for legal brothel; Ottawa's support sought for safe, prostitute-run facility that would cater to Olympic visitors. *Vancouver Sun,* 12 November, A1.

Malarek, V. 2003. *The Natashas: The new global sex trade.* Toronto: Viking Canada.

Marshall, P., and S. Thatun. 2005. Miles away: The trouble with prevention in the Greater Mekong Sub-region. In *Trafficking and prostitution reconsidered: New perspectives on migration, sex work, and human rights,* ed. K. Kempadoo with J. Sanghera and B. Pattanaik, 43-63. Boulder: Paradigm.

McDonald, M. 2000. Olympic flame fails to heat brothel trade. *Ottawa Citizen,* 30 September, D5.

Milivojević, S., and S. Pickering. 2008. Football and sex: The 2006 FIFA World Cup and sex trafficking. *Temida* 11, 2: 21-47.

Montgomery, C. 2008. No 'co-op' brothel before Games, say Tories. *Vancouver Province,* 8 February, A18.

MP calls for action to combat human trafficking. 2006. *canada.com,* 8 December. http://www.canada.com/.

Musto, J.L. 2009. What's in a name? Conflations and contradictions in contemporary U.S. discourses of human trafficking. *Women's Studies International Forum* 32, 4: 281-87.

Office of the High Commissioner for Human Rights. 2002. Recommended principles and guidelines on human rights and human trafficking. Addendum to the Report of the United Nations High Commissioner for Human Rights to the Economic and Social Council. E/2002/68/Add. 1.

Ogrodnik, L. 2010. *Towards the development of a national data collection framework to measure trafficking in persons.* Ottawa: Canadian Centre for Justice Statistics, Statistics Canada.

195 women 'sex slaves': Greece. 2003. *AFP*, 17 December.

One Is Too Many: A Citizens' Summit on Human Trafficking at the Vancouver 2010 Olympic Games and Beyond: Declaration. 2009. April.

Prasad, N., and B. Rohner. 2006a. *Dramatic increase in forced prostitution? The 2006 World Cup and the consequences of an unscreened rumour.* Berlin: Ban Ying.

–. 2006b. *Where are the 40.000? Statement on trafficking during the World Cup.* Berlin: Ban Ying.

REED. 2007. Sam Sullivan campaign, Dec. 5th 2007. http://embracedignity.org/.

–. 2009. Buying sex is not a sport. http://www.embracedignity.org/.

Rosen, R. 1982. *The lost sisterhood: Prostitution in America, 1900-18.* London: Johns Hopkins University Press.

Sanghera, J. 2005. Unpacking trafficking discourse. In *Trafficking and prostitution reconsidered: New perspectives on migration, sex work, and human rights,* ed. K. Kempadoo with J. Sanghera and B. Pattanaik, 3-24. Boulder: Paradigm.

Sinoski, K. 2009. Sex trade workers decry Salvation Army posters: Graphic images wrongly portray them as slaves, they say. *Vancouver Sun,* 25 September, A5.

Sutdhibhasilp, N. 2002. Migrant sex-workers in Canada. In *Transnational prostitution: Changing global patterns,* ed. S. Thorbek and B. Pattanaik, 173-92. London: Zed.

Tavella, A.M. 2007. Sex trafficking and the 2006 World Cup in Germany: Concerns, actions and implications for future international sporting events. *Northwestern Journal of International Human Rights* 6, 1: 196-217.

Thomas, S. 2010. Exotic dancer denounces protest. *Vancouver Courier,* 26 February, 11.

United Nations. 2000. Protocol to prevent, suppress and punish trafficking in persons, especially women and children, supplementing the United Nations Convention against Transnational Organized Crime. http://www.uncjin.org/Documents/Conventions/dcatoc/final_documents_2/convention_%20traff_eng.pdf.

US House of Representatives Committee on International Relations, Subcommittee on Africa, Global Human Rights and International Operations. 2006a. Germany's World Cup brothels: 40,000 women and children at risk of exploitation through trafficking. Washington, DC. http://digitalcommons.unl.edu/.

–. 2006b. *Modern day slavery: Spotlight on the 2006 "Trafficking in Persons Report," forced labor, and sex trafficking at the World Cup.* Washington, DC. http://digitalcommons.unl.edu/.

Vancouver sex workers angry at Sally Ann ads. 2009. *Canada News,* 7 October.

West Coast LEAF (Legal Education and Action Fund). 2009. Position paper on human trafficking for sexual exploitation. Vancouver.

17

A Wolf in Sheep's Clothing: Canadian Anti-Pimping Law and How It Harms Sex Workers

KARA GILLIES

The established literature on the effects of the Canadian Criminal Code focuses almost exclusively on those sections or applications of the criminal law that directly penalize sex workers by sanctioning their activities. Little attention has been paid to the criminalization of third parties involved in the sex trade (managers, or "pimps") and the effect this may have on sex workers themselves (van der Meulen 2010). In fact, the nature and purpose of women's relationships with sex trade managers have largely gone uninvestigated. The only formal Canadian research to concentrate exclusively on these relationships was conducted nearly fifteen years ago (Hodgson 1997) and was confined to an analysis of street-based management, excluding the much larger off-street trade.

This chapter, then, will present the results of a multi-site study involving in-depth qualitative interviews and focus groups with twenty-five woman-identified sex workers in Halifax, Montreal, Toronto, and Edmonton (Currie and Gillies 2006; see also Chapter 12 in this volume).[1] Additional interviews were conducted with social service workers, advocates promoting sex workers' rights, and law enforcement officers. The study, and thus this chapter, is grounded in the principle that sex workers are the best positioned to understand and comment on how public policies affect their lives and work, yet their voices have been unheard, appropriated, or tokenized in most public policy debates.

Sex workers are not a homogeneous community, and social locations including race, sexuality, gender, and socio-economic class dramatically shape their experiences of, and treatment by, public policies, laws, and institutions. Consequently, this study sought out and included participants with a diversity of identities and socio-demographic characteristics, including five Aboriginal women, four black women, and three trans women. Participants also had a range of relationships with prostitution, from career-oriented (both on- and off-street) through subsistence and transactional sex.

Street-based workers, though comprising only about 10 percent of the trade, are generally the most visible, marginalized, and likely to be targeted (and have their professional and personal relations targeted) by the law. In this study, thirteen participants had experience with street-based sex work. At the time of the interviews, all the street-based workers were independent, although many had worked for managers in the past. This is a reflection of a well-documented shift in the street sex trade that has seen an immense reduction in street managerial involvement in general and an almost complete elimination of the stereotypical "street pimp," whom women described as a predominantly American phenomenon.

A Note on Terminology

The term "third party" used throughout this chapter denotes any person involved in the sex trade transaction other than the worker and client. This term has been selected for its neutrality. The chapter also uses "employer," "manager," and "operator" synonymously with "third party" where the role and relationship of the individual to the sex worker makes this application appropriate. I have expressly avoided the label "pimp" as it is mired in dangerous constructs of sex workers and their professional and personal relations. At worst, the word conjures and reinforces stereotypical and racist imagery. At best, it serves to Other sex workers and their relations, especially given that we don't manufacture or employ language specific to managers or personal partners of women in other occupations. As a result, "pimp" is used in this chapter only when referencing stereotypical characterizations or when directly quoting participants.

History and Scope of the Procuring Law

The procuring law has undergone many permutations over the past two hundred years. Initially influenced by English statutes and common law, Canada's prostitution legislation has changed over time in accordance with shifting (and frequently conflicting) social and legal positions on the subject. These positions were typically informed by gendered, classed, and racialized perspectives on issues as diverse (yet connected) as morality, women's social status, sexuality, urbanization, industrialization, immigration, and nationalism (Backhouse 1985; McLaren and Lowman 1990; McLaren 1996). What distinguishes the procuring law from other Criminal Code prostitution offences is its presumed objective of protecting women in general from the perceived harms of prostitution while shielding active sex workers from abusive or exploitative individuals.

In its current configuration, the procuring law contains multiple sections and subsections (*Criminal Code* 1985).[2] Taken together, they criminalize any third-party involvement in prostitution. In basic terms, the procuring law prohibits such activities as the following: soliciting someone to engage in prostitution (ibid., s. 212(1)(a)) or to become a prostitute (section 212(1)(d)); living on the earnings of someone else's prostitution (sections 212(1)(j) and 212(3)); aiding or compelling someone to engage in prostitution for one's own gain by controlling or influencing his or her movements (section 212(1)(h)); and administering an intoxicating substance to someone in order to enable any person to have sex with him or her (section 212(1)(i)).

Benefits of Working for an Individual or Business

Despite these legal restrictions, many sex workers have experience working for a third party. Interestingly, the majority of the sex workers interviewed considered working for an individual or business to be a viable and valuable option. Although some preferred working for a third party, whereas others favoured independent work, there was agreement that working for someone else can offer concrete benefits. This is in contrast to the state's supposition that such arrangements are so inherently damaging and exploitative as to require blanket prohibition.

Overall, management's provision of support services and infrastructure such as administration, security, drivers, and advertising was cited as a key reason for choosing to work for a third party instead of as an independent operator. Karla, a Halifax escort, stated, "*I find it easier to work for an [escort] service because that way the work is done for you. You're picked up, dropped off, you know what I mean? It's more footwork if you have to get clients yourself.*" In addition, many participants explained that they preferred to leave the work of client management and public relations to a third party because of the emotional labour and infringement on personal space that such service-industry interactions can entail. Jane, a Montreal escort, remarked, "*The reason I chose to work for an agency was because I was not interested in the relationship aspect of the work. When I say relationship, I don't really want to spend the time to nurture a relationship with a client.*"

Financial considerations were another factor behind many women's partiality for working for an agency or other third party. Although they agreed that independent sex work results in women retaining the full client payment instead of a percentage or wage, many participants calculated that the decreased overhead and increased volume of clients associated with third-party work often culminates in greater net profit. This was particularly attractive for women seeking temporary or occasional income or for those with limited financial resources. Samantha, a sex worker and activist in Montreal, commented, *"If you don't have the money to invest in a work apartment, in a working telephone, in a working all the rest of it, it's much easier just to hook up with an agency and have it taken care of."* Throughout the study, participants described the social isolation that accompanies working in a criminalized and stigmatized field; the camaraderie and mutual support available from both colleagues and managers were commonly seen as benefits of working for an agency or individual.

Occupational health and safety factored prominently in women's choices to work for an agency, in-call service, or street-level manager. Overwhelmingly, they valued the potential for enhanced security provided by managers or employers and felt that safety initiatives were a vital component of successful managerial services. Many participants outlined employers' detailed safety protocols, including confirmation of client information, recording of licence plate numbers, workers checking in by telephone at both the start and end of sessions, the use of drivers as bodyguards, and lists of abusive or difficult clients. Angela, a Montreal escort and former agency owner, stated, *"They did the screening of the clients ... They call you at the beginning, they call you at the end of the hour, and they pick you up. And the drivers were very, very reliable, and so, in terms of protection, it was good to have a system, and they used it."* Several street-based workers similarly described the role that street-level managers can play in redressing violence, an important consideration for a population of women who experience elevated levels of violence and who overwhelmingly report poor access to, and inappropriate responses from, the police and legal system. Cora, a street and indoor worker in Halifax, said, *"Protection – you feel safer because the bottom line when you're out there and the only person that's in the car with you is some guy that's going to stab you – you feel more protected, you have someone to go to."* Sex workers expressed both confusion and anger at the criminalization of services that they found to be helpful, especially those pertaining to security. As Jane, a Montreal escort, put it, *"I see it that these laws get in the way of my protection because I am paying someone to protect me, and these laws are saying that that protection I'm asking for is illegal."* It is important to recognize that, in the current legal context, any supportive measures undertaken

Kara Gillies

by sex trade managers on behalf of their workers are entirely voluntary and at the discretion of the individual employer. And indeed, not all managers are as rigorous in promoting workplace safety, leading many workers to critique the lack of an industry standard.

Impact of the Procuring Law on Women's Labour Experiences

Ironically, the criminalization of managerial functions was seen by women as undermining the quality and effectiveness of the very administrative and occupational health and safety services they were seeking in the first place. Women reported that managers and employers are forced to distance themselves from any association with the sexual nature of the business in an attempt to avoid procuring charges. This can create a climate of tension, confusion, and potential danger.

One of the most serious impacts of the law is the inability of managers or their agents (such as receptionists) to clearly establish the terms and conditions of service when screening and booking clients. As a result, sex workers' boundaries such as condom use, types of service offered, and additional fees are typically not communicated to clients prior to the in-person meeting. This was seen to undermine workers' safety, income, professional reputation, health, and personal sense of agency.

Concern about the procuring law also prevents employers from providing clear job descriptions and expectations during the hiring process. This culminates in misunderstandings about specific work duties or, in some cases, newly hired workers being unaware of the sexual nature of the job. In fact, a recurrent finding was the disproportionate impact of the procuring provisions on women who were new to the business. Uniformly, women advised that access to support, training, and information were critical for their skills building and occupational health and safety when they first started the trade. However, the procuring law discourages managers and colleagues from providing such assistance.

Experienced sex workers perceived the procuring law as a barrier to career advancement. Several women spoke of establishing or managing a massage parlour, escort agency, or in-call service as an obvious and reasonable goal, especially for older women with a wealth of sex work experience to bring to the role. However, the fear of serious criminal charges frequently quashed these options.

Women's narratives make it clear that the procuring law interferes with both management and workers' efforts to create and maintain safe and supportive work environments. In fact, the criminalization of managerial activities frequently jeopardizes women's safety and well-being, which is in direct contrast to the state's goal of enhancing security through the procuring law. Women took exception to the criminalization of managerial involvement and the underlying premise that any third-party engagement in prostitution is inherently abusive and more exploitative than managerial/employer involvement in other types of work (see also Chapter 7 in this volume). Participants stressed that the potential for exploitation lies in the labour-management power differential that is common to all job sectors and that neither the nature nor the magnitude of such exploitation changes when the labour happens to be sex work. A Toronto escort named Linda explained that *"it's not explicit to sex work. It's not because it's sex work. It's any type of work. You have people who wish to exploit and, on the other hand, people who wish to run nice, decent, ethical businesses. I believe there are ethics in any line of work."* Cora, a Halifax street-based and indoor worker, agreed: *"And I'm not saying that none of that shit happens because it does. But, like, you've got bad people in every job."*

Like other workers, women in the sex trade reported incidents of unfair labour practices and substandard work conditions such as unpaid wages, safety hazards, long hours, and discriminatory or deceptive hiring practices. Participants voiced the strong opinion that labour and employment laws would not only advance their rights and status but would serve to reduce exploitation and abuse. As Jane, a Montreal escort, summarized, *"I think bosses should be accountable to their workers, so I think there should be laws that make bosses accountable to their workers. If your boss is sexually harassing you, if your boss isn't paying you, if your boss isn't responsible to their workers, I think there should be laws – not criminal laws, but labour laws."* Unlike other workers, however, sex workers are unable to reduce exploitation or seek redress through labour or employment laws. This is due to the doctrine of *paramountcy*, which gives federal laws, including the criminal sanctions against procuring, precedence over provincial laws such as labour, employment, and human rights legislation. In this manner, the criminalization of managerial involvement in prostitution effectively precludes sex workers from accessing the labour protections afforded other workers.

The procuring law was seen as too broad and heavy-handed an instrument for addressing cases of labour exploitation; women were interested in promoting healthy work environments, not abolishing worksites or imprisoning managers or operators for labour practices that they characterized as unfair but certainly not criminal. In the absence of the procuring law, workers would be able to prevent, minimize, or redress labour exploitation by accessing occupational health and safety regulations and other mechanisms such as human rights tribunals and employment standards.

Kara Gillies

Beyond the Procuring Law

As previously outlined, job safety was a recurring theme in the women's narratives; under federal, provincial, and territorial occupational health and safety legislation, workers have a fundamental right to be informed of known or predictable workplace hazards and to participate in the prevention of occupational injuries. If prostitution businesses were legitimately covered by such legislation, many safety challenges would be mitigated. For example, the training and information sharing that research participants declared essential to their well-being would not only become permissible, but necessary. The right to refuse dangerous work without fear of reprisal is another basic tenet of occupational health and safety law; if sex workers were able to access this protection, they would be empowered to avoid risk situations without threat of fines, income loss, or job termination, all common scenarios in the current legal climate. Chris, an Edmonton escort, explained, *"If [the manager] throws you a call and you don't stay – the guy's mean to you and you don't stay – you still have to pay him $100 for the call."*

Further, though the details vary, all Canadian jurisdictions have regulations regarding safety for persons working alone. As the women revealed, working in relative isolation is common in prostitution, and therefore these provisions are of particular relevance to sex workers. These regulations provide for the development of safety assessments and procedures, and they typically mandate contact between isolated workers and employers. This latter measure is similar to the "check-in, check-out" system employed by many sex work managers. However, the implementation and regular use of such protocols presently lie at the discretion of individual employers; the application of occupational health and safety regulations would formalize these procedures and ensure equal coverage for workers in the sex trade.

Several provinces have enacted regulations aimed directly at eliminating or reducing the risk of workplace violence through provisions that include employee training about the nature and extent of such violence, how to recognize and respond to it, and how to prevent, reduce, and report/document it. Although many managers of sex trade businesses record information about so-called bad dates, it is not a requirement, and the consistency and effectiveness of these initiatives vary. The duty to document violent incidents and notify workers of general and specific risks could be applied to sex trade businesses to ensure that proper records of abusive individuals are maintained and that all workers have access to this information.

Many women reported discriminatory and racist hiring or management practices within the current legal structure of the sex trade. Racialized women described being denied employment outright, relegated to unpopular shifts, or receiving a minimal number of clients. Many participants spoke of race-based quotas whereby management limits the number of women of colour who are hired or assigned to each shift or location. Several women discussed experiencing age-based discrimination in hiring and work assignments. The transsexual women stated that the vast majority of escort agencies and massage parlours refuse to hire transsexual/transgendered women and that those that do frequently pay them a lower rate than cisgendered women (see also Chapter 4 in this volume). These forms of discrimination are in clear breach of human rights codes, and sex workers who have experienced them should have access to appropriate remedies without the current fear that a complaint will turn into procuring charges against managers or employers and a subsequent shuttering of their workplaces.

The development of professional associations/colleges, other self-regulatory bodies, and unions was also advanced by participants as a viable strategy for building workers' rights and status (see also Chapter 8 in this volume). However, the women cautioned that these should not be used to limit their access or choices. In particular, excessive professionalization such as mandatory training, accreditation, or registration could shut out the most marginalized individuals (including migrant and street-based workers) and create a two-tiered system. It was noted that sex work offers income opportunities for many women who either cannot or choose not to find employment in mainstream regulated jobs. Women therefore suggested that membership in unions or professional associations should be voluntary and involve a minimum of barriers.

Some participants questioned the practicability of applying labour laws and rights to street-based workers, given the atypical structure and organization of their work. However, other non-standard personnel have successfully mobilized to shift the norms of what constitutes recognized worksites, relationships, and practices. One participant drew a parallel between street-based sex workers and bicycle messengers, noting that the latter had recently organized in Quebec to enhance occupational health and safety, and to develop minimum industry standards (Lejtenji 2002).

Conclusion

Although the procuring law prohibits managerial involvement in prostitution on the assumption that such engagement is necessarily abusive, many sex workers

Kara Gillies

report concrete benefits to this arrangement. Specifically, women stated that managers can assist with occupational health and safety as well as provide administrative support and other services. However, the procuring law undermines the quality and safety of sex-working women's work environments by criminalizing services they seek from third parties and precluding access to basic labour and human rights protections.

Sex workers were firm in their position that the current procuring law as it pertains to adults is detrimental to their well-being and must be revisited. Women were especially concerned that the broad scope of the legislation criminalizes benevolent and helpful activities as readily as it captures abusive conduct. Several participants recommended that the procuring law should be amended to specifically and solely address abuse and coercion, whereas the majority recommended that it be abolished outright.

In its place, women suggested the extension or adaptation of existing labour standards and other administrative mechanisms to the sex trade, with the caveat that such mechanisms not be more repressive than those imposed on other work sectors or used by the state as another means of controlling women's work and bodies. The best way to achieve this goal is to ensure that sex workers themselves take the lead in the development, implementation, and evaluation of new legislative or regulatory schemes.

Notes

1 Although this chapter focuses on the impact of the procuring law on women's work experiences and relationships, it's based on a broader study (funded by Status of Women Canada) that also examined the law's impact on women's personal relationships as well as their experiences of violence.
2 This chapter focuses exclusively on the procuring law as it pertains to adult women and does not consider sections that relate to persons under the age of eighteen.

References

Backhouse, C.B. 1985. Nineteenth-century Canadian prostitution law: Reflection of a discriminatory society. *Social History* 18, 36: 397-423.

Criminal Code, R.S.C. 1985, c. C-46.

Currie, N., and K. Gillies. 2006. Bound by law: How Canada's protectionist policies in the areas of both rape and prostitution limit women's choices, agency and activities. Unpublished manuscript. Status of Women, Ottawa.

Hodgson, J.F. 1997. *Games pimps play: Pimps, players and wives-in-law.* Toronto: Canadian Scholars' Press.

Lejtenji, P. 2002. Courier casualties: Bike messengers fight for respect in the wake of a colleague's death. *Montreal Mirror,* 26 September, n.p.

McLaren, J. 1996. Recalculating the wages of sin: The social and legal construction of prostitution 1850-1920. *Manitoba Law Journal* 23: 524-55.

McLaren, J., and J. Lowman. 1990. Enforcing Canada's prostitution laws 1892-1920: Rhetoric and practice. In *Securing compliance: Seven case studies*, ed. M.C. Friedland, 21-87. Toronto: University of Toronto Press.

van der Meulen, E. 2010. Illegal lives, loves, and work: How the criminalization of procuring affects sex workers in Canada. *Wagadu: A Journal of Transnational Women's and Gender Studies* 8: 217-40.

18

Still Punishing to "Protect": Youth Prostitution Law and Policy Reform

STEVEN BITTLE

In Canada, discourses pertaining to the sexual abuse of children and youth significantly shape the state's response to youth working in prostitution. To cohere with this dominant knowledge claim, several jurisdictions across Canada have introduced legal and policy reforms aimed at "rescuing" young women who are sexually exploited through prostitution. Key strategies for realizing this goal include secure care legislation and enhanced child welfare schemes, permitting authorities to detain young prostitutes for their own "protection," programs to encourage youth to end their involvement in prostitution, and (largely unfulfilled) promises to criminalize male "sexual predators" (customers and pimps) (Martin 2002; Busby 2003).

Critics note that conceptualizing youth prostitution as sexual abuse and exploitation fails to protect youth engaged in sex work. They argue that forced detainment through secure care legislation is an unduly harsh measure that pushes prostitution underground and drives youth engaged in sex work from accessing (increasingly disappearing) social services (Martin 2002; Busby 2003). Critics also suggest that the "rhetoric of victimhood" (Phoenix 2002a, 361) does little to address the material and social conditions that make sex work a viable option for some young people (Martin 2002; Busby 2003; Phoenix 2007). As Phoenix (2007, 91) suggests, "Such a simple and naive understanding of the conditions in which women get involved in prostitution belies the economic and social realities so widely documented in two centuries of research." However, despite these concerns, the sexual exploitation discourse is the dominant means of understanding and responding to youth prostitution in Canada

– the hegemonic common sense that animates the state's legal and policy framework.

Building from my previous work in this area (Bittle 2002, 2006), and integrating insights from related research (Martin 2002; Phoenix 2002a, 2002b, 2007; Busby 2003), this chapter critically examines official responses to youth prostitution in Canada, which are rooted in the language of sexual abuse and exploitation.[1] I argue that treating young women engaged in sex work as "always and already victims" (Phoenix 2002a, 354) individualizes the youth prostitution "problem," that a dominant familial ideology underpins efforts to confront youth prostitution as sexual exploitation, and that the current legal and policy nexus reaffirms the state's coercive control of young women engaged in sex work. The state provides counselling and support to youth in the sex trade who accept their victim status (even if this help is not of their choosing), but those who resist their victim identity are labelled as problematic and detained "for their own protection," or risk criminalization through their marginalized status as street-involved youth (Phoenix 2002a, 2002b; Busby 2003). In essence, the state treats youth working in prostitution as victims "*except* when they are offenders" (Phoenix 2002b, 69, emphasis in original), further entrenching the historically rooted distinction "between good women and bad women" (Brock 2000, 80).

To develop these arguments, the chapter examines youth prostitution legal and policy developments in the Canadian provinces of Alberta, British Columbia, and Manitoba. Many of the youth-prostitution-related measures introduced in these jurisdictions exemplify the growing concern in recent decades with the sexual abuse and exploitation of young people through prostitution. Thus, the chapter focuses on the state's response to women under the age of eighteen engaged in sex work, as they constitute the primary target of these initiatives (Busby 2003). Young men involved in prostitution, whose experiences are marginalized within the sexual abuse discourse and who are not subject to the same level of regulation and control as their female counterparts, are therefore beyond the scope of this discussion.[2]

The chapter's theoretical approach builds from Canadian socio-legal feminist scholars who situate issues of gender and law within their broader social context (Smart 1995; Chunn and Lacombe 2000; Comack 2006; Snider 2006). This line of inquiry explores how law and related policy are constitutive of a hegemonic process in which various discourses coalesce within state institutions and practices to (re)create dominant social formations (Chunn and Lacombe 2000; see also Bonnycastle 2000; Comack 2006). Never predetermined or absolute, these processes reflect ongoing ideological struggles about the nature of gender, race, and class relations in society. As Chunn and Lacombe (2000, 9) suggest,

Steven Bittle

"Far from being fixed and immutable, state, law and patriarchy are historically and culturally specific constructs embedded in particular social relations, and they assume new forms with different content over time." Law is, therefore, a site where meanings are contested and certain ideological beliefs take root to animate law-as-legislation and as practice (ibid.; Comack and Balfour 2004; Comack 2006).

The overall goal of the chapter is to demonstrate how current responses to youth sex work in Canada reinforce and reproduce gender, race, and class inequalities (Chunn and Lacombe 2000; Comack and Balfour 2004). Of particular interest are the dominant discourses that animate official responses to youth prostitution, focusing on the "meanings and assumptions embedded in different forms of language use, ways of making sense of the world, and their corresponding practices" (Comack 2006, 61). As we shall see, (re)conceptualizing youth prostitution as sexual abuse and exploitation inspired a range of repressive and ineffectual legal and policy innovations that reinforce a "constructed normality about gender stereotypes and gender power relations" (Bonnycastle 2000, 61). As a result, while young women are punished and controlled under the guise of protection, the conditions that give rise to youth prostitution continue unabated.

Historical Contradictions of Youth Prostitution Law and Policy

Historically, official responses to youth prostitution in Canada oscillated between treating young prostitutes as fallen women who require punishment and as victims in need of sympathy and protection (Lowman 1987; Brock 2000). In many instances we find a blurring between these seemingly contradictory positions, resulting in what Busby (2003, 104) describes as a "slippage between criminal justice and social welfare responses." In practice, young women in prostitution are singled out for censure and control, whereas the men who procure their sexual services are relatively unfettered to pursue, in prevailing heterosexual terms, their (supposedly biologically determined) sexual proclivities. Even under the limited circumstances where the actions of male customers are subject to moral approbation, the nature and extent of the state's response pale in comparison to the regulation and control of women in the sex trade (Sullivan 1986; Martin 2002; Busby 2003). Female sex workers are "quintessentially gendered criminals," as Martin (2002, 363) argues, "cast as immoral, sexually loose, irresponsible breeders of poverty and disorder and punished accordingly."

The dominant knowledge claims of twentieth-century moral reformers, who argued that prostitution was an affront to women's purity, significantly shaped early prostitution laws (Backhouse 1985, 1991; McLaren 1986; Valverde 1991; Minaker 2006). Throughout this period, the state enacted stringent child protection laws aimed at keeping young women from entering the sex trade. As a result, many young women, particularly those from immigrant and working-class backgrounds, found themselves serving lengthy sentences in women's reformatories under the pretence that it was necessary to save them from immorality, to eliminate vice, and to attain social purity (Brock 2000; see also Sullivan 1986; Valverde 1991; Minaker 2006). As we shall see, and as Minaker (2006, 81) notes, these strategies to help "erring females" were early harbingers of the protectionist discourses that animate contemporary state responses to youth prostitution.

The history of prostitution law in Canada also reveals that sex workers of all ages were (and are) subject to discriminatory legislation and unequal law enforcement (Sullivan 1986; Lowman 1987; Brock 2000; Martin 2002). Until 1972, for instance, street prostitution was a gender-specific offence that criminalized "a common prostitute or nightwalker" who was "found in a public place" and could not "give a good account of herself" (Backhouse 1985; Brock 2000; see also the Introduction in this volume). When gender-neutral legislation that criminalized public solicitation for the purposes of prostitution replaced vagrancy laws, it was prostitutes, not their male customers, who were most often charged and convicted (Brock 2000). What is more, throughout the 1980s, as various community groups and politicians across Canada decried that street prostitution was a public nuisance – a perceived blight to community standards – women sex workers were subject to court injunctions that restricted where they could ply their trade and to persistent harassment by police and angry residents who wanted prostitution removed from their neighbourhoods (Lowman 1986, 1990; Brock 1998, 2000). When the federal government reacted by introducing the communicating law, criminalizing communicating for the purpose of prostitution, it was prostitutes who, yet again, faced the greatest burden as a result of the policing of sex work. The *Bedford* case is a stark reminder of how Canada's prostitution laws force many sex workers to meet clients in secluded and dangerous locations so as to avoid running afoul of the law – a policy decision with deadly consequences for many women (*Bedford v. Canada* 2010; see also Chapter 15 in this volume).[3] Together these legal developments underscore the dominant belief that prostitution was, and is, a female crime deserving of punishment and control.

Youth prostitution law and policy started to take a (theoretically) different direction during the 1980s within the context of growing concerns about sexual offences against children and youth. At the forefront of this transformation was the work of the Committee on Sexual Offences against Children and Youth (Badgley Committee 1984), mandated by the federal government to conduct nation-wide research and consultations concerning childhood sexual abuse. The Badgley Report argued that addressing the harms that young prostitutes "bring upon themselves" required using the criminal law against them "so that social intervention can take place" (ibid., 1046, quoted in Busby 2003, 104). Although criticized for individualizing the causes of youth prostitution and misconstruing punishment as help (Busby 2003; see also Lowman 1987; Brock 1998), this recommendation nevertheless set the tone for creating sexual offences that hinged on differentiating between adults and youth (Brock 1998). As Lowman (2001, 2) notes, the Badgley Report represented a "decisive point in the Canadian literature because it helped introduce the idea that although the Canadian age of consent is 14 [which has since been raised to age sixteen], prostitution involving 14 to 17 year-olds is a form of sexual abuse."

The sexual abuse and exploitation discourse continued to gain momentum following the Badgley Report, creating new "ways of objectifying and speaking the truth" (Burchell 1996, 31) and encouraging politicians to implement legal and policy reforms. In 1986, for instance, Ottawa enacted legislation that criminalized purchasing or attempting to purchase the sexual services of a young person under the age of eighteen (*Criminal Code* 1985, s. 212(4)). It quickly became evident, however, that this law would fall into a state of virtual disuse (Hornick and Bolitho 1992; Lowman and Fraser 1996). According to Busby (2003, 104), the perception among law enforcement is that "gathering evidence for these cases is very difficult and therefore charges against those who exploit minors are almost never laid." The alternative is to charge young sex workers under the communicating law (even if less frequently than in the past) or with offences such as drug crimes that are often associated with life on the streets. However, despite failing to produce a "crackdown" on male customers, the enactment of sexual procurement legislation further signalled the growing belief that young women engaged in sex work were victims of sexual abuse and exploitation.

During the 1990s, several municipal task forces and federal and provincial initiatives concluded that youth prostitution constituted child sexual abuse and should be dealt with accordingly (British Columbia Ministry of Attorney General 1996; Manitoba Child and Youth Secretariat 1996; Alberta Task Force on Children Involved in Prostitution 1997). Key among these was the Alberta Task Force on Children Involved in Prostitution (1997), charged with exploring programs for addressing youth prostitution. Its Forsyth Report (ibid., 3) made its philosophical orientation clear in arguing that children involved in prostitution, "if not abused while at home, are certainly victims of sexual abuse when they are used by either a pimp or john." The report recommended a system of "collaborative case management," more procuring charges, a media campaign to raise public awareness about the issue, and most prominently, secure care legislation to provide "legislative support for a continuum of services for children involved in prostitution" (ibid.).

On 1 February 1999, in response to the Forsyth Report, the Province of Alberta became the first and still only Canadian jurisdiction to enact secure care legislation to address the sexual exploitation of children and youth in prostitution. The Protection of Children Involved in Prostitution Act, amended in 2007 as the Protection of Sexually Exploited Children Act to "reflect the true circumstances of these children's lives" (Government of Alberta 2007), empowers police and child welfare workers to detain children involved in, or at risk of becoming involved in, prostitution. A judge must approve the power to apprehend, although the police can do so without a court order if they believe the youth is in serious and imminent danger (Government of Alberta 2010). Unless there is a "suitable" guardian, authorities will place the young person (most commonly a young woman) in a "protective safe house" where she is held for up to five days "to ensure the safety of the child and to assess the child" (ibid., 6); more specifically, the state conducts "tests for drug and alcohol use, sexually transmitted diseases, HIV and pregnancy" (Busby 2003, 105). The act also permits the Children and Youth Services director to apply for two additional periods of detainment of up to twenty-one days each so that the youth can receive further treatment and counselling to "break the cycle of abuse" (ibid., 7).

Alberta's secure care legislation is the most visible and controversial response to the redefinition of youth prostitution as sexual abuse and exploitation. Although other jurisdictions contemplated similar measures, including British Columbia, where a government-led Secure Care Working Group advocated a "safe care" strategy, as well as Saskatchewan, Nova Scotia, and Ontario, they have yet to enact secure care laws. At the same time, however, many jurisdictions drew from the sexual abuse and exploitation discourse to develop their youth-prostitution-related policies and programs. In British Columbia, for instance, the government established community action teams, comprising service providers, police, government officials, and community members, to help eliminate "the exploitation of children and youth through prostitution" (BC – MPSSG 2011a). It also published a handbook for parents and teachers to identify risk factors for youth involvement in prostitution and proclaimed a "stop the

Steven Bittle

sexual exploitation of children and youth awareness week" (BC – MPSSG 2011b). Meanwhile, as part of its sexual exploitation strategy, the Manitoba government amended the Child and Family Services Act to increase penalties to a maximum of a $50,000 fine and two years in prison for "causing a child to be in need of protection" (Manitoba 2009).[4] Special sexual exploitation investigators work with StreetReach programs set up throughout the province, which operate similarly to British Columbia's community action teams, to strengthen the "safety net for youth who have been sexually exploited or are at high risk of being victimized" (ibid.). The government also participates in an annual "stop child sexual exploitation" awareness week.

Together these developments reflect a shift in official strategies to govern and control youth engaged in sex work, who are no longer seen as deviants in need of punishment. The current legal and policy landscape begins from the premise that youth engaged in sex work are victims of sexual abuse and exploitation who require protection (Martin 2002; Busby 2003). However, as the next section demonstrates, this transformation accomplishes little in terms of altering the historical trend that holds young women to account for their decision to prostitute, and it fails to address the material and social conditions that give rise to youth prostitution, effectively reinforcing and reproducing status quo gender, race, and class inequalities (Martin 2002; Snider 2006).

Individualizing the Youth Prostitution "Problem"

As the predominant discourse animating the state's legal and policy framework, defining youth prostitution as sexual abuse and exploitation abstracts the individual sex worker from her social circumstances, obscuring the broader social conditions that shape a young woman's decision to work in prostitution (Martin 2002; Phoenix 2002a, 2002b). Further, as this discourse was taken up by, and interpreted through, an increasingly neoliberal lens, the individual became responsible for both her decision to prostitute and making the "prudent" choice (cf. Hannah-Moffat 2001) to end her "cycle of abuse." These are acutely gendered expectations in that male procurers are not held to the same account (Martin 2002; Busby 2003), and neoliberalism compounds the feminization of poverty, drastically reducing social programs and employment opportunities for young street-involved women (Martin 2002; see also Chunn and Gavigan 2004; Mosher and Hermer 2010).

In contemporary Western societies, law derives its legitimacy through claims of "fairness, stability and justice" (Woodiwiss 2006, 525; see also Smart 1989; Fudge and Cossman 2002; Comack 2006). Naffine (1990, 52, quoted in Comack

2006, 22) argues that law asserts this status by abstracting individuals from their complex and varied social contexts to "examine the merits of their individual cases." Despite the reality that we are not all "equally located structurally" (Morrison 1995, 213), and critical examinations of law that debunk its claims to neutrality (Chunn and Lacombe 2000), this legal sleight of hand ensures that everyone is treated as "free, capable and competitive" subjects whose social circumstances are irrelevant to rendering legal judgments (Comack 2006, 22). Law therefore obscures and individualizes complex social matters, as Snider (2006, 323) reminds us, rendering legal institutions and practices incapable of delivering "empowerment or amelioration" to the very populations they claim to defend.

The current youth prostitution legal and policy environment abstracts the female sex worker from her social context by formalizing her status as a victim of sexual abuse and exploitation. Underpinning Alberta's secure care legislation is the principle that "sexually exploited children are victims of sexual abuse" who require "protection services and support" (Government of Alberta 2010, 5). Similarly, the Manitoba government amended its Child and Family Services Act to "deter predators and protect children in danger of being harboured and sexually exploited," and the British Columbia government notes that the "sexual exploitation of children and youth is never considered prostitution or consensual" (Manitoba Family Services and Consumer Affairs 2011; BC – MPSSG 2011a). These official positions underscore the notion that young women are sexually exploited and abused through their involvement in prostitution, regardless of their individual circumstances and varied histories.

Viewing young prostitutes as "always and already victims" (Phoenix 2002a, 367) obscures the conditions that make sex work a viable option for some young women (ibid.; Phoenix 2002b). There is an extensive literature that documents how many young women in prostitution ran away or were thrown away from emotionally, physically, and sexually abusive home environments – abuse committed primarily by male family members and acquaintances (Lowman 1986; Sullivan 1986; O'Neill 2001). This literature further documents that following the decision to run away, the desire for autonomy and money pulled some young women to the streets, and that the situational poverty of street-involved youth, along with a steady male demand for sexual services, made sex work a feasible survival option. These factors are particularly germane for understanding the overrepresentation of young Aboriginal women in prostitution, whose experiences are also shaped significantly by a history of colonialism (Badgley Committee 1984; Lowman 1986, 1987; Brock 1998). Unfortunately,

Steven Bittle

however, these complex factors are ignored, or pushed to the background, in favour of directing the legal and policy lens almost exclusively at the abuse that occurs in the context of exchanging sexual services for money (Phoenix 2002a). As a result, there is a silencing of some young women's desire to exercise their autonomy and develop a life outside of an abusive home environment – dominant voices equate prostitution with sexual coercion and exploitation, not as a decision that young people make within a particular gendered, racialized, and class context.

Phoenix (2002a, 367) argues that framing youth prostitution as sexual abuse and exploitation conflates important sociological differences between the sexual abuse that young women experience in "intimate and/or familial relationships" and the commercial exchange of sexual services. In particular, Phoenix (ibid.) suggests that "the relationships and activities constituting the institution of prostitution have little meaning outside of the exchange of sex for money." Although she does not deny that young women may experience harm and abuse through their involvement in sex work, her point is that reducing prostitution to "another form of child abuse" glosses over the "economic, political and ideological" context of youth prostitution – the very elements that make prostitution possible. Absent this recognition, abuse and exploitation through prostitution become something to confront and control, not an indication of larger structural problems that require transformation.

The abstraction of young women working in prostitution from their social circumstances also emerges through the convergence of legal and sexual abuse discourses with neoliberal ideals that celebrate the accomplishments of the white male captain of industry and downplay the need for, and effectiveness of, state-sponsored social welfare programs (Fudge and Cossman 2002; Glasbeek 2002). Growing concerns with declining corporate profit levels and economic recessions throughout the 1980s and early 1990s helped propel the now well-documented "tectonic shift" in public policy toward privatization (Fudge and Cossman 2002, 3). This transformation allowed influential neoliberal voices to caution against "government overreach and overload" and to question the state's responsibility for addressing social and economic ills (Rose and Miller 1992, 198; see also Barry, Osborne, and Rose 1996; Fudge and Cossman 2002; Resnick and Wolff 2010). The state responded by reshaping its regulatory responsibilities in pro-business and market-friendly ways, freeing up corporate capitalists to pursue avenues of unprecedented wealth – and, ironically, for corporations to commit serious and devastating crimes (Pearce and Tombs 1998; Glasbeek 2002; Snider 2009). The state also disassembled its welfare regime, introducing crippling cutbacks to unemployment insurance and provincial transfers for "welfare, social services, and post secondary institutions" (Fudge and Cossman 2002, 15-16). And with the state largely out of the social welfare business, matters of poverty, homelessness, and unemployment became individual problems (Comack and Balfour 2004). The dominant neoliberal message was, and is, that overcoming poor social circumstances is a matter of choice for which individuals, along with their families and communities, must work to achieve (Martin 2002; Comack and Balfour 2004).

Neoliberal ideals are evident throughout various measures that attempt to address youth sex work as sexual abuse and exploitation. For instance, the BC government's Secure Care Working Group argued that some *"out of control"* children and youth resist help and therefore place *"themselves* at a great risk of harm" (SCWG 1998, 5, 16, emphasis added). Likewise, the Forsyth Report (Alberta Task Force on Children Involved in Prostitution 1997, 11, emphasis added) acknowledged the victim status of young prostitutes but also demanded that they "take *responsibility* for their actions" and understand that there are consequences for their decisions, including whether to leave the streets. The fact that Alberta's secure care legislation permits authorities to detain young female prostitutes so that they can receive treatment to "break the cycle of abuse" (Deis et al. 2000; Government of Alberta 2010) underscores the belief that the decision to prostitute – or, to turn the dominant discourse on its head, the decision to be sexually exploited – is an individual choice. To echo Carlen's (2002, 235) critique of neoliberal reforms of women's imprisonment, "the problem is in their heads, not their social circumstances."

The development of various community-based initiatives, including sexual exploitation awareness weeks, community action teams, and tool kits for parents and communities to identify youth at risk of sexual exploitation, also reflects dominant neoliberal ideals. More than benevolent attempts by the state to co-ordinate efforts against youth prostitution, these measures reflect the state backing away from its claim to be the sole provider of safety and security, recasting the issue as a normative problem to be addressed through community and state (correctional) partnerships (Garland 2000). In situations where the state enlists Aboriginal communities to address the sexual exploitation of young Aboriginal women (Manitoba 2009; BC – MPSSG 2011a), this reconfiguration of responsibilities obscures the complex socio-economic factors that give rise to Aboriginal youth involvement in sex work, conditions that fade to the background in favour of strategies that focus on the exploitation that occurs within the context of prostitution. In this respect, as Garland (2000, 348) notes, the neoliberal state acts "through civil society and not upon it."

Steven Bittle

Reinforcing Familial Ideology

Current youth prostitution law and policy also help reinforce a dominant familial ideology, espousing the benefits of the "idealized white, Christian, heterosexual, bourgeois, patriarchically organized family" (Martin 2002, 361). Regardless of the fact that many young women engaged in sex work describe their home environments as intolerable, a perception shaped by their experiences of sexual, physical, and emotional abuse in the family unit (Badgley Committee 1984; Lowman 1987), the (patriarchal) family remains a primary solution to the youth prostitution "problem"; young women must be returned to it or with proper intervention encouraged to stay. Underlying this commitment is a hegemonic belief that the nuclear family is the most obvious and normal place for women and men to fulfill their socially ascribed gender roles and responsibilities (Chunn and Lacombe 2000). It also conforms to neoliberal knowledge claims that the family is a more appropriate vehicle for delivering the care and support that was once considered within the state's charge (Fudge and Cossman 2002). Within this context the child's best interests become synonymous with maintaining the family unit (Boyd 2000), whether it is the traditional family or state substitute, such as foster care.

Examples of this familial ideology emerge through the development and implementation of different youth-prostitution-related policies and programs. For instance, both the Forsyth Report and the Secure Care Working Group argued for empowering the family to protect young prostitutes and to remove them from the sex trade. As the Forsyth Report suggested, "Parents wishing to help and support their children to leave prostitution often feel powerless and at the mercy of social service agencies and police ... This is not helpful or supportive of families" (Alberta Task Force on Children Involved in Prostitution 1997, 29). Alberta's secure care framework therefore provides for the family's active involvement in a young sex worker's care while she is in protective confinement (Government of Alberta 2010). Families also play a central role in educational programs and prevention strategies to prevent the sexual exploitation of children and youth. "Education is a parent's best weapon against sexual exploitation; you can never know too much when protecting your children," notes Alberta's Children and Youth Services (2011). Similarly, the BC government funds educational programs and support services for parents of sexually exploited youth, which include helping them determine if their children are on the verge of being coerced into a life of prostitution and removing them from sexually exploitative circumstances (BC – MPSSG 2011a).

This is not to deny that families are caring and supportive environments for many young people, or that the state does not recognize through these initiatives that some children and youth experience abuse in the family. However, the ultimate goal of keeping young women in, or returning them to, the family unit overshadows the role of harmful familial relationships in shaping some young women's decision to engage in sex work. The centrality and supremacy of the nuclear family, along with the gender-based power imbalances that contribute to the harm of young women, are reinforced and reproduced, not challenged or transformed (Martin 2002). It is the decision to leave the family that becomes problematic, not the organization of the patriarchal family itself.

Young Women Still Criminalized and Controlled

The redefinition of youth prostitution as sexual abuse and exploitation also helps reinforce a "disturbing hypocrisy" (ibid., 364) in that the state affords some young women sympathy and protection as victims of sexual abuse and exploitation, whereas it criminalizes and punishes those who reject their victim identity, refuse care, or continue their involvement in prostitution (Phoenix 2002a, 2002b; Busby 2003). As Phoenix (2002b, 78) argues, equating youth prostitution as child sexual abuse "reconstructs the 'problem' of youth prostitution in a binary fashion: as child (sexual) abuse, except where voluntarism can be established in which case it is a crime problem." We therefore find a continued blurring of "criminal justice and social welfare responses," a historically rooted contradiction that ultimately holds the erring female to account for her engagement in sex work (Busby 2003, 104; see also Lowman 1987; Minaker 2006).

Secure care punishes and controls young women in prostitution through their forced detainment and treatment, despite the questionable adequacy of this strategy for dealing with youth prostitution. After all, those who face detention in "protective confinement" to help them end their cycle of abuse are the young women, not the "predators" who procure their sexual services (still no secure care treatment for male customers). In addition, many young prostitutes report negative experiences with child welfare services, citing their distrust and suspicion of "any helping agency" (Nixon et al. 2002, 1039; see also Chapter 5 in this volume). Focus group discussions conducted by Busby et al. (2000, 13; Busby 2003, 120) confirm that young female prostitutes in Alberta perceive secure care as an "ineffective and even counter-productive" form of punishment in which many detainees "simply sleep out their time before being released back to the street." Forcing young women into secure care therefore risks discouraging them from voluntarily seeking help from service agencies, as well as drives youth sex work underground where women are even more vulnerable to violence and exploitation.

Non-secure-care strategies also increase the governance and control of young female prostitutes. For instance, British Columbia and Manitoba's community action teams share information and work with communities to identify youth at risk of sexual exploitation and safeguard those perceived as trapped in the sex trade. Although these coordinating efforts appear laudable, we cannot overlook the fact that the comprising agencies (police, social welfare officials, and service providers) typically structure their work around "traditional child protection methods" (Phoenix 2007, 85). This means that there will be instances in which the police will doff their "helping hat" to detain young women who persistently prostitute or who commit a street crime. In addition, these co-ordinating strategies are limited to provide help in the form of counselling and educating youth about the dangers of sexual exploitation and are not equipped to address the material and social conditions that shape some young women's decision to work in prostitution.

Finally, we need to situate the governance and control of many young female sex workers within their lived realities as street-involved youth. In recent decades, as the state was busy befriending business, it was simultaneously sharpening its teeth when it came to dealing with traditional street crimes (Garland 2001; Wacquant 2009). Despite official rhetoric citing the demise of the overly burdensome and bureaucratic state, those who do not measure up to dominant neoliberal ideals have come under greater surveillance and control (Martin 2002; Comack and Balfour 2004). This includes young women working in prostitution who risk being charged with prostitution-related offences (particularly if they resist their victim identity through persistent involvement in sex work), as well as for crimes associated with life on the streets, such as theft and drug use (Busby 2003).[5] It would thus appear that, as a result of dominant neoliberal thinking, there is improved (economic) freedom for the privileged few but greater state control for the most marginalized and disadvantaged.

Conclusion

This chapter demonstrates the limitations of (re)conceptualizing young women in prostitution as victims of sexual abuse and exploitation. As the dominant knowledge claim that animates the state's legal and policy response, it abstracts young female sex workers from their complex social histories, particularly for young Aboriginal women, individualizing the decision to prostitute and overshadowing the gender, race, and class inequalities that make prostitution both plausible and possible (Phoenix 2002a). It also reinforces and reproduces a familial ideology wherein the ultimate goal is to return young women to, or keep them in, the patriarchal family unit, despite its inherent gender and power imbalances (Martin 2002). There is no room for agency here, no acknowledgment that the decision to engage in sex work is made in conditions that are not of a young person's choosing (Lowman 1987; Phoenix 2007). The young female sex worker is either a victim of sexual abuse and exploitation who requires help and protection, essentially a euphemism for incarceration, or an erring female who needs to be punished and controlled (Phoenix 2002a, 2002b). It would thus appear that the good girl/bad girl duality is firmly entrenched (Minaker 2006), ensuring that young women working in prostitution continue to face the disproportionate burden for the regulation and control of the youth prostitution "problem."

All of this does not suggest that the state, and through it law and policy, automatically or necessarily contributes to the ongoing marginalization of young sex workers. The factors underlying the desire to help are too complex for such simple formulae. What is more, there are signs of resistance to the sexual abuse and exploitation discourse, underscoring that this language is constitutive of larger ideological struggles that are never complete and always subject to change (Chunn and Lacombe 2000). In addition to the fact that Alberta remains the only Canadian jurisdiction to enact secure care legislation, there have been attempts, albeit unsuccessful, to challenge its constitutionality (see *Alberta (Director of Child Welfare) v. K.B.* 2000), and service providers question the wisdom of locking up young women in the name of protection (Busby 2003). However, despite these dissenting voices, the victim-oriented approach to youth sex work continues to shape the legal and policy landscape, effectively reinforcing and reproducing the "material and ideological conditions" (Smart 1995, 144; see also Chunn and Lacombe 2000) within which youth prostitution flourishes. The challenge therefore becomes finding ways to transcend the hegemonic status quo to situate youth prostitution within its broader social, economic, and historical context.

In the end, characterizing young women in prostitution as victims of sexual abuse and exploitation might make for good politics, providing a convenient and easy target so that governments can *seem* to be doing something about youth prostitution, but it fails to deal with root causes. Quite simply, young women are incarcerated for their own "protection," whereas the conditions that give rise to youth involvement in prostitution remain untouched. Instead of casting the regulatory lens down the social hierarchy at young, marginalized women, the state should redirect its efforts toward the "underlying structural

Steven Bittle

constraints (race, class and gender inequalities)" (Minaker 2006, 93) that influence some young women's decision to engage in sex work. Developing intervention strategies around these matters stands a far better chance of ameliorating the lives of young women working in prostitution than efforts that purport to do so under the guise of protection.

Acknowledgment
I would like to acknowledge Samantha McAleese for her research assistance and Jennifer Kilty for her helpful comments on an earlier version of this chapter.

Notes
1 Throughout the chapter I use terms such as "sex work" and "youth involved in prostitution," unless referring specifically to various programs and initiatives that employ the language of "sexually exploited" or "sexually abused" youth. In doing so, I do not deny that some young women experience harms through their involvement in prostitution; instead, my intention is to underscore the need for transcending the sexual abuse discourse to situate youth sex work within its broader socio-economic context. As Phoenix (2007, 91) notes, "Whilst many street working women suffer from some form of victimization and exploitation, they are not all victims waiting to be saved ... Many are just poor women struggling to survive."
2 For an examination of male sex work, see Visano (1987) or McIntyre (2008).
3 Recent research also documents how sex trade workers continue to experience harassment and violence at the hands of police and customers (see Chapter 19 in this volume), as well as how municipal bylaws compound the level of surveillance and control experienced by women who work in massage parlours and escort agencies (van der Meulen and Durisin 2008).
4 The Manitoba government launched its sexual exploitation strategy, dubbed Tracia's Trust, in response to the suicide death of Tracia Owen, a fourteen-year-old Aboriginal youth with an extensive history of abuse and neglect, contact with child welfare officials, drug use, and involvement in prostitution. A coroner's inquest recommended changes to the province's child welfare provisions and services to combat drug use and sexual exploitation of young people on the streets (Guy 2008).
5 Although young women involved in prostitution are no longer charged routinely with communicating offences under the Criminal Code, they are still charged occasionally with prostitution offences. In 2006, for instance, forty-eight youth were accused of prostitution-related offences, and twenty-six were charged (Taylor-Butts and Bressan 2006).

References
Alberta, Children and Youth Services. 2011. Child sexual exploitation. http://www.child. alberta.ca/.

Alberta Task Force on Children Involved in Prostitution (Forsyth Report). 1997. *Children involved in prostitution.* Edmonton: Ministry of Family and Social Services.

Backhouse, C.B. 1985. Nineteenth-century Canadian prostitution law: Reflection of a discriminatory society. *Social History* 17 (November): 387-423.

–. 1991. *Petticoats and prejudice: Women and law in nineteenth century Canada.* Toronto: Osgoode Society.

Badgley Committee (Committee on Sexual Offences against Children and Youth). 1984. *Sexual offences against children and youth.* Ottawa: Department of Supply and Services.

Barry, A., T. Osborne, and N. Rose. 1996. *Foucault and political reason: Liberalism, neoliberalism and rationalities of government.* Chicago: University of Chicago Press.

BC – MPSSG (British Columbia Ministry of Public Safety and Solicitor General). 2011a. Preventing sexual exploitation of children and youth. http://www.pssg.gov.bc.ca/.

–. 2011b. Stopping the sexual exploitation of children and youth. Crime prevention information series 2. http://www.pssg.gov.bc.ca/crimeprevention/publications/docs/crime-prev -series2-sexual-exploitation-children-youth.pdf.

Bittle, S. 2002. When protection is punishment. *Canadian Journal of Criminology and Criminal Justice* 44, 3: 317-50.

–. 2006. From villain to victim: Secure care and young women in prostitution. In *Criminalizing women*, ed. G. Balfour and E. Comack, 195-216. Halifax: Fernwood.

Bonnycastle, K. 2000. Rape uncodified: Reconsidering Bill C-49 amendments to Canadian sexual assault laws. In *Law as a gendering practice*, ed. D.E. Chunn and D. Lacombe, 60-78. Toronto: Oxford University Press.

Boyd, S. 2000. Custody, access, and relocation in a mobile society: (En)gendering the best interests principle. In *Law as a gendering practice*, ed. D.E. Chunn and D. Lacombe, 158-80. Toronto: Oxford University Press.

British Columbia Ministry of Attorney General. 1996. *Community consultation on prostitution in British Columbia: Overview of results*. N.p.: Ministry of Attorney General.

Brock, D.R. 1998. *Making work, making trouble: Prostitution as a social problem*. Toronto: University of Toronto Press.

–. 2000. Victim, nuisance, fallen women, outlaw, worker? Making the identity 'prostitute' in Canadian criminal law. In *Law as a gendering practice*, ed. D.E. Chunn and D. Lacombe, 79-99. Toronto: Oxford University Press.

Burchell, G. 1996. Liberal government and techniques of the self. In *Foucault and political reason: Liberalism, neo-liberalism and rationalities of government*, ed. A. Barry, T. Osborne, and N. Rose, 19-36. Chicago: University of Chicago Press.

Busby, K. 2003. The protective confinement of girls involved in prostitution. In *Being heard: The experience of young women in prostitution*, ed. K. Gorkoff and J. Runn, 103-25. Halifax: Fernwood.

Busby, K., P. Downe, K. Gorkoff, K. Nixon, L. Tutty, and E.J. Ursel. 2000. Examination of innovative programming for children and youth involved in prostitution. http://www.vancouver.sfu.ca/.

Carlen, P. 2002. New discourses of justification and reform for women's imprisonment in England. In *Women and punishment: The struggle for justice*, ed. P. Carlen, 220-36. Portland, OR: Willan.

The Child and Family Services Act, C.C.S.M., c. C.80.

Chunn, D., and S. Gavigan. 2004. Welfare law, welfare fraud, and the moral regulation of the 'never deserving poor.' *Social and Legal Studies* 13, 2: 219-43.

Chunn, D.E., and D. Lacombe. 2000. Introduction. In *Law as a gendering practice*, ed. D.E. Chunn and D. Lacombe, 2-18. Toronto: Oxford University Press.

Comack, E., ed. 2006. *Locating law: Race/class/gender connections*. 2nd ed. Halifax: Fernwood.

Comack, E., and G. Balfour. 2004. *The power to criminalize: Violence, inequality and the law*. Halifax: Fernwood.

Criminal Code, R.S.C. 1985, c. C-46.

Deis, M., K. Rokosh, S. Sagert, B. Robertson, and I. Kerr-Fitzsimmons. 2000. *A historical act – Bill 1: Protection of children involved in prostitution*. N.p.: Government of Alberta.

Fudge, J., and B. Cossman. 2002. Introduction. In *Privatization, law and the challenge to feminism*, ed. B. Cossman and J. Fudge, 3-37. Toronto: University of Toronto Press.

Garland, D. 2000. The culture of high crime societies: Some preconditions of recent 'law and order' policies. *British Journal of Criminology* 40, 3 (Summer): 347-75.

Steven Bittle

–. 2001. *The culture of control: Crime and social order in contemporary society.* Chicago: University of Chicago Press.

Glasbeek, H. 2002. *Wealth by stealth: Corporate crime, corporate law, and the perversion of democracy.* Toronto: Between the Lines.

Government of Alberta. 2007. New law better protects sexually exploited children. News release. Alberta Children's Services.

–. 2010. *Protection of sexually exploited children and youth.* N.p.: Crown in Right of the Government of Alberta.

Guy, J. 2008. The Fatality Inquiries Act in the Matter of Tracia Owens. Provincial Court of Manitoba. Report on Inquest of the Honourable Judge John Guy. 11 January. http://www.manitobacourts.mb.ca/.

Hannah-Moffat, K. 2001. *Punishment in disguise: Penal governance and federal imprisonment of women in Canada.* Toronto: University of Toronto Press.

Hornick, J.P., and F. Bolitho. 1992. *A review of the implementation of the child sexual abuse legislation in selected sites: Studies on the sexual abuse of children in Canada.* Ottawa: Ministry of Supply and Services.

Lowman, J. 1986. You can do it, but don't do it here: Some comments on proposals for the reform of Canadian prostitution law. In *Regulating sex: An anthology of commentaries on the findings and recommendations of the Badgley and Fraser Reports,* ed. J. Lowman, M. Jackson, T. Palys, and S. Gavigan, 193-213. Burnaby, BC: School of Criminology, Simon Fraser University.

–. 1987. Taking young prostitutes seriously. *Canadian Review of Sociology and Anthropology* 24, 1: 99-116.

–. 1990. Against street prostitution. *British Journal of Criminology* 32, 1: 400.

–. 2001. *Identifying research gaps in the prostitution literature.* Ottawa: Department of Justice Canada, Research and Statistics Division.

Lowman, J., and L. Fraser. 1996. *Violence against persons who prostitute: The experience in British Columbia.* Ottawa: Department of Justice Canada.

Manitoba. 2009. First 'Stop Child Sexual Exploitation Awareness Week' proclaimed in Manitoba. News release. 11 May. http://www.gov.mb.ca/.

Manitoba Child and Youth Secretariat. 1996. *Report of the Working Group on Juvenile Prostitution.* Winnipeg: Child and Youth Secretariat.

Manitoba Family Services and Consumer Affairs. 2011. Responding to sexual exploitation: Tracia's Trust. http://www.gov.mb.ca/.

Martin, D. 2002. Both pitied and scorned: Child prostitution in an era of privatization. In *Privatization, law and the challenge to feminism,* ed. B. Cossman and J. Fudge, 355-402. Toronto: University of Toronto Press.

McIntyre, S. 2008. *Under the radar: The sexual exploitation of young men – Western Canadian edition.* Hindsight Group. http://www.hindsightgroup.com/.

McLaren, J. 1986. Chasing the social evil: Moral fervour and the evolution of Canada's prostitution laws, 1867-1917. *Canadian Journal of Law and Society* 1, 1: 125-66.

Minaker, J. 2006. Sluts and slags: The censuring of the erring female. In *Criminalizing women,* ed. G. Balfour and E. Comack, 79-94. Halifax: Fernwood.

Morrison, W. 1995. *Theoretical criminology: From modernity to post-modernity.* London: Cavendish.

Mosher, J., and J. Hermer. 2010. Welfare fraud: The constitution of social assistance as crime. In *Constructing crime: Contemporary processes of criminalization,* ed. J. Mosher and J. Brockman, 17-52. Vancouver: UBC Press.

Naffine, N. 1990. *The law and the sexes: Exploration in feminist jurisprudence.* Sydney: Allen and Unwin.

Nixon, K., L. Tutty, P. Downe, K. Gorkoff, and J. Ursel. 2002. The everyday occurrence: Violence in the lives of girls exploited through prostitution. *Violence against Women* 8, 9: 1016-43.

O'Neill, M. 2001. *Prostitution and feminism: Towards a politics of feeling.* Cambridge: Polity Press.

Pearce, F., and S. Tombs. 1998. *Toxic capitalism: Corporate crime and the chemical industry.* Toronto: Canadian Scholars' Press.

Phoenix, J. 2002a. In the name of protection: Youth prostitution policy reform in England and Wales. *Critical Social Policy* 22, 2: 353-75.

–. 2002b. Youth prostitution policy reform: New discourse, same old story. In *Women and punishment: The struggle for justice,* ed. P. Carlen, 67-93. Portland, OR: Willan.

–. 2007. Governing prostitution: New formations, old agendas. *Canadian Journal of Law and Society* 22, 2: 73-94.

Protection of Children Involved in Prostitution Act, S.A. 1999, c. P-19.3.

Protection of Sexually Exploited Children Act, R.A.A. 2000, c. P-30.3.

Resnick, S., and R. Wolff. 2010. The economic crisis: A Marxian interpretation. *Rethinking Marxism: A Journal of Economics, Culture and Society* 22: 170-86.

Rose, N., and P. Miller. 1992. Political power beyond the state: Problematics of government. *British Journal of Sociology* 43, 2: 172-205.

SCWG (Secure Care Working Group). 1998. Report of the Secure Care Working Group. Commissioned by the Minister of Children and Families, Province of British Columbia.

Smart, C. 1989. *Feminism and the power of the law: Essays in feminism.* London: Routledge.

–. 1995. *Law, crime and sexuality.* London: Sage.

Snider, L. 2006. Making change in neo-liberal times. In *Criminalizing women,* ed. G. Balfour and E. Comack, 323-42. Halifax: Fernwood.

–. 2009. Accommodating power: The common sense of regulators. *Social and Legal Studies* 18, 2: 179-97.

Sullivan, T. 1986. The politics of juvenile prostitution. In *Regulating sex: An anthology of commentaries on the findings and recommendations of the Badgley and Fraser Reports,* ed. J. Lowman, M. Jackson, T. Palys, and S. Gavigan, 177-92. Burnaby, BC: School of Criminology, Simon Fraser University.

Taylor-Butts, A., and A. Bressan. 2006. Youth crime in Canada. Statistics Canada Catalogue no. 85-002-XIE, *Juristat* 28, 3. http://www.statcan.gc.ca/.

Valverde, M. 1991. *The age of light, soap, and water: Moral reform in English Canada 1885-1925.* Toronto: McClelland and Stewart.

van der Meulen, E., and E.M. Durisin. 2008. Why decriminalize? How Canada's municipal and federal regulations increase sex workers' vulnerability. *Canadian Journal of Women and the Law* 20: 289-311.

Visano, L. 1987. *This idle trade.* Concord: VistaSana Books.

Wacquant, L. 2009. *Punishing the poor: The neoliberal government of social insecurity.* Durham, NC: Duke University Press.

Woodiwiss, A. 2006. International law. *Theory, Culture and Society* 23, 2-3: 524-25.

Cases Cited

Alberta (Director of Child Welfare) v. K.B. (2000), 279 A.R. 328, [2000] A.J. No. 1570 (Q.B.) (QL) [K.B. (Q.B.)].

Bedford v. Canada (Attorney General), [2010] O.J. No. 4057 (Ont. Sup. Ct.).

19

To Serve and Protect?
Structural Stigma, Social Profiling, and
the Abuse of Police Power in Ottawa

CHRIS BRUCKERT AND STACEY HANNEM

I have never been arrested but I have been working the streets
for a very long time, so [the police] know me very well: "If I get one more
complaint about you, Jeanette, I'll yank you off the street by the fucking
ponytail and cut it off!" or "I'll punch you in the rotten mouth because
you have such a rotten mouth." I don't like those words, they're not me.

— Jeanette

I got strip-searched on the street, in front of everybody, right in front of Hartman's
[grocery store], by male police officers; they left with my phone book. I get
tickets for jaywalking, loitering as soon as they run my name in their computer.

— Holly

How do we make sense of these narratives by sex workers? Are their experiences at the hands of police officers, sworn to serve and protect, the inevitable by-product of working in a marginalized and criminalized sector? Are they the result of the proverbial few bad apples that can be found in any large urban police service? In this chapter we argue that they speak to something more profound and systemic. Drawing on archival research and twenty-seven interviews with street-based sex workers in Ottawa, we suggest that stigmatic assumptions regarding sex work are not only interactionally realized but are embedded in social structures and subsequently reflected in institutional policy and practice. We submit that the intersection of structural and interpersonal stigma creates the conditions of possibility for social profiling and ensuing violations of human and civil rights such as those described above.[1]

Theorizing the Social Profile

The writings of Goffman, Foucault's insights on power-knowledge, the work of risk theorists, and Hannem's reflections on structural stigma provide us with much-needed conceptual tools. We begin with Goffman's (1963, 4) insight that stigma is engendered by the "relationship between attribute and stereotype." That is, an attribute is defined negatively by others on the basis of a stereotype; those who define the attribute as undesirable react to its bearer with avoidance or discriminatory behaviour. This discriminatory behaviour is the observable evidence of stigma (see also Chapter 13 in this volume). We have argued previously that stigmatic assumptions not only condition interaction between individuals but also (when they are bound up with notions of risk and danger) become embedded at the structural level in the policies and practices of institutions (Hannem and Bruckert 2012). Characterizing members of the stigmatized group as posing a risk of harm to themselves or others legitimates interventions that endeavour to *manage* the perceived risk (Hannem 2012). The institution responds not to individual characteristics, but on the basis of statistically derived categories and risk factors. Thus, structural stigma is less about the individual possession of an undesirable attribute(s) and more about the individual's membership in a marked group that is subject to risk management practices.

Structural stigma also elucidates the interdependence of power and knowledge. As Foucault (1972, 1980, 1997) repeatedly emphasized, power plays an integral role in shaping knowledge – but knowledge also transforms the structures and institutions of power that give rise to that "truth." In this dialectic, knowledges of risk and the classifications of risky populations that emerge from the application of power then transform the practices of institutions, which begin to engage in risk management strategies, employ new technologies, and alter their daily operations to respond to this knowledge. The power-knowledge of risk that underlies structural stigma also alters interactions between the stigmatized and the stigmatizers, perpetuating stigma at the interpersonal level.

The intersection of power-knowledge-stigma provides fertile ground for social profiles to take hold. Stigmatized attributes are bound up with other characteristics that are assumed to accompany the primary attribute: it is this *constellation of statuses* that underlies a *social profile,* indicating the type of person who fits into this stigmatized category. On the basis of this constellation of statuses, institutions identify the risks that they believe need to be addressed

Chris Bruckert and Stacey Hannem

and managed. Individuals whose profile fits this category are targeted for intervention and management through the (often arbitrary) application of legal and institutional policies. Laws, bylaws, and policies that are rarely enforced with the general public are used as tools to target, control, and govern "undesirable" (read: risky) populations (CDPDJ 2009a).

In the case of sex workers, homeless people, substance users, and many other deviantized populations, the constellation of statuses that accompanies the spoiled identity is based on moral stigma or blemish of character (Goffman 1963), which are not immediately evident. The social profile functions to construct and attach a schema of (visible) physical attributes believed to signify the moral stigma, thereby allowing agents of social control to quickly recognize discreditable individuals and render them *discredited*. Social profiling, like racial profiling, is about reading people (based on some visible attribute) to determine the kind of person they are, and the level of risk management and governance to which they should be subject. Social profiling is a visible manifestation of stigma operating at the structural level.

Structural Stigma: Policing Risky Workers

Structural stigma is clearly evident in the policies of the Ottawa Police Service (OPS). The public discourse about prostitution that is presented in official police communication echoes, amplifies, and significantly extends the stereotypes of sex workers as dirty, drug-addicted, and dangerous to the community, at the same time as workers are delegitimized when they are (paradoxically) portrayed as incompetent and irrational victims in need of salvation. As then OPS chief of police Vern White put it, "There are bigger issues involved with prostitution than just prostitution ... A lot of them have either addictions or medical issues – mental health or other. Our job is ... to try to get them some help" (quoted in *Ottawa Citizen* 2008). In justifying its approach, the OPS draws heavily on the rhetoric of community concerns and in the process engages in a "cruel and inaccurate construction of street workers as outside of family, home and community" (Sanchez 2004, 869) and speciously envisions this (sanitized) community as homogeneously united in opposition to street-based sex work(ers).[2] According to the OPS, aggressive tactics to deal with "prostitution and prostitution related problems" (OPS 2012, n.p.) are a legitimate response to the fact that "these communities have been victimized by sex trade activities and crack cocaine use in their neighbourhood, with crime (thefts), public nuisance, safety and security concerns. Consequently, the Ottawa Police Service has dedicated both resources and strategies to deal with these concerns" (OPS 2010, n.p.).

This official claims making about the problem of sex work and risk posed to the community reaffirms social stereotypes and justifies policing strategies *that do not respond to individual law-breaking activities but target sex workers as a group.* Such targeted group-based intervention, legitimated by discourses of risk, is the epitome of structural stigma.

How does this stigma materialize in policy? Several campaigns have been implemented to address these community concerns. One of these is the sending of community safety letters to individuals who are identified as (or suspected of being) clients of sex workers in order to educate them about "the negative impact they are having in our communities" (ibid.) and to dissuade potential clients. Recipients are informed that "there is a clear correlation between street prostitution and drug use, including crack cocaine, as well as a variety of health concerns including H.I.V. [sic] and Hepatitis" (OPS, n.d.) and that the presence of sex workers poses a danger to children and results in the deterioration of community life. The safety letter program perpetuates the stigmatic assumption that sex work is risky and dangerous to the community and also demonstrates how notions of contagion are structurally embedded in law enforcement practices. The letters are sent to individuals "found in the company of a sex trade worker" (OPS 2010, n.p.), which suggests that not only are sex workers presumed guilty, but those found in their company are immediately suspect by association, a phenomenon Goffman (1963) referred to as "courtesy stigma."

In November of 2007, the OPS created a ten-member street crime unit tasked with policing disorder on Ottawa streets. This unit undertakes regular "prostitution sweeps" during which officers proactively attempt to identify and arrest sex workers and clients, using undercover operatives (*Ottawa Citizen* 2008; OPS 2012, n.p.). This policy and its accompanying discourse, which perpetuate the notion that sex workers are a threat to the community and need to be excluded, are profoundly stigmatizing. Indeed, the linguistic coding of "prostitution sweeps" speaks to a sanitized city in which the dirt (sex workers) has been swept away.

The OPS appears to be committed to proactively addressing street sex work through the use of the street crime unit, street sweeps, and community safety letters. By definition, proactive policing requires that officers identify potentially risky persons *before* they have committed an illegal act, so that they can be targeted for intervention; social profiling is one tool of such pre-detection. In 2009, social profiling was recognized as discriminatory and in contravention of the Quebec Charter of Human Rights and Freedoms by the Commission des droits de la personne et des droits de la jeunesse. The commission found that

Chris Bruckert and Stacey Hannem

social profiling is comparable to racial profiling: "In the case of racial profiling, skin colour is the factor that triggers police intervention, in the case of social profiling, the trigger is more likely to be the visible signs of poverty or marginality" (CDPDJ 2009a, n.p.). In the coming section, we turn to the experiences of Ottawa area street-based sex workers to examine social profiling in the formal interactions between them and OPS officers.

Formal Police Interactions

In order to examine how OPS policies are enacted, we draw on twenty-seven interviews with Ottawa area street-based sex workers, which were conducted as part of a larger needs assessment undertaken by POWER (Prostitutes of Ottawa-Gatineau Work, Educate and Resist) between April 2009 and February 2010.[3] Most participants were white, and five identified as Aboriginal. The ages of the twenty-six women (two of whom were transgendered) and one man ranged from twenty to fifty-six. The average age of entry into sex work was twenty-two years. At the time of the interview, about half the participants considered sex work a part-time job. When we examine the narratives of these workers, we see that the OPS public commitment to "clean up" the streets of Ottawa and to eliminate the visible signs of disorder culminates in three types of formal legal interaction that move beyond conventional *reactive* law enforcement strategies: targeting "known" prostitutes, overcharging, and boundary restrictions (red-zones).

Targeting Known Prostitutes

Until 1972, the regulation of street-based sex work in Canada fell under the purview of the Vagrancy C provisions of the Canadian Criminal Code (s. 175(1)(c)), which read, "a common prostitute or nightwalker found in a public place and who does not, when required, give a good account of herself [is guilty of vagrancy]." In the face of feminist mobilizing against this gender-specific status offence (the *status* of being a common prostitute, not her actions, was illegal), section 195.1, which criminalized soliciting "in a public place for the purpose of prostitution," was enacted in 1972; this law was subsequently replaced by the communicating statute in 1985. In practice, some police officers operate as if the Vagrancy C statute is still in force and read sex work not as an activity but rather as an indicator of a deviant and criminal status. Workers' testimonies suggest that police engage in social profiling, assessing individuals on the basis of visible signs (including appearance, behaviours, attitude, or dress), and that those who are read as sex workers are subject to intense (and disproportionate) monitoring. As Julie put it, *"Just because of how I dress, I get stopped. I get very insulted."*

In short, street-based sex workers' interactions with police appear to be conditioned by the workers' master status (Hughes 1945) and the stereotypical attributes that inform it. Once an individual is *known* by police as a sex worker (which does not necessarily mean that he or she has been *charged*), future interactions are affected, and the person becomes the object of surveillance and über-policing. At times sex workers are required to account for themselves when they are evidently not soliciting clients and the police do not have the objective "reasonable grounds" that would justify detention. Sometimes they are even charged when they are clearly not working: *"Once, I had ordered a pizza, I was waiting downstairs for my pizza, in the lobby of my apartment, no shoes on, and I got taken in"* (Lauren). At other times they are subject to short-term detention on the street: *"They harass me. Every time they see me, if I am walking around in the market, they stop me. They pull me right over 'Hey Mallory, how are you?'"* Indeed, this appears to be OPS policy. Inspector Tyron Cameron stated, "We're stopping them, talking to them ... Are we trying to dissuade people from going to them? Absolutely. We make no apologies for that" (quoted in Butler 2010, n.p.). It is notable that the police make "no apology" for behaviour that appears to violate the Canadian Charter of Rights and Freedoms, which prohibits arbitrary detention, including the physical or psychological restraint of an individual's freedom of movement (Pivot 2002).

Overcharging

In addition to facing criminal charges related to their work, Ottawa-area street-based sex workers are also regularly charged with a variety of other offences including jaywalking, loitering, mischief, vagrancy, and trespassing – municipal and provincial regulations that otherwise are rarely enforced. Thus, this marginalized population is singled out and burdened with economic sanctions for behaviours that are rarely used as reasons to regulate the activities of the general public. Workers speak of this as an additional regulatory tool employed by the police: *"If they can't charge you for sex work, they charge you for public mischief. They harass us. They push us around. They're aggressive, especially the rookies. The jail is jam-packed. People are sleeping on the floor and they are still arresting us for ridiculous stuff"* (Julie). When *"almost every day they stop me or fine me"* (Kayla), police charging comes perilously close to harassment. Certainly, Lucy's story appears to indicate excessive regulation: *"I have 163 trespassing tickets. And those are from me getting charged when I am at friends' houses, houses in*

Chris Bruckert and Stacey Hannem

which I have been invited into. Because of who I am and of my record, they never leave me alone. Sometimes I get picked up, brought to the station, and then let go without charges." Again, we see the spectre of social profiling emerge. According to the Quebec Human Rights Commission, "The issue of large numbers of tickets for minor offences affected the homeless in particular, and lead to a prison term, in a high percentage of cases, for non-payment of tickets" (CDPDJ 2009a, 1). This was seen as evidence that city bylaws were being applied and enforced in discriminatory ways. Arguably then, the OPS overcharging of street-based sex workers is discriminatory.

Boundary Restrictions

The financial penalties and criminal charges that result from targeted policing contribute to sex workers' figurative exclusion from social life, whereas the final formal police tactic that we will discuss, boundary restrictions, speaks to a literal corporeal exclusion from the community. Probation conditions (imposed by the courts) and promise-to-appear conditions (imposed by the police) can include a variety of requirements, such as *"probation, good behaviour, having to go to court on certain dates, not drinking alcohol, red zones, a curfew"* (Marci). Of these conditions, boundary restrictions, or red-zones (precisely delimited areas of the city that the individual is prohibited from entering), are notable for their exclusionary impact (see also Chapter 11 in this volume; McGechie forthcoming).[4]

Like many other people, sex workers tend to work in the same geographic areas where they live, shop, socialize, and access health and other services. Given that many of Ottawa's social support services (including food banks, emergency shelters, drop-ins, methadone clinics, health clinics, needle-exchange programs, and social housing) are clustered within the three commonly designated red-zones, these are essentially zones of social exclusion. As Bianca explained, *"[I have a] pretty big red-zone. It was from the end of St-Laurent Boulevard to Charlotte, then to Montreal Road to MacArthur to Beechwood, then to King Edward, Rideau all the way back down to St-Patrick, Vanier and the Market ... It has constricted me in many, many ways. My whole social network is gone. I can't go nowhere, can't talk to anyone."*

In drug courts red zoning is discursively framed as a way to protect addicted persons from the risk posed by a toxic environment (Moore, Freman, and Krawcyk 2011). In assigning red-zones to sex workers, there is not even the pretence of therapeutic intervention: the lack of support and the punitive nature of the sanction suggest that it is the *worker* who is the toxin, the risk that must be evicted to preserve the integrity of the community. The end result of this enactment of power relations is a sanitized city in which "undesirables" are denied access to certain parts of the urban landscape (Davis 2002; Moore, Freman, and Krawcyk 2011).

According to the Quebec Human Rights Commission, bylaws and municipal ordinances "passed with the evident goal of restricting access by the homeless to public spaces" are discriminatory and unreasonable (CDPDJ 2009a, 4). In *Victoria (City) v. Adams* (2008), bylaws that prohibited homeless people from setting up tents in a public park were ruled unconstitutional. Arguably then, the use of red-zones to exclude sex workers from public space on the basis of their occupation is similarly discriminatory and violates their human and civil rights.

Informal Police Interactions

Each of the strategies discussed above can be viewed as exclusionary practices that contribute to the social and civic marginality of street-based sex workers. These workers are excluded precisely because their work is assumed to be an identity and because that (stigmatized) identity is tied up in notions of immorality and toxicity. The preceding police tactics are policies of the OPS and operate at the institutional level, reflecting the structural stigma that has been constructed around sex work as a risky practice. Turning from structural to interpersonal stigma allows us to examine how these scripts play out in the interactions between street-based sex workers and police officers. It is here that we see how social profiling, in conjunction with sex work stigma and the "discourse of disposal" (Lowman 2000, 1003), creates the conditions of possibility for officers to read any woman who carries the markers of street-based sex work not only as undesirable and a threat to order, but as someone who is dirty/drug-addicted/immoral and whose claim to the rights of citizenship and humanity is suspect and therefore violable. This conceptual framework is rendered visible in police actions including verbal abuse, call-outs and outing, public shaming rituals, physical violence, sexual abuse, endangerment, and negligence.

Verbal Abuse
In principle, police are to use respect in their dealings with the public. All of the street-based sex workers who took part in the research spoke of police disrespect, and nineteen out of the twenty-seven explicitly communicated incidents of verbal misconduct. Mallory stated, *"They are rude, disrespectful to us. When they arrest us, they are insulting. They treat us badly. Once I got arrested,*

Chris Bruckert and Stacey Hannem

they'd make fun of me and ask me like 'How much do you weigh? Eighty pounds?'
They just assume I'm a drug addict."

Section 11(d) of the Canadian Charter of Rights and Freedoms states that every citizen has the right "to be presumed innocent until proven guilty according to the law in a fair and public hearing by an independent and impartial tribunal." Charlotte's story speaks to seeming disregard for this principle, and her comments also demonstrate how hateful "uncalled for or offensive remarks" (CDPDJ 2009a, 3) can be: *"They see me from a mile away and they stop me, call me names. Both myself and my boyfriend are really well known by the police. They can't tell if I am working or not. For them I am always just 'that junkie ho.' I could be going to the store; 'Oh Charlotte, what are you doing?' Some of them are assholes too, asking me stuff like 'Charlotte, how much do you charge? In case one day I'm desperate, I can come and see you.'"*

Call-Outs and Outing

Sometimes harassment takes the form of uniformed police officers calling workers out in public spaces, cueing them that they are under surveillance and publicly identifying them as the kind of person known to the police: *"They harass me all the time, even when I am not working. Even like, if I'm at a restaurant eating, they'll come right in 'Whatcha doing Holly?'"* These call-outs are not restricted to the street, where the police could, at least in principle, presume workers are "communicating for the purposes of prostitution." This raises the question as to whether these practices are about law enforcement or are the enactment of an undesirability script. Certainly, the latter would appear to be the case when police officers disclose sex workers' labour activity to their family, friends, and employers:

> *They make sure that whomever I am with knows that they are with a prostitute.*
> *Anyone they see me with, they try to put me down in front of them. Working*
> *or not working. Once I was going to the corner store with a friend of mine.*
> *They asked me, in front of her, if I was training her ... Another time, I was*
> *showing my new neighbour around, walking him up to the food bank. And as*
> *we were walking, one cop turned around and told the young man I was with*
> *"Do you know you are with a prostitute? You could get in trouble for that." He*
> *yelled at the cop "She is my neighbour and I don't care what she does for a*
> *living, she is helping me out. She is still a person." (Jeanette)*

Although rationalizing this approach as a strategy of law enforcement would require cerebral gymnastics, it speaks to courtesy stigma (Goffman 1963) – not only are sex workers "risky" but those found in their company are suspect. Outing also has potentially significant repercussions, increasing the social isolation of the targeted individuals and ensuring that stigma adheres to workers even after they have left the industry. Sometimes, as in the following story by Fiona, ensuring the endurance of the stigma appears deliberate: *"One time, I was working, it was a straight job and they [the police] came in and told my boss what I did."*

Public Shaming

The image of streets needing to be swept clean, which permeates institutional policy, is enacted by individual officers: *"They don't like us, they think we're dirty, they think we're bad for the community ... Let's just say that they don't treat you very nicely. They treat us like we're pieces of shit"* (Bianca). Police are in a position of power; when they abuse that power and operate in accordance with their own (or societal) biases and prejudices, discriminatory actions ensue. Britney stated, *"Once, I was standing on the corner and the police arrested me, and before taking me away, the officers opened the car door and showed me to the people in the building across the street, telling them to take a good look at me, that they were cleaning up their neighbourhood. It was really embarrassing. The cops see me as a prostitute no matter what I say and despite the fact that I wasn't doing anything that day, I was just standing there."*

Such behaviour suggests that assumptions of riskiness and toxicity justify the imposition of an extra-legal punishment in the form of public shaming.[5] Jeanette commented that *"they make sure to harass me every time they see me, even if I am not working. They try to empty my pockets all the time. Once they found an empty condom wrapper in my pocket. They bugged me because of it. They did that in front of people at the bus stop, with the lights flashing and everything."*

When clothes are removed by police officers in populated public spaces, public shaming takes the form of a brutally humiliating extra-legal, and decidedly gendered, sanction. Faye stated, *"I got arrested a couple times and it was not good. Once I got arrested and I was in front of a bunch of people and they pulled my pants down. A lady came up to them and asked if she could pull my pants back up and they told her 'no,' to get the fuck away. My twat, my butt, was there for everybody to see. I wasn't even doing anything! They put me in jail and I wasn't able to complain. Nobody would have believed me."*

Public shaming rituals such as the ones discussed above evidently violate human rights – they also enact a script that denigrates, and in the process further legitimate that denigration. The power-knowledge feedback loop is

Chris Bruckert and Stacey Hannem

interactionally realized. We now turn to instances where the process is corporally manifest in the form of physical violence, sexual abuse, endangerment, and/or negligence.

Physical and Sexual Violence

The Criminal Code of Canada authorizes police to use force only if it is required to arrest someone who is fleeing, to capture someone from a penitentiary, or "for the self-preservation of the person or the preservation of any one under that person's protection from death or grievous bodily harm" (*Criminal Code*, s. 25(3)). Ottawa-area sex workers' accounts of their experiences suggest that these parameters are not always respected.[6] They speak of being physically restrained without charge; what lawyers call "illegal confinement," workers refer to as "jack-ups," "starlight tours," and sometimes "being taken for a ride": "*Cops drive you far away and then they beat us up. They drive us to Orleans at two or three in the morning and they make us walk back. There are no buses. They make you walk back from the woods. The next day, you see the same cops and they don't say anything. If you say something, they arrest you for obstruction*" (Faye).

Sex workers also report acts of extreme violence at the hands of police: "*Four of them attacked me, they were really violent. That is why I cannot see out of this eye and why I have a prosodic ear because of what they did to me*" (Maud). Holly also suffered long-term damage from an assault by police officers: "*Oh fuck yeah, they even broke my arm and everything. They beat me up. They jumped on me and broke my arm, kicked me in the face, all that at the station [shows scar on her neck]. That's the way it is.*"

Stories told of sexual misconduct by police are deeply troubling:

An undercover picked me up once, they were doing a sweep in Vanier. I kind of felt like something was off, so I asked him if he was a cop and then he said "Would a cop do this?" and then he grabbed my hand and forcefully put it on his crotch. So then I told him it would cost sixty dollars, but he ended up being a cop. When another cop came to pick me up, I asked him if his partner was allowed to do that, and he said he was but I still think it was a little strange. (Britney)

A number of participants also spoke of sexual assaults when they were confined. Fiona's horrific experience, which included verbal assaults and physical violence, left her emotionally and psychologically scarred: "*I've been hurt bad by female officers that arrested me. They ripped my clothes off, threw me in the shower, told me I smelled and that I was a dirty whore and stuff like that. I have had to sit in the waiting cell, naked, for twenty-four hours, waiting for someone to come and talk to me. I'm still in counselling for that. It does happen. It's traumatic. It's not right."*

These instances of sexual and physical violence go beyond misuse of authority and speak to criminal violence enacted on a marginalized population by police officers with apparent impunity, precisely because of the power differential and stigma that delegitimize and silence sex workers. That these workers have limited capacity to protest or protect themselves against such abuses of power draws our attention to the subjugation of civil rights: *"The police. The law. They have so much power over us. We're so defenceless when it comes to them and I hate the powerlessness"* (Fiona).

Endangerment

There is ample evidence that providing drug users with clean equipment is one of the most effective ways of slowing the spread of infectious diseases, including the potentially fatal HIV and hepatitis C. Put simply, harm reduction saves lives (World Health Organization 2007). The City of Ottawa's (2011) own website states that "the availability of these programs has been deemed a necessary public health measure to prevent the spread of communicable diseases." By confiscating and/or destroying crack pipes and syringes (both of which are distributed by authorized community organizations), Ottawa police officers undermine this public health initiative and enact the "discourse of disposal" (Lowman 2000, 1003) by putting the safety and well-being of sex workers at risk: *"I get searched a lot. They would dump my purse on Montreal Road. There is this one cop [name withheld] who has a hard-on about smashing people's crack pipes. He did that to me a few times. And then he looks and laughs at us 'What are you gonna do now?'"* (Charlotte).

There is another equally counterintuitive way that police practices may undermine sex workers' ability to keep themselves healthy. Sex workers are highly motivated to engage in safe sex practices in order to protect themselves and their clients from infectious disease. Their ability to do so is thwarted when police confiscate their condoms. Moreover, it is a significant disincentive for sex workers to carry, and therefore to use, barrier protection when officers construct these as evidence of sex work: *"They asked me to empty my pockets at times. One time, I had a handful of condoms and a handful of money, so they were like 'We know what you're up to'"* (Brook).

Condom usage is understood by most Canadians as a legitimate and effective option to reduce the risk of sexually transmitted infection; by carrying condoms, sex workers *increase* their risk of arrest or harassment by police: *"It's bad enough that they take our pipes from us, they also take the condoms. I can't fight the law. What am I supposed to do? If they know you're a street worker, they will take the condoms first. They want the condoms. That's what they are looking for on you. If they find some, I get busted"* (Adrienne). It is here that the bifurcated images of sex workers as at risk and risky collide. The OPS routinely sends "Community Safety Letters" to individuals seen in the company of a known sex worker (suspected clients), warning them of the dangers of contracting HIV and hepatitis (OPS, n.d.). Ironically, the officers' use of condoms as evidence of sex work undermines workers' ability to protect themselves and their clients, perpetuating the risk of the sexually transmitted infections that the organization claims to be concerned about and thereby justifying the community safety letter policy.

Negligence

According to Ontario's Police Services Act (1990, s. 1), "Police services shall be provided throughout Ontario in accordance with the following principles, including safeguarding the fundamental rights guaranteed by the *Canadian Charter of Rights and Freedoms* and the *Human Rights Code*." The question of these *in principle* rights (including the right to equal treatment) may be, practically speaking, irrelevant. Sex workers report that police officers are often negligent, either failing to respond to violence against them or not adequately investigating such incidents (Benoit and Millar 2001; Cler-Cunningham 2001; Pivot 2004; DERA 2006; Jeffrey and MacDonald 2006). Again we see discrimination rooted in stigma when police officers operate under the assumption that sex workers are immoral and therefore untrustworthy – individuals who, in the absence of clear evidence to the contrary, are assumed to be lying:

> *I called the police once when someone pulled a gun on me. It was in a parking lot. They didn't believe me at first, up until they saw the security tape. Then they drove me home. Nothing happened. They never found the guy. When they responded to that call, they knew I was a sex worker. If it would have been a "normal woman," it would have been different.*[7] *I was out there on the street at four or five in the morning, and I was known so they didn't take me seriously.* (Bianca)

At other times, police officers' denial of sex workers' humanity is expressed when they fail to respond to victimization, a clear violation of their sworn duty to serve and protect. Beth stated, *"I've been raped twice. This one time, I was just coming out of an alley, I had just been raped, I have been hit over my head with a brick. My head was gushing blood. I flagged a cop and he told me to call my own fucking ambulance. He called me a fucking crack whore and told me he had no time for me. Then he left ... They didn't give a shit. I couldn't walk even. I ended up just sticking my piece of gum in the hole in my head."*

Conclusion

What justification is there for men and women who are sworn to "protect and serve" the public to perpetrate harassment, physical violence, sexual assault, theft, and destruction or confiscation of property? Police certainly have no legal mandate to perpetuate social stigma by outing sex workers to friends, family, and employers, and it is arguably difficult to rationalize this behaviour as a strategy of law enforcement or order-maintenance. How, then, can we make sense of this? Is this the dark side of community policing, evident in its "territorial logic ... and exclusionary zoning" (Sanchez 2004, 871)? Or is it a result of a legal situation that does not prohibit sex work but criminalizes so many aspects that sex workers themselves become conceptualized as *criminal?* Although these dynamics provide a point of entry to think about the often antagonistic relationship between sex workers and police, they are hardly sufficient to explain the abuse. Here issues of power are implicated. As Bruckert and Chabot (2010, 61) have argued, "When we juxtapose the power and authority of police officers ... to that of marginal street-based sex workers, the potential for abuse comes into sharp focus. As feminists working on the issues of violence against women have demonstrated, such differentials of power set up the conditions of possibility for abuse to occur." We must also consider the power-knowledge feedback loop and how stigma reproduces power differentials and social stratifications.

All of this brings us back to stigma. We have argued that these abuses of sex workers are indicative of a larger systemic problem of stigma attached to sex work, in the consciousness of individual citizens (including police officers) and in institutional policy. When individuals are marked as Other – as fundmentally different from "normal" citizens – stigma legitimizes the denial of rights and privileges, including the right to protection and criminal justice redress. This denial of rights is compounded and aggravated by a lack of response and outrage on the part of citizens, allowing abuse and neglect to go unremarked and unpunished. It is incumbent on us to demand that police services and individual officers be held accountable and afford all citizens the same respect and dignity. The denial of human rights has implications for all of us – street-based sex workers might just be the proverbial canaries in the coalmine.

Notes

1 Social profiling is defined as a form of discrimination on the basis of visible signs of poverty or marginality (CDPDJ 2009a, 2009b).
2 See O'Neil et al. (2010) for a discussion on the differing degrees of tolerance found within communities. The Parliamentary Standing Committee on Justice and Human Rights' Sub-committee on Solicitation Laws also identified a range of community responses and noted that though some are punitive, others "prefer a collaborative approach with prostitutes' advocacy groups to find alternative solutions to protect both prostitutes and the community in general" (Parliament of Canada 2006, 35).
3 For this research, a total of forty-three interviews were conducted (sixteen with indoor workers and the remainder with street-based workers). The interviews, which lasted between forty-five and ninety minutes, were conducted by POWER members or allies trained in research methods, interviewing techniques, and ethical considerations. For more on the research methodology, see Bruckert and Chabot (2010).
4 Failure to comply with boundary restrictions is considered a breach of probation for which the individual can be criminally charged and immediately sent to jail. Notably, the potential sanction for breach of a probation order is greater than the maximum six-month penalty for communicating for the purposes of prostitution (*Criminal Code*, s. 787(1)).
5 These public shaming rituals may also increase individual sex workers' vulnerability to violence. When workers elect to solicit clients in more secluded areas where they are free of police surveillance, they also become easier targets for aggressors who might otherwise be deterred by witnesses.
6 The issue of police assaulting sex workers is mentioned in a number of research projects (Pivot 2002; Bruckert, Parent, and Pouliot 2006; Jeffrey and MacDonald 2006; Lewis, Maticka-Tyndale, and Shaver 2006). In our research, sixteen of the workers had experienced physical violence at the hands of the police and described physical assaults, excessive use of force during arrest, and illegal confinement.
7 It is notable that Bianca herself has internalized the distinction between sex workers and "normal" women.

References

Benoit., C., and A. Millar. 2001. *Dispelling myths and understanding realities: Working conditions, health status, and exiting experiences of sex workers.* Vancouver: PEERS.
Bruckert, C., and F. Chabot. 2010. *Challenges: Ottawa area sex workers speak out.* Ottawa: POWER.
Bruckert, C., C. Parent, and D. Pouliot. 2006. *How to respond to the needs of street sex workers in the Ottawa-Gatineau region.* Ottawa: Status of Women Canada.
Butler, D. 2010. Abuse standard treatment: Sex workers. *Ottawa Citizen,* 1 December. http://www2.canada.com/.
CDPDJ (Commission des droits de la personne et les droits de la jeunesse). 2009a. The judiciarization of the homeless in Montréal: A case of social profiling – executive summary of the opinion of the commission. http://www3.cdpdj.qc.ca/publications/Documents/Homeless_SumSumm.pdf.

–. 2009b. The judiciarization of the homeless in Montréal: A case of social profiling – fact sheet 1: Social profiling – definition. http://www.intraspec.ca/Fact_sheet_1_social_profiling _definition.pdf.

City of Ottawa. 2011. Clean needle syringe program. http://www.ottawa.ca.

Cler-Cunningham, L.C. 2001. *Violence against women in Vancouver's street level sex trade and the police response.* Vancouver: Ministry of Status for Women, BC Attorney General and BC Ministry for Women's Equality.

Criminal Code of Canada, R.S.C. 1985, c. C-46.

Davis, M. 2002. *Dead cities and other tales.* New York: New Press.

DERA (Dancers Equal Rights Association of Ottawa). 2006. *Erotic dancers' labour needs assessment.* Ottawa: Status of Women Canada.

Foucault, M. 1972. *The archaeology of knowledge.* London: Routledge.

–. 1980. *Power/knowledge.* New York: Pantheon.

–. 1997. *The politics of truth.* Los Angeles: Semiotext(e).

Goffman, E. 1963. *Stigma: Notes on the management of a spoiled identity.* Englewood Cliffs, NJ: Prentice-Hall.

Hannem, S. 2012. Theorizing stigma and the politics of resistance. In *Stigma revisited: Negotiations, resistance and the implications of the mark,* ed. S. Hannem and C. Bruckert, 10-28. Ottawa: University of Ottawa Press.

Hannem, S., and C. Bruckert, eds. 2012. *Stigma revisited: The implications of the mark.* Ottawa: University of Ottawa Press.

Hughes, E. 1945. Dilemmas and contradictions of status. *American Journal of Sociology* 50, 5: 353-59.

Jeffrey, L.A., and G. MacDonald. 2006. *Sex workers in the Maritimes talk back.* Vancouver: UBC Press.

Lewis, J., E. Maticka-Tyndale, and F.M. Shaver. 2006. *Safety, security and the well-being of sex workers: A report submitted to the House of Commons Subcommittee on Solicitation Laws.* Windsor: Sex Trade Advocacy and Research.

Lowman, J. 2000. Violence and the outlaw status of (street) prostitution in Canada. *Violence against Women* 6, 9: 987-1011.

McGechie, H. Forthcoming. *The impacts of release conditions on criminalized sex workers in Ottawa.* Ottawa: Salvation Army.

Moore, D., L. Freman, and M. Krawcyk. 2011. Spacio-therapeutics: Drug treatment courts and urban space. *Social and Legal Studies* 20, 2: 157-72.

O'Neil, M., R. Campbell, P. Hubbard, J. Pitcher, and J. Scoular. 2010. Living with the Other: Street sex work, contingent communities and degrees of intolerance. *Crime Media Culture* 4, 1: 73-93.

OPS (Ottawa Police Services). 2010. Community Safety Letters. http://www.ottawapolice.ca.

–. 2012. Ottawa police arrest 14 in prostitution sweep. http://www.ottawapolice.ca/.

–. n.d. OPS sample community safety letter. http://www.ottawapolice.ca/.

Ottawa Citizen. 2008. Detention centre bursting after sweep. 15 November. http://www.canada. com/ottawacitizen/.

Parliament of Canada. 2006. *Report of the Standing Committee on Justice and Human Rights – the challenge of change: A study of Canada's criminal prostitution laws.* Ottawa: Government of Canada.

Pivot. 2002. *To serve and protect: A report on policing in Vancouver's Downtown Eastside.* Vancouver: Pivot Legal Society. http://www.chodarr.org/sites/default/files/chodarr0312.pdf.

–. 2004. Voices for dignity: A call to end the harms caused by Canada's sex trade laws. Pivot Legal Society. http://www.plri.org/sites/plri.org/files/Voices_for_dignity.pdf.

Police Services Act, R.S.O 1990, c. P-15.

Sanchez, L. 2004. The global e-rotic subject, the ban, and the prostitution-free zone: Sex work and the theory of differential exclusion. *Society and Space* 22: 861-83.

World Health Organization. 2007. *Guide to starting and managing needle exchange programs.* Geneva: WHO Press.

Case Cited

Victoria (City) v. Adams, 2008 BCSC 1363, 299 D.L.R. (4th) 193.

20

Beyond the Criminal Code: Municipal Licensing and Zoning Bylaws

EMILY VAN DER MEULEN AND MARIANA VALVERDE

The regulation of sexual services happens primarily at the federal level through the Canadian Criminal Code. Sex workers and others who violate the federal provisions risk arrest and criminal charges. But what of other government levels and jurisdictions? Municipalities too have instituted a series of bylaws aimed at controlling and limiting local sex industries. Although most Canadians know that city governments fix potholes and provide parks, few people, even those with legal training, understand the peculiarities of municipal law, a subject that is given little attention in law school education and legal scholarship.

Debates about how Canadian municipalities might go about regulating establishments in which sex work takes place need to be informed by a basic knowledge of what cities can and cannot do, legally, and of how municipal legal regulation functions in general. Thus, we will begin this chapter with a brief background about the powers of municipalities before turning to a consideration of the main legal tools – namely, zoning bylaws and licensing schemes – that have been used to regulate sex work and sexually oriented businesses at the local level.

Municipal Powers: Property, Not Persons

Municipalities have very little power to act on persons; unlike criminal law, municipal bylaws cannot prohibit certain acts absolutely, and unlike civil law, they cannot regulate personal relationships. Despite these restrictions, however, municipalities have significant powers regarding property, both private and public, and how it is used. Indeed, they can regulate spaces and activities by imposing noise bylaws, garbage bylaws, and rules about the use of parks and sidewalks. However, the ability to regulate spaces and activities exists only as an extension of the power to look after the interests of property owners and to control how people use their private property.

Although the extent of municipal power can differ slightly from location to location, in Canada municipalities generally have the power to revoke both business and individual licences, and to inspect business premises for bylaw adherence. Municipalities also have jurisdiction over where businesses can be located within the city, the types of signage they are allowed to display, and the type and price of licences they require. The full extent of these regulations varies by province and according to local pressures and desires. For example, a municipality is able to restrict the number of a certain kind of establishment or licence (such as taxi and street food vendor licences) and can implement exorbitantly high licensing fees for business owners and workers, effectively deterring individuals from working in that particular sector (Childs et al. 2006). These tactics are much more common for sex industry businesses than for others.

Despite the criminalization of their common work activities, across the country there are tens of thousands of people working in legal sex industry establishments, including massage/body rub parlours, dating and escort services, steam baths, exotic dance venues, and others. Although legal sex industry establishments might seem contradictory to the criminalization of bawdy-houses and owner/operators through the Criminal Code (in particular sections 210 and 212), cities and sex-related businesses are able to circumvent the federal provisions by denying that the direct exchange of sexual services is occurring at the worksite; establishments are providing a massage or companionship, not a sexual service for remuneration. Indeed, municipalities must maintain a veneer of ignorance.

In instances where municipalities have attempted to restrict the sale of sexual services in sex industry establishments or on the street, the courts have deemed these actions out of their jurisdiction as only Ottawa has this power (*Pimenova v. City of Brampton* 2004). For example, case law has determined that municipalities are unable to implement bylaws that outright prohibit street-based sex work from occurring (*Westendorp v. The Queen* 1983). According to the Canadian Constitution, municipalities may not engage in prohibitions for moral purposes (Childs et al. 2006). Instead, they institute bylaws that regulate and control the business aspects of sex industry establishments.

Regulating Buildings and Their Uses: Control through Zoning

In North America, zoning is one of the biggest legal sticks that municipalities can wield against individuals or businesses. For example, if you buy a home or business premise in good faith and later find out that the previous owners had built an illegal addition, you can be compelled to tear it down at your own expense for no reason other than it contravenes the local zoning bylaw. Although this rarely occurs, the likelihood of it happening dramatically increases if a neighbour makes a complaint to the city. Since municipal zoning regulations are so complex – the City of Toronto's zoning bylaw is longer than the federal Income Tax Act – it is very difficult for the average person to know what is and is not legal. And since zoning variances (that is, exceptions) are easily obtained, looking at the neighbours' house to judge the legality of your own will not be helpful since they may have received a variance that you might well be denied.

Generally, municipalities are divided into different zoning or land use areas that regulate the types of development that can occur there: these include residential zones, industrial zones, and commercial zones, among others. However, the zoning rules do not amount to a coherent overall system. There are different rules in different neighbourhoods, even in different blocks, and it's not uncommon for areas within one city to have their own separate bylaws. In order to determine where sex industry establishments can reside, some municipalities have instituted bylaws that prohibit sex industry parlours or agencies from setting up businesses in residential neighbourhoods; instead, sexual service establishments are relegated to industrial zones far from the downtown core and thus far from readily accessible public transit.

The assumed purpose of these bylaws is to prevent residential zones from having sex businesses in their vicinity, but their consequence is that it can be much more difficult and dangerous for sex workers to get to and from work (van der Meulen and Durisin 2008). Conversely, in other municipalities such as Vancouver, licensed body rub parlours are permitted to provide services only in the "Downtown District" zone (Childs et al. 2006). Indeed, each municipality will institute its own series of zoning regulations that specify which sex industry establishments are permitted and in which zones. Businesses that violate the zoning bylaws can face stiff penalties: for example, the penalty in Vancouver is up to $2,000 or two months in prison (City of Vancouver, Bylaw No. 3575, s. 8.2).

The complexity and lack of uniformity of zoning rules can encourage political interference with planning decisions. An individual who wants a zoning variance

Emily van der Meulen and Mariana Valverde

for his or her property or business might be more likely to call a city councillor than to spend the money on a planning lawyer. In return, the councillor may be more willing to support his or her constituent's request as this is one way to build political capital if the request is unlikely to upset other members of the community. This politicization of zoning has serious implications for those involved in businesses that might be unpopular and lead to NIMBY (not in my back yard) sentiments.

Regulating Small Entrepreneurs: Control through Licensing

In addition to zoning bylaws, licensing is a common measure through which municipalities restrict and control local sex industries. A key irony of local business regulation is that whereas large corporations such as banks, factories, offices, and warehouses can establish themselves in any industrially or commercially zoned building without needing municipal permission, the self-employed entrepreneurs who operate variety stores, drive taxis, or sell hot dogs on the street are often subject to expensive, time consuming, and onerous regulations. In Canadian cities, there are two primary types of licences for regulating, and in many cases deterring, the sex trade: business licences for owners, managers, and operators of sex industry establishments; and licences for the individual workers themselves.

Business Licences for Sex Industry Establishments

Mandating that business owners and operators must have a licence in order to manage their establishment provides an effective way for municipalities to "control the number and nature of businesses within their boundaries, ensure compliance with health and safety guidelines, and collect licensing fees for city revenue" (Childs et al. 2006, 36). In order to get a business licence, the business owner will be required to fill out the necessary paperwork at the local city hall, including his or her personal contact information, submit to a criminal record check, produce valid identification, and pay a fee. Municipalities can refuse to grant business licences if the applicant has a criminal record. As a condition of granting the licence, it is not uncommon for operators of body rub parlours and dating services, for example, to have to agree that they will supply the city and/ or the local police with the names and addresses of their employees (City of Toronto Municipal Code, No. 545-328, s. D; City of Vancouver, Bylaw No. 4450).

Cities can also set licence fees without much, if any, scrutiny. Thus, business owner licence fees can be quite expensive and considerably higher than for almost all other licences; for instance, owner/operator licences are upward of

$8,000 per year in Vancouver (Childs et al. 2006; City of Vancouver, Bylaw No. 4450, Schedule A), $3,600 in Calgary (City of Calgary, Bylaw No. 32M98), $4,000 in Edmonton (City of Edmonton, Bylaw No. 13138), and just over $10,000 in Toronto (City of Toronto Municipal Code, No. 545-333, Appendix A). To put the high cost of licences for sex-related establishments into perspective, City of Toronto owner/operator licences for nightclubs, bars, and/or restaurants are just under $400 (ibid.).

Not surprisingly, establishments that commonly provide sexual services to clients are subject to considerably more bylaws, both in number and in severity, than most other businesses. For example, in Vancouver, there are bylaws that regulate the size of body rub rooms (City of Vancouver, Bylaw No. 5156, s. 11.5(5)), the levels of lighting that must remain on (ibid.), and the length of the workers' clothing (City of Vancouver, Bylaw No. 4450, s. 11.5(7)).[1] Vancouver's dating services must notify the City within seventy-two hours if they hire a new employee or if an employee leaves the service (City of Vancouver, Bylaw No. 5156, s. 13.1), and escort services must submit to the city inspector or the police the list of all employees and customers if requested (ibid., s. 25.3).[2]

Similarly, the City of Toronto bylaws regulating body rub parlours dictate that parlours cannot be used for sleeping (City of Toronto Municipal Code, No. 545-342) and that body rub rooms cannot have doors that lock (City of Toronto Municipal Code, No. 545-343, s. A). Further, body rub parlour owners must retain the licences of their employees and must post them in a "conspicuous place," thus compromising worker privacy and anonymity (City of Toronto Municipal Code, No. 545-338, s. B). For whatever reason, Toronto body rub bylaws also stipulate that "foot baths" are prohibited (City of Toronto Municipal Code, No. 545-345, s. J).

In Edmonton, bylaws mandate that escort agency office doors must remain unlocked during business hours and that someone must remain on the premises (Childs et al. 2006), making it extremely difficult for one sex worker to run a sole-proprietor agency. Indeed, as soon as she sees a client during office hours, she is subjecting herself to a possible $2,500 fine. These various bylaw provisions are clear violations of sex workers' privacy, security, and labour rights.

Individual and Worker's Licences

The other main way that municipalities rely on licensing bylaws to restrict and control the sex industry is through the allocation of licences to individual sex workers. Since licensing systems are not subject to much, if any, legal scrutiny, municipalities have a great deal of leeway in deciding what activities they will subject to licensing. Each major municipality, therefore, will differ in what

Emily van der Meulen and Mariana Valverde

licences it requires and for what areas of work. For example, in Ontario, the City of Niagara Falls requires licences for escorts, whereas neither Toronto nor Ottawa do. Although escort licensing is not common among most other Canadian municipalities, most do require licences for exotic dancers and massage/body rub attendants. In some places, where police crackdowns on body rub parlours are common and where municipalities restrict the number of body rub licences they grant to individual workers, some sex workers apply for "holistic health practitioner" or "health enhancement" licences.

Sex workers are not the only category of workers who must obtain a licence. Taxi drivers, for instance, must acquire a specific driver's licence and plate licence that are over and above the standard provincial driver's and plate licence requirements. However, it is somewhat peculiar for municipalities to mandate licences for exotic dancers or massage attendants while exempting restaurant workers, bartenders, and non-erotic masseuses from the same requirement.

In some municipalities, licensing bylaws prohibit workers from employment at more than one business at a time. For example, in Toronto, a licensed body rub attendant is permitted to work at only one body rub parlour (City of Toronto Municipal Code, No. 545-338, s. A). If she wants to work at another parlour, both the business owner and the licensed worker are required to notify the City in writing within forty-eight hours of the termination of employment (ibid., s. C). The worker must then apply for employment at a new parlour, which is required to notify the City in writing within forty-eight hours of the new hire (ibid.).

Like the fees for business owner and operator licences, the annual cost of a sex worker's licence can be very high. In Edmonton, for instance, where independent escorts are licensed, the fee is just over $1,500 (City of Edmonton, Bylaw Nos. 13138, 12452). This amount is cost-prohibitive for many sex workers and can make it difficult for street-based sex workers to move indoors. Further, if a sex worker receives a licence in one municipality, it is not transferable to another; sex workers must apply for and purchase licences in each city where they will work. For some, such as exotic dancers who travel as part of their job, this can be very expensive.

In instances where a licensed massage attendant provides sexual services in a licensed massage parlour, she could be charged under the federal Criminal Code's bawdy-house provisions (for providing a sexual service in a fixed location), could have her licence revoked or suspended, and could perhaps be fined (for violating the terms of the bylaw) (Childs et al. 2006). Bylaw fines can vary widely within a jurisdiction and between jurisdictions. In Vancouver, for example, fines range from $100 to $2,000. If the licensed sex worker is convicted of the offence, a permanent notice could be placed in her city record, which could then prevent her from gaining a licence in future. Further, if her fines go unpaid, she could be charged with contempt of court and could face possible imprisonment (ibid.).

Although, on the one hand, municipalities must deny the sexual nature of the services provided in a licensed sex industry establishment (or risk contravening the Criminal Code), on the other hand, some municipalities have included mandatory medical examinations as part of the licensing process. In Toronto, body rub attendants must bring in a form "signed by a duly qualified medical practitioner certifying that such person is free from communicable diseases and is medically fit to perform or receive body-rubs" (City of Toronto Municipal Code, No. 545-333, s. A). Why such certification is necessary if the worker is not providing direct-contact sexual services is unclear. Further, if body rub parlour owners suspect that an employee or patron has been exposed to or has a communicable disease, they must exclude the employee or patron from the premises (City of Toronto Municipal Code, No. 545-346, s. B).

Licensing Implications for Sex Businesses

There are three main features of licensing that are particularly important for sex businesses. First, the licence represents, according to law, the privilege to operate a business that would otherwise be banned. This means that the licence holder is subject to all sorts of rules that wouldn't be legal in other circumstances. Further, in recent years, courts have ruled that though municipalities must have a reason to deny someone a licence, cities can legally decide to set an unreasonably low maximum number of licences for particular businesses, thus imposing an artificial limit on a market. For example, the City of Toronto permits only twenty-five owner/operator licences for body rub parlours (City of Toronto Municipal Code, No. 545-394), meaning that others attempting to operate such establishments in the absense of available licences will be acting in defiance of the bylaw and could be shut down by the City if discovered.

The second key feature of importance for sex businesses is that through licensing, the business or the person is subject to instant unannounced inspections that would probably be deemed unconstitutional in other circumstances. Police enforcing the criminal law are not supposed to enter a private business without cause. For instance, without probable cause, a police officer cannot go into a department store and start questioning staff or request to see the day's cash intake. However, police can enter a business that is municipally licensed, such as a strip club or massage parlour, at any time, for no reason, and demand to see the workers' licences.[3]

Third, since a licence is a legal document, specific conditions can be attached to it, conditions that can differ from business to business. For instance, bars can have time conditions attached to their liquor licence (such as no serving liquor on the patio after 10:00 p.m.) for which there is no legal recourse, no matter how economically devastating the conditions might be. Any business that draws negative attention from neighbours, such as an erotic massage parlour, and that operates by means of a municipal licence, can thus be faced with arbitrary rules that apply solely to it, not to anyone else.

Conclusion

Zoning and licensing bylaws not only are complicated and confusing, but can be onerous for sex workers who might not know how to navigate the complex bureaucracy of many city halls or how to access the specific bylaw details (Lewis and Maticka-Tyndale 2000; Bruckert, Parent, and Robitaille 2003). Further, Canadian sex workers have reported that licensing does not improve their workplace conditions, their safety, or their ability to organize for better rights (Childs et al. 2006; van der Meulen and Durisin 2008). Indeed, it's rare for people working in licensed sex industry establishments to speak out against abuses as any attempt to rectify exploitative working conditions could lead to federal criminal charges, bylaw fines, licence cancellation, or even the closure of the business itself (Childs et al. 2006; van der Meulen and Durisin 2008; van der Meulen 2010). It's not uncommon, then, for sex workers to forgo licensing and take their chances working illegally and subject to federal criminal charges.

Notes
1 Clothing must be "non-transparent" and must cover the worker's body from neck to knee.
2 Interestingly, Vancouver has a bylaw that expressly forbids three types of businesses: ones that offer massage services in any location aside from a licensed parlour; ones that offer "erotic telephone calls"; and ones that provide "nude encounters" (City of Vancouver, Bylaw No. 5156).
3 This also applies to any establishment holding a liquor licence, where police may enter without cause.

References
Bruckert, C., C. Parent, and P. Robitaille. 2003. *Erotic service/erotic dance establishments: Two types of marginalized labour.* Ottawa: Law Commission of Canada.
Childs, M., et al. 2006. *Beyond decriminalization: Sex work, human rights and a new framework for law reform.* Vancouver: Pivot Legal Society.
City of Calgary, Bylaw No. 32M98, *Business Licence Bylaw.*
City of Edmonton, Bylaw No. 12452, *Escort Licensing Bylaw.*
City of Edmonton, Bylaw No. 13138, *Business Licence Bylaw.*

City of Toronto Municipal Code, *Licensing*, Article XXXI, No. 545-328, Chapter 545 Licensing.
City of Toronto Municipal Code, *Licensing*, Article XXXI, No. 545-333, Chapter 545 Licensing.
City of Toronto Municipal Code, *Licensing*, Article XXXI, No. 545-338, Chapter 545 Licensing.
City of Toronto Municipal Code, *Licensing*, Article XXXI, No. 545-342, Chapter 545 Licensing.
City of Toronto Municipal Code, *Licensing*, Article XXXI, No. 545-343, Chapter 545 Licensing.
City of Toronto Municipal Code, *Licensing*, Article XXXI, No. 545-345, Chapter 545 Licensing.
City of Toronto Municipal Code, *Licensing*, Article XXXI, No. 545-346, Chapter 545 Licensing.
City of Toronto Municipal Code, *Licensing*, Article XXXI, No. 545-394, Chapter 545 Licensing.
City of Vancouver, Bylaw No. 3575, *Zoning and Development By-Law.*
City of Vancouver, Bylaw No. 4450, *License Bylaw* (23 September 1969).
City of Vancouver, Bylaw No. 5156, *A By-law to prohibit the carrying on of sundry business, trades, professions and other occupations.* (11 April 1978).
Lewis, J., and E. Maticka-Tyndale. 2000. Licensing sex work: Public policy and women's lives. *Canadian Public Policy* 26, 4: 437-49.
van der Meulen, E. 2010. Illegal lives, loves, and work: How the criminalization of procuring affects sex workers in Canada. *Wagadu: A Journal of Transnational Women's and Gender Studies* 8: 217-40.
van der Meulen, E., and E.M. Durisin. 2008. Why decriminalize? How Canada's municipal and federal regulations increase sex workers' vulnerability. *Canadian Journal of Women and the Law* 20, 2: 289-312.

Cases Cited

Pimenova v. Brampton (City), [2004] OJ No. 2450 (Ont. Sup. Ct.).
Westendorp v. The Queen, [1983] 1 S.C.R. 43 (QL).

Afterword

ALAN YOUNG

Here's an easy recipe for a public policy nightmare. Take one powerful, instinctive drive. Add a pinch of hysteria, a sprinkling of fear, and a whole lot of misinformation. Pour it into the pre-shaped mould of state control called criminal justice. Let it stew for many years and never check on the simmering concoction to see if it tastes good. This is precisely the formula adopted in Canada to deal with the issue of prostitution, and it tastes awful.

The public policy crisis we have found ourselves in has resulted from an unrealistic and irrational approach to the purchase and sale of commercial sex, a system that says prostitution is legal but makes it nearly impossible for many sex workers to work in safety. Every politician and prohibitionist who supports the current policy approach of criminalization should read this anthology so they can see that there are many informed and insightful sex workers and scholars whose voices can provide the blueprint for an escape from the current public policy nightmare we have constructed to deal with the sex trade.

Sex workers have had an enormous fall from grace in the past millennium, going from sacred temple harlots to marginalized outcasts exposed to all manner of violence, abuse, and ridicule. We will continue to dig up dead bodies of sex workers on pig farms and secluded urban alleys while we maintain ineffective and irrational criminal prohibitions on commercial sex. Our species is always on the lookout for sexual outlets, and when the pleasure does not present itself, some will go to the marketplace to buy a fleeting moment of sexual gratification or physical comfort. There is nothing the state can do about this. This is a bottomless market.

Prostitution flourished in Biblical times, and when Jesus reprimanded the priestly caste for wanting to stone a prostitute, this should have signalled the end of the punitive approach to this social dilemma. Jesus said that only those without sin should cast the first stone, and somehow over the ages this has been transformed into a licence for a multitude of petty sinners to cast many stones in the direction of sex workers. Last I looked, we have been casting about eight to ten thousand criminal charges a year in Canada, but the business continues to thrive despite the sanctimonious stone throwing.

In order to dodge the stones, sex workers are compelled to work in an environment laden with risks and dangers. The recent Pickton trial has finally brought the issue out of the shadows, but it is a mistake to believe that workplace violence for sex workers involves only the predatory street trolling of monsters such as Gary Ridgway (the Green River Killer, forty-eight victims), Peter Sutcliffe (the Yorkshire Ripper, thirteen victims, late 1970s), Arthur Shawcross (Genesee River killer, ten victims, late 1980s), and Joel Rifkin (New York City, nine victims, early 1990s). There is no question that many who work in the sex trade are easy targets for violent criminals. However, the real problem is that the daily existence of the sex worker on the street is marked by the threat of assault and psychological terror, and due to the social marginalization and legal stigmatization of sex work, this violence is simply ignored or routinely addressed with utter indifference by all public officials.

With no political solution on the horizon, Terri-Jean Bedford, Amy Lebovitch, and Valerie Scott, current and former sex workers, retained me to mount a constitutional challenge in 2007 to three prostitution-related criminal prohibitions. The challenge was based upon the well-recognized constitutional doctrine that the principles of fundamental justice under section 7 of the Charter of Rights and Freedoms prohibit the enactment of arbitrary and irrational laws that do greater harm than good. The constitutional challenge was designed to attack the law's complicity in, or its contribution to, the daily risk of violence faced by sex workers. As is the case in most constitutional challenges, the concerns being raised involve an assessment of the legitimacy and rationality of state policy rather than a resolution of the divergent moral perspectives regarding sex for sale.

The illogical and sinister arbitrariness of the law is demonstrated by the manner in which it proclaims the act of prostitution to be legal, and yet in the same breath it takes away every legal option for pursuing this work in a safe and secure manner. Section 213(1)(c) of the Criminal Code prohibits the act of communicating for the purpose of prostitution, so it is actually illegal to do any rudimentary screening of customers before entering their cars. Section

Alan Young

212(1)(j) prohibits the act of living on the avails (earnings) of prostitution, and despite this provision's mistaken association with the act of pimping, it does not require proof of any parasitic or exploitive relationship, making it illegal for anyone to work for a sex worker regardless of whether this employment is legitimately required for the personal security of the sex worker. Finally, section 210 prohibits the act of keeping a bawdy-house on a habitual and frequent basis, so, despite the obvious dangers of the street trade, the law makes it illegal to move into a more secure and safe indoor setting.

On 28 September 2010, Madame Justice Himel of the Superior Court of Ontario allowed our application in its entirety and invalidated three sections of the Criminal Code: section 210, the bawdy-house provision; section 212(1)(j), the living on the avails provision; and section 213(1)(c), the communication provision (*Bedford v. Canada*, 2010 ONSC 4264). She held that these laws violated the principles of fundamental justice in that they operated in an arbitrary and overbroad manner, and that their harmful effects were grossly disproportionate to any public benefits they might achieve. The Court of Appeal for Ontario was largely in agreement with Justice Himel with respect to the factual underpinning of the constitutional claim (that the law contributes to a risk of harm) but reached a different conclusion in terms of remedy. The court upheld section 213(1)(c) (communication) on the basis that it did not believe it significantly contributed to an increased risk of harm; however, it invalidated section 210 (bawdy-house) on the basis that the prohibition on indoor sex work constituted a major obstacle to securing a safer work environment. Finally, the court reinterpreted section 212(1)(j) (avails) so that it could operate in a constitutionally sound manner: a conviction for living on the avails now requires proof of an exploitive relationship (*Canada (Attorney General) v. Bedford*, 2012 ONCA 186).

On 25 March 2012, the attorney general of Canada filed its leave to appeal application in the Supreme Court of Canada. As this publication goes to print, the fate of the constitutional challenge and the law now lies in the hands of that court. A few more years will elapse before we have a firm and certain understanding of how the law will be changed.

Of course, even with a change in the law, commercial sex work is not an ideal career choice for everyone. In the five years I have been engaged in the constitutional challenge, I have been inundated with horror stories about sex work from police officers, prosecutors, former sex workers, and moral entrepreneurs masquerading as scholars. The horror stories are real and shocking, and these are the stories that tend to dominate media and public portrayals of sex work. The public policy nightmare we have constructed is largely based upon the mistake of allowing the horror stories to serve as the conventional paradigm for understanding sex work. It takes a publication of this nature to set the record straight. However, whether or not decriminalization of sex work or some other meaningful legislative reform is achieved through the constitutional challenge, it is important to remember that while we try to build a safe environment for those who wish to make a living from sex work, we must strive to develop and maintain social safety nets for those who should never have entered, or who wish to exit, the profession.

It remains unclear to me what we hope to accomplish with prohibitions on commercial sex; however, for many people, the issue is not a matter of rational discourse but a visceral reaction to the commodification of sex. Religious objections have now been replaced by the scholarly discourse on the evils of degradation and dehumanization. In this discourse, sex is sacred and transcends the marketplace ethos. It is all about "making love," and the commodification and commercialization of sexuality are seen as morally repugnant and degrading. This Hallmark card approach to sex is fine for some, but in a pluralistic secular society, the sanitized and sanctified vision of sexuality is just one of many competing moral perspectives.

The ubiquity of sex work is what has earned it the title of the world's oldest profession. As no legal or political regime has ever eradicated sex work, it is time we stop the futile quest for a prostitution-free society and start to construct a legal regime that respects the safety and security of anyone who freely chooses to earn a living through the sale of sexual services.

Contributors

JOYCE ARTHUR is a founding member of FIRST, a national group of feminists who advocate for the rights of sex workers and for the decriminalization of prostitution in Canada. She moderates the popular FIRST e-mail listserv and writes and speaks publicly on sex worker rights issues. She was the 2010 recipient of the Naked Truth Adult Entertainment award for "Favourite Feminist Activist." Joyce is a former topless dancer, who currently works as a writer and pro-choice activist. She is the founder and executive director of the Abortion Rights Coalition of Canada, a national pro-choice group in Canada.

CHERYL AUGER is finishing her dissertation in political science at the University of Toronto. Her research explores sex work policy and policy debates in Canada, and her interests include sexual politics, urban politics, social movements, and feminism. She received her master's degree from Queen's University in political studies. Cheryl loves to dance, knit, and take photos of friends and interesting places.

STEVEN BITTLE is an assistant professor in the Department of Criminology, University of Ottawa. His previous publications on youth prostitution law and policy reform include "From Villain to Victim: Secure Care and Young Women Involved in Prostitution" (2006). His current research interests are in the area of corporate crime and regulation. He is the author of *Still Dying for a Living: Corporate Criminal Liability after the Westray Mine Disaster* (2012) and (with L. Snider) "Moral Panics Deflected: The Failed Legislative Response to Canada's Safety Crimes and Markets Fraud Legislation" (2011).

CHRIS BRUCKERT is an associate professor in the Department of Criminology at the University of Ottawa. Over the past twenty years, she has devoted much of her energy to examining diverse sectors of the sex industry; to that end, she has undertaken qualitative research into street-based sex work, erotic dance, the in-call sector, escorts, clients, male sex workers, and managers. She endeavours to put the principles of committed scholarship into practice and is active in the sex worker rights movement. Her engagement includes being a founding member and active participant in POWER (Prostitutes of Ottawa-Gatineau Work, Educate and Resist), Ottawa's first by-and-for sex worker rights group.

JENN CLAMEN has been active in the Canadian and global sex worker rights movements since 2000. Her passion and work are around mobilizing sex workers into meaningful participation in policies and practices that have an impact on their lives. She has been an active member of Stella, Montreal's sex worker organization, since 2002. In 2003, she co-founded the Canadian Guild for Erotic Labour. Jenn is also an educator in university and community settings, teaching on issues and realities affecting criminalized and marginalized communities, in particular around human rights, public space and poverty, women in conflict with the law, and community organizing.

DEBORAH CLIPPERTON teaches in the Department of Humanities at York University, where she studies issues of culture and identity. She is currently finishing a book based on interviews with strippers who enjoy their work. She is also writing a contemporary history of burlesque in Toronto, exploring issues of performativity, pleasure, and the retranscription of gender.

ANNA-LOUISE CRAGO became involved in the sex workers' rights movement fifteen years ago as a street sex worker in Montreal. She is the former coordinator of clinical and outreach services at Stella, Montreal's organization by and for sex workers, and she is currently pursuing a PhD. Her publications include *Rights Not Rescue: Female, Male, and Trans Sex Workers' Human Rights in Botswana, Namibia, and South Africa* (2008), *Our Lives Matter: Sex Workers Unite for Health and Rights* (2008), and *Arrest the Violence* (2010), a sex-worker-led community research project on physical and sexual violence by police against sex workers in eleven Central Eastern European and Central Asian countries.

SUSAN DAVIS has been an active sex worker in Vancouver for over twenty-five years and finds it rewarding. She is involved in sex worker labour organizing and is development coordinator for Canada's first sex worker cooperative, the West Coast Cooperative of Sex Industry Professionals. Susan sits on numerous committees striving to stabilize the safety of Vancouver sex workers. She has done extensive research on Vancouver's historical sex industry, has lectured on her experiences at universities and colleges, testified to the Parliamentary Subcommittee on Solicitation Laws, and also testified at the constitutional challenge of Canada's prostitution laws by three Ontario sex workers *(Bedford v. Canada).*

JANE DOE is the pseudonym for the woman who successfully sued the Toronto police for negligence and gender discrimination in the investigation of her rape. Her case set Canadian legal precedent and is taught in law schools across Canada and internationally. Her book *The Story of Jane Doe* (2004) is curriculum content for numerous high schools, colleges, and universities. Jane Doe is also a lecturer, researcher, teacher, community organizer, and long-time sex worker ally. She has been awarded honorary doctorates in law at the University of Ottawa and Concordia University.

ELYA M. DURISIN is a doctoral candidate in the Department of Political Science at York University, Toronto, where she is conducting research on Canadian anti-trafficking policies. She holds a master's degree in environmental studies from York University, where she studied the influence of federal and municipal regulations on the working conditions of indoor sex workers in Ontario. Durisin has worked in varying capacities on research projects related to sex work, including projects about management in the sex industry and Aboriginal women in sex work. Recent publications can be found in *Canadian Journal of Women and the Law* (20, 2) and *Canadian Woman Studies* (28, 1).

TOR FLETCHER is a queer mixed-race trans man living and working in Hamilton, Ontario. He graduated with a master's degree from Ontario Institute for Studies in Education – University of Toronto, where he did research with racialized transgender men. He sits on the board of Big Susie's, an advocacy group run by and for sex workers, and he has a twenty-year history of queer, anti-racist, feminist activism.

KARA GILLIES has been working in the sex trade since 1987. During this time, she has been active in many aspects of the sex workers' rights movement. In

1998, she co-founded the Toronto Migrant Sex Workers Advocacy Group, and in 2003, she co-founded the Canadian Guild for Erotic Labour. She has been involved with Maggie's: Toronto Sex Workers Action Project, for over twenty years, providing outreach, education, and workshops to sex workers and health/ social service providers. She is currently the executive director at a Toronto-based abortion clinic, where she continues the fight for women's sexual and reproductive rights.

MICHAEL GOODYEAR is an assistant professor of medicine at Dalhousie University, Halifax. His academic background is in public health, women's health, feminist health care ethics, health law, social justice, research as culture, and knowledge sharing. His recent work focuses on the effects of social exclusion on self-determination and access in health. He has developed networks of communities of practice and knowledge in several regions of the world as a demonstration of the utility of knowledge translation, uniting researchers, sex workers, and program providers in a collaborative model to inform public policy.

STACEY HANNEM is assistant professor of criminology at Wilfrid Laurier University's Brantford Campus and is chair of the policy review committee for the Canadian Criminal Justice Association. She holds a PhD in sociology from Carleton University (2008), where she researched the effects of incarceration on prisoners' families. She is a member of the editorial board for the *Journal of Prisoners on Prisons* and is active in public criminology, researching and writing about the effects of social stigma and discriminatory justice policy for marginalized persons.

SARAH HUNT is a PhD candidate in the Department of Geography at Simon Fraser University. Her current research examines how Canadian law and Indigenous law are being used to address the normalization of violence against Indigenous people in BC and how "law" and "violence" are understood in these relations of legal pluralism. She has worked as a community-based researcher, educator, and advocate in Indigenous communities across British Columbia for more than ten years and is a member of the Kwagiulth Band of the Kwakwaka'wakw First Nation.

JJ is a youth activist, sister, and auntie who believes that to meet people where they are at requires more listening and supporting and less telling them what they should do. She has worked on the front lines doing youth and community organizing work for the past seventeen years, and supports the direct resistance of youth and communities against violence from the state and the self-determination of rights over body and space.

LESLIE ANN JEFFREY is a professor of political science at the University of New Brunswick in Saint John. She has authored two books on sex work, *Sex and Borders: Gender, National Identity and Prostitution Policy in Thailand* (2002) and, with Gayle MacDonald, *Sex Workers in the Maritimes Talk Back* (2006). She focuses on issues of sex work policy in Canada, Australia, New Zealand, and Europe, and on the debates surrounding sex worker migration/trafficking.

TUULIA LAW is a PhD student in the Department of Criminology at the University of Ottawa whose research interests include labour relationships and conditions in the sex industry, and the effects of stigma. For her master's research in women's studies at the University of Ottawa, she examined women's transitions from indoor sex work to mainstream jobs. She is a founding member of Students for Sex Worker Rights, a sex worker and ally group at the University of Ottawa that focuses on public education. Law is also a member of the Sex Professionals of Canada, a by-and-for sex workers political group advocating decriminalization.

ANNALEE LEPP is an associate professor and chair of the Department of Women's Studies at the University of Victoria, British Columbia. She is a founding member of the Global Alliance against Traffic in Women (GAATW) Canada (1996), a member organization of GAATW, whose international secretariat is located in Bangkok. Since 1997, she has participated in crisis intervention, advocacy, assessments of the impact of anti-trafficking measures on human rights internationally, and various collaborative research projects, which examine Canadian state policies and practices as they relate to trafficking in persons and irregular cross-border movements.

JACQUELINE LEWIS is an associate professor in the Department of Sociology, Anthropology and Criminology at the University of Windsor. Her research focuses on issues tied to crime, deviance, and socio-legal studies – the impact of public policy on health and well-being, identity and stigma management, adapting to illness, and drugs and drug policy. She has led three government-funded studies exploring the impact of policy on various forms of sex work. The most recent, the Sex Trade Advocacy and Research (STAR) project, brought academics and community partners together for a SSHRC-funded study of the impact of public policy on the health and well-being of sex workers in two Canadian cities.

VICTORIA LOVE is a sex worker and activist based in Toronto. She entered the Ontario sex industry as a youth and has experience in a number of sectors, including erotic dance, massage, and escort. She is a frequent guest speaker at community events, conferences, trainings, and university classrooms. She has also written about her experiences in the sex industry and has conducted numerous interviews for both media and academic research. Love is a member of Maggie's: Toronto Sex Workers Action Project.

JOHN LOWMAN is a professor in the School of Criminology at Simon Fraser University. Since 1977, he has studied prostitution, prostitution law, and prostitution law enforcement in Canada. His research includes the *Vancouver Field Study of Prostitution* (1984), *Street Prostitution, Assessing the Impact of the Law, Vancouver* (1989), *Violence against Persons Who Prostitute in British Columbia* (with Laura Fraser, 1996), *Men Who Buy Sex* (with Chris Atchison and Laura Fraser, 1997), and *Beyond Decriminalization* (with Pivot Legal Society, 2006). He has given testimony before various parliamentary committees and public inquiries, and he appeared as an expert witness in *Bedford v. Canada*.

GAYLE MacDONALD is a professor of sociology at St. Thomas University in Fredericton, where she also serves as assistant vice-president, research. Her research is on marginalized populations, sex workers, social control, and social justice. She is past president of AIDS NB and is involved with JustUs fair trade products promotion. She's the mother of two teenagers and has a dog and two cats, just in case the two teens aren't paying enough attention to her.

KAROLYN MARTIN is a master's candidate at Trent University in the interdisciplinary Theory, Culture and Politics Program. Her research interests include policy analysis, sexual assault awareness campaigns, and feminist theory. She has been involved with the pan-Canadian RebELLEs movement since 2008. Currently, she is studying the 2011 elimination of the New Brunswick Advisory Council on the Status of Women. Her approach involves analyzing how language works with other elements of social life to create the worlds we inhabit, with the hope of creating worlds lacking any form of oppression.

ELEANOR MATICKA-TYNDALE received her doctorate in 1989 from the University of Calgary, Alberta. She holds a Tier 1 Canada Research Chair in Social Justice and Sexual Health and is university professor in the Department of Sociology, Anthropology and Criminology at the University of Windsor, Ontario. Her research focuses on sexual health and rights within the context of globalization and includes projects in Canada, Europe, Africa, and South/Southeast Asia. Three projects focused on sex work in southwestern Ontario. Her publications number close to two hundred and include academic work, technical reports, government briefs, training manuals and curricula, and civil society publications.

RIVER REDWOOD has been involved in various aspects of the sex industry, from street-level participation to working for mainstream porn companies. His film work has won a variety of awards. He also co-founded and ran his own alternative porn company and has produced a number of films that have appeared at gay and lesbian film festivals around the globe. He currently sits on the board of directors for Big Susie's in Hamilton, Ontario. Big Susie's is an organization run by and for sex workers. Its purpose is to fight back against the stigma that dehumanizes sex workers.

RENE ROSS graduated with a political science degree from Acadia University and is a former United Nations intern, where she focused on violence against women in conflict zones. For the past seven years, she has been involved with Stepping Stone, the only outreach agency exclusively for sex workers in Atlantic Canada. Ross is currently its executive director. Stepping Stone is a charitable not-for-profit organization that offers supportive programs and outreach to women, men, and transgender sex workers as well as former sex workers. Ross is also a contributor to numerous research projects about sex work and is a local anti-poverty advocate.

TRISH SALAH is a lecturer at the Ontario Institute for Studies in Education at the University of Toronto. As a member of CUPE 3903, she worked to put trans workers' rights and sex worker solidarity on the union agenda, and she was the first trans representative to sit on CUPE's National Pink Triangle Committee. Her writing appears in recent issues of *Feminist Studies* and the *Cordite Review,* and in the collection *Féminismes électriques;* new work is forthcoming in the *Journal of the Medical Humanities* and in the anthology *Contested Imaginaries.*

She is the author of *Wanting in Arabic* (TSAR 2002) and recently completed a new poetry manuscript titled *Lyric Sexology*.

ESTHER SHANNON is a long-time Vancouver feminist activist. She is a founding member of FIRST, a national coalition of feminists advocating for the decriminalization of sex work. Esther worked with Vancouver sex workers to establish MAP, a mobile service delivering support to street-based sex workers. She received the inaugural BC Coalition of Experiential Women's Honorary Whore Award (2006) and the inaugural Naked Truth Adult Entertainment Award for "Favourite Feminist Activist" (2009). She has expert-level knowledge on women's issues and on international trafficking and the Olympic Games, as regards their impact on marginalized communities.

FRANCES M. SHAVER is a professor in the Department of Sociology and Anthropology at Concordia University. She is currently involved in a CIHR Team Grant that draws together a multi-disciplinary team of knowledge users, collaborators, scholars, and trainees. The team is working collaboratively to identify key factors linked to violence and vulnerabilities in the Canadian sex industry at systems, social, and individual levels; to estimate the impact of gender on violence-related links between sex workers, clients, romantic partners, supervisors, and regulators; and to ensure that the knowledge generated informs policies and practices aimed at improving the safety and health of sex workers at work and in their personal lives.

MARIANA VALVERDE is director of the Centre of Criminology and Sociolegal Studies at the University of Toronto. Notable published works include *Sex, Power, and Pleasure* (1985), *The Age of Light, Soap and Water: Moral Reform in English Canada, 1885-1925* (1991, 2009), *Diseases of the Will: Alcohol and the Dilemmas of Freedom* (1998), *Law's Dream of a Common Knowledge* (2003), *Law and Order: Signs, Meanings, Myths* (2006), *The Force of Law* (2010), and *Making Law on the Street: Urban Governance and the Challenges of Diversity* (forthcoming). She has also published over forty scholarly articles in a wide variety of journals.

EMILY VAN DER MEULEN is an assistant professor in the Department of Criminal Justice and Criminology at Ryerson University. Her research is community-based and action-oriented, focusing on issues of gender, sexuality, labour, and the law. Her current projects include a two-site study with Aboriginal sex workers, a pilot project on gender, video surveillance, and urban security in Toronto, and research on criminalized mothers.

ALAN YOUNG is an associate professor at Osgoode Hall Law School and the co-founder and director of the Innocence Project, which investigates suspected cases of wrongful conviction and imprisonment. He has brought constitutional challenges to gambling, obscenity, bawdy-house, and drug laws, and for more than a decade has provided free legal services for people whose lifestyles have brought them into conflict with the law. In 2010, in *Bedford v. Canada,* he persuaded the Superior Court of Ontario to overturn three key provisions of the Criminal Code related to prostitution. He is also the author of *Justice Defiled: Perverts, Potheads, Serial Killers and Lawyers* (2003).

Index

ASTTeQ. *See* Action Santé Travesti(e)s/
Transsexuel(le)s du Québec
(ASTTeQ)
Athens Olympic Games, 253-55
Auger, Cheryl, 327
autonomy. *See* agency
AWAN. *See* Aboriginal Women's Action
Network (AWAN)
awards for adult entertainment, 138
AWCEP. *See* Asian Women Coalition for
Ending Prostitution (AWCEP)

B

bad dates, 52, 137, 172, 275
lists of, 131, 139, 167, 175
non-reporting of, 67, 221
Badgley Report, 283, 289
bawdy-house legislation, 5, 6, 8, 10, 11-12,
16, 67, 118, 183, 215, 315, 319,
325
2012 revision, 13-14, 325
See also Bedford v. Canada 2010
BC Coalition of Experiential Commun-
ities (BCCEC), 138-39, 140-41,
259-60
BCCEC. *See* BC Coalition of Experiential
Communities (BCCEC)
BEAVER, 8
Bedford, Terri-Jean, 324
See also Bedford v. Canada 2010
Bedford v. Canada 2010, 13-14, 67, 200, 201,
230-44, 282, 324-25
Benedet, Janine, 243, 248n28
Bertha, 105, 106, 107, 108, 109n1
Beth, 310
Better End All Vicious Erotic Repression.
See BEAVER
Bianca, 303, 306, 309
Bittle, Steven, 327
Bloc Québecois, 202, 223
body rub parlours. *See* massage parlours
Bonella, Amanda, 136
boundaries. *See* boundary restrictions
boundary restrictions, 173-74, 176, 221,
301, 303-4, 311n4
Bowen, Raven, 142
Bravo, Karina, 159
Britain
International Union of Sex Workers
(IUSW), 114, 117, 119

British Columbia
Missing Women Commission of Inquiry,
134
sex work in rural areas, 89-90
underage sex workers, 284-85, 286, 288,
289, 291
See also Vancouver
Britney, 306, 307
Brook, 308
brothels, 9
co-op, 142, 259-60
See also bawdy-house legislation
Bruckert, Chris, 328
burlesque, 29, 30-31
new burlesque, 41-42, 43
Buying Sex is NOT a Sport campaign,
261-62

C

Cabiria, 160
Callahora, Sauci, 42
Canada. Criminal Code, 6-7
1972 amendments, 7-8
1985 amendments (Bill C-49), 9-10, 149
Bedford v. Canada 2010, 13-14, 67, 200,
201, 230-44, 282, 324-25
*Canada (Attorney General) v. Bedford
2012,* 13-14, 325
definition of exploitation, 266n1
Vagrancy C provisions, 7, 282, 301
See also constitutional challenges;
legislation
Canada. Indian Act, 84-86
Canada. Supreme Court, 8, 38, 39
*Canada (Attorney General) v. Bedford
2012,* 13-14, 325
ruling on lap dancing, 39, 43n9
See also constitutional challenges
Canadian Association of Burlesque Enter-
tainers (CABE), 36, 43n7
Canadian Charter of Rights and Freedoms,
13-14, 223, 302, 305, 309
See also constitutional challenges
Canadian Guild for Erotic Labour (CGEL),
119-20
relations with CUPE, 121-24
Canadian Labour Congress (CLC), 116,
124-26
Canadian Organization for the Rights of
Prostitutes, 8

Canadian Union of Public Employees
(CUPE)
support/non-support for sex workers,
113-28
Canadians for Decency, 36
career advancement, 273
Carstensen, Jacquie, 133-34
CASH, 8
CGEL. See Canadian Guild for Erotic
Labour (CGEL)
Charlotte, 305, 308
Charter challenges. See constitutional
challenges
child sexual abuse, 231, 232-33
conceptualization of youth prostitution
as, 279-93
Christian missionary morality, 77, 79
cisgender, 72n4, 72n5
cisman, 72n4
cissexual, 72n4, 72n5
ciswoman, 72n4
Citizen's Summit on Human Trafficking,
261
citizenship, 198-206, 217, 222, 225, 304,
310-11
Clamen, Jenn, 162n2, 328
views on CUPE, 113-28
Claudia, 156, 157-58
CLC. See Canadian Labour Congress
(CLC)
CLES. See Concertation des luttes contre
l'exploitation sexuelle (CLES)
clients, 6-7, 51-52
criminalization of, 14-15, 149, 157, 172-
73, 217, 221, 230, 243, 245
effects on process of transition, 103-4
male sex workers and, 47, 51-52, 54-55,
73n6
relationships with workers, 62-63, 103-4
screening of, 52, 67, 244, 260, 271-73, 324
targeted during Vancouver Olympics,
261-63
trans sex workers and, 67-69
underage sex workers and, 12, 283, 290
See also bad dates
Clipperton, Deborah, 328
La Coalition pour les droits des travailleuses et travailleurs du sexe, 152-54,
156, 157, 158, 159, 160
colonialism. See colonization

colonization, 18-19, 77, 134, 135, 286
construction of Indigenous women, 83,
84-88, 92-93, 95-96
Committee against Human Trafficking, 260
Committee Against Street Harassment. See
CASH
Committee on Sexual Offences against
Children and Youth, 283
communicating/solicitation legislation, 8,
12-14, 21n4, 67, 149-50, 215, 282
See also Bedford v. Canada 2010
Concertation des luttes contre l'exploitation
sexuelle (CLES), 161
Condor Club (San Francisco), 31-32
Conn, Melanie, 142
Conservative Party of Canada
government funding cuts, 196n3
government positions on prostitution,
200-3
harm reduction and, 176-77, 202-3
Subcommittee on Solicitation Laws
Review, 200-3, 216, 223
constitutional challenges, 9-10, 13, 136
Bedford v. Canada 2010, 13-14, 67, 200,
201, 230-44, 282, 324-25
Canada (Attorney General) v. Bedford
2012, 13-14, 325
Contagious Diseases Act, 5-6
Le Coq d'Or (Toronto), 32
Cora, 272, 274
CORP. See Canadian Organization for the
Rights of Prostitutes
Cowessess First Nation, 79
Crago, Anna-Louise, 162n2, 222, 328
Craig, Carol, 32
Criminal Code. See Canada. Criminal
Code
criminalization, 293n5
constructed as victim rescue, 74, 182,
193, 203, 219, 225, 264, 280, 282
of clients, 14-15, 149, 157, 172-73, 217,
221, 230, 243, 245
of sexually assaulted women, 183, 186,
189, 195n2
of third parties, 118-19, 269-77
of youth involved in sex trade, 74, 280,
281-82, 290-93
related to harmful working conditions,
11-14, 118-19, 149-50, 157, 200, 204,
221, 323-26

related to violence against sex workers, 9, 10, 18, 81, 149-51, 152, 157

See also legislation; police repression; municipal bylaws

CUPE. *See* Canadian Union of Public Employees (CUPE)

customers. *See* clients

D

D'Angelo, Raigen, 222

Davies, Libby, 223

Davis, Susan, 132, 143, 329

De Wet, Paul Henry, 235

decriminalization, 16-17, 67, 136

as harm reduction process, 67, 172, 221

Indigenous sex workers and, 96-97

labour unions and, 122, 125-26

prohibitionist vs sex-radical feminist viewpoints, 14-17, 142-43, 168-69

resistance by prohibitionist organizations, 135

screening of clients and, 52, 67, 244, 260, 271-73, 324

support of CUPE, 116-17

young sex workers and, 81

See also human rights issues

demand-side prohibition. *See* Swedish model

democratic governance, 211

deQuatros, Sally, 131

Developing Capacity for Change, 140

deviant constructs, 199, 212-13, 224, 299

as discourse of exclusion, 14-15, 126-27, 165-66, 169-70, 182-94, 216-20, 281-82, 287-88, 290-92, 299-300

of female sexuality, 182-83, 188-89, 190-91, 192, 193, 194, 195, 217

of Indigenous women, 83, 84-88, 92-93, 95-96

of sex workers, 88-89, 213, 214, 216-18, 219-20, 223, 224, 225, 301

Subcommittee on Solicitation Laws Review and, 216-18, 223, 224, 225

discourses of exclusion, 211, 212

deviance and victimhood, 14-15, 76-78, 126-27, 165-66, 169-70, 182-94, 203-4, 214, 216-20, 281-82, 287-88, 290-92, 299-300

prostitute vs citizen, 198-206, 217-18

See also boundary restrictions; criminalization; deviant constructs; silencing

of sex workers; social profiling; stigmatization

discourses of inclusion, 211, 216, 217, 220-22

discriminatory practices

application of municipal bylaws, 154-56, 299, 302-5

workplace discrimination, 107-8, 115, 133, 274, 276

See also racism; social profiling; stigmatization

Dlite, Roxi, 42

Dodo, Carol Ann, 31

Doe, Jane, 183-84, 190-91, 329

drivers, 12, 70, 119, 271, 272

drug use, 53, 300, 308

Durbar Mahila Samanwaya Committee, 160, 196n9

Durisin, Elya M., 329

E

economic conditions, 114

benefits of working for a third party, 272

role in career choice, 93-94, 98, 103, 136-37, 169, 286

transition to mainstream work and, 106-7

See also neoliberalism

Ecuador, 159

Edmonton, 88, 269, 275

municipal bylaws, 318, 319

Project KARE, 187-88

emerging social movements

access to power, 211, 214, 217, 226

employees of sex workers, 12, 70, 119, 244

employers. *See* employment; licensing; managers

employment, 9, 12, 119

benefits of working for a third party, 269-74, 276-77

See also licensing; mainstream employment; working conditions

escort work, 62-64

EVE. *See* Exploited Voices Now Educating (EVE)

exclusion. *See* discourses of exclusion

exit strategies. *See* transition to mainstream employment

exotic dancers, 114, 261-62

attempt to unionize, 133-34

NakedTruth.ca, 137-38

P

PACE Society, 132, 139, 140
Pacey, Karen, 142
Paralympic Games, 141, 251-66
Parisien, Nicole, 242-43
Parker, R., 199
PEERS Vancouver, 136
Pheterson, G., 195
pimps. *See* managers
Pinzer, Maimie, 148
Pivot Legal Society, 136
pole-dancing, 38
police
  abusive attitudes toward sex workers,
    221, 297-311
  improved relations with sex workers,
    141, 160
  protection rackets in Montreal, 148-49
  relationship of outreach programs with,
    174-75
  sexually assaulted women and, 182, 183-
    84, 186-88, 190-91, 193, 195n2,
    195n10
  See also police repression
police repression, 221, 293n3
  Halifax, 172-75
  Montreal, 149-50, 152-55, 157-58
  Ottawa, 297-311
  sexual harassment, 155, 307-8
  Vancouver, 246
  See also geographic displacements; social
    profiling
politics of exclusion/inclusion. *See* discourses of exclusion; discourses of
  inclusion
pornographic films, 47-48, 49-51
Porth, Kerry, 132, 144
post-traumatic stress disorder (PTSD),
  234-35
Poulin, Richard, 230, 231-33, 234, 241-42,
  245, 246n4, 247n26, 248n27
poverty. *See* economic conditions
POWER, 131, 301
Presland, Don, 139
pro-sex feminism. *See* sex-radical feminism
procurers. *See* managers
procuring legislation. *See* living on the
  avails legislation

prohibitionist feminism, 14-15, 16, 134-35,
  168-71, 185
  attacks on sex worker organizations, 161,
    170
  commonalities with pro-sex feminism,
    135, 177-78
  prohibitionist vs sex-radical viewpoints,
    14-17, 126-27, 142-43, 168-71, 177-78
Project KARE, 187-88
"prostitute," 2-3
"prostituted" women, 219
Prostitutes of Ottawa-Gatineau Work,
    Educate and Resist (POWER). *See*
    POWER
prostitution
  history, 323-24
  lap dancing and, 39, 43n9
  legal definitions, 11, 43n9
  terminological choices, 2-3, 219
psychological harms, 102, 234-37
PTSD. *See* post-traumatic stress disorder
    (PTSD)
public shaming, 305-6, 311n5

Q

Quebec, 43n9
  biker gangs, 148-49
  Charter of Human Rights and Freedoms,
    300
  Council on the Status of Women, 161
  Human Rights Commission, 300, 304
  Indemnisation des victimes d'actes
    criminels, 155-56
  See also Montreal

R

R. v. Pelletier 1999, 39, 43n9
racialized women, 69, 71, 194, 263-65, 276
  See also Indigenous sex workers; Indigen-
    ous women; migrant sex workers
racism, 18-19, 56, 98n2, 107-8, 151, 190, 276
  trans people and, 67, 69
  See also colonization; racialized women
radical feminism. *See* prohibitionist
  feminism
rape. *See* sexual assault
Rape Relief. *See* Vancouver Rape Relief and
  Women's Shelter

British Columbia, 284-85, 286, 288, 289, 291
    claim of average age of entry into prostitution, 231-32
    legislation concerning, 215, 282-85
    Manitoba, 285, 286, 291, 293n4
    social contexts, 46, 81, 285-87, 289-93
    See also youth involved in sex trade
unions. *See* labour unions
United States
    Exotic Dancers' Union, 114
Urry, Faye, 125

V

vagrancy legislation, 5, 6, 7, 20n1, 282, 301
Valverde, Mariana, 334
van der Meulen, Emily, 334-35
Vancouver, 236, 237, 238-39, 240
    Aboriginal Women's Action Network, 91
    Downtown Eastside, 82, 83-84, 97, 130, 133, 134, 159, 236, 237
    history of sex industry, 130-31, 140
    Indigenous sex workers, 82, 83, 84, 89
    missing and murdered women, 82, 83-84, 87, 97, 130, 133, 134, 135, 144, 159, 215, 241, 242, 245-46
    Olympic Games, 141, 251-66
    police relations with sex workers, 141, 246
    regulation of sex trade, 316, 317, 318, 319, 320, 321n2
    sex worker movement, 8, 130-44
    Women's Memorial March, 134
Vancouver Rape Relief and Women's Shelter, 135, 142
verbal abuse, 304-5
victim constructs
    as discourses of exclusion, 15, 126-27, 165-66, 169-70, 182-94, 216-20, 281-82, 287-88, 290-92, 299-300
    as future murder victims, 187-88, 218
    criminalization and, 74, 182, 193, 203, 219, 225, 264, 280, 282
    of female sexuality, 182-83, 188-89, 190-91, 192, 193, 194, 195, 217
    of Indigenous sex workers, 89, 90, 91, 95
    of youth involved in sex trade, 75-78, 81, 279, 280, 283-88, 290-92, 293n1
    sexual assault compared with prostitution, 181, 182-94

violence
    fear of, 102-3
    against Indigenous people, 86, 87, 88
    inherent in prostitution, 231, 233-43
    institutionalization of anti-violence services, 184-85
    against women, 186
    See also sexual assault; violence against sex workers
violence against sex workers, 324
    as support for victim constructs, 117
    Halifax, 167
    indifference of police, 134, 155, 309-10, 324
    indifference of social system, 155-56, 324
    Montreal, 149, 151, 155-56, 157
    perpetrated by police, 306-8, 311n6
    related to criminalization, 9, 10, 18, 81, 149-51, 152, 157
    related to criminalization of clients, 172-73
    related to work settings, 237-43
    reporting to police, 160-61
    See also bad dates; murdered sex workers
Vivian, 103, 106, 108, 109n1
voice. *See* agency; silencing of sex workers

W

warnings, 95-96, 188-89, 196n6
WCCSIP. *See* West Coast Cooperative of Sex Industry Professionals (WCCSIP)
West Coast Cooperative of Sex Industry Professionals (WCCSIP), 142
WISH Drop-In Centre, 131, 139
Woodman, Shelly, 136
working conditions, 114, 118-19, 140, 153-54
    benefits of working for a third party, 269-74, 276-77
    Canadian Guild for Erotic Labour, 120
    pornography industry, 49-51
    related to unionization, 118, 123
    stripping, 30-31, 32-34, 35, 36-41, 43, 133
    unfair labour practices, 274-76
    See also criminalization; discriminatory practices; police repression; violence against sex workers

Y

Young, Alan, 335
youth
    need for sex-positive sex education, 78-79
youth involved in sex trade
    constructed as victims, 75-78, 81, 279, 280, 283-88, 290-92, 293n1
    effects of stigma on, 75, 79, 80, 81
    Indigenous youth, 74-81, 90, 286, 288, 291
    interview with Ivo, 74-81
    lack of appropriate services for, 76-81, 285
    obscuring of social contexts, 81, 285-87, 289-93
    See also underage sex workers

Z

zoning bylaws, 316-17